Level I

Microsoft®

access

2007

BENCHMARK SERIES

Nita Rutkosky
Pierce College at Puyallup
Puyallup, Washington

Audrey Rutkosky Roggenkamp
Pierce College at Puyallup
Puyallup, Washington

Managing Editor	Sonja Brown
Production Editor	Donna Mears
Cover and Text Designer	Leslie Anderson
Copy Editor	Susan Capecchi
Desktop Production	John Valo, Desktop Solutions
Proofreader	Laura Nelson
Indexer	Nancy Fulton

Acknowledgments: The authors and editors wish to thank Pamela J. Silvers, Chairperson, Business Computer Technologies, Asheville-Buncombe Technical Community College, Asheville, North Carolina, for testing the instruction and exercises for accuracy.

Care has been taken to verify the accuracy of information presented in this book. However, the authors, editors, and publisher cannot accept responsibility for Web, e-mail, newsgroup, or chat room subject matter or content, or for consequences from application of the information in this book, and make no warranty, expressed or implied, with respect to its content.

Photo Credits: Introduction page 1 (clockwise from top), Lexmark International, Inc., courtesy of Dell Inc., all rights Hewlett-Packard Company, Logitech, Micron Technology, Inc.; page 1, © Corbis; photos in Student Resources CD, courtesy of Kelly Rutkosky and Michael Rutkosky.

Trademarks: Microsoft is a trademark or registered trademark of Microsoft Corporation in the United States and/or other countries. Some of the product names and company names included in this book have been used for identification purposes only and may be trademarks or registered trade names of their respective manufacturers and sellers. The authors, editors, and publisher disclaim any affiliation, association, or connection with, or sponsorship or endorsement by, such owners.

We have made every effort to trace the ownership of all copyrighted material and to secure permission from copyright holders. In the event of any question arising as to the use of any material, we will be pleased to make the necessary corrections in future printings. Thanks are due to the aforementioned authors, publishers, and agents for permission to use the materials indicated.

ISBN 978-0-76382-987-2 (Text)
ISBN 978-0-76383-002-1 (Text + CD)

© 2008 by Paradigm Publishing Inc., a division of EMC Corporation
875 Montreal Way
St. Paul, MN 55102
E-mail: educate@emcp.com
Web site: www.emcp.com

Printed in the United States of America

17 16 15 14 13 12 11 10 09 08 07   1 2 3 4 5 6 7 8 9 10

CONTENTS

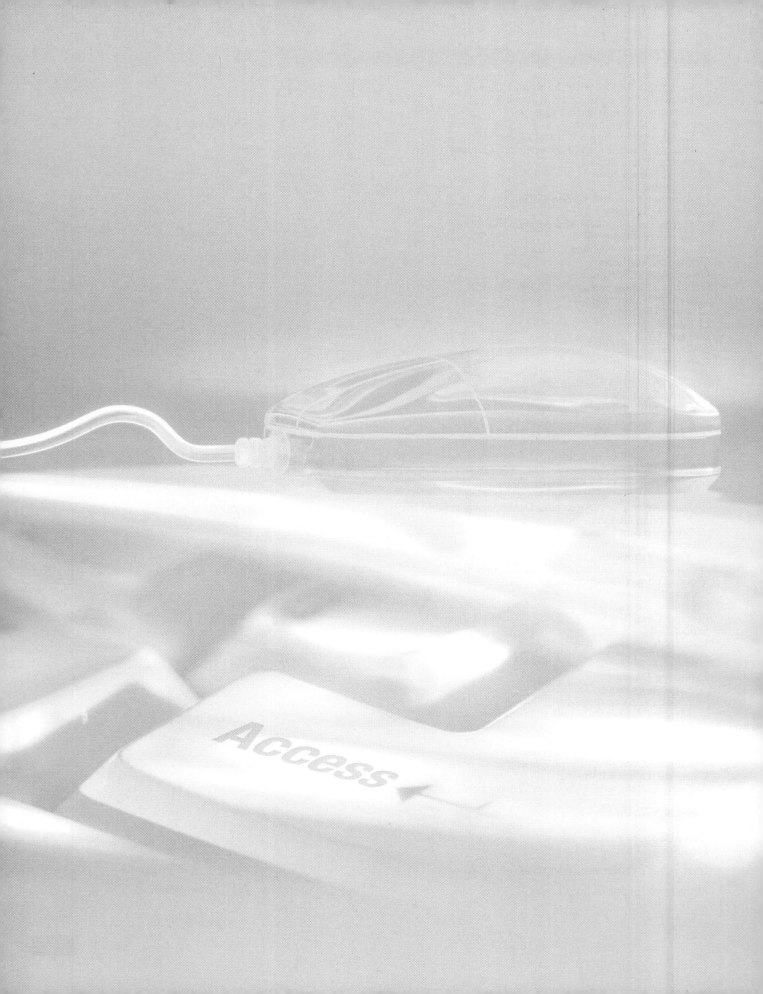

Benchmark Microsoft Access 2007 is designed for students who want to learn how to use this feature-rich data management tool to track, report, and share information. No prior knowledge of database management systems is required. After successfully completing a course using this textbook, students will be able to

- Create database tables to organize business or personal records
- Modify and manage tables to ensure that data is accurate and up-to-date
- Perform queries to assist with decision-making
- Plan, research, create, revise, and publish database information to meet specific communication needs
- Given a workplace scenario requiring the reporting and analysis of data, assess the information requirements and then prepare the materials that achieve the goal efficiently and effectively

In addition to mastering Access skills, students will learn the essential features and functions of computer hardware, the Windows XP operating system, and Internet Explorer 7.0. Upon completing the text, they can expect to be proficient in using Access to organize, analyze, and present information.

Achieving Proficiency in Access 2007

Since its inception several Office versions ago, the Benchmark Series has served as a standard of excellence in software instruction. Elements of the book function individually and collectively to create an inviting, comprehensive learning environment that produces successful computer users. On this and following pages, take a visual tour of the structure and features that comprise the highly popular Benchmark model.

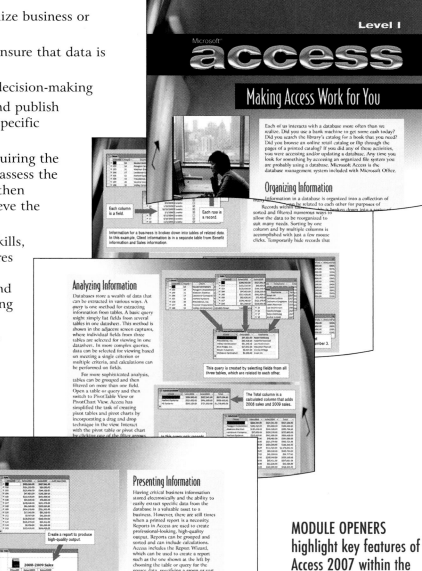

MODULE OPENERS highlight key features of Access 2007 within the context of organizing, analyzing, and presenting information.

Level 1

Microsoft®

access

Unit 1: Creating Tables and Queries

➤ Creating Database Tables
➤ Creating Relationships between Tables
➤ Modifying and Managing Tables
➤ Performing Queries

UNIT OPENERS display the unit's four chapter titles. Each level has two units, which conclude with a comprehensive unit performance assessment.

CHAPTER 3

Modifying and Managing Tables

Access

CHAPTER OPENERS present the Performance Objectives and highlight the practical relevance of the skills students will learn.

PERFORMANCE OBJECTIVES

Upon successful completion of Chapter 3, you will be able to:

- Modify a table by adding, deleting, or moving fields
- Assign a default value and validate a field entry
- Insert a Total row
- Use the Input Mask Wizard and the Lookup Wizard
- Complete a spelling check on data in a table
- Find specific records in a table
- Find specific data in a table and replace with other data
- Backup a database
- Compact and repair a database
- Use the Help feature

access Chapter 3

CD icon identifies a folder of data files students copy to a storage medium.

An Access database requires maintenance to keep the database up to date. Maintenance might include modifying the table by inserting or deleting fields, defining values and validating field entries, inserting a Total row, using wizards to identify data type, and sorting data in tables. In this chapter, you will learn how to modify tables as well as how to use the spelling checker to find misspelled words in a table and how to use the find and replace feature to find specific records in a table or find specific data in a table and replace with other data. As you continue working with a database, consider compacting and repairing the database to optimize performance and back up the database to protect your data from accidental loss or hardware failure. Microsoft Office contains an on-screen reference manual containing information on features and commands for each program within the suite. In this chapter, you will learn to use the Help feature to display information about Access.

Note: Before beginning computer projects, delete the Access2007L1C2 folder from your storage medium. Next, copy the Access2007L1C3 subfolder from the Access2007L1 folder on the CD that accompanies this textbook to your storage medium and make Access2007L1C3 the active folder.

A prominent note reminds students to copy the appropriate chapter data folder and make it active.

access Level 1
Modifying and Managing Tables **65**

New! PROJECT APPROACH: Builds Skill Mastery within Realistic Context

Project 1 Manage Data and Define Data Types

You will modify tables by adding and deleting fields, assign data types and default values to fields, validate field entries, insert a total row, and use the Input Mask Wizard and the Lookup Wizard. You will also move fields in a table and sort records in ascending and descending order.

Modifying a Table

Maintaining a table involves adding and/or deleting records as needed. It can also involve adding, moving, changing, or deleting fields in the table. Modify the structure of the table in Datasheet view or Design view. In Datasheet view, click the Table Tools Datasheet tab and then use options in the Fields & Columns group to insert or delete fields. To display a table in Design view, open the table, and then click the View button in the Views group in the Home tab. You can also change to Design view by clicking the View button arrow and then clicking *Design View* at the drop-down list or by clicking the Design View button located in the View area at the right side of the Status bar.

In Design view, *Field Name, Data Type,* and *Description* display at the top of the window and *Field Properties* displays toward the bottom of the window. In Design view, you can add fields, remove fields, and change the order of fields. When you switch to Design view, the Table Tools Design tab displays as shown in Figure 3.1. Use buttons in this tab to insert and delete rows and perform a variety of other tasks.

Figure 3.1 Table Tools Design Tab

HINT
Use options in the Data Type & Formatting group in the Table Tools Datasheet tab to set the data type.

Adding a Field

Situations change within a company, and a table must be flexible to accommodate changes that occur with new situations. Adding a field is a change that may need to be made to an existing table. For example, more information may be required to manage the data or an additional field may be needed for accounting purposes.

You can add a new field in Datasheet view or in Design view. One method for creating a new field is to simply type new records into a blank table or in the *Add New Field* column that displays at the right side of the last field in the table. Access sets a data type for each new field you type based on the type of data entered. For example, a column that contains dates is automatically assigned the Date/Time data type. You can also insert a new field by clicking the Table Tools Datasheet tab and then clicking the Insert button in the Fields & Columns group.

To add a row for a new field in Design view, position the insertion point on any text in the row that will be located immediately *below* the new field and then click the Insert Rows button in the Tools group in the Table Tools Design tab or

66   Chapter Three

Instruction and practice are organized into multipart projects that focus on related program features. A project overview identifies the tasks to accomplish and the key features to use in completing the work.

Following the project overview and between project parts, the text presents instruction on the features and skills necessary to accomplish the next tasks.

Typically, a file remains open throughout a project. Students save their work incrementally.

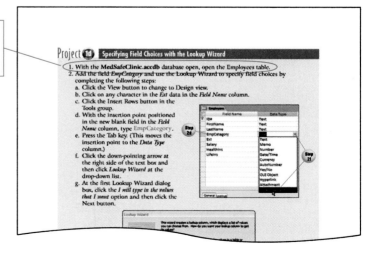

Project 1d Specifying Field Choices with the Lookup Wizard

1. With the **MedSafeClinic.accdb** database open, open the Employees table.
2. Add the field *EmpCategory* and use the Lookup Wizard to specify field choices by completing the following steps:
   a. Click the View button to change to Design view.
   b. Click on any character in the *Ext* data in the *Field Name* column.
   c. Click the Insert Rows button in the Tools group.
   d. With the insertion point positioned in the new blank field in the *Field Name* column, type EmpCategory.
   e. Press the Tab key. (This moves the insertion point to the *Data Type* column.)
   f. Click the down-pointing arrow at the right side of the text box and then click *Lookup Wizard* at the drop-down list.
   g. At the first Lookup Wizard dialog box, click the *I will type in the values that I want* option and then click the Next button.

Each project exercise guides students step by step to the desired outcome. Screen captures illustrate what the screen should look like at key points.

Text in magenta identifies material to type.

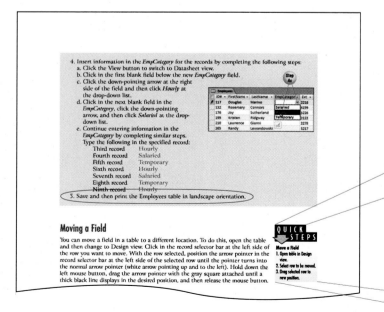

At or near the end of the project, students save and print their work. Locked, watermarked model answers in PDF format on the Student Resources CD allow students to check their results. This option rewards careful effort and builds software mastery.

Quick Steps provide feature summaries for reference and review.

Move a Field
1. Open table in Design view.
2. Select row to be moved.
3. Drag selected row to new position.

CHAPTER REVIEW ACTIVITIES: A Hierarchy of Learning Assessments

CHAPTER summary

- Modifying a table can include adding, moving, or deleting a field.
- Add a new field in Datasheet or Design view. Type new records in a blank database or in the *Add New Field* column or add a row for a new field in Design view. Click the Insert Rows button in the Tools group to insert a new field.
- To delete a field, display the table in Design view, select the record you want deleted, and then click the Delete Rows button. Click Yes at the message.
- Select a row by clicking the record selector bar that displays at the left side of the row.
- Use the *Default Value* property in the *Field Properties* section to insert the most common field entry.
- Use the *Validation Rule* property to enter a statement containing a conditional test. Enter in the *Validation Text* property the error message you want to display if the data entered violates the v[...]
- Click the Totals button in the Re[...] a row at the bottom of the datas[...] down-pointing arrow in the Tota[...] the drop-down list.
- Use the Input Mask Wizard to s[...]
- Use the Lookup Wizard to confi[...] items.
- Sort records in a table in ascendi[...] Sort & Filter group or in descend[...]
- Use the spelling checker to find [...]
- The spelling checker compares t[...] If a match is found, the word is [...] checker will select the word and [...]
- Begin the spelling checker by cli[...] in the Home tab.
- Use options at the Find and Rep[...] search for specific field entries in[...] the Find button in the Find grou[...]
- Use options at the Find and Rep[...] to search for specific data and re[...] by clicking the Replace button i[...]
- Back up a database on a consiste[...] from accidental loss or from any[...] the Office button, point to *Mana*[...]
- Compact and repair a database t[...] Compact and repair a database b[...] *Manage*, and then clicking *Compa*[...]
- Display the Access Help window[...] button located in the upper right[...]

CHAPTER SUMMARY captures the purpose and execution of key features.

COMMANDS review

FEATURE	RIBBON TAB, GROUP	BUTTON, OPTION	KEYBOARD SHORTCUT
Add field	Table Tools Design, Tools	Insert Rows	
Delete field	Table Tools Design, Tools	Delete Rows	
Sort records ascending	Home, Sort & Filter		
Sort records descending	Home, Sort & Filter		
Spelling checker	Home, Records	Spelling	F7
Find and Replace dialog box with Find tab selected	Home, Find		Ctrl + F
Find and Replace dialog box with Replace tab selected	Home, Find	Replace	Ctrl + H
Back up database		Manage, Back Up Database	
Compare and repair database		Manage, Compact and Repair Database	
Access Help window			F1

COMMANDS REVIEW summarizes visually the major features and command options.

CONCEPTS CHECK questions assess knowledge recall.

CONCEPTS check

Test Your Knowledge

Completion: For each description, indicate the correct term, symbol, or character.

1. Select a row by clicking this bar that displays at the left side of the row.

2. If most records are likely to contain the same field value, use this property to insert the most common field entry.

3. Use this property to enter a statement containing a conditional test that is checked each time data is entered into a field.

4. Use this wizard to set a pattern for how data is entered in a field.

5. Use this wizard to confine data entered in a field to a specific list of items.

6. The Ascending and Descending sort buttons are located in this group in the Home tab.

7. The Spelling button is located in this group in the Home tab.

8. This is the keyboard shortcut to begin spell checking.

9. Use options at the Find and Replace dialog box with this tab selected to search for specific data and replace with other data.

10. To back up a database, click the Office button, point to this option, and then click *Back Up Database*.

11. Perform this action on a database to optimize the performance of the database.

12. This is the keyboard shortcut to display the Access Help window.

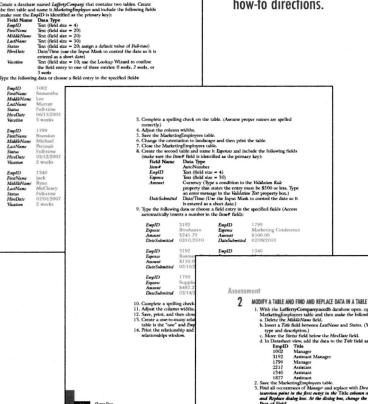

SKILLS CHECK exercises ask students to develop both standard and customized kinds of database elements without how-to directions.

The chapter CASE STUDY requires planning and executing multi-part workplace projects.

Students strengthen their analytical and writing skills by using Microsoft Word to describe best uses of Access features or to explain the decisions they made in completing the Case Study.

UNIT PERFORMANCE ASSESSMENT: Cross-Disciplinary, Comprehensive Evaluation

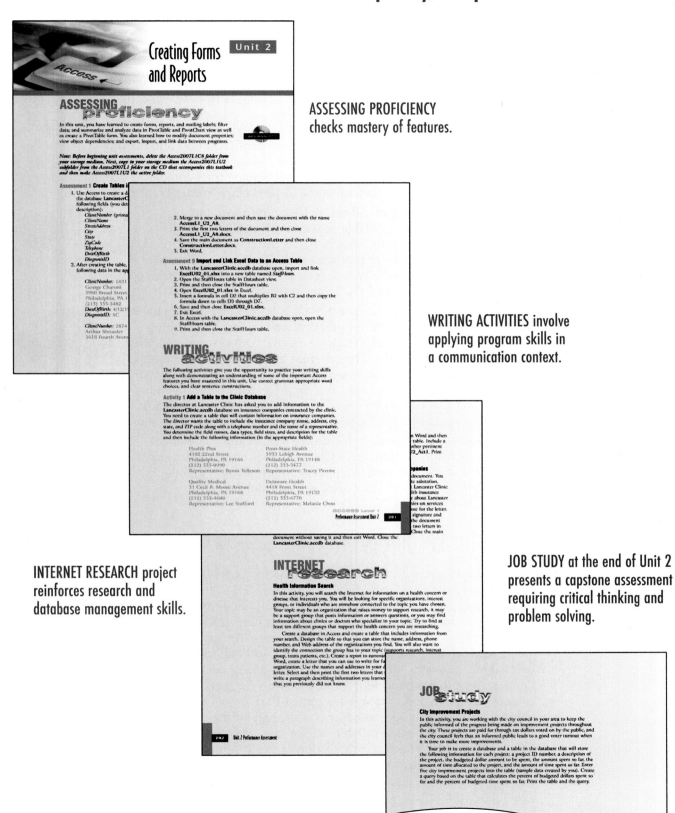

ASSESSING PROFICIENCY checks mastery of features.

WRITING ACTIVITIES involve applying program skills in a communication context.

INTERNET RESEARCH project reinforces research and database management skills.

JOB STUDY at the end of Unit 2 presents a capstone assessment requiring critical thinking and problem solving.

Student Courseware

Student Resources CD Each Benchmark Series textbook is packaged with a Student Resources CD containing the data files required for completing the projects and assessments. A CD icon and folder name displayed on the opening page of chapters reminds students to copy a folder of files from the CD to the desired storage medium before beginning the project exercises. Directions for copying folders are printed on the inside back cover. The Student Resources CD also contains the model answers in PDF format for the project exercises within chapters. Files are locked and watermarked, but students can compare their completed documents with the PDF files, either on screen or in hard copy (printed) format.

Internet Resource Center Additional learning tools and reference materials are available at the book-specific Web site at www.emcp.net/BenchmarkAccess07XP. Students can locate and use the same resources that are on the Student Resources CD along with study aids, Web links, and tips for working with computers effectively in academic and workplace settings.

SNAP Training and Assessment SNAP is a Web-based program that provides hands-on instruction, practice, and testing for learning Microsoft Office 2007 and Windows. SNAP course work simulates operations of Office 2007. The program is comprised of a Web-based learning management system, multimedia tutorials, performance skill items, a concept test bank, and online grade book and course planning tools. A CD-based set of tutorials teaching the basics of Office and Windows is also available for additional practice not requiring Internet access.

Class Connections Available for both WebCT and Blackboard e-learning platforms, Paradigm's Class Connection provides self-quizzes and study aids and facilitates communication among students and instructors via e-mail and e-discussion.

Instructor Resources

Curriculum Planner and Resources Instructor support for the Benchmark Series has been expanded to include a *Curriculum Planner and Resources* binder with CD. This all-in-one print resource includes planning resources such as Lesson Blueprints, teaching hints, and sample course syllabi; presentation resources such as PowerPoint presentations and handouts; and assessment resources including an overview of assessment venues, live program and PDF model answers for intrachapter projects, and live program and annotated PDF model answers for end-of-chapter and end-of-unit assessments. Contents of the *Curriculum Planner and Resources* binder are also available on the Instructor's CD and on the password-protected Instructor's section of the Internet Resource Center for this title at www.emcp.com.

Computerized Test Generator Instructors can use ExamView test generating software and the provided bank of multiple-choice items to create customized Web-based or print tests.

System Requirements

This text is designed for the student to complete projects and assessments on a computer running a standard installation of Microsoft Office 2007, Professional Edition, and the Microsoft Windows XP operating system with Service Pack 2 or later. To effectively run this suite and operating system, your computer should be outfitted with the following:

- 500 MHz processor or higher; 256 MB RAM or higher
- DVD drive
- 2 GB of available hard-disk space
- CD-ROM drive
- 800 by 600 minimum monitor resolution; 1024 by 768 recommended
  Note: Screen captures in this book were created using 1024 by 768 resolution; screens with a higher resolution may look different.
- Computer mouse, or compatible pointing device

About the Authors

Nita Rutkosky began teaching business education courses at Pierce College in Puyallup, Washington, in 1978. Since then she has taught a variety of software applications to students in postsecondary Information Technology certificate and degree programs. In addition to co-authoring texts in the *Benchmark Office 2007 Series*, she has co-authored *Signature Word 2007*, *Marquee Office 2007*, and *Using Computers in the Medical Office: Microsoft Word, Excel, and PowerPoint 2003*. Other textbooks she has written for Paradigm Publishing include books on previous versions of Microsoft Office along with WordPerfect, desktop publishing, keyboarding, and voice recognition.

Audrey Rutkosky Roggenkamp has been teaching courses in the Business Information Technology department at Pierce College in Puyallup including keyboarding, skill building, and Microsoft Office programs. In addition to titles in the *Benchmark Office 2007 Series*, she has co-authored *Using Computers in the Medical Office*, *Marquee Office 2007*, and *Signature Word 2007*.

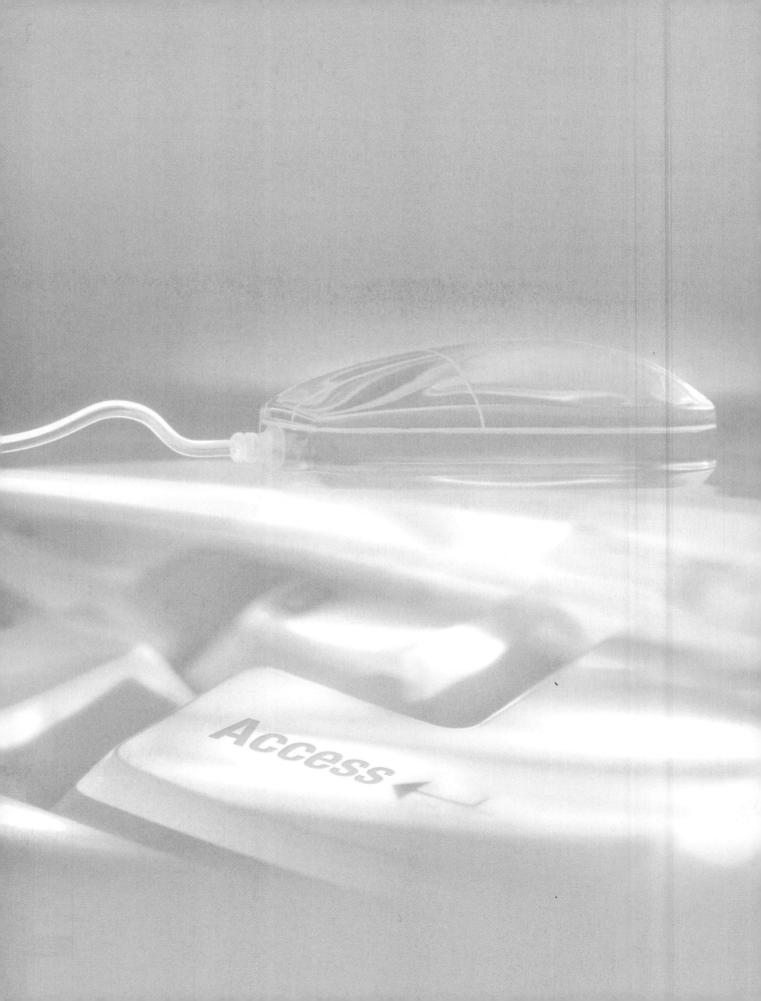

Getting Started in Office 2007

In this textbook, you will learn to operate several computer application programs that combine to make an application "suite." This suite of programs is called Microsoft Office 2007. The programs you will learn to operate are the software, which includes instructions telling the computer what to do. Some of the application programs in the suite include a word processing program named Word, a spreadsheet program named Excel, a database program named Access, and a presentation program named PowerPoint.

Identifying Computer Hardware

The computer equipment you will use to operate the suite of programs is referred to as hardware. You will need access to a microcomputer system that should consist of the CPU, monitor, keyboard, printer, drives, and mouse. If you are not sure what equipment you will be operating, check with your instructor. The computer system shown in Figure G.1 consists of six components. Each component is discussed separately in the material that follows.

Figure G.1 Microcomputer System

CPU

CPU stands for Central Processing Unit and it is the intelligence of the computer. All the processing occurs in the CPU. Silicon chips, which contain miniaturized circuitry, are placed on boards that are plugged into slots within the CPU. Whenever an instruction is given to the computer, that instruction is processed through circuitry in the CPU.

Monitor

The monitor is a piece of equipment that looks like a television screen. It displays the information of a program and the text being input at the keyboard. The quality of display for monitors varies depending on the type of monitor and the level of resolution. Monitors can also vary in size—generally from 14-inch size up to 21-inch size or larger.

Keyboard

The keyboard is used to input information into the computer. Keyboards for microcomputers vary in the number and location of the keys. Microcomputers have the alphabetic and numeric keys in the same location as the keys on a typewriter. The symbol keys, however, may be placed in a variety of locations, depending on the manufacturer. In addition to letters, numbers, and symbols, most microcomputer keyboards contain function keys, arrow keys, and a numeric keypad. Figure G.2 shows an enhanced keyboard.

Figure G.1 Microcomputer System

The 12 keys at the top of the enhanced keyboard, labeled with the letter F followed by a number, are called *function keys*. Use these keys to perform functions within each of the suite programs. To the right of the regular keys is a group of *special* or *dedicated keys*. These keys are labeled with specific functions that will be performed when you press the key. Below the special keys are arrow keys. Use these keys to move the insertion point in the document screen.

In the upper right corner of the keyboard are three mode indicator lights. When you select certain modes, a light appears on the keyboard. For example, if you press the Caps Lock key, which disables the lowercase alphabet, a light appears next to Caps Lock. Similarly, pressing the Num Lock key will disable the special functions on the numeric keypad, which is located at the right side of the keyboard.

Disk Drives

Depending on the computer system you are using, Microsoft Office 2007 is installed on a hard drive or as part of a network system. Whether you are using Office on a hard drive or network system, you will need to have available a DVD or CD drive and a USB drive or other storage medium. You will insert the CD (compact disc) that accompanies this textbook in the DVD or CD drive and then copy folders from the CD to your storage medium. You will also save documents you complete at the computer to folders on your storage medium.

Printer

A document you create in Word is considered soft copy. If you want a hard copy of a document, you need to print it. To print documents you will need to access a printer, which will probably be either a laser printer or an ink-jet printer. A laser printer uses a laser beam combined with heat and pressure to print documents, while an ink-jet printer prints a document by spraying a fine mist of ink on the page.

Mouse

Many functions in the suite of programs are designed to operate more efficiently with a mouse. A mouse is an input device that sits on a flat surface next to the computer. You can operate a mouse with the left or the right hand. Moving the mouse on the flat surface causes a corresponding mouse pointer to move on the screen. Figure G.1 shows an illustration of a mouse.

Using the Mouse

The programs in the Microsoft Office suite can be operated using a keyboard or they can be operated with the keyboard and a mouse. The mouse may have two or three buttons on top, which are tapped to execute specific functions and commands. To use the mouse, rest it on a flat surface or a mouse pad. Put your hand over it with your palm resting on top of the mouse and your wrist resting on the table surface. As you move the mouse on the flat surface, a corresponding pointer moves on the screen.

When using the mouse, you should understand four terms—point, click, double-click, and drag. When operating the mouse, you may need to point to a specific command, button, or icon. Point means to position the mouse pointer on the desired item. With the mouse pointer positioned on the desired item, you may need to click a button on the mouse. Click means quickly tapping a button on the mouse once. To complete two steps at one time, such as choosing and then executing a function, double-click a mouse button. Double-click means to tap the left mouse button twice in quick succession. The term drag means to press and hold the left mouse button, move the mouse pointer to a specific location, and then release the button.

Using the Mouse Pointer

The mouse pointer will change appearance depending on the function being performed or where the pointer is positioned. The mouse pointer may appear as one of the following images:

- The mouse pointer appears as an I-beam (called the I-beam pointer) in the document screen and can be used to move the insertion point or select text.

- The mouse pointer appears as an arrow pointing up and to the left (called the arrow pointer) when it is moved to the Title bar, Quick Access toolbar, ribbon, or an option in a dialog box. For example, to open a new document with the mouse, position the I-beam pointer on the Office button located in the upper left corner of the screen until the pointer turns into an arrow pointer and then click the left mouse button. At the drop-down menu that displays, make a selection by positioning the arrow pointer on the desired option and then clicking the left mouse button.

- The mouse pointer becomes a double-headed arrow (either pointing left and right, pointing up and down, or pointing diagonally) when performing certain functions such as changing the size of an object.

- In certain situations, such as moving an object or image, the mouse pointer becomes a four-headed arrow. The four-headed arrow means that you can move the object left, right, up, or down.

- When a request is being processed or when a program is being loaded, the mouse pointer may appear with an hourglass beside it. The hourglass image means "please wait." When the process is completed, the hourglass image is removed.

- The mouse pointer displays as a hand with a pointing index finger in certain functions such as Help and indicates that more information is available about the item.

Choosing Commands

Once a program is open, you can use several methods in the program to choose commands. A command is an instruction that tells the program to do something. You can choose a command using the mouse or the keyboard. When a program such as Word or PowerPoint is open, the ribbon contains buttons for completing tasks and contains tabs you click to display additional buttons. To choose a button on the Quick Access toolbar or in the ribbon, position the tip of the mouse arrow pointer on a button and then click the left mouse button.

The Office suite provides access keys you can press to use a command in a program. Press the Alt key on the keyboard to display KeyTips that identify the access key you need to press to execute a command. For example, press the Alt key in a Word document and KeyTips display as shown in Figure G.3. Continue pressing access keys until you execute the desired command. For example, if you want to begin spell checking a document, you would press the Alt key, press the R key on the keyboard to display the Review tab, and then press the letter S on the keyboard.

Figure G.3 Access Key KeyTips

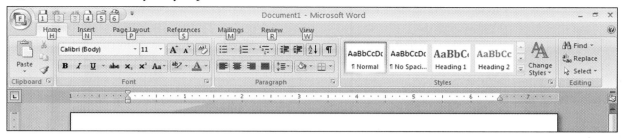

Choosing Commands from Drop-Down Lists

To choose a command from a drop-down list with the mouse, position the mouse pointer on the desired option and then click the left mouse button. To make a selection from a drop-down list with the keyboard, type the underlined letter in the desired option.

Some options at a drop-down list may be gray-shaded (dimmed), indicating that the option is currently unavailable. If an option at a drop-down list displays preceded by a check mark, that indicates that the option is currently active. If an option at a drop-down list displays followed by an ellipsis (…), a dialog box will display when that option is chosen.

Choosing Options from a Dialog Box

A dialog box contains options for applying formatting to a file or data within a file. Some dialog boxes display with tabs along the top providing additional options. For example, the Font dialog box shown in Figure G.4 contains two tabs—the Font tab and the Character Spacing tab. The tab that displays in the front is the

Figure G.4 Word Font Dialog Box

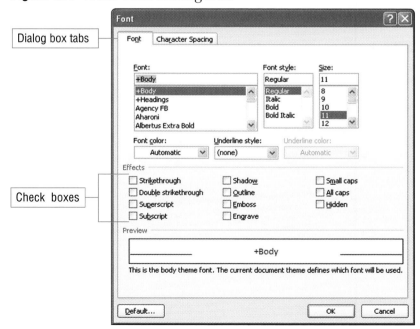

active tab. To make a tab active using the mouse, position the arrow pointer on the desired tab and then click the left mouse button. If you are using the keyboard, press Ctrl + Tab or press Alt + the underlined letter on the desired tab.

To choose options from a dialog box with the mouse, position the arrow pointer on the desired option and then click the left mouse button. If you are using the keyboard, press the Tab key to move the insertion point forward from option to option. Press Shift + Tab to move the insertion point backward from option to option. You can also hold down the Alt key and then press the underlined letter of the desired option. When an option is selected, it displays with a blue background or surrounded by a dashed box called a marquee. A dialog box contains one or more of the following elements: text boxes, list boxes, check boxes, option buttons, spin boxes, and command buttons.

Text Boxes

Some options in a dialog box require you to enter text. For example, the boxes below the *Find what* and *Replace with* options at the Excel Find and Replace dialog box shown in Figure G.5 are text boxes. In a text box, you type text or edit existing text. Edit text in a text box in the same manner as normal text. Use the Left and Right Arrow keys on the keyboard to move the insertion point without deleting text and use the Delete key or Backspace key to delete text.

Figure G.5 Excel Find and Replace Dialog Box

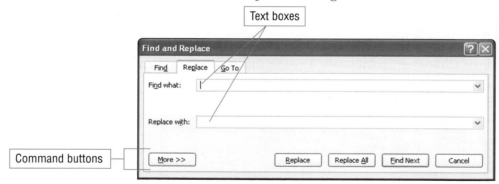

List Boxes

Some dialog boxes such as the Word Open dialog box shown in Figure G.6 may contain a list box. The list of files below the *Look in* option is contained in a list box. To make a selection from a list box with the mouse, move the arrow pointer to the desired option and then click the left mouse button.

Figure G.6 Word Open Dialog Box

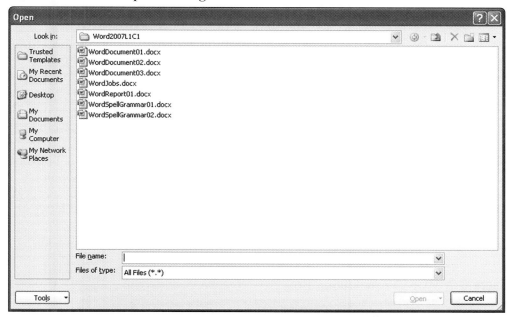

Some list boxes may contain a scroll bar. This scroll bar will display at the right side of the list box (a vertical scroll bar) or at the bottom of the list box (a horizontal scroll bar). You can use a vertical scroll bar or a horizontal scroll bar to move through the list if the list is longer than the box. To move down through a list on a vertical scroll bar, position the arrow pointer on the down-pointing arrow and hold down the left mouse button. To scroll up through the list in a vertical scroll bar, position the arrow pointer on the up-pointing arrow and hold down the left mouse button. You can also move the arrow pointer above the scroll box and click the left mouse button to scroll up the list or move the arrow pointer below the scroll box and click the left mouse button to move down the list. To move through a list with a horizontal scroll bar, click the left-pointing arrow to scroll to the left of the list or click the right-pointing arrow to scroll to the right of the list.

To make a selection from a list using the keyboard, move the insertion point into the box by holding down the Alt key and pressing the underlined letter of the desired option. Press the Up and/or Down Arrow keys on the keyboard to move through the list.

In some dialog boxes where enough room is not available for a list box, lists of options are inserted in a drop-down list box. Options that contain a drop-down list box display with a down-pointing arrow. For example, the *Underline style* option at the Word Font dialog box shown in Figure G.4 contains a drop-down list. To display the list, click the down-pointing arrow to the right of the *Underline style* option box. If you are using the keyboard, press Alt + U.

Check Boxes

Some dialog boxes contain options preceded by a box. A check mark may or may not appear in the box. The Word Font dialog box shown in Figure G.4 displays a variety of check boxes within the *Effects* section. If a check mark appears in the box, the option is active (turned on). If the check box does not contain a check mark, the option is inactive (turned off). Any number of check boxes can be active. For example, in the Word Font dialog box, you can insert a check mark in any or all of the boxes in the *Effects* section and these options will be active.

To make a check box active or inactive with the mouse, position the tip of the arrow pointer in the check box and then click the left mouse button. If you are using the keyboard, press Alt + the underlined letter of the desired option.

Option Buttons

The Word Print dialog box shown in Figure G.7 contains options in the *Print range* section preceded by option buttons. Only one option button can be selected at any time. When an option button is selected, a green circle displays in the button. To select an option button with the mouse, position the tip of the arrow pointer inside the option button and then click the left mouse button. To make a selection with the keyboard, hold down the Alt key and then press the underlined letter of the desired option.

Figure G.7 Word Print Dialog Box

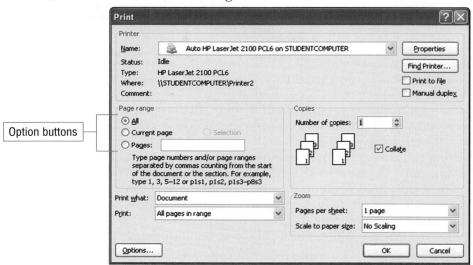

Option buttons

Spin Boxes

Some options in a dialog box contain measurements or numbers you can increase or decrease. These options are generally located in a spin box. For example, the Word Paragraph dialog box shown in Figure G.8 contains spin boxes located after the *Left*, *Right*, *Before*, and *After* options. To increase a number in a spin box, position the tip of the arrow pointer on the up-pointing arrow to the right of the desired option and then click the left mouse button. To decrease the number, click the down-pointing arrow. If you are using the keyboard, press Alt + the underlined letter of the desired option and then press the Up Arrow key to increase the number or the Down Arrow key to decrease the number.

Figure G.8 Word Paragraph Dialog Box

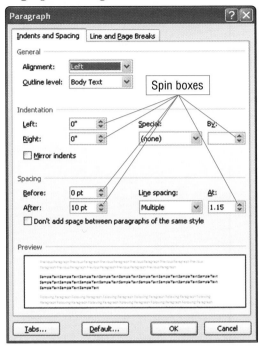

Command Buttons

In the Excel Find and Replace dialog box shown in Figure G.5, the boxes along the bottom of the dialog box are called command buttons. Use a command button to execute or cancel a command. Some command buttons display with an ellipsis (...). A command button that displays with an ellipsis will open another dialog box. To choose a command button with the mouse, position the arrow pointer on the desired button and then click the left mouse button. To choose a command button with the keyboard, press the Tab key until the desired command button contains the marquee and then press the Enter key.

Choosing Commands with Keyboard Shortcuts

Applications in the Office suite offer a variety of keyboard shortcuts you can use to executive specific commands. Keyboard shortcuts generally require two or more keys. For example, the keyboard shortcut to display the Open dialog box in an application is Ctrl + O. To use this keyboard shortcut, hold down the Ctrl key, type the letter O on the keyboard, and then release the Ctrl key. For a list of keyboard shortcuts, refer to the Help files.

Choosing Commands with Shortcut Menus

The software programs in the suite include menus that contain commands related to the item with which you are working. A shortcut menu appears in the file in the location where you are working. To display a shortcut menu, click the right mouse button or press Shift + F10. For example, if the insertion point is positioned in a paragraph of text in a Word document, clicking the right mouse button or pressing Shift + F10 will cause the shortcut menu shown in Figure G.9 to display in the document screen.

Figure G.9 Word Shortcut Menu

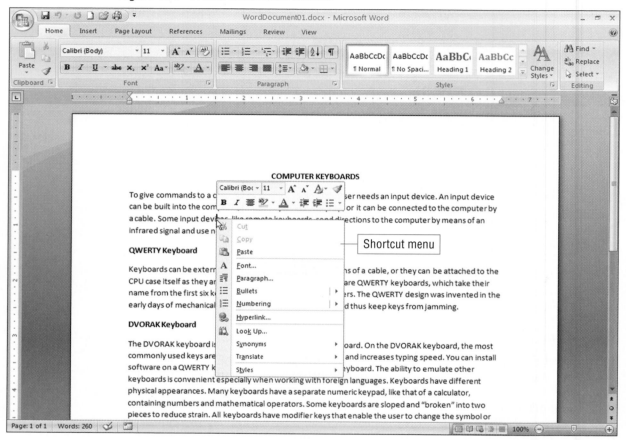

To select an option from a shortcut menu with the mouse, click the desired option. If you are using the keyboard, press the Up or Down Arrow key until the desired option is selected and then press the Enter key. To close a shortcut menu without choosing an option, click anywhere outside the shortcut menu or press the Esc key.

Working with Multiple Programs

As you learn the various programs in the Microsoft Office suite, you will notice how executing commands in each is very similar. For example, the steps to save, close, and print are virtually the same whether you are working in Word, Excel, or PowerPoint. This consistency between programs greatly enhances a user's ability to transfer knowledge learned in one program to another within the suite. Another appeal of Microsoft Office is the ability to have more than one program open at the same time. For example, you can open Word, create a document, and then open Excel, create a spreadsheet, and copy the spreadsheet into Word.

When you open a program, the name of the program displays in the Taskbar. If you open a file within the program, the file name follows the program name on the button on the Taskbar. If you open another program, the program name displays on a button positioned to the right of the first program button. Figure G.10 shows the Taskbar with Word, Excel, and PowerPoint open. To move from one program to another, click the button on the Taskbar representing the desired program file.

Figure G.10 Taskbar with Word, Excel, and PowerPoint Open

Completing Computer Projects

Some computer projects in this textbook require that you open an existing file. Project files are saved on the Student CD that accompanies this textbook. The files you need for each chapter are saved in individual folders. Before beginning a chapter, copy the necessary folder from the CD to your storage medium. After completing projects in a chapter, delete the chapter folder before copying the next chapter folder. (Check with your instructor before deleting a folder.)

The Student CD also contains model answers in PDF format for the project exercises within (but not at the end of) each chapter so you can check your work. To access the PDF files, you will need to have Adobe Acrobat Reader installed on your computer's hard drive. A free download of Adobe Reader is available at Adobe Systems' Web site at www.adobe.com.

Copying a Folder

As you begin working in a chapter, copy the chapter folder from the CD to your storage medium using the My Computer window by completing the following steps:

1. Insert the CD that accompanies this textbook in the CD drive.
2. Insert your storage medium in the appropriate drive.
3. At the Windows XP desktop, open the My Computer window by clicking the Start button and then clicking *My Computer* at the Start menu.
4. Double-click the CD drive in the contents pane (probably displays as *Office2007_Bench* or *Word2007, Excel 2007*, etc. followed by the drive letter).
5. Double-click the *StudentDataFiles* folder in the contents pane.
6. Double-click the desired folder name in the contents pane. (For example, if you are copying a folder for a Word Level 1 chapter, double-click the *Word2007L1* folder.)
7. Click once on the desired chapter subfolder name to select it.
8. Click the <u>Copy this folder</u> hyperlink in the *File and Folder Tasks* section of the task pane.
9. At the Copy Items dialog box, click the drive where your storage medium is located and then click the Copy button.
10. After the folder is copied to your storage medium, close the My Computer window by clicking the Close button (white X on red background) that displays in the upper right corner of the window.

Deleting a Folder

Before copying a chapter folder onto your storage medium, delete any previous chapter folders. Do this in the My Computer window by completing the following steps:

1. Insert your storage medium in the appropriate drive.
2. At the Windows XP desktop, open the My Computer window by clicking the Start button and then clicking *My Computer* at the Start menu.
3. Double-click the drive where you storage medium is located in the contents pane.
4. Click the chapter folder in the list box.
5. Click the <u>Delete this folder</u> hyperlink in the *File and Folder Tasks* section of the task pane.
6. At the message asking if you want to remove the folder and all its contents, click the Yes button.
7. If a message displays asking if you want to delete a read-only file, click the Yes to All button.
8. Close the My Computer window by clicking the Close button (white X on red background) that displays in the upper right corner of the window.

Viewing or Printing the Project Model Answers

If you want to access the PDF model answer files, first make sure that Adobe Acrobat Reader is installed on your hard drive. Double-click the folder, double-click the desired chapter subfolder name, and double-click the appropriate file name to open the file. You can view and/or print the file to compare it with your own completed exercise file.

Customizing the Quick Access Toolbar

The four applications in the Office 2007 suite covered in this textbook — Word, Excel, PowerPoint, and Access — each contain a Quick Access toolbar that displays at the top of the screen. By default, this toolbar contains three buttons: Save, Undo, and Redo. Before beginning chapters in this textbook, customize the Quick Access toolbar by adding three additional buttons: New, Open, and Quick Print. To add these three buttons to the Word Quick Access toolbar, complete the following steps:

1. Open Word.
2. Click the Customize Quick Access Toolbar button that displays at the right side of the toolbar.
3. At the drop-down list, click *New*. (This adds the New button to the toolbar.)
4. Click the Customize Quick Access Toolbar button and then click *Open* at the drop-down list. (This adds the Open button to the toolbar.)
5. Click the Customize Quick Access Toolbar button and then click *Quick Print* at the drop-down list. (This adds the Quick Print button to the toolbar.)

Complete the same steps for Excel, Access, and PowerPoint. You will only need to add the buttons once to the Quick Access toolbar. These buttons will remain on the toolbar even when you exit and then reopen the application.

Using Windows XP

A computer requires an operating system to provide necessary instructions on a multitude of processes including loading programs, managing data, directing the flow of information to peripheral equipment, and displaying information. Windows XP Professional is an operating system that provides functions of this type (along with much more) in a graphical environment. Windows is referred to as a ***graphical user interface*** (GUI—pronounced *gooey*) that provides a visual display of information with features such as icons (pictures) and buttons. In this introduction, you will learn the basic features of Windows XP:

- Use desktop icons and the Taskbar to launch programs and open files or folders
- Organize and manage data, including copying, moving, creating, and deleting files and folders
- Customize the desktop by changing the theme, background, colors, and settings, and adding a screen saver
- Use the Help and Support Center features
- Customize monitor settings

Historically, Microsoft has produced two editions of Windows—one edition for individual users (on desktop and laptop computers) and another edition for servers (on computers that provide service over networks). Windows XP is an upgrade and a merging of these two Windows editions and is available in two versions. The Windows XP Home Edition is designed for home use and Windows XP Professional is designed for small office and workstation use. Whether you are using Windows XP Home Edition or Windows XP Professional, you will be able to complete the steps in the exercises in this introduction.

Before using one of the software programs in the Microsoft Office suite, you will need to start the Windows XP operating system. To do this, turn on the computer. Depending on your computer equipment configuration, you may also need to turn on the monitor and printer. If you are using a computer that is part of a network system or if your computer is set up for multiple users, a screen will display showing the user accounts defined for your computer system. At this screen, click your user account name and, if necessary, type your password and then press the Enter key. The Windows XP operating system will start and, after a few moments, the desktop will display as shown in Figure W.1. (Your desktop may vary from what you see in Figure W.1.)

Figure W.1 Windows XP Desktop

icon

Taskbar

Exploring the Desktop

When Windows XP is loaded, the main portion of the screen is called the *desktop*. Think of the desktop in Windows as the top of a desk in an office. A business person places necessary tools—such as pencils, pens, paper, files, calculator—on the desktop to perform functions. Like the tools that are located on a desk, the desktop contains tools for operating the computer. These tools are logically grouped and placed in dialog boxes or panels that you can display using icons on the desktop. The desktop contains a variety of features for using your computer and software programs installed on the computer. The features available on the desktop are represented by icons and buttons.

Using Icons

Icons are visual symbols that represent programs, files, or folders. Figure W.1 identifies the *Recycle Bin* icon located on the Windows XP desktop. The Windows XP desktop on your computer may contain additional icons. Programs that have been installed on your computer may be represented by an icon on the desktop. Also, icons may display on your desktop representing files or folders. Double-click an icon and the program, file, or folder it represents opens on the desktop.

Using the Taskbar

The bar that displays at the bottom of the desktop (see Figure W.1) is called the Taskbar. The Taskbar, shown in Figure W.2, contains the Start button, a section that displays task buttons representing open programs, and the notification area.

Figure W.2 Windows XP Taskbar

Start button   Task button area   Notification area

Click the Start button, located at the left side of the Taskbar, and the Start menu displays as shown in Figure W.3 (your Start menu may vary). You can also display the Start menu by pressing the Windows key on your keyboard or by pressing Ctrl + Esc. The left column of the Start menu contains *pinned programs*, which are programs that always appear in that particular location on the Start menu, and links to the most recently and frequently used programs. The right column contains links to folders, the Control Panel, online help, and the search feature.

Figure W.3 Start Menu

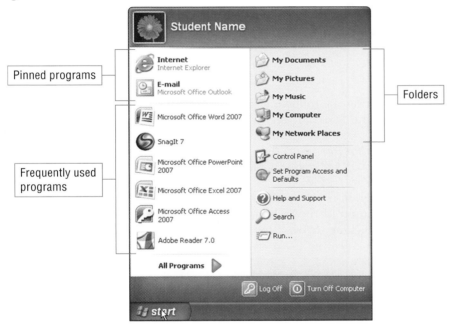

To choose an option from the Start menu, drag the arrow pointer to the desired option (referred to as *pointing*) and then click the left mouse button. Pointing to options at the Start menu that are followed by a right-pointing arrow will cause a side menu to display with additional options. When a program is open, a task button representing the program appears on the Taskbar. If multiple programs are open, each program will appear as a task button on the Taskbar (a few specialized tools may not).

Project ① Opening Programs and Switching between Programs

1. Open Windows XP. (To do this, turn on the computer and, if necessary, turn on the monitor and/or printer. If you are using a computer that is part of a network system or if your computer is set up for multiple users, you may need to click your user account name and, if necessary, type your password and then press the Enter key. Check with your instructor to determine if you need to complete any additional steps.)

2. When the Windows XP desktop displays, open Microsoft Word by completing the following steps:
   a. Position the arrow pointer on the Start button on the Taskbar and then click the left mouse button.
   b. At the Start menu, point to *All Programs* (a side menu displays) and then point to *Microsoft Office* (another side menu displays).
   c. Drag the arrow pointer to *Microsoft Office Word 2007* in the side menu and then click the left mouse button.
   d. When the Microsoft Word program is open, notice that a task button representing Word displays on the Taskbar.

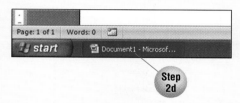

Step 2d

3. Open Microsoft Excel by completing the following steps:
   a. Position the arrow pointer on the Start button on the Taskbar and then click the left mouse button.
   b. At the Start menu, point to *All Programs* and then point to *Microsoft Office*.
   c. Drag the arrow pointer to *Microsoft Office Excel 2007* in the side menu and then click the left mouse button.
   d. When the Microsoft Excel program is open, notice that a task button representing Excel displays on the Taskbar to the right of the task button representing Word.

4. Switch to the Word program by clicking the task button on the Taskbar representing Word.

Step 4

Step 6

5. Switch to the Excel program by clicking the task button on the Taskbar representing Excel.
6. Exit Excel by clicking the Close button that displays in the upper right corner of the Excel window.
7. Exit Word by clicking the Close button that displays in the upper right corner of the Word window.

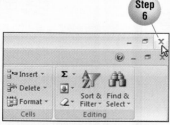

Exploring the Notification Area

The notification area is located at the right side of the Taskbar and contains the system clock along with small icons representing specialized programs that run in the background. Position the arrow pointer over the current time in the notification area of the Taskbar and today's date displays in a small yellow box above the time. Double-click the current time displayed on the Taskbar and the Date and Time Properties dialog box displays as shown in Figure W.4.

Figure W.4 Date and Time Properties Box

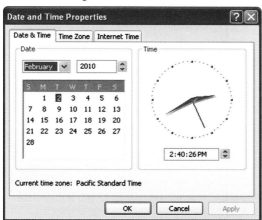

Change the date with options in the *Date* section of the dialog box. For example, to change the month, click the down-pointing arrow at the right side of the option box containing the current month and then click the desired month at the drop-down list. Change the year by clicking the up- or down-pointing arrow at the right side of the option box containing the current year until the desired year displays. To change the day, click the desired day in the monthly calendar that displays in the dialog box. To change the time, double-click either the hour, minute, or seconds and then type the appropriate time or use the up- and down-pointing arrows to adjust the time.

Some programs, when installed, will add an icon to the notification area of the Taskbar. Display the name of the icon by positioning the mouse pointer on the icon and, after approximately one second, the icon label displays in a small yellow box. Some icons may display information in the yellow box rather than the icon label. If more icons have been inserted in the notification area than can be viewed at one time, a left-pointing arrow button displays at the left side of the notification area. Click this left-pointing arrow button and the remaining icons display.

Setting Taskbar Properties

By default, the Taskbar is locked in its current position and size. You can change this default setting, along with other default settings, with options at the Taskbar and Start Menu Properties dialog box, shown in Figure W.5. To display this dialog box, position the arrow pointer on any empty spot on the Taskbar and then click the right mouse button. At the shortcut menu that displays, click *Properties*.

Figure W.5 Taskbar and Start Menu Properties Box

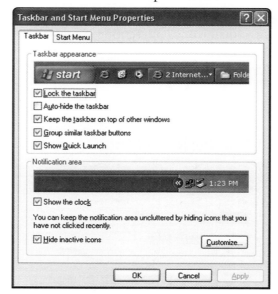

Each property is controlled by a check box. Property options containing a check mark are active. Click the option to remove the check mark and make the option inactive. If an option is inactive, clicking the option will insert a check mark in the check box and turn on the option (make it active).

Project ②   Changing Taskbar Properties

1. Make sure Windows XP is open and the desktop displays.
2. Hide the Taskbar and remove the display of the clock by completing the following steps:
   a. Position the arrow pointer on any empty area on the Taskbar and then click the *right* mouse button.
   b. At the shortcut menu that displays, click *Properties*.
   c. At the Taskbar and Start Menu Properties dialog box, click *Auto-hide the taskbar*. (This inserts a check mark in the check box.)
   d. Click *Show the clock*. (This removes the check mark from the check box.)
   e. Click the Apply button.
   f. Click OK to close the dialog box.

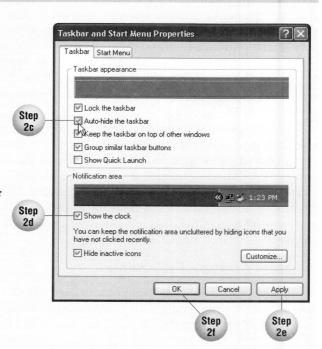

3. Display the Taskbar by positioning the mouse pointer at the bottom of the screen. When the Taskbar displays, notice that the time no longer displays at the right side of the Taskbar.
4. Return to the default settings for the Taskbar by completing the following steps:
   a. With the Taskbar displayed (if it does not display, position the mouse pointer at the bottom of the desktop), position the arrow pointer on any empty area on the Taskbar and then click the *right* mouse button.
   b. At the shortcut menu that displays, click *Properties*.
   c. At the Taskbar and Start Menu Properties dialog box, click *Auto-hide the taskbar*. (This removes the check mark from the check box.)
   d. Click *Show the clock*. (This inserts a check mark in the check box.)
   e. Click the Apply button.
   f. Click OK to close the dialog box.

Turning Off the Computer

When you are finished working with your computer, you can choose to shut down the computer completely, shut down and then restart the computer, put the computer on standby, or tell the computer to hibernate. Do not turn off your computer until your screen goes blank. Important data is stored in memory while Windows XP is running and this data needs to be written to the hard drive before turning off the computer.

To shut down your computer, click the Start button on the Taskbar and then click *Turn Off Computer* at the Start menu. At the Turn off computer window, shown in Figure W.6, click the *Stand By* option and the computer switches to a low power state causing some devices such as the monitor and hard drives to turn off. With these devices off, the computer uses less power. Stand By is particularly useful for saving battery power for portable computers. Tell the computer to "hibernate" by holding down the Shift key while clicking the *Stand By* option. In hibernate mode, the computer saves everything in memory, turns off the monitor and hard drive, and then turns off the computer. Click the *Turn Off* option if you want to shut down Windows XP and turn off all power to the computer. Click the *Restart* option if you want to restart the computer and restore the desktop exactly as you left it. You can generally restore your desktop from either standby or hibernate by pressing once on the computer's power button. Usually, bringing a computer out of hibernation takes a little longer than bringing a computer out of standby.

Figure W.6 Turn Off Computer Window

Managing Files and Folders

As you begin working with programs in Windows XP, you will create files in which data (information) is saved. A file might contain a Word document, an Excel workbook, or a PowerPoint presentation. As you begin creating files, consider creating folders into which those files will be stored. You can complete file management tasks such as creating a folder and copying and moving files and folders at the My Computer window. To display the My Computer window shown in Figure W.7, click the Start button on the Taskbar and then click My Computer. The various components of the My Computer window are identified in Figure W.7.

Figure W.7 My Computer Window

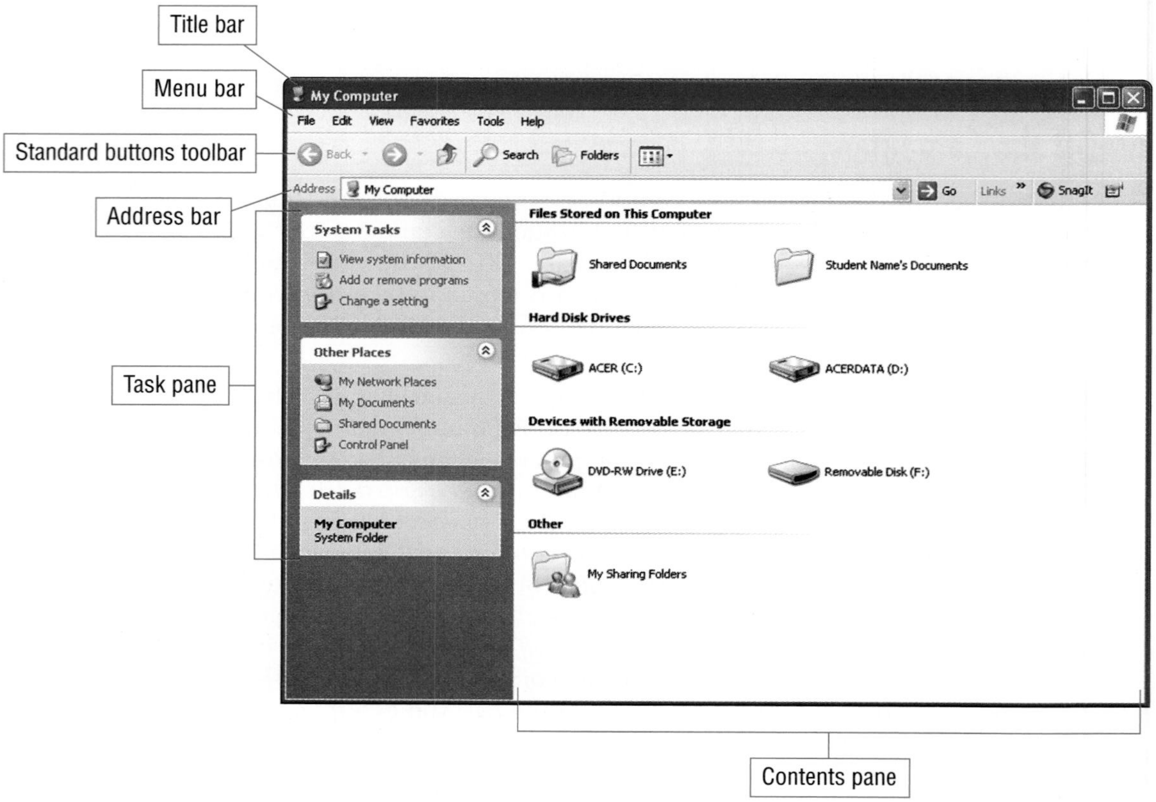

Copying, Moving, and Deleting Files/Folders

File and folder management activities might include copying and moving files or folders from one folder or drive to another, or deleting files or folders. The My Computer window offers a variety of methods for copying, moving, and deleting files/folders. You can use options in the task pane, drop-down menu options, or shortcut menu options. This section will provide you with the steps for copying, moving, and deleting files/folders using options in the task pane.

To copy a file/folder to another folder or drive, first display the file in the contents pane by identifying the location of the file. If the file is located in the My Documents folder, click the <u>My Documents</u> hyperlink in the *Other Places* section of the task pane. If the file is located on the hard drive, double-click the desired drive in the contents pane; if the file is located on a USB drive, DVD, or CD, double-click the desired drive letter. Next, click the folder or file name in the contents pane that you want to copy. This changes the options in the task pane to include management options such as renaming, moving, copying, and deleting folders or files. Click the Copy this folder (or Copy this file) hyperlink in the task pane and the Copy Items dialog box displays as shown in Figure W.8. At the Copy Items dialog box, click the desired folder or drive and then click the Copy button.

Figure W.8 Copy Items Dialog Box

To move adjacent files/folders, click the first file or folder, hold down the Shift key, and then click the last file or folder. This selects and highlights all files/folders from the first file/folder you clicked to the last file/folder you clicked. With the adjacent files/folders selected, click the Move the selected items hyperlink in the File and Folder Tasks section of the task pane and then specify the desired location at the Move Items dialog box. To select nonadjacent files/folders, click the first file/folder to select it, hold down the Ctrl key, and then click any other files/folders you want to move or copy.

You can easily remove (delete) a file or folder from the My Computer window. To delete a file or folder, click the file or folder in the contents pane, and then click the Delete this folder (or Delete this file) hyperlink in the task pane. At the dialog box asking you to confirm the deletion, click Yes. A deleted file or folder is sent to the Recycle Bin. You will learn more about the Recycle Bin in the next section.

In Exercise 3, you will insert the CD that accompanies this book into the DVD or CD drive. When the CD is inserted, the drive may automatically activate and a dialog box may display on the screen telling you that the disk or device contains more than one type of content and asking what you want Windows to do. If this dialog box displays, click Cancel to remove the dialog box.

Project 3 Copying a File and Folder and Deleting a File

1. At the Windows XP desktop, insert the CD that accompanies this textbook into the appropriate drive. If a dialog box displays telling you that the disk or device contains more than one type of content and asking what you want Windows to do, click Cancel.
2. At the Windows XP desktop, open the My Computer window by clicking the Start button on the Taskbar and then clicking *My Computer* at the Start menu.
3. Copy a file from the CD that accompanies this textbook to the drive containing your storage medium by completing the following steps:
   a. Insert your storage medium in the appropriate drive.
   b. In the contents pane, double-click the drive containing the CD (probably displays as *Office2007_Bench* followed by a drive letter). (Make sure you double-click the mouse button because you want the contents of the CD to display in the contents pane.)
   c. Double-click the *StudentDataFiles* folder.
   d. Double-click the *WindowsXP* folder in the contents pane.
   e. Click **WordDocument01.docx** in the contents pane to select it.
   f. Click the <u>Copy this file</u> hyperlink located in the *File and Folder Tasks* section of the task pane.

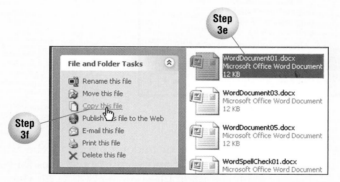

   g. At the Copy Items dialog box, click in the list box the drive containing your storage medium.
   h. Click the Copy button.

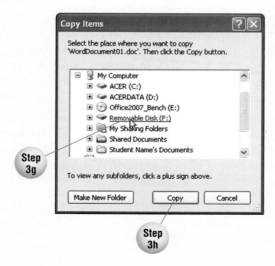

4. Delete **WordDocument01.docx** from your storage medium by completing the following steps:
   a. Click the <u>My Computer</u> hyperlink located in the *Other Places* section of the task pane.
   b. Double-click in the contents pane the drive containing your storage medium.
   c. Click ***WordDocument01.docx***.
   d. Click the <u>Delete this file</u> hyperlink in the *File and Folder Tasks* section of the task pane.

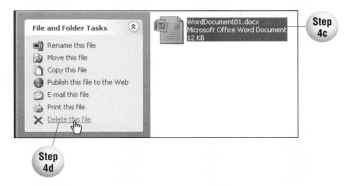

   e. At the message asking you to confirm the deletion, click Yes.
5. Copy the WindowsXP folder from the CD drive to the drive containing your storage medium by completing the following steps:
   a. Click the My Computer hyperlink in the *Other Places* section of the task pane.
   b. In the contents pane, double-click the drive containing the CD (probably displays as *Office2007_Bench* followed by a drive letter).
   c. Double-click the *StudentDataFiles* folder.
   d. Click the *WindowsXP* folder in the contents pane to select it.
   e. Click the <u>Copy this folder</u> hyperlink in the *File and Folder Tasks* section of the task pane.
   f. At the Copy Items dialog box, click the drive containing your storage medium.
   g. Click the Copy button.
6. Close the window by clicking the Close button (contains a white *X* on a red background) located in the upper right corner of the window. (You can also close the window by clicking File on the Menu bar and then clicking *Close* at the drop-down list.)

Selecting Files/Folders

You can move, copy, or delete more than one file or folder at the same time. Before moving, copying, or deleting files/folders, select the desired files or folders. Selecting files/folders is easier when you change the display in the contents pane to List or Details. To change the display, open the My Computer window and then click the Views button on the Standard Buttons toolbar. At the drop-down list that displays, click the *List* option or the *Details* option.

    To move adjacent files/folders, click the first file or folder, hold down the Shift key, and click the last file or folder. This selects and highlights all files/folders from the first file/folder you clicked to the last file/folder you clicked. With the adjacent files/folders selected, click the <u>Move the selected items</u> hyperlink in the *File and Folder Tasks* section of the task pane and then specify the desired location at the Move Items dialog box. To select nonadjacent files/folders, click the first file/folder to select it, hold down the Ctrl key, and then click any other files/folders you want to move or copy.

Project ④ Copying and Deleting Files

1. At the Windows XP desktop, open the My Computer window by clicking the Start button and then clicking *My Computer* at the Start menu.
2. Copy files from the CD that accompanies this textbook to the drive containing your storage medium by completing the following steps:
   a. Make sure the CD that accompanies this textbook and your storage medium are inserted in the appropriate drives.
   b. Double-click the CD drive in the contents pane (probably displays as *Office2007_Bench* followed by the drive letter).
   c. Double-click the *StudentDataFiles* folder in the contents pane.
   d. Double-click the *WindowsXP* folder in the contents pane.
   e. Change the display to Details by clicking the Views button on the Standard Buttons toolbar and then clicking *Details* at the drop-down list.

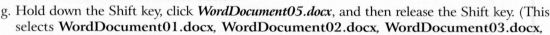

   f. Position the arrow pointer on **WordDocument01.docx** in the contents pane and then click the left mouse button.
   g. Hold down the Shift key, click **WordDocument05.docx**, and then release the Shift key. (This selects **WordDocument01.docx, WordDocument02.docx, WordDocument03.docx, WordDocument04.docx,** and **WordDocument05.docx**.)
   h. Click the <u>Copy the selected items</u> hyperlink in the *File and Folder Tasks* section of the task pane.

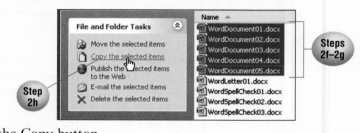

   i. At the Copy Items dialog box, click the drive containing your storage medium and then click the Copy button.
3. Display the files and folder saved on your storage medium by completing the following steps:
   a. Click the <u>My Computer</u> hyperlink in the *Other Places* section of the task pane.
   b. Double-click the drive containing your storage medium.
4. Delete the files from your storage medium that you just copied by completing the following steps:
   a. Change the view by clicking the Views button on the Standard Buttons toolbar and then clicking *List* at the drop-down list.
   b. Click **WordDocument01.docx** in the contents pane.
   c. Hold down the Shift key, click **WordDocument05.docx**, and then release the Shift key. (This selects **WordDocument01.docx, WordDocument02.docx, WordDocument03.docx, WordDocument04.docx,** and **WordDocument05.docx**.)
   d. Click the <u>Delete the selected items</u> hyperlink in the *File and Folder Tasks* section of the task pane.

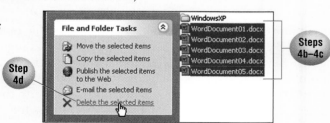

   e. At the message asking you to confirm the deletion, click Yes.
5. Close the window by clicking the Close button (white *X* on red background) that displays in the upper right corner of the window.

Manipulating and Creating Folders

As you begin working with and creating a number of files, consider creating folders in which you can logically group the files. To create a folder, display the My Computer window and then display in the contents pane the drive where you want to create the folder. Click File on the Menu bar, point to *New*, and then click *Folder* at the side menu. This inserts a folder icon in the contents pane and names the folder *New Folder*. Type the desired name for the new folder and then press Enter.

Project ⑤ Creating a New Folder

1. At the Windows XP desktop, open the My Computer window.
2. Create a new folder by completing the following steps:
   a. Double-click in the contents pane the drive that contains your storage medium.
   b. Double-click the *WindowsXP* folder in the contents pane. (This opens the folder.)
   c. Click File on the Menu bar, point to *New*, and then click *Folder*.

   d. Type **SpellCheckFiles** and then press Enter. (This changes the name from *New Folder* to *SpellCheckFiles*.)
3. Copy **WordSpellCheck01.docx**, **WordSpellCheck02.docx**, and **WordSpellCheck03.docx** into the SpellCheckFiles folder you just created by completing the following steps:
   a. Click the Views button on the Standard Buttons toolbar and then click *List* at the drop-down list.

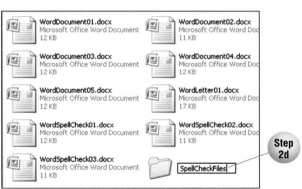

   b. Click once on the file named *WordSpellCheck01.docx* located in the contents pane.
   c. Hold down the Shift key, click once on the file named *WordSpellCheck03.docx*, and then release the Shift key. (This selects **WordSpellCheck01.docx, WordSpellCheck02.docx,** and **WordSpellCheck03.docx**.)
   d. Click the <u>Copy the selected items</u> hyperlink in the *File and Folder Tasks* section of the task pane.
   e. At the Copy Items dialog box, click in the list box the drive containing your storage medium.
   f. Click *WindowsXP* in the list box.
   g. Click *SpellCheckFiles* in the list box.
   h. Click the Copy button.
4. Display the files you just copied by double-clicking the *SpellCheckFiles* folder in the contents pane.

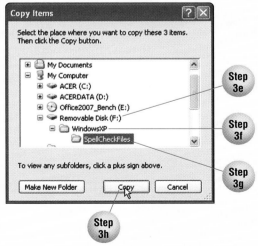

5. Delete the SpellCheckFiles folder and its contents by completing the following steps:
   a. Click the Up button on the Standard Buttons toolbar. (This displays the contents of the Windows folder which is up one folder from the SpellCheckFiles folders.)
   b. Click the *SpellCheckFiles* folder in the contents pane to select it.
   c. Click the <u>Delete this folder</u> hyperlink in the *File and Folder Tasks* section of the task pane.
   d. At the message asking you to confirm the deletion, click Yes.
6. Close the window by clicking the Close button located in the upper right corner of the window.

Using the Recycle Bin

Deleting the wrong file can be a disaster but Windows XP helps protect your work with the Recycle Bin. The Recycle Bin acts just like an office wastepaper basket; you can "throw away" (delete) unwanted files, but you can "reach in" to the Recycle Bin and take out (restore) a file if you threw it away by accident.

Deleting Files to the Recycle Bin

A file/folder or selected files/folders deleted from the hard drive are sent automatically to the Recycle Bin. Files/folders deleted from a disk are deleted permanently. (Recovery programs are available, however, that will help you recover deleted text. If you accidentally delete a file/folder from a disk, do not do anything more with the disk until you can run a recovery program.)

One method for deleting files is to display the My Computer window and then display in the contents pane the file(s) and/or folder(s) you want deleted. Click the file or folder or select multiple files or folders and then click the appropriate delete option in the task pane. At the message asking you to confirm the deletion, click Yes. Another method for deleting a file is to drag the file to the *Recycle Bin* icon on the desktop. Drag a file icon to the Recycle Bin until the *Recycle Bin* icon is selected (displays with a blue background) and then release the mouse button. This drops the file you are dragging into the Recycle Bin.

Recovering Files from the Recycle Bin

You can easily restore a deleted file from the Recycle Bin. To restore a file, double-click the *Recycle Bin* icon on the desktop. This opens the Recycle Bin window shown in Figure W.9. (The contents of the Recycle Bin will vary.) To restore a file, click the file you want restored, and then click the <u>Restore this item</u> hyperlink in the *Recycle Bin Tasks* section of the task pane. This removes the file from the Recycle Bin and returns it to its original location. You can also restore a file by positioning the arrow pointer on the file, clicking the right mouse button, and then clicking *Restore* at the shortcut menu.

Figure W.9 Recycle Bin Window

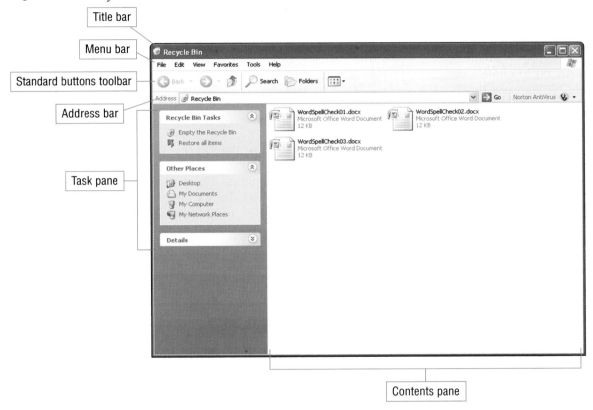

Title bar
Menu bar
Standard buttons toolbar
Address bar
Task pane
Contents pane

Project ⑥ Deleting Files to and Recovering Files from the Recycle Bin

Before completing this exercise, check with your instructor to determine if you can copy files to the hard drive.

1. At the Windows XP desktop, open the My Computer window.
2. Copy files from your storage medium to the My Documents folder on your hard drive by completing the following steps:
    a. Double-click in the contents pane the drive containing your storage medium.
    b. Double-click the *WindowsXP* folder in the contents pane.
    c. Click the Views button on the Standard Buttons toolbar and then click *List* at the drop-down list.
    d. Position the arrow pointer on **WordSpellCheck01.docx** and then click the left mouse button.
    e. Hold down the Shift key, click ***WordSpellCheck03.docx***, and then release the Shift key.

f. Click the Copy the selected items hyperlink in the *File and Folder Tasks* section of the task pane.

g. At the Copy Items dialog box, click *My Documents* in the list box.

h. Click the Copy button.

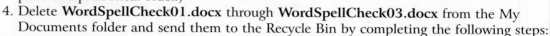

3. Click the <u>My Documents</u> hyperlink in the *Other Places* section of the task pane. (The files you copied, **WordSpellCheck01.docx** through **WordSpellCheck03.docx**, will display in the contents pane in alphabetical order.)

4. Delete **WordSpellCheck01.docx** through **WordSpellCheck03.docx** from the My Documents folder and send them to the Recycle Bin by completing the following steps:

a. Select **WordSpellCheck01.docx** through **WordSpellCheck03.docx** in the contents pane. (If these files are not visible, you will need to scroll down the list of files.)

b. Click the <u>Delete the selected items</u> hyperlink in the *File and Folder Tasks* section of the task pane.

c. At the message asking you to confirm the deletion to the Recycle Bin, click Yes.

5. Click the Close button to close the window.

6. At the desktop, display the contents of the Recycle Bin by double-clicking the *Recycle Bin* icon.

7. At the Recycle Bin window, restore **WordSpellCheck01.docx** through **WordSpellCheck03.docx** to the My Documents folder by completing the following steps:

a. Select **WordSpellCheck01.docx** through **WordSpellCheck03.docx** in the contents pane of the Recycle Bin window. (If these files are not visible, you will need to scroll down the list of files.)

b. With the files selected, click the <u>Restore the selected items</u> hyperlink in the *Recycle Bin Tasks* section of the task pane.

8. Close the Recycle Bin window by clicking the Close button located in the upper right corner of the window.

9. Display the My Computer window.

10. Click the <u>My Documents</u> hyperlink in the *Other Places* section of the task pane.

11. Delete the files you restored by completing the following steps:

a. Select **WordSpellCheck01.docx** through **WordSpellCheck03.docx** in the contents pane. (If these files are not visible, you will need to scroll down the list of files. These are the files you recovered from the Recycle Bin.)

b. Click the <u>Delete the selected items</u> hyperlink in the *File and Folder Tasks* section of the task pane.

c. At the message asking you to confirm the deletion, click Yes.

12. Close the window.

Emptying the Recycle Bin

Just like a wastepaper basket, the Recycle Bin can get full. To empty the Recycle Bin, position the arrow pointer on the *Recycle Bin* icon on the desktop and then click the *right* mouse button. At the shortcut menu that displays, click *Empty Recycle Bin*. At the message asking you to confirm the deletion, click Yes. You can also empty the Recycle Bin by double-clicking the *Recycle Bin* icon. At the Recycle Bin window, click the <u>Empty the Recycle Bin</u> hyperlink in the *Recycle Bin Tasks* section of the task pane. At the message asking you to confirm the deletion, click Yes. (You can also empty the Recycle Bin by clicking File on the Menu bar and then clicking *Empty Recycle Bin* at the drop-down menu.)

Emptying the Recycle Bin deletes all files/folders. You can delete a specific file/folder from the Recycle Bin (rather than all files/folders). To do this, double-click the *Recycle Bin* icon on the desktop. At the Recycle Bin window, select the file/folder or files/folders you want to delete. Click File on the Menu bar and then click *Delete* at the drop-down menu. (You can also right-click a selected file/folder and then click *Delete* at the shortcut menu.) At the message asking you to confirm the deletion, click Yes.

Project ⑦ Emptying the Recycle Bin

Before completing this exercise, check with your instructor to determine if you can delete files/folders from the Recycle Bin.

1. At the Windows XP desktop, double-click the *Recycle Bin* icon.
2. At the Recycle Bin window, empty the contents of the Recycle Bin by completing the following steps:
   a. Click the <u>Empty the Recycle Bin</u> hyperlink in the *Recycle Bin Tasks* section of the task pane.

Step 2a

   b. At the message asking you to confirm the deletion, click Yes.
3. Close the Recycle Bin window by clicking the Close button located in the upper right corner of the window.

When you empty the Recycle Bin, the files cannot be recovered by the Recycle Bin or by Windows XP. If you have to recover a file, you will need to use a file recovery program such as Norton Utilities. These utilities are separate programs, but might be worth their cost if you ever need them.

Creating a Shortcut

If you use a file or program on a consistent basis, consider creating a shortcut to the file or program. A shortcut is a specialized icon that represents very small files that point the operating system to the actual item, whether it is a file, a folder, or an application. If you create a shortcut to a Word document, the shortcut icon is not the actual document but a path to the document. Double-click the shortcut icon and Windows XP opens the document in Word.

One method for creating a shortcut is to display the My Computer window and then display the drive or folder where the file is located. Right-click the desired file, point to *Send To*, and then click *Desktop (create shortcut)*. You can easily delete a shortcut icon from the desktop by dragging the shortcut icon to the Recycle Bin icon. This deletes the shortcut icon but does not delete the file to which the shortcut pointed.

Project ⑧ Creating a Shortcut

1. At the Windows XP desktop, display the My Computer window.
2. Double-click the drive containing your storage medium.
3. Double-click the *Windows* folder in the contents pane.
4. Change the display of files to a list by clicking the Views button on the Standard Buttons toolbar and then clicking *List* at the drop-down list.
5. Create a shortcut to the file named **WordLetter01.docx** by right-clicking on **WordLetter01.docx**, pointing to *Send To*, and then clicking *Desktop (create shortcut)*.

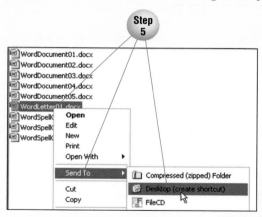

6. Close the My Computer window by clicking the Close button located in the upper right corner of the window.
7. Open Word and the file named **WordLetter01.docx** by double-clicking the *WordLetter01.docx* shortcut icon on the desktop.
8. After viewing the file in Word, exit Word by clicking the Close button that displays in the upper right corner of the window.
9. Delete the *WordLetter01.docx* shortcut icon by completing the following steps:
   a. At the desktop, position the mouse pointer on the *WordLetter01.docx* shortcut icon.
   b. Hold down the left mouse button, drag the icon on top of the *Recycle Bin* icon, and then release the mouse button.

Customizing the Desktop

You can customize the Windows XP desktop to fit your particular needs and preferences. For example, you can choose a different theme, change the desktop background, add a screen saver, and apply a different appearance to windows, dialog boxes, and menus. To customize the desktop, position the arrow pointer on any empty location on the desktop and then click the *right* mouse button. At the shortcut menu that displays, click *Properties*. This displays the Display Properties dialog box with the Themes tab selected as shown in Figure W.10.

Figure W.10 Display Properties Dialog Box

Changing the Theme

A Windows XP theme specifies a variety of formatting such as fonts, sounds, icons, colors, mouse pointers, background, and screen saver. Windows XP contains two themes—Windows XP (the default) and Windows Classic (which appears like earlier versions of Windows). Other themes are available as downloads from the Microsoft Web site. Change the theme with the *Theme* option at the Display Properties dialog box with the Themes tab selected.

Changing the Desktop

With options at the Display Properties dialog box with the Desktop tab selected, as shown in Figure W.11, you can choose a different desktop background and customize the desktop. Click any option in the *Background* list box and preview the results in the preview screen. With the *Position* option, you can specify that the background image is centered, tiled, or stretched on the desktop. Use the *Color* option to change the background color and click the Browse button to choose a background image from another location or Web site.

Figure W.11 Display Properties Dialog Box with Desktop Tab Selected

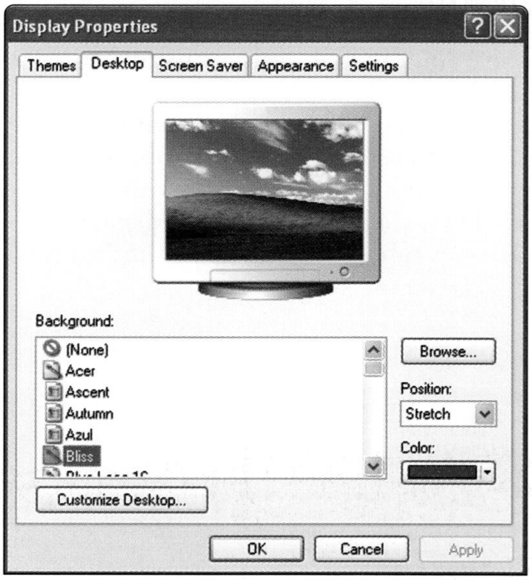

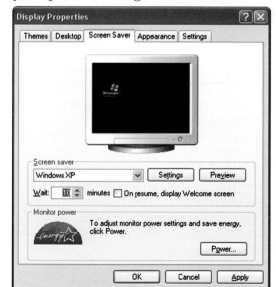

Adding a Screen Saver

If your computer sits idle for periods of time, consider adding a screen saver. A screen saver is a pattern that changes constantly, thus eliminating the problem of an image staying on the screen too long. To add a screen saver, display the Display Properties dialog box and then click the Screen Saver tab. This displays the dialog box as shown in Figure W.12.

Figure W.12 Display Properties Dialog Box with Screen Saver Tab Selected

Click the down-pointing arrow at the right side of the *Screen saver* option box to display a list of installed screen savers. Click a screen saver and a preview displays in the monitor located toward the top of the dialog box. Click the Preview button and the dialog box is hidden and the screen saver displays on your monitor. Move the mouse or click a button on the mouse and the dialog box will reappear. Click the Power button in the *Monitor power* section and a dialog box displays with options for choosing a power scheme appropriate to the way you use your computer. The dialog box also includes options for specifying how long the computer can be left unused before the monitor and hard disk are turned off and the system goes to standby or hibernate mode.

Changing Colors

Click the Appearance tab at the Display Properties dialog box and the dialog box displays as shown in Figure W.13. At this dialog box, you can change the desktop scheme. Schemes are predefined collections of colors used in windows, menus, title bars, and system fonts. Windows XP loads with the Windows XP style color scheme. Choose a different scheme with the Windows and buttons option and choose a specific color with the Color scheme option.

Figure W.13 Display Properties Dialog Box with Appearance Tab Selected

Changing Settings

Click the Settings tab at the Display Properties dialog box and the dialog box displays as shown in Figure W.14. At this dialog box, you can set color and screen resolution. The *Color quality* option determines how many colors your monitor displays. The more colors that are shown, the more realistic the images will appear. However, a lot of computer memory is required to show thousands of colors. Your exact choice is determined by the specific hardware you are using. The *Screen resolution* slide bar sets the screen's resolution. The higher the number, the more you can fit onto your screen. Again, your actual values depend on your particular hardware.

Figure W.14 Display Properties Dialog Box with Settings Tab Selected

Project ⑨ Customizing the Desktop

Before completing this exercise, check with your instructor to determine if you can customize the desktop.

1. At the Windows XP desktop, display the Display Properties dialog box by positioning the arrow pointer on an empty location on the desktop, clicking the *right* mouse button, and then clicking *Properties* at the shortcut menu.

2. At the Display Properties dialog box, change the desktop background by completing the following steps:

   a. Click the Desktop tab.

   b. If a background is selected in the *Background* list box (other than the *(None)* option), make a note of this background name.

   c. Click *Blue Lace 16* in the *Background* list box. (If this option is not available, choose another background.)

   d. Make sure *Tile* is selected in the *Position* list box.

   e. Click OK to close the dialog box.

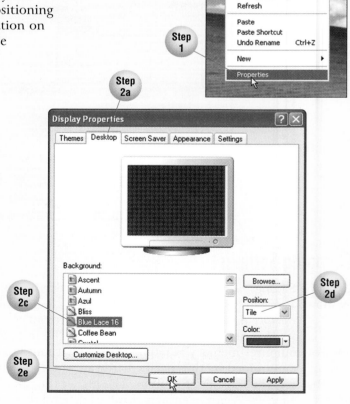

3. After viewing the desktop with the Blue Lace 16 background, remove the background image and change the background color by completing the following steps:
    a. Display the Display Properties dialog box.
    b. At the Display Properties dialog box, click the Desktop tab.
    c. Click *(None)* in the *Background* list box.
    d. Click the down-pointing arrow at the right side of the *Color* option and then click the dark red option at the color palette.
    e. Click OK to close the Display Properties dialog box.

4. After viewing the desktop with the dark red background color, add a screen saver and change the wait time by completing the following steps:
    a. Display the Display Properties dialog box.
    b. At the Display Properties dialog box, click the Screen Saver tab. (If a screen saver is already selected in the *Screen saver* option box, make a note of this screen saver name.)
    c. Click the down-pointing arrow at the right side of the *Screen saver* option box.
    d. At the drop-down list that displays, click a screen saver that interests you. (A preview of the screen saver displays in the screen located toward the top of the dialog box.)
    e. Click a few other screen savers to see how they will display on the monitor.
    f. Click OK to close the Display Properties dialog box.

5. Return all settings back to the default by completing the following steps:
    a. Display the Display Properties dialog box.
    b. Click the Desktop tab.
    c. If a background and color were selected when you began this exercise, click that background name in the *Background* list box and change the color back to the original color.
    d. Click the Screen Saver tab.
    e. At the Display Properties dialog box with the Screen Saver tab selected, click the down-pointing arrow at the right side of the *Screen saver* option box, and then click *(None)*. (If a screen saver was selected before completing this exercise, return to that screen saver.)
    f. Click OK to close the Display Properties dialog box.

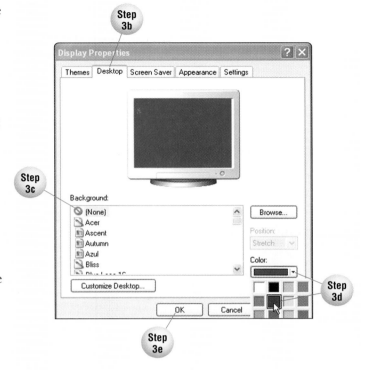

Step 3b

Step 3c

Step 3d

Step 3e

Exploring Windows XP Help and Support

Windows XP includes an on-screen reference guide providing information, explanations, and interactive help on learning Windows features. The on-screen reference guide contains complex files with hypertext used to access additional information by clicking a word or phrase.

Using the Help and Support Center Window

Display the Help and Support Center window shown in Figure W.15 by clicking the Start button on the Taskbar and then clicking *Help and Support* at the Start menu. The appearance of your Help and Support Center window may vary slightly from what you see in Figure W.15.

If you want to learn about a topic listed in the *Pick a Help topic* section of the window, click the desired topic and information about the topic displays in the window. Use the other options in the Help and Support Center window to get assistance or support from a remote computer or Windows XP newsgroups, pick a specific task, or learn about the additional help features. If you want help on a specific topic and do not see that topic listed in the *Pick a Help topic* section of the window, click inside the *Search* text box (generally located toward the top of the window), type the desired topic, and then press Enter or click the Start searching button (white arrow on a green background).

Figure W.15 Help and Support Center Window

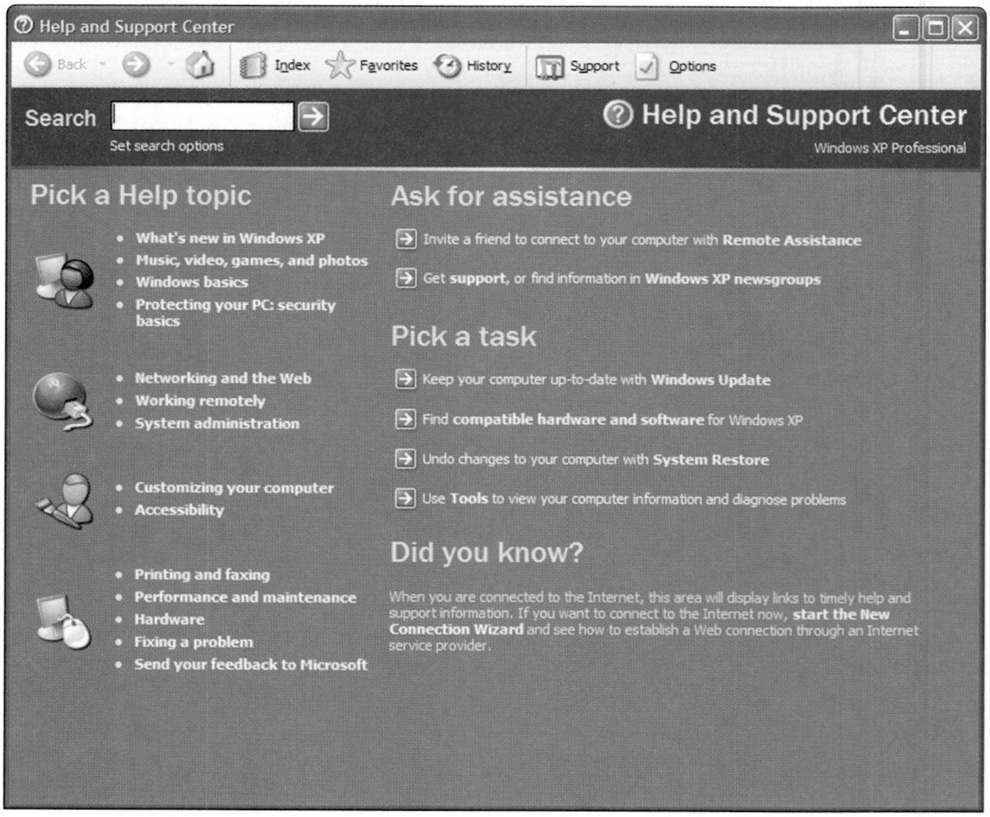

1. At the Windows XP desktop, use the Help and Support feature to learn about new Windows XP features by completing the following steps:
   a. Click the Start button on the Taskbar and then click *Help and Support* at the Start menu.
   b. At the Help and Support Center window, click the <u>What's new in Windows XP</u> hyperlink located in the *Pick a Help topic* section of the window.

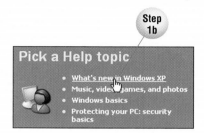

Step 1b

   c. Click the <u>What's new</u> hyperlink located in the *What's new in Windows XP* section of the window. (This displays a list of Help options at the right side of the window.)
   d. Click the <u>What's new in Windows XP</u> hyperlink located at the right side of the window below the subheading *Overviews, Articles, and Tutorials*.
   e. Read the information about Windows XP that displays at the right side of the window.
   f. Print the information by completing the following steps:
      1) Click the Print button located on the toolbar that displays above the information titled *What's new in Windows XP Professional*.

Step 1d

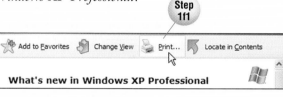

Step 1f1

      2) At the Print dialog box, make sure the correct printer is selected and then click the Print button.
2. Return to the opening Help and Support Center window by clicking the Home button located on the Help and Support Center toolbar.
3. Use the *Search* text box to search for information on deleting files by completing the following steps:
   a. Click in the *Search* text box located toward the top of the Help and Support Center window.
   b. Type deleting files and then press Enter.
   c. Click the <u>Delete a file or folder</u> hyperlink that displays in the *Search Results* section of the window (below the *Pick a task* subheading).

Step 3b

Step 3c

d. Read the information about deleting a file or folder that displays at the right side of the window and then print the information by clicking the Print button on the toolbar and then clicking the Print button at the Print dialog box.

e. Click the <u>Delete or restore files in the Recycle Bin</u> hyperlink that displays in the *Search Results* section of the window.

f. Read the information that displays at the right side of the window about deleting and restoring files in the Recycle Bin and then print the information.

4. Close the Help and Support Center window by clicking the Close button located in the upper right corner of the window.

Displaying an Index of Help and Support Topics

Display a list of help topics available by clicking the Index button on the Help and Support Center window toolbar. This displays an index of help topics at the left side of the window as shown in Figure W.16. Scroll through this list until the desired topic displays and then double-click the topic. Information about the selected topic displays at the right side of the window. If you are looking for a specific topic or keyword, click in the *Type in the keyword to find* text box, type the desired topic or keyword, and then press Enter.

Figure W.16 Help and Support Center Window with Index Displayed

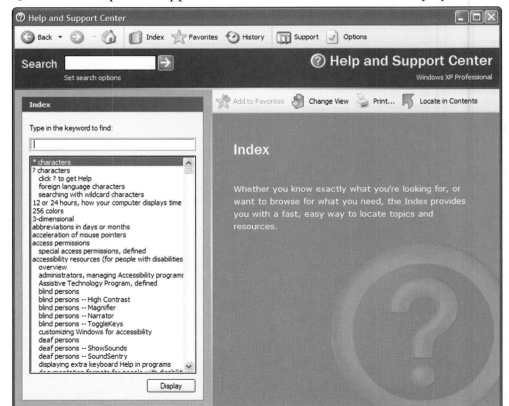

Project 11 Using the Index to Search for Information

1. At the Windows XP desktop, use the Index to display information on accessing programs by completing the following steps:
   a. Click the Start button on the Taskbar and then click *Help and Support* at the Start menu.
   b. Click the Index button on the Help and Support Center window toolbar.
   c. Scroll down the list of Index topics until *accessing programs* is visible and then double-click the subheading *overview* that displays below *accessing programs*.

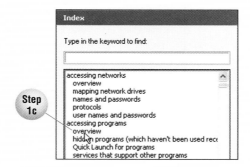

Step 1c

   d. Read the information that displays at the right side of the window and then print the information.
2. Find information on adding a shortcut to the desktop by completing the following steps:
   a. Select and delete the text *overview* that displays in the *Type in the keyword to find* text box and then type shortcuts.
   b. Double-click the subheading *for specific programs* that displays below the *shortcuts* heading.

Step 2a

Step 2b

   c. Read the information that displays at the right side of the window and then print the information.
3. Close the Help and Support Center window by clicking the Close button located in the upper right corner of the window.

Customizing Settings

Before beginning computer projects in this textbook, you may need to customize the monitor settings and turn on the display of file extensions. Projects in the chapters in this textbook assume that the monitor display is set to 1024 by 768 pixels and that the display of file extensions is turned on. To change the monitor display to 1024 by 768, complete the following steps:

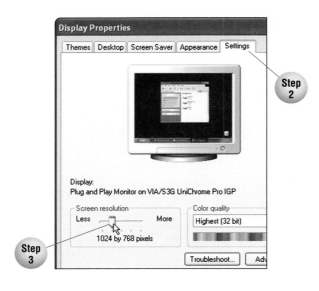

1. At the Windows XP desktop, right-click on any empty location on the desktop and then click *Properties* at the shortcut menu.
2. At the Display Properties dialog box, click the Settings tab.
3. Using the mouse, drag the slide bar button in the *Screen resolution* section to the left or right until *1024 by 768* displays below the slider bar.
4. Click the Apply button.
5. Click the OK button.

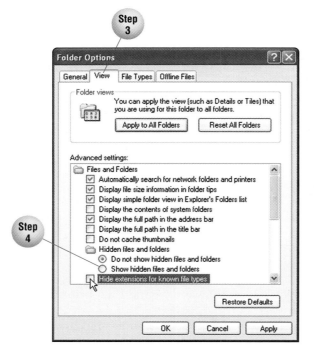

To turn on the display of file extensions, complete the following steps:

1. At the Windows XP desktop, click the Start button and then click *My Computer*.
2. At the My Computer window, click Tools on the Menu bar and then click *Folder Options* at the drop-down list.

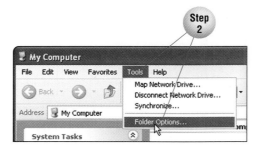

3. At the Folder Options dialog box, click the View tab.
4. Click the *Hide extentions for known file types* check box to remove the check mark.
5. Click the Apply button.
6. Click the OK button.

Browsing the Internet
Using Internet Explorer 7.0

Microsoft Internet Explorer 7.0 is a Web browser program with options and features for displaying sites as well as navigating and searching for information on the Internet. The *Internet* is a network of computers connected around the world. Users access the Internet for several purposes: to communicate using instant messaging and/or e-mail, to subscribe to newsgroups, to transfer files, to socialize with other users around the globe in "chat" rooms, and also to access virtually any kind of information imaginable.

Using the Internet, people can find a phenomenal amount of information for private or public use. To use the Internet, three things are generally required: an Internet Service Provider (ISP), a program to browse the Web (called a *Web browser*), and a *search engine*. In this section, you will learn how to:

- Navigate the Internet using URLs and hyperlinks
- Use search engines to locate information
- Download Web pages and images

Browsing the Internet

You will use the Microsoft Internet Explorer Web browser to locate information on the Internet. Uniform Resource Locators, referred to as URLs, are the method used to identify locations on the Internet. The steps for browsing the Internet vary but generally include: opening Internet Explorer, typing the URL for the desired site, navigating the various pages of the site, navigating to other sites using links, and then closing Internet Explorer.

To launch Internet Explorer 7.0, double-click the *Internet Explorer* icon on the Windows desktop. Figure IE.1 identifies the elements of the Internet Explorer, version 7.0, window. The Web page that displays in your Internet Explorer window may vary from what you see in Figure IE.1.

Figure IE.1 Internet Explorer Window

title bar

navigation bar

address bar

instant search box

toolbar

tabbed browsing—display multiple Web pages by inserting new tabs

status bar

change zoom level

If you know the URL for the desired Web site, click in the Address bar, type the URL, and then press Enter. The Web site's home page displays in a tab within the Internet Explorer window. URLs (Uniform Resource Locators) are the method used to identify locations on the Internet. The format of a URL is *http://server-name.path*. The first part of the URL, *http*, stands for HyperText Transfer Protocol, which is the protocol or language used to transfer data within the World Wide Web. The colon and slashes separate the protocol from the server name. The server name is the second component of the URL. For example, in the URL http://www.microsoft.com, the server name is *microsoft*. The last part of the URL specifies the domain to which the server belongs. For example, *.com* refers to "commercial" and establishes that the URL is a commercial company. Other examples of domains include *.edu* for "educational," *.gov* for "government," and *.mil* for "military."

Project ① Browsing the Internet Using URLs

1. Make sure you are connected to the Internet through an Internet Service Provider and that the Windows desktop displays. (Check with your instructor to determine if you need to complete steps for accessing the Internet such as typing a user name and password to log on.)
2. Launch Microsoft Internet Explorer by double-clicking the *Internet Explorer* icon located on the Windows desktop.
3. At the Internet Explorer window, explore the Web site for Yosemite National Park by completing the following steps:
   a. Click in the Address bar, type www.nps.gov/yose, and then press Enter.

Step 3a

b. Scroll down the home page for Yosemite National Park by clicking the down-pointing arrow on the vertical scroll bar located at the right side of the Internet Explorer window.

c. Print the home page by clicking the Print button located on the Internet Explorer toolbar.

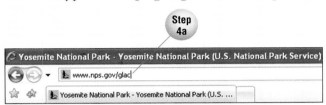

4. Explore the Web site for Glacier National Park by completing the following steps:

a. Click in the Address bar, type www.nps.gov/glac, and then press Enter.

b. Print the home page by clicking the Print button located on the Internet Explorer toolbar.

5. Close Internet Explorer by clicking the Close button (contains an X) located in the upper right corner of the Internet Explorer window.

Navigating Using Hyperlinks

Most Web pages contain "hyperlinks" that you click to connect to another page within the Web site or to another site on the Internet. Hyperlinks may display in a Web page as underlined text in a specific color or as images or icons. To use a hyperlink, position the mouse pointer on the desired hyperlink until the mouse pointer turns into a hand, and then click the left mouse button. Use hyperlinks to navigate within and between sites on the Internet. The navigation bar in the Internet Explorer window contains a Back button that, when clicked, takes you to the previous Web page viewed. If you click the Back button and then want to return to the previous page, click the Forward button. You can continue clicking the Back button to back your way out of several linked pages in reverse order since Internet Explorer maintains a history of the Web sites you visit.

Project ② Navigating Using Hyperlinks

1. Make sure you are connected to the Internet and then double-click the *Internet Explorer* icon on the Windows desktop.

2. At the Internet Explorer window, display the White House Web page and navigate in the page by completing the following steps:

a. Click in the Address bar, type whitehouse.gov, and then press Enter.

b. At the White House home page, position the mouse pointer on a hyperlink that interests you until the pointer turns into a hand, and then click the left mouse button.

c. At the linked Web page, click the Back button. (This returns you to the White House home page.)

d. At the White House home page, click the Forward button to return to the previous Web page viewed.

e. Print the Web page by clicking the Print button on the Internet Explorer toolbar.

3. Display the Web site for Amazon.com and navigate in the site by completing the following steps:

a. Click in the Address bar, type www.amazon.com, and then press Enter.

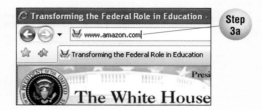

b. At the Amazon.com home page, click a hyperlink related to books.

c. When a book Web page displays, click the Print button on the Internet Explorer toolbar.

4. Close Internet Explorer by clicking the Close button (contains an X) located in the upper right corner of the Internet Explorer window.

Searching for Specific Sites

If you do not know the URL for a specific site or you want to find information on the Internet but do not know what site to visit, complete a search with a search engine. A search engine is a software program created to search quickly and easily for desired information. A variety of search engines are available on the Internet, each offering the opportunity to search for specific information. One method for searching for information is to click in the *Instant Search* box (displays the text *Live Search*) located at the right end of the navigation bar, type a keyword or phrase related to your search, and then click the Search button or press Enter. Another method for completing a search is to visit the Web site for a search engine and use options at the site.

Project ③ Searching for Information by Topic

1. Start Internet Explorer.

2. At the Internet Explorer window, search for sites on bluegrass music by completing the following steps:

a. Click in the *Instant Search* box (currently displays *Live Search*) located at the right end of the of the navigation bar.

b. Type bluegrass music and then press Enter.

c. When a list of sites displays in the Live Search tab, click a site that interests you.

d. When the page displays, click the Print button.

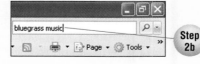

3. Use the Yahoo! search engine to find sites on bluegrass music by completing the following steps:
   a. Click in the Address bar, type www.yahoo.com, and then press Enter.
   b. At the Yahoo! Web site, with the insertion point positioned in the *Search* text box, type bluegrass music and then press Enter. (Notice that the sites displayed vary from sites displayed in the earlier search.)

Step 3b

   c. Click hyperlinks until a Web site displays that interests you.
   d. Print the page.
4. Use the Google search engine to find sites on jazz music by completing the following steps:
   a. Click in the Address bar, type www.google.com, and then press Enter.
   b. At the Google Web site, with the insertion point positioned in the search text box, type jazz music and then press Enter.

   c. Click a site that interests you.

Step 4b

   d. Print the page.
5. Close Internet Explorer.

Completing Advanced Searches for Specific Sites

The Internet contains an enormous amount of information. Depending on what you are searching for on the Internet and the search engine you use, some searches can result in several thousand "hits" (sites). Wading through a large number of sites can be very time-consuming and counterproductive. Narrowing a search to very specific criteria can greatly reduce the number of hits for a search. To narrow a search, use the advanced search options offered by the search engine.

Web Search

Project ④ Narrowing a Search

1. Start Internet Explorer.
2. Search for sites on skydiving in Oregon by completing the following steps:
   a. Click in the Address bar and then type www.yahoo.com.
   b. At the Yahoo! Web site, click the Web Search button next to the Search text box and then click the Advanced Search hyperlink.

   c. At the Advanced Web Search page, click in the search text box next to *all of these words*.
   d. Type skydiving Oregon tandem static line. (This limits the search to Web pages containing all of the words typed in the search text box.)

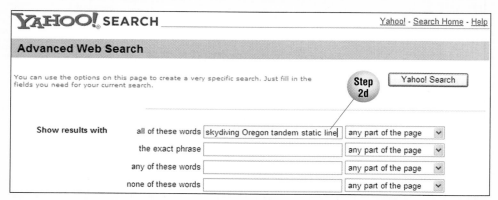

   e. Choose any other options at the Advanced Web Search page that will narrow your search.
   f. Click the Yahoo! Search button.
   g. When the list of Web sites displays, click a hyperlink that interests you.
   h. Print the page.
3. Close Internet Explorer.

Downloading Images, Text, and Web Pages from the Internet

The image(s) and/or text that display when you open a Web page as well as the Web page itself can be saved as a separate file. This separate file can be viewed, printed, or inserted in another file. The information you want to save in a separate file is downloaded from the Internet by Internet Explorer and saved in a folder of your choosing with the name you specify. Copyright laws protect much of the information on the Internet. Before using information downloaded from the Internet, check the site for restrictions. If you do use information, make sure you properly cite the source.

Project ⑤ Downloading Images and Web Pages

1. Start Internet Explorer.
2. Download a Web page and image from Banff National Park by completing the following steps:
   a. Search for sites on the Internet for Banff National Park.
   b. From the list of sites that displays, choose a site that contains information about Banff National Park and at least one image of the park.
   c. Save the Web page as a separate file by clicking the Page button on the Internet Explorer toolbar, and then clicking *Save As* at the drop-down list.
   d. At the Save Webpage dialog box, click the down-pointing arrow at the right side of the *Save in* option and then click the drive you are using as your storage medium at the drop-down list.
   e. Select the text in the *File name* text box, type BanffWebPage, and then press Enter.

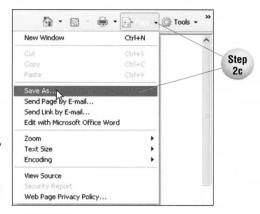

Step 2c

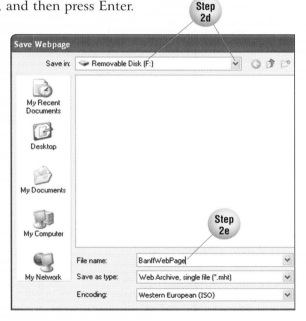

Step 2d

Step 2e

3. Save an image file by completing the following steps:
   a. Right-click an image that displays on the Web site. (The image that displays may vary from what you see below.)
   b. At the shortcut menu that displays, click *Save Picture As*.

Step 3b

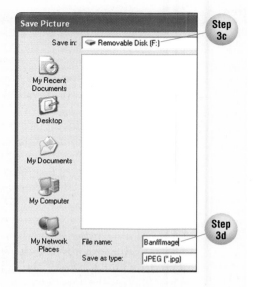

c. At the Save Picture dialog box, change the *Save in* option to your storage medium.

d. Select the text in the *File name* text box, type BanffImage, and then press Enter.

4. Close Internet Explorer.

OPTIONAL

Project   Opening the Saved Web Page and Image in a Word Document

1. Open Microsoft Word by clicking the Start button on the Taskbar, pointing to *All Programs*, pointing to *Microsoft Office*, and then clicking *Microsoft Office Word 2007*.

2. With Microsoft Word open, insert the image in a document by completing the following steps:

a. Click the Insert tab in the ribbon and then click the Picture button in the Illustrations group.

b. At the Insert Picture dialog box, change the *Look in* option to the location where you saved the Banff image and then double-click *BanffImage.jpg*.

c. When the image displays in the Word document, print the document by clicking the Print button on the Quick Access toolbar.

d. Close the document by clicking the Office button and then clicking *Close* at the drop-down menu. At the message asking if you want to save the changes, click No.

3. Open the **BanffWebPage.mht** file by completing the following steps:

a. Click the Office button and then click *Open* at the drop-down menu.

b. At the Open dialog box, change the *Look in* option to the location where you saved the Banff Web page and then double-click *BanffWebPage.mht*.

c. Print the Web page by clicking the Print button on the Quick Access toolbar.

d. Close the **BanffWebPage.mht** file by clicking the Office button and then *Close*.

4. Close Word by clicking the Close button (contains an X) that displays in the upper right corner of the screen.

Microsoft® access

Making Access Work for You

Each of us interacts with a database more often than we realize. Did you use a bank machine to get some cash today? Did you search the library's catalog for a book that you need? Did you browse an online retail catalog or flip through the pages of a printed catalog? If you did any of these activities, you were accessing and/or updating a database. Any time you look for something by accessing an organized file system you are probably using a database. Microsoft Access is the database management system included with Microsoft Office.

Organizing Information

Information in a database is organized into a collection of *tables* that can be related to each other for purposes of exchanging data. Each table is broken down into a series of columns (called *fields*) and rows (called *records*). If you are familiar with a spreadsheet program such as Excel, you will be comfortable viewing a datasheet in Access. Much thought is put into the design of a database and its tables since all of the data a business collects in a database must

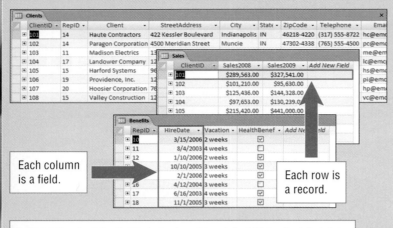

Each column is a field.

Each row is a record.

Information for a business is broken down into tables of related data. In this example, Client information is in a separate table from Benefit information and Sales information.

be organized into logical groups. Defining a *relationship* between two tables enables data from more than one table to be shared or exchanged for viewing, updating, or reporting purposes. Access allows for three kinds of relationships that can be created: one-to-one, one-to-many, and many-to-many.

Records within tables can be sorted and filtered numerous ways to allow the data to be reorganized to suit many needs. Sorting by one column and by multiple columns is accomplished with just a few mouse clicks. Temporarily hide records that

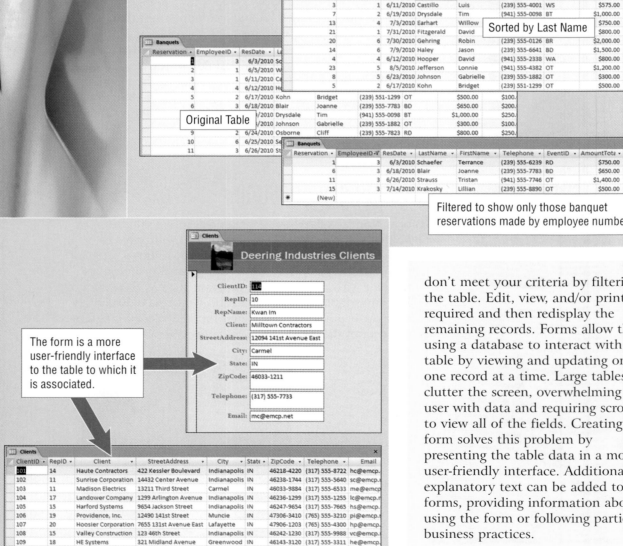

Sorted by Last Name

Original Table

Filtered to show only those banquet reservations made by employee number 3.

The form is a more user-friendly interface to the table to which it is associated.

Deering Industries Clients

don't meet your criteria by filtering the table. Edit, view, and/or print as required and then redisplay the remaining records. Forms allow those using a database to interact with the table by viewing and updating only one record at a time. Large tables clutter the screen, overwhelming the user with data and requiring scrolling to view all of the fields. Creating a form solves this problem by presenting the table data in a more user-friendly interface. Additional explanatory text can be added to forms, providing information about using the form or following particular business practices.

Analyzing Information

Databases store a wealth of data that can be extracted in various ways. A *query* is one method for extracting information from tables. A basic query might simply list fields from several tables in one datasheet. This method is shown in the adjacent screen captures, where individual fields from three tables are selected for viewing in one datasheet. In more complex queries, data can be selected for viewing based on meeting a single criterion or multiple criteria, and calculations can be performed on fields.

For more sophisticated analysis, tables can be grouped and then filtered on more than one field. Open a table or query and then switch to PivotTable View or PivotChart View. Access has simplified the task of creating pivot tables and pivot charts by incorporating a drag and drop technique in the view. Interact with the pivot table or pivot chart by clicking one of the filter arrows, selecting or deselecting the items you want to view, and then clicking OK. The data in the view is instantly updated to reflect the new settings.

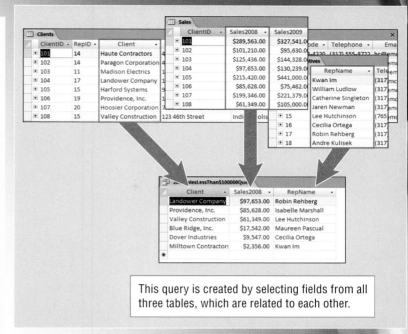

This query is created by selecting fields from all three tables, which are related to each other.

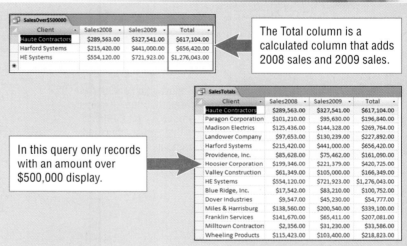

The Total column is a calculated column that adds 2008 sales and 2009 sales.

In this query only records with an amount over $500,000 display.

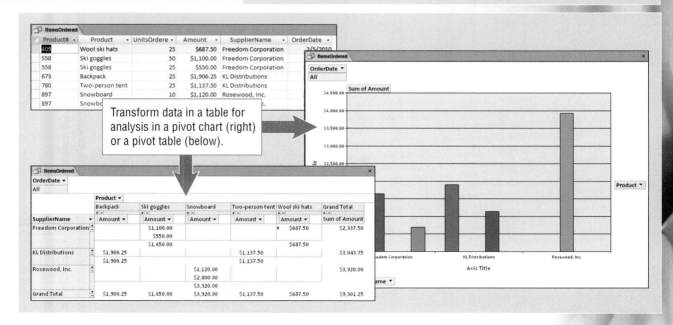

Transform data in a table for analysis in a pivot chart (right) or a pivot table (below).

Create a report to produce high-quality output.

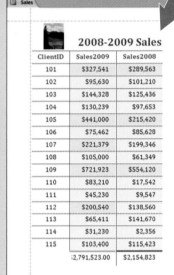

Report with conditional formatting that displays amounts over $199,999 with green shading and amounts under $200,000 with red shading.

Presenting Information

Having critical business information stored electronically and the ability to easily extract specific data from the database is a valuable asset to a business. However, there are still times when a printed report is a necessity. Reports in Access are used to create professional-looking, high-quality output. Reports can be grouped and sorted and can include calculations. Access includes the Report Wizard, which can be used to create a report such as the one shown at the left by choosing the table or query for the source data, specifying a group or sort order, and choosing from predefined styles and layouts. Once the report is generated, you can easily modify its design by moving, resizing, adding, or deleting objects, changing the layout or sort order, adding a calculation, applying gridlines, and so on.

Having a well designed database that is easy to update and maintain is a necessity for most businesses. Microsoft Access is a database management system that is easy to learn and use. In just a few pages, you will be exploring the world of databases and learning how to access the technology that drives business success.

Report created from a query that displays Indianapolis and Muncie sales over $75,000.

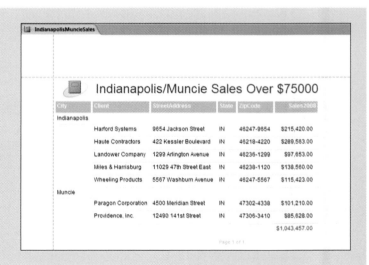

Microsoft®

access

Unit 1: Creating Tables and Queries

➤ Creating Database Tables

➤ Creating Relationships between Tables

➤ Modifying and Managing Tables

➤ Performing Queries

Access

access Level 1

Benchmark Microsoft® Access 2007 Level 1

Microsoft Certified Application Specialist Skills—Unit 1

Reference No.	Skill	Pages
1	**Structuring a Database**	
1.2	Define and print table relationships	
1.2.1	Create relationships	35-46
1.2.2	Modify relationships	40-50
1.2.3	Print table relationships	43, 46
1.3	Add, set, change, or remove primary keys	
1.3.1	Define and modify primary keys	37-40
2	**Creating and Formatting Database Elements**	
2.1	Create databases	
2.1.2	Create blank databases	8, 13-21
2.2	Create tables	
2.2.1	Create custom tables in Design view	13-21
2.3	Modify tables	
2.3.1	Modify table properties	66-70
2.3.5	Summarize table data by adding a Total row	70-72
2.4	Create fields and modify field properties	
2.4.1	Create commonly used fields	13-19
2.4.2	Modify field properties	70-76
3	**Entering and Modifying Data**	
3.1	Enter, edit, and delete records	26-28, 49-50
3.3	Find and replace data	84-86
4	**Creating and Modifying Queries**	
4.1	Create queries	99-105
4.1.1	Create queries based on single tables	99-105
4.1.2	Create queries based on more than one table	105-128
4.1.4	Create crosstab queries	121-123
4.2	Modify queries	
4.2.4	Create calculated fields in queries	116-118
4.2.6	Create sum, average, min/max, and count queries	118-121
5	**Presenting and Sharing Data**	
5.1	Sort data	
5.1.1	Sort data within tables	80-81
5.1.2	Sort data within queries	108-109
5.6	Print database objects	80-81
6	**Managing and Maintaining Databases**	
6.1	Perform routine database operations	
6.1.2	Back up databases	86-89
6.1.3	Compact and repair databases	87-89
6.2	Manage databases	
6.2.2	Configure database options	11-12

Note: The Level 1 and Level 2 texts each address approximately half of the Microsoft Certified Application Specialist skills. Complete coverage of the skills is offered in the combined Level 1 and Level 2 text titled *Benchmark Series Microsoft® Access 2007: Levels 1 and 2,* which has been approved as certified courseware and which displays the Microsoft Certified Application Specialist logo on the cover.

CHAPTER 1

Creating Database Tables

PERFORMANCE OBJECTIVES

Upon successful completion of Chapter 1, you will be able to:

- Open and close objects in a database
- Design a table
- Determine fields and assign data types in a table
- Enter data in a table
- Open, save, print, and close a table
- Add and delete records in a table

access Chapter 1

Managing information in a company is an integral part of operating a business. Information can come in a variety of forms, such as data about customers, including names, addresses, and telephone numbers; product data; purchasing and buying data; information on services performed for customers or clients; and much more. Most companies today manage data using a database management system software program. Microsoft Office Professional includes a database management system software program named *Access*. With Access, you can organize, store, maintain, retrieve, sort, and print all types of business data.

As an example of how Access might be used to manage data in an office, suppose a bookstore decides to send a mailer to all customers who have purchased a certain type of book in the past month (such as autobiographies). The bookstore uses Access and maintains data on customers, such as names, addresses, types of books purchased, and types of books ordered. With this data in Access, the manager of the bookstore can easily select those customers who have purchased or ordered autobiographies in the past month and send a mailer announcing a visit by an author who has written a recently-published autobiography. The bookstore could also use the information to determine what types of books have been ordered by customers in the past few months and use this information to determine what inventory to purchase.

Use the information in a database to perform a wide variety of functions. This chapter contains just a few ideas. With a properly designed and maintained database management system, a company can operate smoothly with logical, organized, and useful information. The Access program displays in the Start pop-up menu preceded by a picture of a key. The key symbolizes the importance of managing and maintaining data to a company's survival and success.

Note: Before beginning computer projects, copy to your storage medium the Access 2007L1C1 subfolder from the Access2007L1 folder on the CD that accompanies this textbook. Steps on how to copy a folder are presented on the inside of the back cover of this textbook. Do this every time you start a chapter's projects.

Project 1 Explore an Access Database

You will open a database and open and close objects in the database including tables, queries, and forms.

Exploring a Database

A database is comprised of a series of objects such as tables, forms, reports, and queries that you use to enter, manage, view, and print data. Data in a database is organized into tables, which contain information for related items such as customers, employees, orders, and products. To view the various objects in a database, you will open a previously created database and then navigate in the database and open various objects.

To open a previously created database, click the Start button on the Taskbar, point to *All Programs*, point to *Microsoft Office*, and then click *Microsoft Office Access 2007*. (These steps may vary depending on your operating system and/or system configuration.) This displays the *Getting Started with Microsoft Office Access* screen shown in Figure 1.1. This window is divided into three sections. Use the *Template Categories* section at the left to preview and download database templates. Start a new database by clicking the Blank Database button in the *New Blank Database* section and open an existing database by clicking a database name in the *Open Recent Database* section.

Opening and Closing a Database

HINT

Only one database can be open at a time.

Office button

To open a database, click the file name located in the *Open Recent Database* section of the *Getting Started with Microsoft Office Access* screen or click the Office button and then click *Open* at the drop-down list. At the Open dialog box, navigate to the desired folder and then double-click the desired database name in the list box. When you open a database, the Access screen displays as shown in Figure 1.2. Refer to Table 1.1 for a description of the Access screen elements. To close a database, click the Office button and then click *Close Database* at the drop-down list. To exit Access, click the Close button that displays in the upper right corner of the screen, or click the Office button and then the Exit Access button that displays in the lower right corner of the drop-down list.

Figure 1.1 Getting Started with Microsoft Office Access Screen

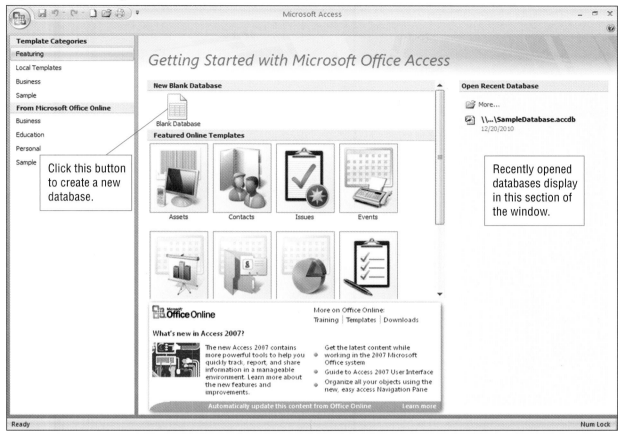

Table 1.1 Access Screen Elements

Feature	Description
Office button	Displays as a Microsoft Office logo and, when clicked, displays a list of options along with the most recently opened databases
Quick Access toolbar	Contains buttons for commonly-used commands
Title bar	Displays database name followed by program name
Tabs	Contains commands and features organized into groups
Ribbon	Area containing the tabs and commands divided into groups
Message bar	Displays security alerts if the database you open contains potentially unsafe content
Navigation pane	Displays names of objects within database grouped by categories
Work area	Area in screen where opened objects display
Status bar	Displays number of pages and words, View buttons, and the Zoom slider bar

Figure 1.2 Access Screen

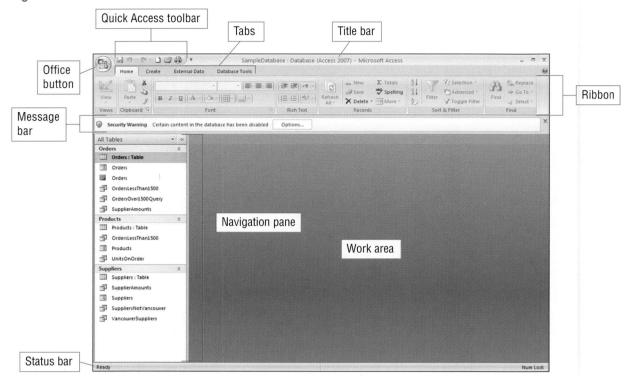

Security features in Access 2007 cause a message bar to display a security alert message below the ribbon. This message displays when you open an Access 2007 database outside of a trusted location (a list of drives and folder names stored in the Trust Center dialog box). If you know that the database is virus-free, click the Options button in the Message bar. At the Microsoft Office Security Options dialog box that displays, click the *Enable this content* option and then click OK. The Message bar closes when you identify the database as a trusted source.

The Navigation pane at the left side of the Access screen displays the objects that are contained in the database. Some common objects found in a database include tables, forms, reports, and queries. Refer to Table 1.2 for a description of these four types of objects.

Table 1.2 Database Objects

Object	Description
Table	Organizes data in fields (columns) and rows (records). A database must contain at least one table. The table is the base upon which other objects are created.
Query	Used to display data from a table that meets a conditional statement and/or to perform calculations. For example, display only those records in which the city is Vancouver.
Form	Allows fields and records to be presented in a different layout than the datasheet. Used to facilitate data entry and maintenance.
Report	Prints data from tables or queries.

Opening and Closing Objects

Database objects display in the Navigation pane. Control what displays in the pane by clicking the Menu bar at the top of the Navigation pane and then clicking the desired option at the drop-down list. For example, to display a list of all saved objects in the database, click the *Object Type* option at the drop-down list. This view displays the objects grouped by type — Tables, Queries, Forms, and Reports. To open an object, double-click the object in the Navigation pane. The object opens in the work area and a tab displays with the object name at the left side of the object.

To view more of an object, consider closing the Navigation pane by clicking the Shutter Bar Open/Close button located in the upper right corner of the pane. Click the button again to open the Navigation pane.

You can open more than one object in the work area. Each object opens with a visible tab. You can navigate to objects by clicking the object tab. To close an object, click the Close button that displays at the right side of the work area.

HINT

Hide the Navigation pane by clicking the button in the upper right corner of the pane (called the Shutter Bar button) or by pressing F11.

Close Object

Project ① Opening and Closing a Database and Objects

1. Open Access by clicking the Start button on the Taskbar, pointing to *All Programs*, pointing to *Microsoft Office*, and then clicking *Microsoft Office Access 2007*. (These steps may vary.)
2. At the Getting Started with Microsoft Office Access screen, click the Office button and then click *Open* at the drop-down list.
3. At the Open dialog box, navigate to the Access2007L1C1 folder on your storage medium and then double-click the database ***SampleDatabase.accdb***.
4. Click the Options button in the Message bar.
5. At the Microsoft Office Security Options dialog box, click *Enable this content* and then click OK.
6. Click the Navigation pane Menu bar and then click *Object Type* at the drop-down list. (This option displays the objects grouped by type — Tables, Queries, Forms, and Reports.)
7. Double-click *Suppliers* in the *Tables* section of the Navigation pane. This opens the Suppliers table in the work area as shown in Figure 1.3. The fields in the table display in the top row of the table and some of the field names are not completely visible.
8. Close the Suppliers table by clicking the Close button in the upper right corner of the work area.
9. Double-click *OrdersLessThan1500* in the *Queries* section of the Navigation pane. A query displays data that meets a conditional statement and this query displays orders that meet the criterion of being less than $1,500.

10. Close the query by clicking the Close button in the upper right corner of the work area.
11. Double-click the *SuppliersNotVancouver* query in the Navigation pane and notice that the query displays information about suppliers that are not located in Vancouver.
12. Click the Close button in the work area.
13. Double-click *Orders* in the *Forms* section of the Navigation pane. This displays an order form. A form is used to view and edit data in a table one record at a time.
14. Click the Close button in the work area.
15. Double-click *Orders* in the *Reports* section of the Navigation pane. This displays a report with information about orders and order amounts.
16. Close the Navigation pane by clicking the Shutter Bar Open/Close button located in the upper right corner of the pane.
17. After viewing the report, click the button again to open the Navigation pane.
18. Click the Close button in the work area.
19. Close the database by clicking the Office button and then clicking *Close Database* at the drop-down list.
20. Exit Access by clicking the Close button (contains an X) that displays in the upper right corner of the screen.

Figure 1.3 Open Suppliers Table

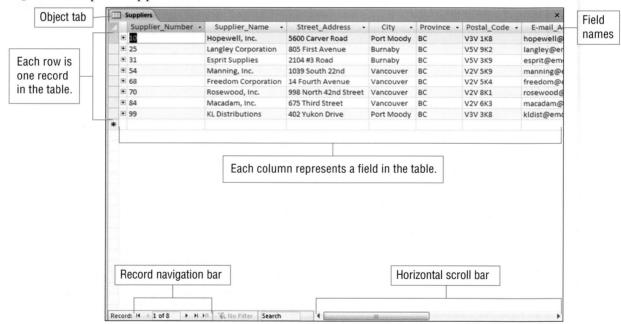

Project 2 Create and Maintain Tables

You will create tables for a Premium database by determining the field names and data types and then entering records in the tables. You will change the page layout and field widths and then print the tables; you will also maintain tables by adding and deleting records.

Organizing Data in a Table

Data is not very useful to a company if it is not organized in a logical manner. Organizing data in a manageable and logical manner allows the data to be found and used for a variety of purposes. As mentioned earlier, the information in a database is organized into tables. A table contains information for related items such as customers, suppliers, inventory, or human resources broken down into individual units of information. Creating a new table generally involves determining fields, assigning a data type to each field, modifying properties, designating the primary key, and naming the table. This process is referred to as defining the table structure.

HINT
Organize data in tables to minimize or eliminate duplication.

Determining Fields

Microsoft Access is a database management system software program that allows you to design, create, input, maintain, manipulate, sort, and print data. Access is considered a relational database in which you organize data in related tables. In this chapter, you will be creating tables as part of a database, and learn how to relate tables in a later chapter.

HINT
A database table contains fields that describe a person, customer, client, object, place, idea, or event.

The first step in creating a table is to determine the fields. A field is one piece of information about a person, a place, or an item. For example, one field could be a customer's name, another field could be a customer's address, and another a customer number. All fields for one unit, such as a customer, are considered a record. For example, in Project 2a, a record is all of the information pertaining to one employee of Premium Health Services. A collection of records becomes a table.

When designing a table, determine fields for information to be included on the basis of how you plan to use the data. When organizing fields, be sure to consider not only current needs for the data but also any future needs. For example, a company may need to keep track of customer names, addresses, and telephone numbers for current mailing lists. In the future, the company may want to promote a new product to customers who purchase a specific type of product. For this situation, a field that identifies product type must be included in the database. When organizing fields, consider all potential needs for the data but also try to keep the fields logical and manageable.

After deciding what data you want included in a table, you need to determine field names. Consider the following guidelines when naming fields in a table:

- Each field must contain a unique name.
- The name should describe the contents of the field.
- A field name can contain up to 64 characters.
- A field name can contain letters, numbers, spaces, and symbols except the period (.), comma (,), exclamation point (!), square brackets ([]), and grave accent (`).
- A field name cannot begin with a space.

In Project 2a, you will create a table containing information on employees of a medical corporation. The fields in this table and the names you will give to each field are shown in Figure 1.4.

Figure 1.4 Field Information and Names for Project 2a

Employee Information	Field Name
ID number	*Emp#*
Last name	*LastName*
First name	*FirstName*
Middle initial	*MI*
Street address	*StreetAddress*
City	*City*
State	*State*
ZIP code	*ZipCode*
Department code	*DeptCode*
Date of hire	*HireDate*
Supplemental health insurance	*Yes/No*

Assigning a Data Type to Fields

HINT

Assign a data type for each field that determines the values that can be entered for the field.

Part of the process of designing a table includes specifying or assigning a data type to each field. The data type specifies the type of data you can enter in a field. Assigning a data type to fields helps maintain and manage the data and helps identify for anyone entering information in the field what type of data is expected. The data types you will use in fields in this chapter include *Text*, *Date/Time*, and *Yes/No*.

Assign the Text data type to a field where text will be entered such as names, addresses, and numbers that do not require calculations, such as telephone numbers, Social Security numbers, and ZIP codes. You can store up to 255 characters in the text data field with 255 as the default. Assign the Date/Time data type to a field where a date and/or time will be entered. You will assign the data types and field sizes shown in Figure 1.5 when you create a table in Project 2a.

Figure 1.5 Data Types for Project 2a

Field Name	Data Type
Emp#	Text (Field Size = 5)
LastName	Text (Field Size = 30)
FirstName	Text (Field Size = 30)
MI	Text (Field Size = 2)
StreetAddress	Text (Field Size = 30)
City	Text (Field Size = 20)
State	Text (Field Size = 2)
ZipCode	Text (Field Size = 5)
DeptCode	Text (Field Size = 2)
HireDate	Date/Time
SuppIns	Yes/No

Data entered for some fields in Project 2a, such as *ZipCode,* will be numbers. These numbers, however, are not values and will not be used in calculations. This is why they are assigned the data type of Text (rather than Number or Currency).

When assigning a field size, consider the data that will be entered in the field, and then shorten or lengthen (up to the maximum number) the number to accommodate any possible entries. For the *FirstName* field or the *LastName* field, for example, shortening the number to 30 would be appropriate, ensuring that all names would fit in the field. The two-letter state abbreviation will be used in the *State* field, so the number of characters is changed to 2.

Creating a Table

When you create a new blank database, the database opens and a blank table displays in the work area in Datasheet view. Datasheet view is used primarily for entering data. To specify fields and identify data types for your table, you need to change to Design view. To do this, click the View button that displays in the View group in the Table Tools Datasheet tab. Before switching to Design view, you must save the table. At the Save As dialog box, type a name for the table and then press Enter or click OK and the table displays in Design view as shown in Figure 1.6.

Create a Table
1. Click Blank Database button.
2. Click Create tab.
3. Click Table button.
4. Click View button.
5. Type name for table.
6. Press Enter or click OK.
7. Type field names, specify types, and include descriptions.

View

Figure 1.6 Table in Design View

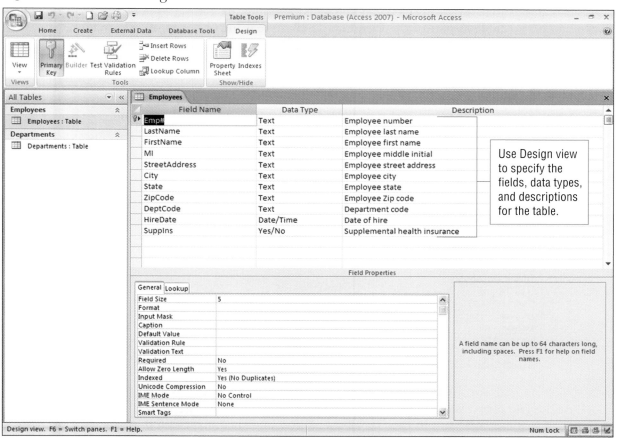

Save

By default, Access provides the *ID* field as the first field in the record and assigns the AutoNumber data type to the field. You can use the *ID* field or type your own field name. Accept the *ID* field name or type a new name and then press the Tab key. This moves the insertion point to the *Data Type* column. In this column, accept the data type or click the down-pointing arrow at the right side of the data type text and then click the desired data type at the drop-down list. Press the Tab key to move the insertion point to the *Description* column and then type a description for the field that specifies what should be entered in the field. Continue typing field names, assigning a data type to each field, and typing a description of all fields. When the table design is complete, save the table by clicking the Save button on the Quick Access toolbar or by clicking the Office button and then clicking *Save* at the drop-down list. Click the View button in the Views group in the Table Tools Design tab to switch to Datasheet view and enter records or click the Close button in the work area to close the table.

At the Table window shown in Figure 1.6, field names are entered, data types are assigned, and descriptions are typed. When assigning a data type, Access displays information in the bottom portion of the window in a section with the General tab selected. Information in this section can be changed to customize a data type for a field. For example, you can specify that only a maximum of two characters can be entered in the *MI* field.

A database can contain more than one table. Tables containing related data are saved in the same database. In Project 2a, you will create a table named Employees that is part of the database named Premium. In Project 2b, you will create another table as part of the Premium database that includes payroll information.

Project 2a — Creating an Employee Table

1. Open Access by clicking the Start button on the Taskbar, pointing to *All Programs*, pointing to *Microsoft Office*, and then clicking *Microsoft Office Access 2007*. (These steps may vary.)
2. At the Getting Started with Microsoft Office Access screen, click the Blank Database button in the *New Blank Database* section.
3. Click the folder icon located at the right side of the *File Name* text box in the *Blank Database* section.

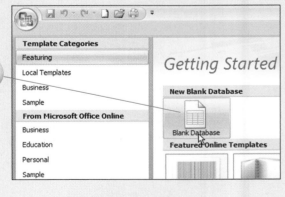

4. At the File New Database dialog box, navigate to the drive where your storage medium is located, type **Premium** in the *File name* text box, and then press Enter.

5. At the Getting Started with Microsoft Office Access screen, click the Create button located below the *File Name* text box in the *Blank Database* section.

6. At the Database window, change to Design view by clicking the View button in the Views group in the Home tab.

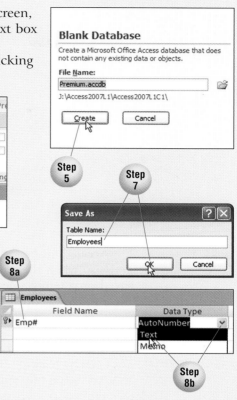

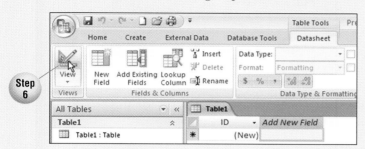

7. At the Save As dialog box, type Employees in the *Table Name* text box and then click OK.

8. In the table, type the fields shown in Figure 1.7 by completing the following steps:

   a. Type Emp# in the *Field Name* text box and then press the Tab key.

   b. Change the *Data Type* to *Text* by clicking the down-pointing arrow located in the *Data Type* box and then clicking *Text* at the drop-down list.

   c. Change the field size from the default of 255 to 5. To do this, select *255* that displays after *Field Size* in the *Field Properties* section of the window and then type 5.

   d. Position the I-beam pointer in the *Description* text box (for the *Emp#*) and then click the left mouse button. Type Employee number in the *Description* text box and then press Tab.

   e. Type LastName in the *Field Name* text box and then press Tab.

   f. Change the field size to 30 and then click in the *Description* text box for the *LastName* field. Type Employee last name and then press Tab.

   g. Type FirstName in the *Field Name* text box and then press Tab.

   h. Change the field size to 30 and then click in the *Description* text box for the *FirstName* field. Type Employee first name and then press Tab.

   i. Continue typing the field names, data types, and descriptions as shown in Figure 1.7. Identify the following sizes: *MI* = 2, *StreetAddress* = 30, *City* = 20, *State* = 2, *ZipCode* = 5, and *DeptCode* = 2. (Refer to Figure 1.5.) To change the data type for the *HireDate* field, click the down-pointing arrow after *Text* and then click *Date/Time* at the drop-down list. To change the data type for the *SuppIns* field, click the down-pointing arrow after *Text* and then click *Yes/No* at the drop-down list.

9. When all of the fields are entered, save the table by clicking the Save button on the Quick Access toolbar.

10. Close the Employees table by clicking the Close button located at the upper right corner of the datasheet.

Figure 1.7 Project 2a

Field Name	Data Type	Description
Emp#	Text	Employee number
LastName	Text	Employee last name
FirstName	Text	Employee first name
MI	Text	Employee middle initial
StreetAddress	Text	Employee street address
City	Text	Employee city
State	Text	Employee state
ZipCode	Text	Employee Zip code
DeptCode	Text	Department code
HireDate	Date/Time	Date of hire
SuppIns	Yes/No	Supplemental health insurance

Employees (window title)

HINT

The active database is saved automatically on a periodic basis and also when you make another record active, close the table, or close the database.

✕ E**x**it Access

Access automatically saves an open (or active) database on a periodic basis and also when the database is closed. If you are working with a database that is saved on a removable storage medium, never remove the storage medium while the database is open because Access saves the database periodically. If the storage medium is not available when Access tries to save it, problems will be encountered and you run the risk of damaging the database. Exit (close) Access by clicking the Close button located in the upper right corner of the Access Title bar (contains an *X*) or by clicking the Office button and then clicking the Exit Access button located in the bottom right corner of the drop-down list.

The Employees table contains a *DeptCode* field. This field will contain a two-letter code identifying the department within the company. In Project 2b, you will create a table named Departments containing only two fields—the department code and the department name. Establishing a department code decreases the amount of data entered in the Employees table. For example, in an employee record, you type a two-letter code identifying the employee department rather than typing the entire department name. Imagine the time this saves when entering hundreds of employee records. This is an example of the power of a relational database.

Project 2b Creating a Department Table

1. At the Premium : Database window, create a new table in Design view. To do this, click the Create tab and then click the Table button in the Tables group.
2. At the Table1 window, click the View button in the Views group.
3. At the Save As dialog box, type Departments and then press Enter.
4. Type the fields shown in Figure 1.8 by completing the following steps:
   a. Type DeptCode in the *Field Name* text box and then press Tab.
   b. Click the down-pointing arrow after *AutoNumber* and then click *Text*.
   c. Change the field size to 2 and then click in the *Description* text box for the *DeptCode* field.
   d. Type Department code in the *Description* text box and then press the Tab key.

Step 1

e. Type Department in the *Field Name* text box and then press Tab.

f. Change the field size to 30 and then click in the *Description* text box for the *Department* field.

g. Type Department name in the *Description* text box.

5. When all of the fields are entered, click the Save button on the Quick Access toolbar.

6. Close the Departments table by clicking the Close button located in the upper right corner of the table.

Figure 1.8 Project 2b

Field Name	Data Type	Description
DeptCode	Text	Department code
Department	Text	Department name

(Table window titled "Departments")

Entering Data in a Table

Enter data in a table in a database in Datasheet view. A table datasheet displays the contents of a table in rows and columns in the same manner as a Word table or Excel worksheet. Each row in a datasheet represents one record. In the Employees table of the Premium database, one record will contain the information for one employee.

When you type data for the first field in the record, another row of cells is automatically inserted below the first row. Type the data for the first record, pressing Tab to move the insertion point to the next field or pressing Shift + Tab to move the insertion point to the previous field. The description you typed for each field when creating the table displays at the left side of the Access Status bar. This description reminds you what data is expected in the field.

If you assigned the Yes/No data type to a field, a square displays in the field. You can leave this square empty or insert a check mark. If the field is asking a yes/no question, an empty box signifies "No" and a box with a check mark signifies "Yes." If the field is asking for a true/false answer, an empty box signifies "False" and a box with a check mark signifies "True." This field can also have an on/off response. An empty box signifies "Off" and a box with a check mark signifies "On." To insert a check mark in the box, tab to the field and then press the spacebar.

As you enter data in fields, the description you typed for each field displays at the left side of the Status bar. The descriptions help identify to the person entering data in the table what data is expected.

QUICK STEPS

Enter Data in a Table
1. Click Open button.
2. Double-click database name.
3. Double-click table name.
4. Make sure table displays in Datasheet view.
5. Type data in fields.

Project 2c Entering Data in the Employees and the Departments Tables

1. At the Premium : Database window, double-click *Employees : Table* in the Navigation pane.
2. At the Employees window, type the following data for five records in the specified fields. (Press Tab to move the insertion point to the next field or press Shift + Tab to move the insertion point to the previous field. When typing data, not all of the data may be visible. You will adjust column widths in a later project. For the *SuppIns* field, press the spacebar to insert a check mark indicating "Yes" and leave the check box blank indicating "No.")

Step 1

Emp#	=	21043
LastName	=	Brown
FirstName	=	Leland
MI	=	C.
StreetAddress	=	112 Kansas Avenue
City	=	Missoula
State	=	MT
ZipCode	=	84311
DeptCode	=	PA
HireDate	=	11/5/2007
SuppIns	=	*Yes (Insert a check mark)*

Emp#	=	19034
LastName	=	Guenther
FirstName	=	Julia
MI	=	A.
StreetAddress	=	215 Bridge West
City	=	Lolo
State	=	MT
ZipCode	=	86308
DeptCode	=	MS
HireDate	=	2/15/2005
SuppIns	=	*No (Leave blank)*

Emp#	=	27845
LastName	=	Oaklee
FirstName	=	Thomas
MI	=	E.
StreetAddress	=	2310 Keating Road
City	=	Missoula
State	=	MT
ZipCode	=	84325
DeptCode	=	HR
HireDate	=	6/8/2009
SuppIns	=	*No (Leave blank)*

Emp#	=	08921
LastName	=	Avery

FirstName	=	Michael
MI	=	W.
StreetAddress	=	23155 Neadham Avenue
City	=	Florence
State	=	MT
ZipCode	=	85901
DeptCode	=	PA
HireDate	=	11/5/2006
SuppIns	=	Yes *(Insert a check mark)*
Emp#	=	30091
LastName	=	Latora
FirstName	=	Gina
MI	=	M.
StreetAddress	=	13221 138th Street
City	=	Missoula
State	=	MT
ZipCode	=	84302
DeptCode	=	HR
HireDate	=	9/16/2010
SuppIns	=	No *(Leave blank)*

3. After typing the data, save the table by clicking the Save button on the Quick Access toolbar.
4. Close the Employees table by clicking the Close button located in the upper right corner of the work area.
5. At the Premium : Database window, double-click *Departments : Table* in the Navigation pane.
6. At the Departments window, type the following data for four departments in the specified fields (press Tab to move the insertion point to the next field or press Shift + Tab to move the insertion point to the previous field):

Step 5

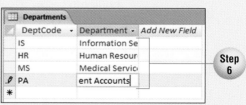

Step 6

DeptCode	=	IS
DepartmentName	=	Information Services
DeptCode	=	HR
DepartmentName	=	Human Resources
DeptCode	=	MS
DepartmentName	=	Medical Services
DeptCode	=	PA
DepartmentName	=	Patient Accounts

7. After typing the data, save the table by clicking the Save button on the Quick Access toolbar.
8. Close the Departments table by clicking the Close button located in the upper right corner of the work area.

Printing a Table

Print a Table
1. Open database.
2. Open table.
3. Click Quick Print button.

Quick Print

Customize Quick
Access Toolbar

Various methods are available for printing data in a table. One method for printing is to open the table and then click the Quick Print button on the Quick Access toolbar. If the Quick Print button is not visible on the Quick Access toolbar, click the Customize Quick Access Toolbar button that displays at the right side of the toolbar and then click *Quick Print* at the drop-down list.

When you click the Quick Print button, the information is sent directly to the printer without any formatting changes. In some fields created in the Employees table, this means that you would not be able to see all printed text in a field if all of the text did not fit in the field. For example, when typing the data in Project 2c, did you notice that the *StreetAddress* data was longer than the field column could accommodate? You can change the table layout to ensure that all data is visible. You will first print the Employees and Departments tables with the default settings, learn about changing the layout, and then print the tables again.

Project 2d — Printing the Employees and Departments Tables with the Default Settings

1. Open the Employees table.
2. Click the Quick Print button on the Quick Access toolbar. (The table will print on two pages.)
3. Close the Employees table.
4. Open the Departments table.
5. Click the Quick Print button on the Quick Access toolbar.
6. Close the Departments table.

Step 2

Look at the printing of the Employees table and notice how the order of records displays differently in the printing (and in the table) than the order in which the records were typed. Access automatically sorted the records by employee number in ascending order. Access automatically sorted the records in the Departments table alphabetically by department name. You will learn more about sorting later in this chapter.

Previewing a Table

Preview a Table
1. Click Office button.
2. Point to *Print*.
3. Click *Print Preview*.

Before printing a table, you may want to display the table in Print Preview to determine how the table will print on the page. To display a table in Print Preview, click the Office button, point to *Print*, and then click *Print Preview*. This displays the table as it will appear when printed as well as the Print Preview tab as shown in Figure 1.9.

Figure 1.9 Print Preview

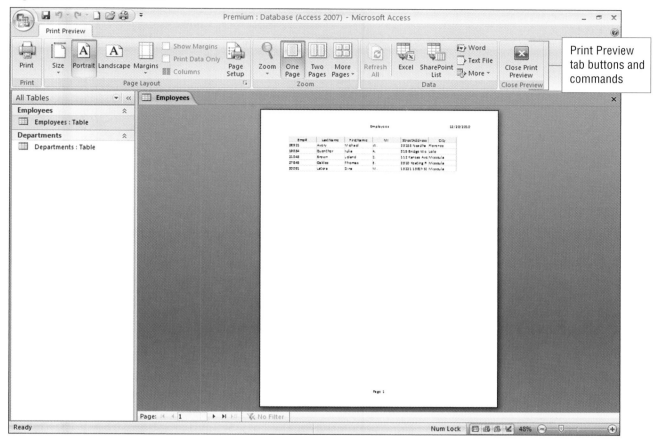

Print Preview tab buttons and commands

Changing Page Layout

The Employees table printed on two pages in portrait orientation with default margins. You can change page orientation and page margins with options in the Page Layout group in Print Preview. By default, Access prints a table in standard page size that is 8.5 inches wide and 11 inches tall. Click the Size button in the Page Layout group and a drop-down list displays with options for changing the page size to legal size, executive size, envelope size, and so on.

Access prints a page in Portrait orientation by default. At this orientation, the page is 8.5 inches wide and 11 inches tall. You can change this orientation to landscape, which makes the page 11 inches wide and 8.5 inches tall. The orientation buttons are located in the Page Layout group. Access uses default top, bottom, left, and right margins of 1 inch. Change these default margins by clicking the Margins button in the Page Layout group and then clicking one of the predesigned margin options.

You can also change page layout with options at the Page Setup dialog box shown in Figure 1.10. To display this dialog box, click the Page Setup button in the Page Layout group. You can also display the dialog box by clicking the Page Layout group dialog box launcher.

QUICK STEPS

Display Page Setup Dialog Box
1. Click Office button, Print, Print Preview.
2. Click Page Setup button.
OR
1. Click Office button, Print, Print Preview.
2. Click Page Layout group dialog box launcher.

Size

Margins

Page Setup

Figure 1.10 Page Setup Dialog Box with Print Options Tab Selected

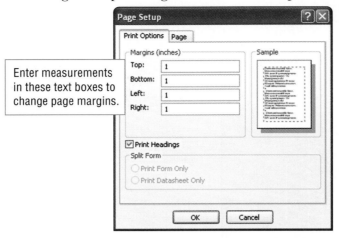

At the Page Setup dialog box with the Print Options tab selected, notice that the default margins are 1 inch. Change these defaults by typing a different number in the desired margin text box. By default, the table name prints at the top center of the page. For example, when you printed the Employees table, *Employees* printed at the top of the page along with the current date (printed at the right side of the page). *Page 1* also printed at the bottom of the page. If you do not want the name of the table and the date as well as the page number printed, remove the check mark from the *Print Headings* option at the Page Setup dialog box with the Print Options tab selected.

Change the table orientation at the Page Setup dialog box with the Page tab selected as shown in Figure 1.11. To change to landscape orientation, click *Landscape*. You can also change the paper size with options in the *Paper* section of the dialog box and specify the printer with options in the *Printer for (table name)* section of the dialog box.

Figure 1.11 Page Setup Dialog Box with Page Tab Selected

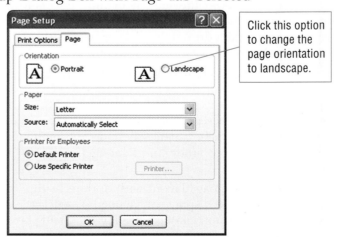

Changing Field Width

In the printing of the Employees table, not all of the data is visible in the *StreetAddress* field. You can remedy this situation by changing the width of the fields. Automatically adjust one field (column) in a table to accommodate the longest entry in the field by positioning the arrow pointer on the column boundary at the right side of the column until it turns into a double-headed arrow pointing left and right with a line between and then double-clicking the left mouse button. Automatically adjust adjacent columns by selecting the columns first and then double-clicking on a column boundary.

QUICK STEPS

Changing Field Width
1. Open table in Datasheet view.
2. Drag column boundary to desired position.

HINT

Automatically adjust column widths in an Access table in the same manner as adjusting column widths in an Excel worksheet.

Project 2e — Changing Page Layout and Printing the Employees Table

1. Open the Employees table.
2. Display the table in Print Preview by clicking the Office button, pointing to *Print*, and then clicking *Print Preview*.
3. Change the page orientation by clicking the Landscape button in the Page Layout group in the Print Preview tab.
4. Change margins by completing the following steps:
   a. Click the Page Setup button in the Page Layout group in the Print Preview tab.
   b. At the Page Setup dialog box with the Print Options tab selected, select *1* in the *Top* text box and then type **2**.
   c. Select *1* in the *Left* text box and then type **0.5**.
   d. Select *1* in the *Right* text box and then type **0.5**.
   e. Click OK to close the dialog box.
5. Click the Close Print Preview button.
6. Automatically adjust columns in the table to accommodate the longest entry by completing the following steps:
   a. Position the arrow pointer on the *Emp#* field name (the arrow pointer turns into a down-pointing black arrow).
   b. Hold down the left mouse button, drag the arrow pointer to the *ZipCode* field name, and then release the mouse button.

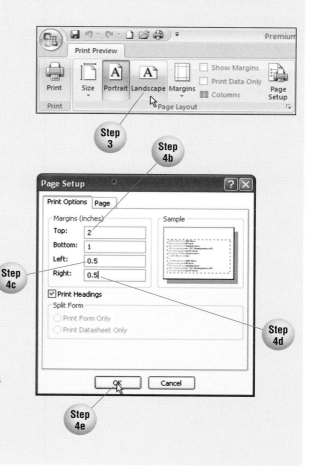

c. Position the arrow pointer on one of the column boundaries until it turns into a double-headed arrow pointing left and right with a line between and then double-click the left mouse button.

d. Click in any entry in the *ZipCode* column.

e. Drag the scroll box on the horizontal scroll bar to the right so the remaining fields (*DeptCode*, *HireDate*, and *SuppIns*) are visible.

f. Position the arrow pointer on the *DepCode* field name until the pointer turns into a down-pointing black arrow.

g. Hold down the left mouse button and then drag to the *SuppIns* field.

h. Double-click a column boundary between two of the selected columns.

i. Drag the scroll box to the left on the horizontal scroll bar so the *Emp#* field name displays.

j. Click in any entry in the *Emp#* field.

7. Send the table to the printer by clicking the Quick Print button on the Quick Access toolbar.

Step 6c

Emp#	LastName	FirstName
08921	Avery	Michael
19034	Guenther	Julia
21043	Brown	Leland
27845	Oaklee	Thomas
30091	Latora	Gina

Employees

Maintaining a Table

Add a Record to a Table
1. Open table in Datasheet view.
2. Click New button in Records group.
OR
1. Open table in Datasheet view.
2. Press Ctrl + Shift + +.

Delete a Record from a Table
1. Open table in Datasheet view.
2. Click Delete button arrow in Records group.
3. Click *Delete Record* at drop-down list.
4. Click Yes.

Once a table is created, more than likely it will require maintenance. For example, newly hired employees will need to be added to the Employees table. A system may be established for deleting an employee record when an employee leaves the company. The type of maintenance required on a table is related to the type of data stored in the table.

Adding a Record to a Table

Add a new record to an existing table by clicking the New button in the Records group in the Home tab or with the keyboard shortcut Ctrl + Shift + +. Type the data in the appropriate fields in the new record.

Deleting a Record in a Table

To delete an existing record in a table, select the row containing the record by clicking in the record selector bar. The record selector bar is the light blue area that displays at the left side of a record. When the mouse pointer is positioned in the record selector bar, the pointer turns into a black, right-pointing arrow. With the record selected, click the Delete button arrow in the Records group in the Home tab and then click *Delete Record* at the drop-down list. A message displays telling you that you will not be able to undo the delete operation and asking if you want to continue. At this message, click Yes.

Project 2f — Adding and Deleting Records in the Employees Table

1. With the Employees table open, add two new records to the table by completing the following steps:
   a. With the Home tab selected, click the New button in the Records group.

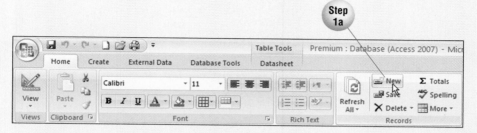

Step 1a

   b. Type the following data in the specified fields:
      Emp#   =   30020
      LastName   =   Pang
      FirstName   =   Eric
      MI   =   R.
      StreetAddress =   15512 Country Drive
      City   =   Lolo
      State   =   MT
      ZipCode   =   86308
      DeptCode   =   IS
      HireDate   =   8/15/2009
      SuppIns   =   Yes (Insert a check mark)
   c. Click the New button in the Records group (or just press the Tab key).
   d. Type the following data in the specified fields:
      Emp#   =   30023
      LastName   =   Zajac
      FirstName   =   Elizabeth
      MI   =   A.
      StreetAddress =   423 Corrin Avenue
      City   =   Missoula
      State   =   MT
      ZipCode   =   84325
      DeptCode   =   HR
      HireDate   =   8/15/2007
      SuppIns   =   Yes (Insert a check mark)

2. Delete a record in the table by completing the following steps:
   a. Select the row containing the record for Julia Guenther by clicking in the record selector bar that displays at the left side of the record. (When the mouse pointer is positioned in the record selector bar it turns into a black, right-pointing arrow.)

b. Click the Delete button arrow in the Records group and then click *Delete Record* at the drop-down list.

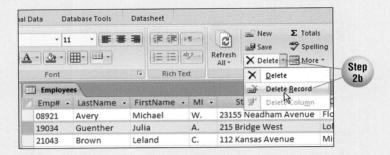

c. At the message telling you that you will not be able to undo the delete operation and asking if you want to continue, click Yes.
3. Click the Save button again on the Quick Access toolbar to save the Employees table.
4. Print the Employees table by completing the following steps:
   a. Click the Office button, point to *Print*, and then click *Print Preview*.
   b. In Print Preview, click the Landscape button in the Page Layout group.
   c. Click the Margins button in the Page Layout group and then click *Normal* at the drop-down list.
   d. Click the Print button at the left side of the Print Preview tab.
   e. Click OK at the Print dialog box.
5. Click the Close Print Preview button.
6. Save and then close the Employees table.
7. Close the **Premium.accdb** database.

CHAPTER summary

- Microsoft Access is a database management system software program that will organize, store, maintain, retrieve, sort, and print all types of business data.

- Open a database by double-clicking the file name in the *Open Recent Database* section of the Getting Started with Microsoft Office Access screen. You can also open a database by double-clicking the desired database at the Open dialog box. Display this dialog box by clicking the Open button on the Quick Access toolbar or clicking the Microsoft Office button and then clicking *Open* at the drop-down list.

- Organize data in Access in related tables in a database.

- The first step in organizing data for a table is determining fields. A field is one piece of information about a person, place, or item. All fields for one unit, such as an employee or customer, are considered a record.

- A field name should be unique and describe the contents of the field. It can contain up to 64 characters including letters, numbers, spaces, and some symbols.

- Part of the process of designing a table is assigning a data type to each field, which helps maintain and manage data and helps identify what type of data is expected for the field.

- When assigning a data type, you can assign a specific field size to a field.

- Access automatically saves a database on a periodic basis and also when the database is closed.

- Enter data in a table in Datasheet view. Type data in a field, pressing the Tab key to move to the next field or pressing Shift + Tab to move to the previous field.

- Print a table by opening the table and then clicking the Quick Print button on the Quick Access toolbar.

- Change margins in a table with the Margins button in the Page Layout group in the Print Preview tab or with options at the Page Setup dialog box with the Print Options tab selected.

- Change the paper size with the Size button in the Page Layout group in the Print Preview tab or with the *Size* option at the Page Setup dialog box with the Page tab selected.

- Click the Landscape button in the Page Layout group in the Print Preview tab to change the page orientation or with options in the *Orientation* section of the Page Layout dialog box with the Page tab selected.

- Adjust field widths in a table in the same manner as column widths in an Excel worksheet. Double-click a column boundary to automatically adjust the width to accommodate the longest entry.

- Maintaining a table can include adding and/or deleting records.

COMMANDS review

FEATURE	RIBBON TAB, GROUP	BUTTON	QUICK ACCESS TOOLBAR	OFFICE BUTTON DROP-DOWN LIST	KEYBOARD SHORTCUT
Open dialog box				Open	Ctrl + O
Close database				Close Database	
Design view	Home, Views	OR			
Datasheet view	Home, Views	OR			
Save database				Save	Ctrl + S
Save As dialog box				Save As	
Print table					
Print Preview				Print, Print Preview	
Portrait orientation	Print Preview, Page Layout				
Landscape orientation	Print Preview, Page Layout				
Page Setup dialog box	Print Preview, Page Layout				
Margins	Print Preview, Page Layout				
Add record	Home, Records	New			Ctrl + Shift + +
Delete record	Home, Records	✗ Delete ▾			

CONCEPTS check

Test Your Knowledge

Completion: For each description, indicate the correct term, symbol, or number.

1. This toolbar contains buttons for commonly used commands. _____

2. This displays the names of objects within a database grouped by categories. _____

3. All fields for one unit, such as an employee or customer, are considered to be this.

_____

4. In a field assigned the Yes/No data type, a check mark in the box in the field asking a yes/no question signifies this.

_____

5. This view is used in a table to define field names and assign data types.

_____

6. Use this view to enter data in fields.

_____

7. Change to landscape orientation by clicking the Landscape button in this group in the Print Preview tab.

_____

8. Add a new record to a table in this view.

_____

9. The Delete button is located in this group in the Home tab.

_____

10. Click this to select the row.

_____

SKILLS check
Demonstrate Your Proficiency

Assessment

1

CREATE AN ORDERS TABLE IN A HEALTHPLUS DATABASE

1. Use Access to create a database for a store that sells vitamins and other health aids. The table you create will keep track of what vitamins are ordered for the store. (This table assumes that the database includes at least two other tables—one table containing information on suppliers and the other containing information on products. You will learn more about how tables are related in Chapter 2.) Use the name of the store, HealthPlus, as the database name, and name the table *Orders*. Create the following fields in the Orders table and assign the data type shown (you determine the Description):

Field Name		Data Type
OrderNumber	=	Text (field size = 3)
ProductCode	=	Text (field size = 2)
SupplierNumber	=	Text (field size = 2)
DateOfOrder	=	Date/Time
AmountOfOrder	=	Currency

2. Save the table.
3. Change to Datasheet view and then enter the following data:

```
OrderNumber      =    214
ProductCode      =    MT
SupplierNumber   =    10
DateOfOrder      =    4/5/2010
AmountOfOrder    =    $875.50

OrderNumber      =    223
ProductCode      =    PA
SupplierNumber   =    27
DateOfOrder      =    4/6/2010
AmountOfOrder    =    $1,005.45

OrderNumber      =    241
ProductCode      =    GS
SupplierNumber   =    10
DateOfOrder      =    4/8/2010
AmountOfOrder    =    $441.95

OrderNumber      =    259
ProductCode      =    AV
SupplierNumber   =    18
DateOfOrder      =    4/8/2010
AmountOfOrder    =    $772.00
```

4. Automatically adjust the width of fields.
5. Save, print, and then close the Orders table.

2 ADD RECORDS TO THE ORDERS TABLE

1. With the **HealthPlus.accdb** database open, open the Orders table and then add the following records (remember to do this in Datasheet view):

```
OrderNumber      =    262
ProductCode      =    BC
SupplierNumber   =    27
DateOfOrder      =    4/9/2010
AmountOfOrder    =    $258.65

OrderNumber      =    265
ProductCode      =    VC
SupplierNumber   =    18
DateOfOrder      =    4/13/2010
AmountOfOrder    =    $1,103.45
```

2. Delete the record for order number 241.
3. Print the table with a top margin of 2 inches.
4. Close the Orders table.

3 CREATE A SUPPLIERS TABLE

1. With the **HealthPlus.accdb** database open, create a new table named Suppliers with the following fields and assign the data type shown (you determine the Description):

Field Name		Data Type
SupplierNumber	=	Text (field size = 2)
SupplierName	=	Text (field size = 20)
StreetAddress	=	Text (field size = 30)
City	=	Text (field size = 20)
State	=	Text (field size = 2)
ZipCode	=	Text (field size = 10)

2. After creating and saving the table with the fields shown above, enter the following data in the table (remember to do this in Datasheet view):

SupplierNumber	=	10
SupplierName	=	VitaHealth, Inc.
StreetAddress	=	12110 South 23rd
City	=	San Diego
State	=	CA
ZipCode	=	97432-1567

SupplierNumber	=	18
SupplierName	=	Mainstream Supplies
StreetAddress	=	312 Evergreen Building
City	=	Seattle
State	=	WA
ZipCode	=	98220-2791

SupplierNumber	=	21
SupplierName	=	LaVerde Products
StreetAddress	=	121 Vista Road
City	=	Phoenix
State	=	AZ
ZipCode	=	86355-6014

SupplierNumber	=	27
SupplierName	=	Redding Corporation
StreetAddress	=	554 Ninth Street
City	=	Portland
State	=	OR
ZipCode	=	97466-3359

3. Automatically adjust the width of fields.
4. Save the Suppliers table.
5. Change the page orientation to landscape and then print the table.
6. Close the Suppliers table.
7. Close the **HealthPlus.accdb** database.

CASE study

Apply Your Skills

Part 1

You are the manager of Miles Music, a small music store that specializes in CDs, DVDs, and Laserdiscs. Recently, the small store has increased its volume of merchandise, requiring better organization and easier retrieval of information. You decide to create a database named *MilesMusic* that contains two tables. Name one table *Inventory* and include fields that identify the category of music, the name of the CD or DVD, the name of the performer or band, and the media type (such as CD or DVD). Create a second table named *Category* that includes a short abbreviation for a category (such as R for Rap, A for Alternative, and C for Country). When entering records in the Inventory table, enter the category abbreviation you established in the Category table (rather than the entire category name). Enter at least eight records in the Inventory table and identify at least five categories of music. Print the Inventory and Category tables.

Part 2

As part of the maintenance of the database, you need to delete and add records as items are sold or orders are received. Delete two records from the Inventory table and then add three additional records. Print the Inventory table and then close the **MilesMusic.accdb** database.

Part 3

In Microsoft Word, create a document that describes the tables you created in the **MilesMusic.accdb** database. In the document, specify the fields in each table, the data types assigned to each field, and the field size (if appropriate). Apply any formatting to the document to enhance the visual appeal and then save the document and name it **Access_C1_CS_P3**. Print and then close **Access_C1_CS_P3.docx**.

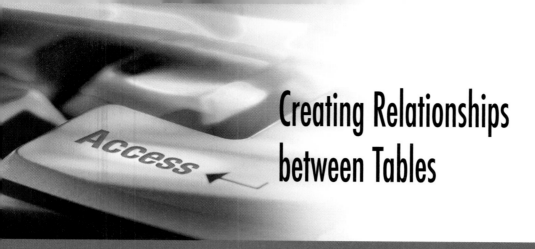

Creating Relationships between Tables

PERFORMANCE OBJECTIVES

Upon successful completion of Chapter 2, you will be able to:

access Chapter 2

- **Create a database table with a primary key and a foreign key**
- **Create a one-to-many relationship between tables**

Access is a relational database program that allows you to create tables that have a relation or connection to each other within the same database. In Chapter 1, you created a table containing information on employees and another containing department information. With Access, you can connect these tables through a common field that appears in both tables.

In this chapter you will learn how to identify a primary key field in a table that is unique to that table. In Access, data can be divided into logical groupings in tables for easier manipulation and management. Duplicate information is generally minimized in tables in the same database. A link or relationship, however, should connect the tables. In this chapter, you will define primary keys and define relationships between tables.

Note: Before beginning computer projects, delete the Access2007L1C1 folder from your storage medium. Next, copy the Access2007L1C2 subfolder from the Access2007L1 folder on the CD that accompanies this textbook to your storage medium and make Access2007L1C2 the active folder.

Project ❶ Establish Relationships between Tables

You will specify primary keys in tables, establish one-to-many and one-to-one relationships between tables, specify referential integrity, and print the relationships. You will also edit and delete a relationship and display records in a datasheet.

Creating Related Tables

Generally, a database management system fits into one of two categories—either a file management system (also sometimes referred to as a *flat file database*) or a relational database management system. In a file management system, data is stored without indexing and sequential processing. This type of system lacks flexibility in manipulating data and requires the same data to be stored in more than one place.

In a relational database management system, like Access, relationships are defined between sets of data allowing greater flexibility in manipulating data and eliminating data redundancy (entering the same data in more than one place). In projects in this chapter, you will define relationships between tables in the insurance company database. Because these tables will be related, information on a client does not need to be repeated in a table on claims filed. If you used a file management system to maintain insurance records, you would need to repeat the client information for each claim filed.

Determining Relationships

Taking time to plan a database is extremely important. Creating a database with related tables takes even more consideration. You need to determine how to break down the required data and what tables to create to eliminate redundancies. One idea to help you determine the necessary tables in a database is to think of the word "about." For example, an insurance company database will probably need a table "about" clients, another "about" the type of coverage, another "about" claims, and so on. A table should be about only one subject, such as a client, customer, department, or supplier.

Along with deciding on the necessary tables for a database, you also need to determine the relationship between tables. The ability to relate, or "join," tables is part of what makes Access a relational database system. Figure 2.1 illustrates the tables and fields that either are or will become part of the SouthwestInsurance.accdb database. Notice how each table is about only one subject—clients, type of insurance, claims, or coverage.

Figure 2.1 SouthwestInsurance.accdb Tables

Clients table	**Insurance table**
ClientNumber	LicenseNumber
Client	ClientNumber
StreetAddress	InsuranceCode
City	UninsuredMotorist
State	
ZipCode	

Claims table	**Coverage table**
ClaimNumber	InsuranceCode
ClientNumber	TypeOfInsurance
LicenseNumber	
DateOfClaim	
AmountOfClaim	

Some fields such as *ClientNumber*, *LicenseNumber*, and *InsuranceCode* appear in more than one table. These fields are used to create a relationship between tables. For example, in Project 1b you will create a relationship between the Clients table and the Insurance table with the *ClientNumber* field.

Creating relationships between tables tells Access how to bring the information in the database back together again. With relationships defined, you can bring information together to create queries, forms, and reports. (You will learn about these features in future chapters.)

Creating a Primary Field

Before creating a relationship between tables, you need to define the primary key in a table. In a table, at least one field must be unique so that one record can be distinguished from another. A field (or several fields) with a unique value is considered a *primary key*. When a primary key is defined, Access will not allow duplicate values in the primary field. For example, the *ClientNumber* field in the Clients table must contain a unique number (you would not assign the same client number to two different clients). If you define this as the primary key field, Access will not allow you to type the same client number in two different records.

In a field specified as a primary key, Access expects a value in each record in the table. This is referred to as *entity integrity*. If a value is not entered in a field, Access actually enters a null value. A null value cannot be given to a primary key field. Access will not let you close a database containing a primary field with a null value.

To define a field as a primary key, open the table and then change to Design view. Position the insertion point somewhere in the row containing the field you want to identify as the primary key and then click the Primary Key button in the Tools group. An image of a key is inserted at the beginning of the row identified as the primary key field. To define more than one field as a primary key, select the rows containing the fields you want as primary keys and then click the Primary Key button in the Tools group.

Creating a Foreign Key

A primary key field in one table may be a foreign key in another. For example, if you define the *ClientNumber* field in the Clients table as the primary key, the *ClientNumber* field in the Insurance table will then be considered a *foreign key*. The primary key field and the foreign key field form a relationship between the two tables. In the Clients table, each entry in the *ClientNumber* field will be unique (it is the primary key), but the same client number may appear more than once in the *ClientNumber* field in the Insurance table (such as a situation where a client has insurance on more than one vehicle). Each table in Figure 2.1 contains a unique field that will be defined as the primary key. Figure 2.2 identifies the primary keys and also foreign keys.

HINT

Access uses a primary key to associate data from multiple tables.

QUICK STEPS

Specify a Primary Key
1. Open table in Design view.
2. Click desired field.
3. Click Primary Key button.
4. Click Save button.

HINT

You must enter a value in the primary key field in every record.

Primary Key

Figure 2.2 Primary and Foreign Keys

Clients table
ClientNumber *(primary key)*
Client
StreetAddress
City
State
ZipCode

Insurance table
LicenseNumber *(primary key)*
ClientNumber *(foreign key)*
InsuranceCode *(foreign key)*
UninsuredMotorist

Claims table
ClaimNumber *(primary key)*
ClientNumber *(foreign key)*
LicenseNumber *(foreign key)*
DateOfClaim
AmountOfClaim

Coverage table
InsuranceCode *(primary key)*
TypeOfInsurance

In Project 1a, you will create another table for the SouthwestInsurance.accdb database, enter data, and then define primary keys for the tables. In the section following Project 1a, you will learn how to create relationships between the tables.

Project 1a   Creating a Table and Defining Primary Keys

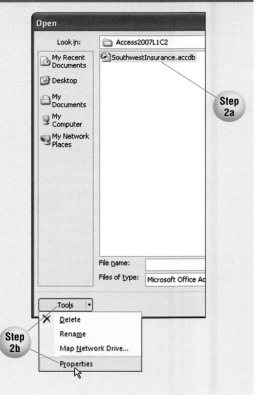

1. Display the Open dialog box and make the Access2007L1C2 folder on your storage medium the active folder.
2. Remove the read-only attribute from **SouthwestInsurance.accdb** by completing the following steps:
   a. Click once on the ***SouthwestInsurance.accdb*** database name.
   b. Click the Tools button located in the lower left corner of the Open dialog box and then click *Properties* at the drop-down list.
   c. At the SouthwestInsurance.accdb Properties dialog box with the General tab selected, click *Read-only* in the *Attributes* section to remove the check mark.
   d. Click OK to close the SouthwestInsurance.accdb Properties dialog box.
3. Open the **SouthwestInsurance.accdb** database.
4. At the SouthwestInsurance : Database window, create a new table by completing the following steps:
   a. Click the Create tab.
   b. Click the Table button in the Tables group.

Step 2a

Step 2b

c. At the Table window, click the View button in the Views group in the Table Tools Datasheet tab.

d. At the Save As dialog box, type **Insurance** in the *Table Name* text box and then press Enter or click OK.

e. Type the fields, assign the data types, and type the descriptions as shown below (for assistance, refer to Chapter 1, Project 1a):

Field Name	Data Type	Description
LicenseNumber	Text (Field Size = 7)	Vehicle license number
ClientNumber	Text (Field Size = 4)	Client number
InsuranceCode	Text (Field Size = 1)	Insurance code
UninsuredMotorist	Yes/No	Uninsured motorist coverage

5. Click the Save button on the Quick Access toolbar.

6. Notice the key that displays at the left side of the *LicenseNumber* field identifying the field as a primary key.

7. Close the Insurance table by clicking the Close button located in the upper right corner of the window.

8. Define primary keys for the other tables in the database by completing the following steps:

a. At the SouthwestInsurance : Database window, double-click *Claims* in the Navigation pane.

b. With the Claims table open, click the View button to switch to Design view.

c. Click anywhere in the text *ClaimNumber* and then click the Primary Key button in the Tools group.

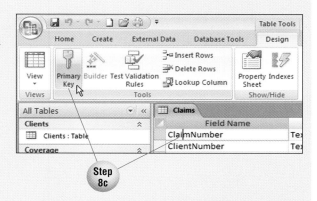

Step 8c

d. Click the Save button on the Quick Access toolbar.

e. Close the Claims table.

f. At the SouthwestInsurance : Database window, double-click *Clients* in the Navigation pane.

g. With the Clients table open, click the View button to switch to Design view.

h. Click anywhere in the text *ClientNumber* and then click the Primary Key button in the Tools group.

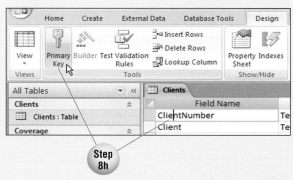

Step 8h

i. Click the Save button on the Quick Access toolbar.

j. Close the Clients table.

k. At the SouthwestInsurance : Database window, double-click *Coverage* in the Navigation pane.

l. With the Coverage table open, click the View button to switch to Design view.

m. Click anywhere in the text *InsuranceCode* and then click the Primary Key button in the Tools group.

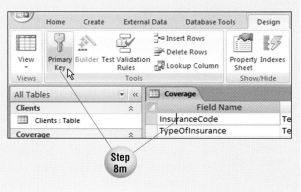

Step 8m

n. Click the Save button on the Quick Access toolbar.

o. Close the Coverage table.

9. Open the Insurance table and then type the following data in the specified fields. (If the *Uninsured Motorist* field is Yes, insert a check mark in the field by pressing the spacebar. If the field is No, leave the check box blank.)

LicenseNumber	=	341 VIT
ClientNumber	=	3120
InsuranceCode	=	F
UninsuredMotorist	=	Yes
LicenseNumber	=	776 ERU
ClientNumber	=	9383
InsuranceCode	=	F
UninsuredMotorist	=	No
LicenseNumber	=	984 CWS
ClientNumber	=	7335
InsuranceCode	=	L
UninsuredMotorist	=	Yes
LicenseNumber	=	877 BNN
ClientNumber	=	4300
InsuranceCode	=	L
UninsuredMotorist	=	Yes
LicenseNumber	=	310 YTV
ClientNumber	=	3120
InsuranceCode	=	F
UninsuredMotorist	=	Yes

Insurance

LicenseNum ⌄	ClientNumb ⌄	InsuranceCo ⌄	UninsuredM ⌄	Add New Field
341 VIT	3120	F	☑	
776 ERU	9383	F	☐	
984 CWS	7335	L	☑	
877 BNN	4300	L	☑	
310 YTV	3120	F	☑	
*			☐	

Step 9

10. Save and then close the Insurance table.

HINT

Defining a relationship between tables is one of the most powerful features of a relational database management system.

Establishing a Relationship between Tables

In Access, one table can be related to another, which is generally referred to as performing a *join*. When tables with a common field are joined, data can be extracted from both tables as if they were one large table. Another reason for relating tables is to ensure the integrity of the data. For example, in Project 1b, you will create a relationship between the Clients table and the Claims table. The relationship that is established will ensure that a client cannot be entered in the Claims table without first being entered in the Clients table. This ensures that a claim is not processed on a person who is not a client of the insurance company. This type of relationship is called a one-to-many relationship, which means that one record in the Clients table will match zero, one, or many records in the Claims table.

In a one-to-many relationship, the table containing the "one" is referred to as the *primary table* and the table containing the "many" is referred to as the *related table*. Access follows a set of rules known as *referential integrity*, which enforces consistency between related tables. These rules are enforced when data is updated in related tables. The referential integrity rules ensure that a record added to a related table has a matching record in the primary table.

HINT

Use the Table Analyzer Wizard to analyze your tables and restructure them to better conform to relational theory. Start the wizard by clicking the Database Tools tab and then clicking the Analyze Table button.

Creating a One-to-Many Relationship

A relationship is specified between existing tables in a database. To create a one-to-many relationship, open the database containing the tables to be related. Click the Database Tools tab and then click the Relationships button in the Show/Hide group. This displays the Show Table dialog box, as shown in Figure 2.3. At the Show Table dialog box, each table that will be related must be added to the Relationships window. To do this, click the first table name to be included and then click Add. Continue in this manner until all necessary table names have been added to the Relationships window and then click the Close button.

Figure 2.3 Show Table Dialog Box

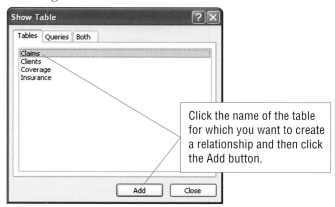

Click the name of the table for which you want to create a relationship and then click the Add button.

At the Relationships window, such as the one shown in Figure 2.4, use the mouse to drag the common field from the primary table (the "one") to the related table (the "many"). This causes the Edit Relationships dialog box to display as shown in Figure 2.5. At the Edit Relationships dialog box, check to make sure the correct field name displays in the *Table/Query* and *Related Table/Query* list boxes and the relationship type at the bottom of the dialog box displays as *One-To-Many*.

Figure 2.4 Relationships Window

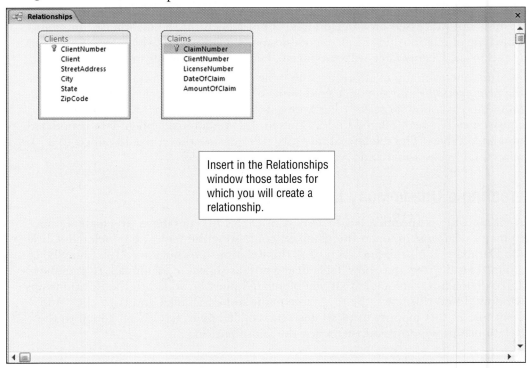

Insert in the Relationships window those tables for which you will create a relationship.

Figure 2.5 Edit Relationships Dialog Box

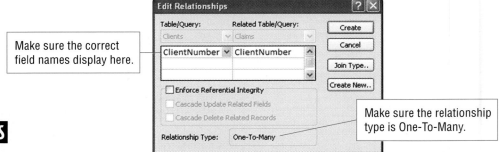

Make sure the correct field names display here.

Make sure the relationship type is One-To-Many.

QUICK STEPS

Create a One-to-Many Relationship
1. Click Database Tools tab.
2. Click Relationships button.
3. At Show Table dialog box, add tables to be related.
4. At Relationship window, drag "one" field from primary table to "many" field in related table.
5. At Edit Relationships dialog box, enforce referential integrity.
6. Click Create button.
7. Click Save button.

Specify the relationship options by choosing *Enforce Referential Integrity*, as well as *Cascade Update Related Fields* and/or *Cascade Delete Related Records*. (These options are explained in the text after these steps.) Click the Create button. This causes the Edit Relationships dialog box to close and the Relationships window to display showing the relationship between the tables.

In Figure 2.6, the Clients table displays with a black line attached along with the number *1* (signifying the "one" side of the relationship). The black line is connected to the Claims table along with the infinity symbol ∞ (signifying the "many" side of the relationship). The black line, called the ***join line***, is thick at both ends if the enforce referential integrity option has been chosen. If this option is not chosen, the line is thin at both ends. Click the Save button on the Quick Access toolbar to save the relationship. Close the Relationships window by clicking the Close button located in the upper right corner of the window.

Figure 2.6 One-to-Many Relationship

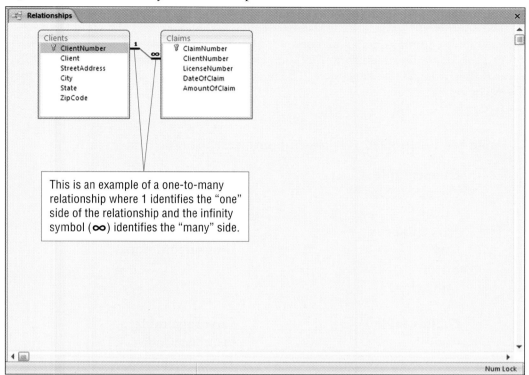

This is an example of a one-to-many relationship where 1 identifies the "one" side of the relationship and the infinity symbol (∞) identifies the "many" side.

Specifying Referential Integrity

Choose *Enforce Referential Integrity* at the Edit Relationships dialog box to ensure that the relationships between records in related tables are valid. Referential integrity can be set if the field from the primary table is a primary key and the related fields have the same data type. When referential integrity is established, a value for the primary key must first be entered in the primary table before it can be entered in the related table.

If you select only *Enforce Referential Integrity* and the related table contains a record, you will not be able to change a primary key value or delete a primary key value in the primary table. If you choose *Cascade Update Related Fields*, you will be able to change a primary key value in the primary table and Access will automatically update the matching value in the related table. Choose *Cascade Delete Related Records* and you will be able to delete a record in the primary table and Access will delete any related records in the related table.

Printing Relationships

You can print a report displaying the relationships between tables. To do this, display the Relationships window and then click the Relationship Report button in the Tools group. This displays the Relationships report in Print Preview. Click the Print button in the Print group in the Print Preview tab. After printing the relationships report, click the Close button that displays at the right side of the Relationships window.

QUICK STEPS

Print Database Relationships
1. Click Database Tools tab.
2. Click Relationships button.
3. Click Relationships Report button.
4. Click Print button.
5. Click OK at Print dialog box.
6. Click Close button.

 Relationship Report

Print

Relating Tables in the SouthwestInsurance Database

The SouthwestInsurance.accdb database contains the four tables shown in Figure 2.1. Each table contains data about something—clients, insurance, claims, and coverage. You can relate these tables so that data can be extracted from more than one table as if they were all one large table. The relationships between the tables are identified in Figure 2.7.

Figure 2.7 Relationships between SouthwestInsurance Tables

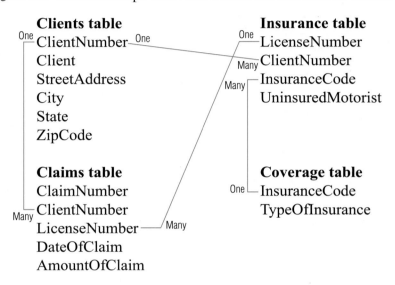

In the relationships shown in Figure 2.7, notice how the primary key is identified as the "one" and the foreign key is identified as the "many." Relate these tables so you can extract information from more than one table. For example, you can design a report about claims that contains information on claims as well as information on the clients submitting the claims.

Project 1b   Creating a One-to-Many Relationship between the Client and Claims Tables

1. With the **SouthwestInsurance.accdb** database open, click the Database Tools tab and then click the Relationships button in the Show/Hide group.

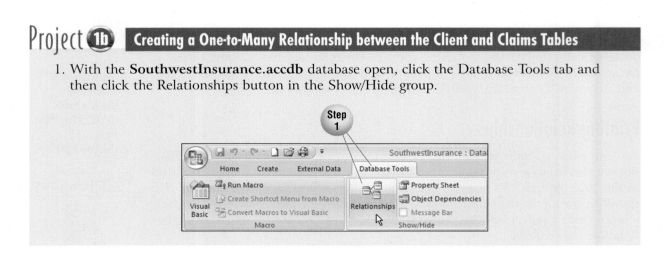

Step 1

2. At the Show Table dialog box, add the Clients and Claims tables to the Relationships window by completing the following steps:
   a. Click *Clients* in the list box and then click Add.
   b. Click *Claims* in the list box and then click Add.
3. Click the Close button to close the Show Table dialog box.
4. At the Relationships window, drag the *ClientNumber* field from the Clients table to the Claims table by completing the following steps:
   a. Position the arrow pointer on the *ClientNumber* field that displays in the Clients table.
   b. Hold down the left mouse button, drag the arrow pointer (with a field icon attached) to the *ClientNumber* field in the *Claims* table, and then release the mouse button. (This causes the Edit Relationships dialog box to display.)

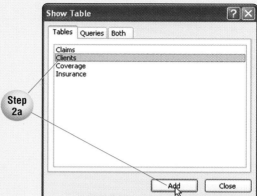

Step 2a

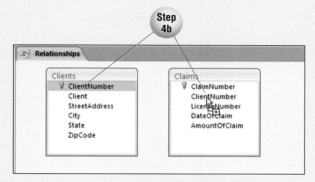

Step 4b

5. At the Edit Relationships dialog box, make sure *ClientNumber* displays in the *Table/Query* and *Related Table/Query* list boxes and the relationship type at the bottom of the dialog box displays as *One-To-Many*.
6. Enforce the referential integrity of the relationship by completing the following steps:
   a. Click *Enforce Referential Integrity*. (This makes the other two options available.)
   b. Click *Cascade Update Related Fields*.
   c. Click *Cascade Delete Related Records*.
7. Click the Create button. (This causes the Edit Relationships dialog box to close and the Relationships window to display showing a thick black line connecting Clients to Claims. At the Clients side, a *1* will appear and an infinity symbol ∞ will display at the Claims side of the thick black line.)

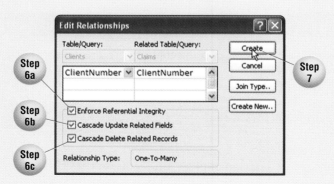

Step 6a

Step 7

Step 6b

Step 6c

8. Click the Save button on the Quick Access toolbar to save the relationship.
9. Print the relationships by completing the following steps:
   a. At the Relationships window, click the Relationship Report button in the Tools group. (This displays the Relationships report in Print Preview.)
   b. Click the Print button in the Print group.

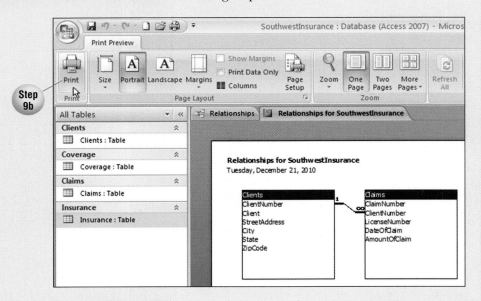

   c. Click OK at the Print dialog box.
   d. Click the Close button that displays at the right side of the Relationships window.
   e. At the message asking if you want to save changes to the design of the report, click No.
10. Close the Relationships window by clicking the Close button that displays at the right side of the Relationships window.

Once a relationship has been established between tables, clicking the Relationships button causes the Relationships window to display (rather than the Show Table dialog box). To create additional relationships, click the Database Tools tab, click the Relationships button in the Show/Hide group, and then click the Show Table button in the Relationships group. This displays the Show Table dialog box where you can specify the tables you need for creating another relationship.

Project 1c Creating Additional One-to-Many Relationships in a Database

1. With the **SouthwestInsurance.accdb** database open, create another one-to-many relationship between the Clients table and the Insurance table. Begin by clicking the Database Tools tab.
2. Click the Relationships button in the Show/Hide group.
3. At the Relationships window, click the Show Table button in the Relationships group.

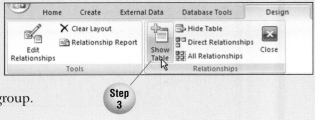

4. At the Show Table dialog box, click *Insurance* in the list box, and then click the Add button. (You do not need to add the Clients table because it was added in Project 1b.)
5. Click the Close button to close the Show Table dialog box.
6. At the Relationships window, drag the *ClientNumber* field from the Clients table to the Insurance table by completing the following steps:
   a. Position the arrow pointer on the *ClientNumber* field that displays in the Clients table.
   b. Hold down the left mouse button, drag the arrow pointer (with a field icon attached) to the *ClientNumber* field in the Insurance table, and then release the mouse button. (This causes the Edit Relationships dialog box to display.)

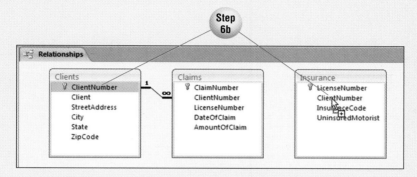

7. At the Edit Relationships dialog box, make sure *ClientNumber* displays in the *Table/Query* and *Related Table/Query* list boxes and the relationship type at the bottom of the dialog box displays as *One-To-Many*.
8. Enforce the referential integrity of the relationship by completing the following steps:
   a. Click *Enforce Referential Integrity*. (This makes the other two options available.)
   b. Click *Cascade Update Related Fields*.
   c. Click *Cascade Delete Related Records*.
9. Click the Create button. (This causes the Edit Relationships dialog box to close and the Relationships window to display showing a thick black line connecting Clients to Insurance. At the Clients side, a *1* will appear and an infinity symbol ∞ will display at the Insurance side of the thick black line.)

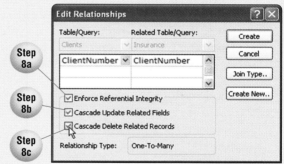

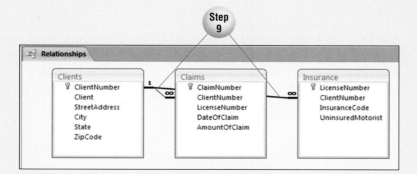

10. Click the Save button on the Quick Access toolbar to save the relationship.

11. With the Relationships window still open, create the following one-to-many relationships by completing steps similar to those in Steps 3 through 10:
   a. Create a relationship between *LicenseNumber* in the Insurance table and the Claims table. (*LicenseNumber* in the Insurance table is the "one" and *LicenseNumber* in the Claims table is the "many.") At the Edit Relationships dialog box, be sure to choose *Enforce Referential Integrity*, *Cascade Update Related Fields*, and *Cascade Delete Related Records*.
   b. Add the Coverage table to the Relationships window and then create a relationship between *InsuranceCode* in the Coverage table and the Insurance table. (*InsuranceCode* in the Coverage table is the "one" and *InsuranceCode* in the Insurance table is the "many." At the Edit Relationships dialog box, be sure to choose *Enforce Referential Integrity*, *Cascade Update Related Fields*, and *Cascade Delete Related Records*.

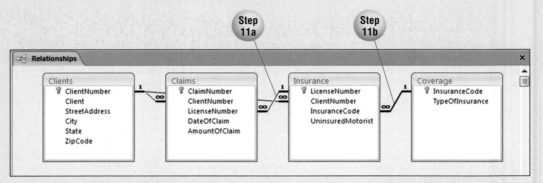

12. Click the Save button on the Quick Access toolbar.
13. Print the relationships by completing the following steps:
   a. At the Relationships window, click the Relationship Report button in the Tools group. (This displays the Relationships report in Print Preview.)
   b. Click the Print button in the Print group and then click OK at the Print dialog box.
   c. Click the Close button that displays at the right side of the Relationships window.
   d. At the message asking if you want to save changes to the design of the report, click No.
14. Close the Relationships window by clicking the Close button that displays at the right side of the Relationships window.

       In the relationship established in Project 1b, a record must first be added to the Clients table before a related record can be added to the Claims table. This is because you chose the *Enforce Referential Integrity* option at the Edit Relationships dialog box. Because you chose the two options *Cascade Update Related Fields* and *Cascade Delete Related Records*, records in the Clients table (the primary table) can be updated and/or deleted and related records in the Claims table (related table) will automatically be updated or deleted.

Project **1d** | **Updating Fields and Adding and Deleting Records in Related Tables**

1. With the **SouthwestInsurance.accdb** database open, open the Clients table.
2. Change two client numbers in the Clients database (Access will automatically change it in the Claims table) by completing the following steps:
   a. Make sure the Clients window displays in Datasheet view.
   b. Click once in the *ClientNumber* field for Paul Vuong containing the number *4300*.
   c. Change the number from *4300* to *4308*.
   d. Click once in the *ClientNumber* field for Vernon Cook containing the number *7335*.
   e. Change the number from *7335* to *7325*.
   f. Click the Save button on the Quick Access toolbar.
   g. Close the Clients table.
   h. Open the Claims table. (Notice that the client numbers for Vernon Cook and Paul Vuong automatically changed.)
   i. Close the Claims table.

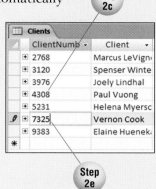

3. Open the Clients table, make sure the table displays in Datasheet view, and then add the following records at the end of the table:

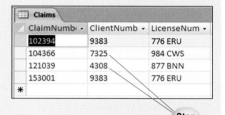

ClientNumber	=	5508
Client	=	Martina Bentley
StreetAddress	=	6503 Taylor Street
City	=	Scottsdale
State	=	AZ
ZipCode	=	85889

ClientNumber	=	2511
Client	=	Keith Hammond
StreetAddress	=	21332 Janski Road
City	=	Glendale
State	=	AZ
ZipCode	=	85310

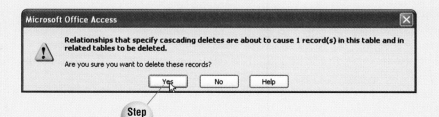

4. With the Clients table still open, delete the record for Elaine Hueneka. At the message telling you that relationships that specify cascading deletes are about to cause records in this table and related tables to be deleted, click Yes.

> **Microsoft Office Access**
>
> ⚠ Relationships that specify cascading deletes are about to cause 1 record(s) in this table and in related tables to be deleted.
>
> Are you sure you want to delete these records?
>
> [Yes] [No] [Help]

Step 4

5. Save, print, and then close the Clients table.
6. Open the Insurance table, make sure the table displays in Datasheet view, and then add the following records at the end of the table:

LicenseNumber	=	422 RTW
ClientNumber	=	5508
InsuranceCode	=	L
UninsuredMotorist	=	Yes

LicenseNumber	=	130 YWR
ClientNumber	=	5508
InsuranceCode	=	F
UninsuredMotorist	=	No

LicenseNumber	=	795 GRT
ClientNumber	=	2511
InsuranceCode	=	L
UninsuredMotorist	=	Yes

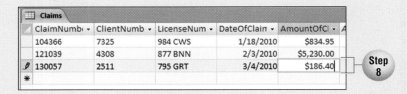

7. Save, print, and then close the Insurance table.
8. Open the Claims table, make sure the table displays in Datasheet view, and then add the following record:

ClaimNumber	=	130057
ClientNumber	=	2511
LicenseNumber	=	795 GRT
DateOfClaim	=	3/4/2010
AmountOfClaim	=	$186.40

9. Save and then print the Claims table.
10. With the Claims table still open, try to enter a record for a client who has not been entered in the Clients table by completing the following steps (Access will not allow this because of the one-to-many relationship that was established in Project 1b):
    a. Add the following record to the Claims table:

ClaimNumber	=	201221
ClientNumber	=	5824
LicenseNumber	=	640 TRS
DateOfClaim	=	3/11/2010
AmountOfClaim	=	$895.25

    b. Click the Close button to close the Claims table. This causes a message to display telling you that the record cannot be added or changed because a related record is required in the Clients table. At this message, click OK.
    c. A message displays warning you that Access cannot save the table, that closing the object will cause the changes to be made, and asking if you want to close the database object. At this warning, click Yes.

Editing and Deleting a Relationship

You can make changes to a relationship that has been established between tables. The relationship can also be deleted. To edit a relationship, open the database containing the tables with the relationship, click the Database Tools tab, and then click the Relationships button in the Show/Hide group. This displays the Relationships window with the related tables displayed in boxes. Click the Edit Relationships button located in the Tools group to display the Edit Relationships dialog box such as the one shown in Figure 2.5, where you can change the current relationship. You can also display the Edit Relationships dialog box by positioning the arrow pointer on the thin portion of one of the black lines that connects the related tables and then clicking the *right* mouse button. This causes a pop-up menu to display. At this pop-up menu, click the left mouse button on Edit Relationship.

To delete a relationship between tables, display the related tables in the Relationships window. Position the arrow pointer on the thin portion of the black line connecting the related tables and then click the *right* mouse button. At the pop-up menu that displays, click the left mouse button on Delete. At the message asking if you are sure you want to permanently delete the selected relationship from your database, click Yes.

Creating a One-to-One Relationship

You can create a one-to-one relationship between tables in which each record in the first table matches only one record in the second table and one record in the second table matches only one record in the first table. A one-to-one relationship is not as common as a one-to-many relationship since the type of information used to create the relationship can be stored in one table. A one-to-one relationship can be helpful in a situation where you divide a table with many fields into two tables.

Edit a Relationship
1. Click Database Tools tab.
2. Click Relationships button.
3. Click Edit Relationships button.
4. At Edit Relationships dialog box, make desired changes.
5. Click OK.

Delete a Relationship
1. Click Database Tools tab.
2. Click Relationships button.
3. Right-click on black line connecting related tables.
4. Click Delete.
5. Click Yes.

HINT
The Relationships window displays any relationship you have defined between tables.

Edit Relationships

Project **1e** ▌ **Creating Tables and Defining a One-to-One Relationship**

1. With the **SouthwestInsurance.accdb** database open, create a new table by completing the following steps:
   a. Click the Create tab.
   b. Click the Table button in the Tables group.
   c. At the Table window, click the View button in the Views group in the Table Tools Datasheet tab.
   d. At the Save As dialog box, type **Assignments** in the *Table Name* text box and then press Enter or click OK.
   e. Type the fields, assign the data types, and type the descriptions as shown below (for assistance, refer to Chapter 1, Project 1a):

Field Name	Data Type	Description
ClientNumber	Text (Field Size = 4)	Client number
AgentNumber	Text (Field Size = 3)	Agent number

2. Make sure a key displays at the left side of the *ClientNumber* field and then click the Save button on the Quick Access toolbar.

3. Click the View button to change to Datasheet view and then type the following in the specified fields:

ClientNumber	2511	ClientNumber	2768
AgentNumber	210	AgentNumber	142

ClientNumber	3120	ClientNumber	3976
AgentNumber	173	AgentNumber	210

ClientNumber	4308	ClientNumber	5231
AgentNumber	245	AgentNumber	173

ClientNumber	5508	ClientNumber	7325
AgentNumber	245	AgentNumber	142

4. Save, print, and then close the Assignments table.
5. At the SouthwestInsurance : Database window, create a new table by completing the following steps:
   a. Click the Create tab.
   b. Click the Table button in the Tables group.
   c. At the Table window, click the View button in the Views group in the Table Tools Datasheet tab.
   d. At the Save As dialog box, type **Agents** in the *Table Name* text box and then press Enter or click OK.
   e. Type the fields, assign the data types, and type the descriptions as shown below (for assistance, refer to Chapter 1, Project 2a):

Field Name	Data Type	Description
AgentNumber	Text (Field Size = 3)	Agent number
FirstName	Text (Field Size = 20)	Agent first name
LastName	Text (Field Size = 20)	Agent last name
Telephone	Text (Field Size = 12)	Agent phone number
Email	Text (Field Size = 30)	Agent e-mail address

6. Make sure a key displays at the left side of the *AgentNumber* field and then click the Save button on the Quick Access toolbar.
7. Click the View button to change to Datasheet view and then type the following in the specified fields:

AgentNumber	142	AgentNumber	173
FirstName	James	FirstName	Tamara
LastName	Moriyama	LastName	Sadler
Telephone	602-555-2676	Telephone	602-555-2698
Email	jmoriyama@emcp.net	Email	tsadler@emcp.net

AgentNumber	210	AgentNumber	245
FirstName	Phillip	FirstName	Dayton
LastName	Cowans	LastName	Hubbard
Telephone	602-555-2683	Telephone	602-555-2644
Email	pcowans@emcp.net	Email	dhubbard@emcp.net

8. Automatically adjust the width of columns.

9. Save, print, and then close the Agents table.
10. Create a one-to-one relationship between the Assignments table and the Clients table by completing the following steps:
   a. Click the Database Tools tab.
   b. Click the Relationships button in the Show/Hide group.
   c. At the Relationships window, click the Show Table button in the Relationships group.
   d. At the Show Table dialog box, click *Assignments* in the list box, and then click the Add button.
   e. Click the Close button to close the Show Table dialog box.
   f. At the Relationships window, drag the *ClientNumber* field from the Assignments table to the *ClientNumber* field in the Clients table.

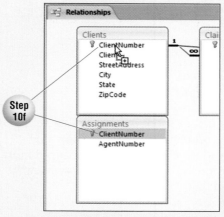

   g. At the Edit Relationships dialog box, make sure *ClientNumber* displays in the *Table/Query* and *Related Table/Query* list boxes and the relationship type at the bottom of the dialog box displays as *One-To-One.*
   h. Enforce the referential integrity of the relationship by completing the following steps:
      1) Click *Enforce Referential Integrity*. (This makes the other two options available.)
      2) Click *Cascade Update Related Fields*.
      3) Click *Cascade Delete Related Records*.

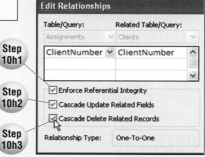

   i. Click the Create button. (This causes the Edit Relationships dialog box to close and the Relationships window to display showing a thick black line connecting the *ClientNumber* field in the Assignments and Clients tables.
   j. Click the Save button on the Quick Access toolbar to save the relationship.
11. Create a one-to-many relationship between the Assignments table and the Agents table by completing the following steps:
   a. With the Relationships window open, click the Show Table button in the Relationships group.
   b. At the Show Table dialog box, click *Agents* in the list box and then click the Add button.
   c. Click the Close button to close the Show Table dialog box.

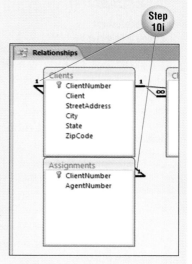

d. At the Relationships window, drag the *AgentNumber* field from the Agents table to the *AgentNumber* field in the Assignments table.

e. At the Edit Relationships dialog box, make sure *AgentNumber* displays in the *Table/Query* and *Related Table/Query* list boxes and the relationship type at the bottom of the dialog box displays as *One-To-Many*.

f. Enforce the referential integrity of the relationship by completing the following steps:
   1) Click *Enforce Referential Integrity*. (This makes the other two options available.)
   2) Click *Cascade Update Related Fields*.
   3) Click *Cascade Delete Related Records*.

g. Click the Create button.

h. Click the Save button on the Quick Access toolbar to save the relationship.

12. Print the relationships by completing the following steps:
   a. At the Relationships window, click the Relationship Report button in the Tools group. (This displays the Relationships report in Print Preview.)
   b. Click the Print button in the Print group.
   c. Click OK at the Print dialog box.
   d. Click the Close button that displays at the right side of the Relationships window.
   e. At the message asking if you want to save changes to the design of the report, click No.

13. Close the Relationships window by clicking the Close button that displays at the right side of the Relationships window.

 Displaying Related Records in a Subdatasheet

Display Subdatasheet
1. Open table in Datasheet view.
2. Click expand indicator at left of desired record.
3. At Insert Subdatasheet dialog box, click desired table.
4. Click OK.

When a relationship is established between tables, you can view and edit fields in related tables with a subdatasheet. Figure 2.8 displays the Clients table with the subdatasheet displayed for the client Keith Hammond. The subdatasheet displays the fields in the Insurance table related to Keith Hammond. Use this subdatasheet to view information and also to edit information in the Clients table as well as the Insurance table. Changes made to fields in a subdatasheet affect the table and any related table.

Access automatically inserts plus symbols (referred to as *expand indicators*) before each record in a table that is joined to another table by a one-to-many relationship. Click the expand indicator and, if the table is related to only one other table, a subdatasheet containing fields from the related table displays below the record as shown in Figure 2.8. To remove the subdatasheet, click the minus sign (referred to as the *collapse indicator*) preceding the record. (The plus symbol turns into the minus symbol when a subdatasheet displays.)

Figure 2.8 Table with Subdatasheet Displayed

Subdatasheet

If a table has more than one relationship defined, clicking the expand indicator will display the Insert Subdatasheet dialog box shown in Figure 2.9. At this dialog box, click the desired table in the Tables list box and then click OK. You can also display the Insert Subdatasheet dialog box by clicking the More button in the Records group in the Home tab, pointing to *Subdatasheet*, and then clicking *Subdatasheet*.

You can display subdatasheets for all records by clicking the More button, pointing to *Subdatasheet*, and then clicking *Expand All*. Remove all subdatasheets by clicking the More button, pointing to *Subdatasheet*, and then clicking *Collapse All*.

Figure 2.9 Insert Subdatasheet Dialog Box

If a table is related to two or more tables, specify the desired subdatasheet at the Subdatasheet dialog box. If you decide to display a different subdatasheet, remove the subdatasheet first before selecting to the next subdatasheet. Do this by clicking the More button, pointing to *Subdatasheet*, and then clicking *Remove*.

1. With the **SouthwestInsurance.accdb** database open, open the Clients table.
2. Display a subdatasheet by completing the following steps:
   a. Click the expand indicator (plus symbol) that displays at the left side of the first row (the row for Keith Hammond).
   b. At the Insert Subdatasheet dialog box, click *Claims* in the list box and then click OK.

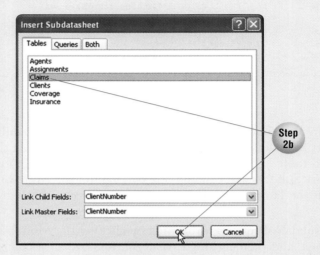

3. Remove the subdatasheet by clicking the collapse indicator (minus sign) that displays at the left side of the record for Keith Hammond.
4. Display subdatasheets for all of the records by clicking the More button in the Records group, pointing to *Subdatasheet*, and then clicking *Expand All*.

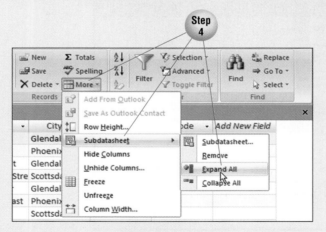

5. Remove the display of all subdatasheets by clicking the More button, pointing to *Subdatasheet*, and then clicking *Collapse All*.
6. Remove the connection between Clients and Claims by clicking the More button, pointing to *Subdatasheet*, and then clicking *Remove*.

7. Suppose that the client, Vernon Cook, has moved to a new address and purchased insurance for a new car. Display the Insurance subdatasheet and make changes to fields in the Clients table and the Insurance table by completing the following steps:
   a. Click the expand indicator (plus symbol) that displays at the left side of the *Vernon Cook* record.
   b. At the Insert Subdatasheet dialog box, click *Insurance* in the list box and then click OK.
   c. Change his street address from *1230 South Mesa* to *22135 Cactus Drive*.
   d. Change his ZIP code from *86201* to *85344*.
   e. Add the following information in the second row in the Insurance subdatasheet:
LicenseNumber	=	430 DWT
InsuranceCode	=	F
UninsuredMotorist	=	*Yes*

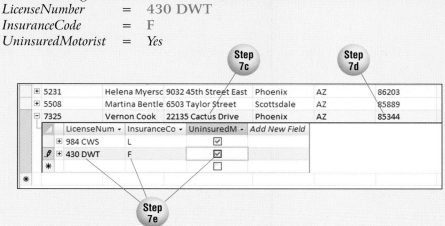

   f. Click the Save button on the Quick Access toolbar.
   g. Close the Clients table.
8. Open the Clients table, print it, and then close it.
9. Open the Insurance table, print it, and then close it.
10. Close the **SouthwestInsurance.accdb** database.

CHAPTER summary

- Access is a relational database software program in which you can create tables that have a relation or connection to one another.
- When planning a table, take time to determine how to break down the required data and what relationships will need to be defined to eliminate data redundancies.
- In a table at least one field must be unique so that one record can be distinguished from another. A field with a unique value is considered a primary key.
- In a field defined as a primary key, duplicate values are not allowed in the primary field and Access also expects a value in each record in the primary key field.
- Define a primary key field with the Primary Key button in the Tools group.
- A primary key field included in another table is referred to as a foreign key. Unlike a primary key field, a foreign key field can contain duplicate data.
- In Access, you can relate a table to another by performing a join. When tables that have a common field are joined, you can extract data from both tables as if they were one large table.
- You can create a one-to-many relationship between tables in a database. In this relationship, a record must be added to the "one" table before it can be added to the "many" table.
- You can create a one-to-one relationship between tables in which each record in the first table matches only one record in the second table and one record in the second table matches only one record in the first table.
- You can edit or delete a relationship between tables.
- To print a relationship, display the Relationships window, click the Relationship Report button in the Tools group, and then click the Print button in the Print Preview tab.
- When a relationship is established between tables, you can view and edit fields in related tables with a subdatasheet.
- To display a subdatasheet for a record, click the expand indicator (plus symbol) that displays at the left side of the record. To display subdatasheets for all records, click the More button in the Reports group in the Home tab, point to *Subdatasheet*, and then click *Expand All*.
- Display the Insert Subdatasheet dialog box by clicking the More button in the Reports group in the Home tab, pointing to *Subdatasheet*, and then clicking *Subdatasheet*.
- Turn off the display of a subdatasheet by clicking the collapse indicator (minus symbol) at the beginning of a record. To turn off the display of subdatasheets for all records, click the More button, point to *Subdatasheet*, and then click *Collapse All*.

COMMANDS review

FEATURE	RIBBON TAB, GROUP	BUTTON, OPTION
Primary key	Table Tools Design, Tools	
Relationships window	Database Tools, Show/Hide	
Edit Relationships window	Relationship Tools Design, Tools	
Show Table dialog box	Relationship Tools Design, Relationships	
Relationship report window	Relationship Tools Design, Tools	Relationship Report
Insert Subdatasheet dialog box	Home, Records	More ▾, Subdatasheet, Subdatasheet

CONCEPTS check

Test Your Knowledge

Completion: For each description, indicate the correct term, symbol, or character.

1. A primary key field must contain unique data while this type of key field can contain duplicate data. _____

2. In Access, one table can be related to another, which is generally referred to as performing this. _____

3. In a one-to-many relationship, the table containing the "one" is referred to as this. _____

4. In a one-to-many relationship, the table containing the "many" is referred to as this. _____

5. In a one-to-many relationship, Access follows a set of rules that enforces consistency between related tables and is referred to as this. _____

6. In related tables, this symbol displays near the black line next to the related table. _____

7. The black line that connects related tables is referred to as this. _____

8. Establish this type of relationship between tables in which each record in the first table matches only one record in the second table and one record in the second table matches only one record in the first table. _____

9. The plus symbol that displays at the beginning of a record in a related table is referred to as this. _____

10. The minus symbol that displays at the beginning of a record in a related table with a subdatasheet displayed is referred to as this. _____

11. Display subdatasheets for all records by clicking the More button, pointing to *Subdatasheet*, and then clicking this option. _____

SKILLS check

Demonstrate Your Proficiency

Assessment

CREATE AUTHORS, BOOKS, AND CATEGORIES TABLES IN A MYBOOKS DATABASE

1. Use Access to create a database for keeping track of books. Name the database *MyBooks*. Create a table named *Authors* that includes the following fields (you determine the data type, field size, and description):

    Field Name
    AuthorNumber (primary key)
    FirstName
    LastName
    MiddleInitial

2. After creating the table with the fields shown above and defining the primary key, save the table. Switch to Datasheet view and then enter the following data in the table:

AuthorNumber	=	1
FirstName	=	Branson
LastName	=	Walters
MiddleInitial	=	A.

AuthorNumber	=	2
FirstName	=	Christiana
LastName	=	Copeland
MiddleInitial	=	M.

AuthorNumber	=	3
FirstName	=	Shirley
LastName	=	Romero
MiddleInitial	=	E.

```
AuthorNumber   =   4
FirstName      =   Jeffrey
LastName       =   Fiedler
MiddleInitial  =   R.
```

3. Automatically adjust the width of columns.
4. Save, print, and then close the Authors table.
5. With the **MyBooks.accdb** database open, create another table named *Books* with the following fields (you determine the data type, field size, and description):

   Field Name
   ISBN (primary key)
   AuthorNumber
   Title
   CategoryCode
   Price

6. After creating the table with the fields shown above and defining the primary key, save the table. Switch to Datasheet view and then enter the following data in the table:

```
ISBN           =   12-6543-9008-7
AuthorNumber   =   4
Title          =   Today's Telecommunications
CategoryCode   =   B
Price          =   $34.95

ISBN           =   09-5225-5466-6
AuthorNumber   =   2
Title          =   Marketing in the Global Economy
CategoryCode   =   M
Price          =   $42.50

ISBN           =   23-9822-7645-0
AuthorNumber   =   1
Title          =   International Business Strategies
CategoryCode   =   B
Price          =   $45.00

ISBN           =   08-4351-4890-3
AuthorNumber   =   3
Title          =   Technological Advances
CategoryCode   =   B
Price          =   $36.95
```

7. Automatically adjust the width of columns (to accommodate the longest entry).
8. Save, print, and then close the Books table.
9. Create another table named *Categories* with the following fields (you determine the data type, field size, and description):

   Field Name
   CategoryCode (primary key)
   Category

10. After creating the table with the fields shown above and defining the primary key, save the table. Switch to Datasheet view and then enter the following data in the table:

    CategoryCode = B
    Category = Business

    CategoryCode = M
    Category = Marketing

11. Save, print, and then close the Categories table.

Assessment

2 CREATE RELATIONSHIPS BETWEEN TABLES

1. With the **MyBooks.accdb** database open, create the following relationships:
   a. Create a one-to-many relationship with the *AuthorNumber* field in the Authors table the "one" and the *AuthorNumber* field in the Books table the "many." (At the Edit Relationships dialog box, choose *Enforce Referential Integrity*, *Cascade Update Related Fields*, and *Cascade Delete Related Records*.)
   b. Create a one-to-many relationship with the *CategoryCode* field in the Categories table the "one" and the *CategoryCode* field in the Books table the "many." (At the Edit Relationships dialog box, choose *Enforce Referential Integrity*, *Cascade Update Related Fields*, and *Cascade Delete Related Records*.)
2. Print the relationships.
3. After creating, saving, and printing the relationships, add the following record to the Authors table:
       AuthorNumber = 5
       FirstName = Glenna
       LastName = Zener-Young
       MiddleInitial = A.
4. Adjust the column width for the *LastName* field.
5. Save, print, and then close the Authors table.
6. Add the following records to the Books table:

    ISBNNumber = 23-8931-0084-7
    AuthorNumber = 2
    Title = Practical Marketing Strategies
    Category = M
    Price = $28.50

    ISBNNumber = 87-4009-7134-6
    AuthorNumber = 5
    Title = Selling More
    Category = M
    Price = $40.25

7. Save, print, and then close the Books table.
8. Close the **MyBooks.accdb** database.

CASE study

Apply Your Skills

You are the owner of White Gloves Cleaning, a small housekeeping and cleaning service for residences and businesses. Since your business is continuing to grow, you decide to manage your records electronically instead of on paper. Create a database named **WhiteGloves** that contains three tables. Create a table named *Clients* that includes fields for a client number; name; address; city, state, ZIP code, contact person, location number, and rate number. Create another table named *Locations* that includes a location number field and a location field. Create a third table named *Rates* that includes a rate number field and a rates field.

In the Locations table, create the following:

Location number	Location
1	Residence
2	Business
3	Construction Site

In the Rates table, create the following:

Rate number	Rate
1	$15.00
2	$25.00
3	$40.00

Assign primary keys in each table and then create a one-to-many relationship with the *Location number* field in the Locations table the "one" and the *Location number* field in the Clients the many. Create another one-to-many relationship with the *Rate number* field in the Rates table the "one" and the *Rate number* field in the Clients table the many. Save and then print the relationships.

Enter six records in the Clients table. Specify that the location number for two records is 1 (residence) and the rate is 1 ($15.00). Specify that the location number for two records is 2 (business) and the rate is 2 ($25.00). Specify that the location number for two records is 3 (construction site) and the rate is 3 ($40.00). Save and print each table (print the Clients table in landscape orientation) and then close the **WhiteGloves.accdb** database.

Your business is growing and you have been hired to provide cleaning services to one additional business and one additional construction company. Add the appropriate information in the fields in the Clients table. One of your clients has cancelled services with your company so delete a client of your choosing from the Clients table. Print the Clients table. You have raised your hourly rates for cleaning a residence to $20.00. Make this change to the Rates table. Print the Rates table.

Part

3

In Microsoft Word, create a document that describes the tables, fields, and relationships you created in the WhiteGloves database. In the document, specify the fields in each table, the data types assigned to each field, the field size (if appropriate), and describe the one-to-many relationships you created. Apply formatting to the document to enhance the visual appeal and then save the document and name it **Access_C2_CS_P3**. Print and then close **Access_C2_CS_P3.docx**.

CHAPTER 3

Modifying and Managing Tables

PERFORMANCE OBJECTIVES

Upon successful completion of Chapter 3, you will be able to:

- Modify a table by adding, deleting, or moving fields
- Assign a default value and validate a field entry
- Insert a Total row
- Use the Input Mask Wizard and the Lookup Wizard
- Complete a spelling check on data in a table
- Find specific records in a table
- Find specific data in a table and replace with other data
- Backup a database
- Compact and repair a database
- Use the Help feature

access Chapter 3

An Access database requires maintenance to keep the database up to date. Maintenance might include modifying the table by inserting or deleting fields, defining values and validating field entries, inserting a Total row, using wizards to identify data type, and sorting data in tables. In this chapter, you will learn how to modify tables as well as how to use the spelling checker to find misspelled words in a table and how to use the find and replace feature to find specific records in a table or find specific data in a table and replace with other data. As you continue working with a database, consider compacting and repairing the database to optimize performance and back up the database to protect your data from accidental loss or hardware failure. Microsoft Office contains an on-screen reference manual containing information on features and commands for each program within the suite. In this chapter, you will learn to use the Help feature to display information about Access.

Note: Before beginning computer projects, delete the Access2007L1C2 folder from your storage medium. Next, copy the Access2007L1C3 subfolder from the Access2007L1 folder on the CD that accompanies this textbook to your storage medium and make Access2007L1C3 the active folder.

Project ① Manage Data and Define Data Types

You will modify tables by adding and deleting fields, assign data types and default values to fields, validate field entries, insert a total row, and use the Input Mask Wizard and the Lookup Wizard. You will also move fields in a table and sort records in ascending and descending order.

Modifying a Table

Maintaining a table involves adding and/or deleting records as needed. It can also involve adding, moving, changing, or deleting fields in the table. Modify the structure of the table in Datasheet view or Design view. In Datasheet view, click the Table Tools Datasheet tab and then use options in the Fields & Columns group to insert or delete fields. To display a table in Design view, open the table, and then click the View button in the Views group in the Home tab. You can also change to Design view by clicking the View button arrow and then clicking *Design View* at the drop-down list or by clicking the Design View button located in the View area at the right side of the Status bar.

In Design view, *Field Name*, *Data Type*, and *Description* display at the top of the window and *Field Properties* displays toward the bottom of the window. In Design view, you can add fields, remove fields, and change the order of fields. When you switch to Design view, the Table Tools Design tab displays as shown in Figure 3.1. Use buttons in this tab to insert and delete rows and perform a variety of other tasks.

Figure 3.1 Table Tools Design Tab

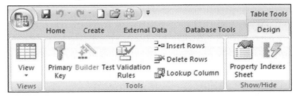

H I N T

Use options in the Data Type & Formatting group in the Table Tools Datasheet tab to set the data type.

Adding a Field

Situations change within a company, and a table must be flexible to accommodate changes that occur with new situations. Adding a field is a change that may need to be made to an existing table. For example, more information may be required to manage the data or an additional field may be needed for accounting purposes.

You can add a new field in Datasheet view or in Design view. One method for creating a new field is to simply type new records into a blank table or in the *Add New Field* column that displays at the right side of the last field in the table. Access sets a data type for each new field you type based on the type of data entered. For example, a column that contains dates is automatically assigned the Date/Time data type. You can also insert a new field by clicking the Table Tools Datasheet tab and then clicking the Insert button in the Fields & Columns group.

To add a row for a new field in Design view, position the insertion point on any text in the row that will be located immediately *below* the new field and then click the Insert Rows button in the Tools group in the Table Tools Design tab or position the insertion point on any text in the row that will be immediately *below* the new field, click the *right* mouse button, and then click *Insert Rows*. If you insert a row for a new field and then change your mind, immediately click the Undo button on the Quick Access toolbar.

Deleting a Field

Delete a field in a table and all data entered in that field is also deleted. When a field is deleted, it cannot be undone with the Undo button. Delete a field only if you are sure you really want it and the data associated with it completely removed from the table.

To delete a field in Datasheet view, click in any entry in the field you want to delete, click the Table Tools Datasheet tab, and then click the Delete button in the Fields & Columns group. To delete a field in Design view, click in the record selector bar at the left side of the row you want to delete and then click the Delete Rows button in the Tools group. At the message asking if you want to permanently delete the field and all of the data in the field, click Yes.

Assigning Data Type

In Chapter 1, you created tables and assigned data types of *Text*, *Date/Time*, or *Yes/No*. Access includes these data types as well as additional types as described in Table 3.1. Assign a data type with the *Data Type* column in Design view.

Table 3.1 Data Types

Data type	Description
Text	Alphanumeric data up to 255 characters in length, such as a name, address, or value such as a telephone number or Social Security number that it used as an identifier and not for calculating.
Memo	Alphanumeric data up to 64,000 characters in length.
Number	Positive or negative values that can be used in calculations. Do *not* use for value that will calculate monetary amounts (see Currency).
Date/Time	Use this type to ensure dates and times are entered and sorted properly.
Currency	Values that involve money. Access will not round off during calculations.
AutoNumber	Access automatically numbers each record sequentially (incrementing by 1) when you begin typing a new record.
Yes/No	Data in the field will be either Yes or No, True or False, or On or Off.
OLE Object	Used to embed or link objects created in other Office applications.
Hyperlink	Field that will store a hyperlink such as a URL.
Attachment	Use this data type to add file attachments to a record such as a Word document or an Excel workbook.
Lookup Wizard	Use the Lookup Wizard to enter data in the field from another existing table or display a list of values in a drop-down list from which the user chooses.

Add a Field to a Table
1. Open table in Design view.
2. Click in row that will follow the new field.
3. Click Insert Rows button.

Delete a Field from a Table
1. Open table in Design view.
2. Click in row to be deleted.
3. Click Delete Rows button.
4. Click Yes.

Undo

1. Remove the read-only attribute from the **MedSafeClinic.accdb** database by completing the following steps:
   a. In Access, display the Open dialog box with the drive active containing your storage medium.
   b. Click once on the **MedSafeClinic.accdb** database name.
   c. Click the Tools button located in the lower left corner of the Open dialog box and then click *Properties* at the drop-down list.
   d. At the MedSafeClinic.accdb Properties dialog box with the General tab selected, click *Read-only* in the *Attributes* section to remove the check mark.
   e. Click OK to close the MedSafeClinic.accdb Properties dialog box.
2. Open the **MedSafeClinic.accdb** database.
3. At the MedSafeClinic : Database window, double-click the *Products* table to open it.
4. Insert a new field by completing the following steps:
   a. Click in the empty field below the *Add New Field* column heading.
   b. Type **50** and then press the Down Arrow key on your keyboard.
   c. Type **50** and then press the Down Arrow key.
   d. Type **125** and then press the Down Arrow key.
   e. Type **100** and then press the Down Arrow key.
   f. Type **150** and then press the Down Arrow key.
   g. Type **100** and then press the Down Arrow key.

UnitsInStock ▾	Field1 ▾	Add New Field
63	50	
38	50	
144	125	
57	100	
122	150	
78	100	

Steps 4b–4g

5. Click the View button to switch to Design view and notice that Access automatically selected the Number data type for the new field you created. Modify the field by completing the following steps:
   a. Select *Field1* that displays in the *Field Name* column and then type **ReorderLevel**.
   b. Click in the *Description* text box for the *ReorderLevel* field and then type **Reorder level number**.

Products

Field Name	Data Type	Desc
ProductID	AutoNumber	Automatic product ID number
ProductName	Text	Product name
SupplierID	Text	Supplier ID number
SupplierRegion	Text	Supplier geographic region
UnitsInStock	Number	Number of units in stock
ReorderLevel	Number	Reorder level number

Step 5a

Step 5b

Step 6b

6. Delete the *SupplierRegion* field by completing the following steps:
   a. Click in the record selector bar at the left side of the *SupplierRegion* row.
   b. Click the Delete Rows button in the Tools group.
   c. At the message stating that the field will be permanently deleted, click Yes.

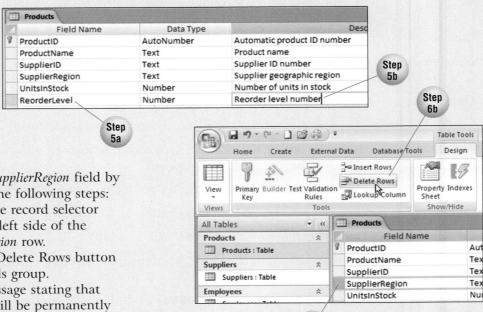

Step 6a

7. Insert a new field by completing the following steps:
   a. Click on any character in the *ReorderLevel* field name.
   b. Click the Insert Rows button in the Tools group.
   c. With the insertion point positioned in the new blank field in the *Field Name* column, type UnitsOnOrder.
   d. Press the Tab key.
   e. Click the down-pointing arrow at the right side of the Text box and then click *Number* at the drop-down list.
   f. Press the Tab key and then type Number of units on order.

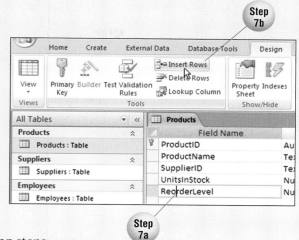

Step 7b

Step 7a

8. Insert a new field by completing the following steps:
   a. Click on any character in the *ReorderLevel* field name.
   b. Click the Insert Rows button in the Tools group.
   c. With the insertion point positioned in the new blank field in the *Field Name* column, type UnitPrice.
   d. Press the Tab key.
   e. Click the down-pointing arrow at the right side of the Text box and then click *Currency* at the drop-down list.
   f. Press the Tab key and then type Unit price.
9. Click the Save button on the Quick Access toolbar to save the modified table.
10. Click the View button to switch to Datasheet view and then enter the following information in the specified fields:

UnitsOnOrder	UnitPrice
0	12.50
50	24.00
0	5.70
100	9.90
150	4.50
100	10.00

11. Click the Save button on the Quick Access toolbar.
12. Display the table in Print Preview, change the orientation to landscape, and then print the table.
13. Close Print Preview and close the Products table.
14. Define a one-to-many relationship between the Suppliers and the Products tables by completing the following steps:
   a. Click the Database Tools tab and then click the Relationships button in the Show/Hide group.
   b. At the Show Table dialog box, click *Suppliers* in the list box and then click Add.
   c. Click *Products* in the list box and then click Add.
   d. Click the Close button to close the Show Table dialog box.
   e. At the Relationships window, drag the *SupplierID* field from the Suppliers table to the *SupplierID* field in the Products table.
   f. At the Edit Relationships dialog box, click *Enforce Referential Integrity*, click *Cascade Update Related Fields*, and then click *Cascade Delete Related Records*.
   g. Click the Create button.

15. Click the Save button on the Quick Access toolbar to save the relationship.
16. Print the relationships by completing the following steps:
    a. At the Relationships window, click the Relationship Report button in the Tools group. (This displays the Relationships report in Print Preview.)
    b. Click the Print button in the Print group.
    c. Click OK at the Print dialog box.
    d. Click the Close button that displays at the right side of the Relationships window.
    e. At the message asking if you want to save changes to the design of the report, click No.
17. Close the Relationships window by clicking the Close button that displays at the right side of the Relationships window.

Assigning a Default Value

In Design view, the available field properties that display in the lower half of the work area vary depending on the data type of the active field. You can use a field property to control how the field displays or how the field interacts with data. For example, you have been using the *Field Size* option in the Field Properties section to limit the numbers of characters allowed when entering data in the field. If most records are likely to contain the same field value, use the *Default Value* property to insert the most common field entry. In Project 1b, you will insert a health insurance field with a Yes/No data type. Since most employees sign up for health insurance benefits, you will set the default value for the field as *Yes*. If you add a new field that contains a default value to an existing table, the existing records will not reflect the default value, only new records entered in the table.

Insert a Total Row
1. Open table in Datasheet view.
2. Click Totals button.
3. Click in Total row.
4. Click down-pointing arrow that appears.
5. Click desired function at drop-down list.

HINT
The Total row option provides a number of aggregate functions which are functions that calculate values across a range of data.

Validating Field Entries

Use the *Validation Rule* property to enter a statement containing a conditional test that is checked each time data is entered into a field. When data is entered that fails to satisfy the conditional test, Access does not accept the entry and displays an error message. By entering a conditional statement in the *Validation Rule* property that checks each entry against the acceptable range, you can reduce errors. Enter in the *Validation Text* property the content of the error message that you want to display.

Inserting a Total Row

A new feature in Access 2007 is the ability to add a total row to a datasheet and then choose from a list of functions to add or to find the average, maximum, minimum, count, standard deviations, or variance result in a numeric column. To insert a total row, click the Totals button in the Records group in the Home tab. Access adds a row to the bottom of the datasheet with the label *Total* at the left. Click in the Total row, click the down-pointing arrow that appears, and then click the desired function at the drop-down list.

1. With the **MedSafeClinic.accdb** database open, open the Employees table.
2. Insert a new field by completing the following steps:
   a. Click the View button to switch to Design view.
   b. Click in the empty field immediately below the *Salary* field in the *Field Name* column and then type **HealthIns**.
   c. Press the Tab key.
   d. Click the down-pointing arrow at the right side of the Text box and then click *Yes/No* at the drop-down list.
   e. Select the current entry in the *Default Value* field property box and then type **Yes**.
   f. Click in the field in the *Description* column for the *HealthIns* field and then type **Employee signed up for health insurance benefits**.

Step 2e

Field Properties	
General Lookup	
Format	Yes/No
Caption	
Default Value	Yes
Validation Rule	
Validation Text	
Indexed	No
Text Align	General

3. Click the Save button on the Quick Access toolbar.
4. Click the View button to switch to Datasheet view. (Notice that the *HealthIns* check box for existing records does not contain a check mark [the default value] but the check box in the new record contains a check mark.)
5. Enter the following new records:

ID#	265		*ID#*	199
FirstName	Randy		*FirstName*	Kristen
LastName	Lewandowski		*LastName*	Ridgway
Ext	3217		*Ext*	2122
Salary	29000		*Salary*	33550
HealthIns	(Press Tab to accept default)		*HealthIns*	(Press Tab to accept default)

6. Click in each of the existing *HealthIns* check boxes to insert a check mark except the check box for *Chris Weaver*.
7. Save the Employees table.
8. Insert a new field by completing the following steps:
   a. Click the View button to switch to Design view.
   b. Click in the empty field immediately below the *HealthIns* field in the *Field Name* column and then type **LifeIns**.
   c. Press the Tab key.
   d. Click the down-pointing arrow at the right side of the Text box and then click *Currency* at the drop-down list.
   e. Click in the *Validation Rule* property box, type **<=100000**, and then press Enter.
   f. With the insertion point positioned in the *Validation Text* property box, type **Enter a value that is equal to or less than $100,000**.

Step 8e

Step 8f

Field Properties	
General Lookup	
Format	Currency
Decimal Places	Auto
Input Mask	
Caption	
Default Value	
Validation Rule	<=100000
Validation Text	Enter a value that is equal to or less than $100,000.
Required	No
Indexed	No
Smart Tags	
Text Align	General

g. Click in the box in the *Description* column for the *HealthIns* field and then type Optional life insurance amount.

9. Click the Save button on the Quick Access toolbar. Since the validation rule was created *after* data was entered into the table, Access displays a warning message indicating that some data may not be valid. At this message, click No.

10. Click the View button to switch to Datasheet view.

11. Click in the first empty field in the *LifeIns* column, type 200000, and then press the Down Arrow key.

12. Access inserts the error message telling you to enter an amount that is equal to or less than $100,000. At this error message, click OK.

13. Edit the amount in the field so it displays as 100000 and then press the Down Arrow key.

14. Type the following entries in the remaining fields in the *LifeIns* column:

    25000
    0
    50000
    50000
    0
    100000
    50000
    25000

15. Save the Employees table.

16. Insert a Total row and insert a function by completing the following steps:

    a. In Datasheet view, click the Totals button in the Records group in the Home tab.

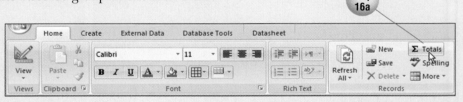

    b. Click in the blank field in the *Salary* column in the Total row.

    c. Click the down-pointing arrow at the left side of the field and then click *Average* at the drop-down list.

    d. Click in any other field.

    e. Save and then print the Employees table.

    f. Click in the field containing the salary average amount.

    g. Click the down-pointing arrow at the left side of the field and then click *Sum* at the drop-down list.

    h. Click in any other field.

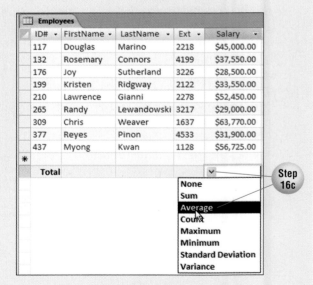

17. Save, print, and then close the Employees table.

Using the Input Mask Wizard

For some fields, you may want to control the data entered in the field. For example, in a *ZipCode* field, you may want the nine-digit ZIP code entered (rather than the five-digit ZIP code); or you may want the three-digit area code included in a telephone number. Use the *Input Mask* field property to set a pattern for how data is entered in a field. An input mask ensures that data in records conforms to a standard format. Access includes an Input Mask Wizard that guides you through creating an input mask.

Use the Input Mask Wizard when assigning a data type to a field. After specifying the *Field Size* in the *Field Properties* section in Design view, click in the Input Mask box. Run the Input Mask Wizard by clicking the Build button (button containing three black dots) that appears to the right of the Input Mask box. This displays the first Input Mask Wizard dialog box as shown in Figure 3.2. In the Input Mask list box, choose which input mask you want your data to look like and then click the Next button. At the second Input Mask Wizard dialog box as shown in Figure 3.3, specify the appearance of the input mask and the desired placeholder character and then click the Next button. At the third Input Mask Wizard dialog box, specify whether you want the data stored with or without the symbol in the mask and then click the Next button. At the fourth dialog box, click the Finish button.

Figure 3.2 First Input Mask Wizard Dialog Box

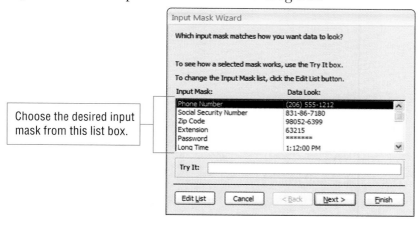

Choose the desired input mask from this list box.

Figure 3.3 Second Input Mask Wizard Dialog Box

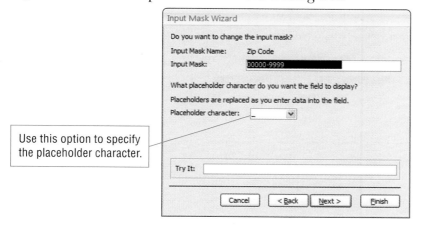

Use this option to specify the placeholder character.

1. With the **MedSafeClinic.accdb** database open, open the Suppliers table.
2. Create a new *ZipCode* field with an Input Mask by completing the following steps:
   a. Click the View button in the Views group.
   b. Click anywhere in the text *Email* that displays in the *Field Name* column.
   c. Click the Insert Rows button in the Tools group.
   d. With the insertion point positioned in the new blank field in the *Field Name* column, type **ZipCode**.
   e. Press the Tab key. (This moves the insertion point to the *Data Type* column.)
   f. Select *255* that displays in the *Field Size* text box in the *Field Properties* section of the window and then type **10**.
   g. Click the Save button to save the table. (You must save the table before using the Input Mask Wizard.)

Step 2c

   h. Click in the *Input Mask* box in the *Field Properties* section of the window.
   i. Click the Build button (button containing three black dots) that displays to the right of the *Input Mask* box.

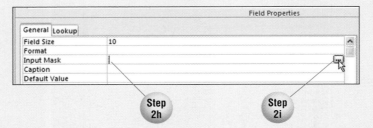

Step 2h   Step 2i

   j. At the first Input Mask Wizard dialog box, click *Zip Code* in the *Input Mask* list box and then click the Next button.

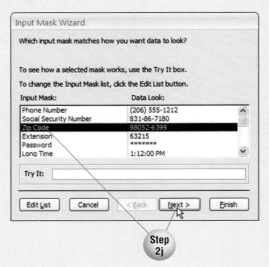

Step 2j

k. At the second Input Mask Wizard dialog box, click the Next button.

l. At the third Input Mask Wizard dialog box, click the *With the symbols in the mask, like this* option.

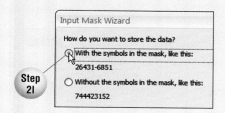

Step 2l

m. Click the Next button.

n. At the fourth Input Mask Wizard dialog box, click the Finish button.

o. Click in the *Description* column in the *ZipCode* row and then type **Supplier nine-digit Zip code.**

3. Create a new *Telephone* field with an Input Mask by completing the following steps:

a. Click anywhere in the text *Email* that displays in the *Field Name* column.

b. Click the Insert Rows button in the Tools group.

c. With the insertion point positioned in the new blank field in the *Field Name* column, type **Telephone.**

d. Press the Tab key. (This moves the insertion point to the *Data Type* column.)

e. Select *255* that displays in the *Field Size* text box in the *Field Properties* section of the window and then type **14.**

f. Click the Save button to save the table. (You must save the table before using the Input Mask Wizard.)

g. Click in the Input Mask box in the *Field Properties* section of the window.

h. Click the Build button (button containing three black dots) that displays to the right of the Input Mask box.

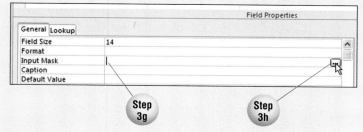

Step 3g

Step 3h

i. At the first Input Mask Wizard dialog box, make sure *Phone Number* is selected in the *Input Mask* list box and then click the Next button.

Step 3i

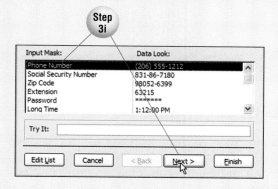

j. At the second Input Mask Wizard dialog box, click the down-pointing arrow at the right side of the *Placeholder character* box and then click # at the drop-down list.

k. Click the Next button.

l. At the third Input Mask Wizard dialog box, click the *With the symbols in the mask, like this* option.

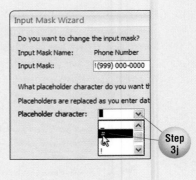

Input Mask Wizard

Do you want to change the input mask?

Input Mask Name: Phone Number

Input Mask: !(999) 000-0000

What placeholder character do you want th

Placeholders are replaced as you enter dat

Placeholder character:

Step 3j

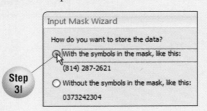

Input Mask Wizard

How do you want to store the data?

● With the symbols in the mask, like this:

(814) 287-2621

○ Without the symbols in the mask, like this:

0373242304

Step 3l

m. Click the Next button.

n. At the fourth Input Mask Wizard dialog box, click the Finish button.

o. Click in the *Description* column in the *Telephone* row and then type **Supplier telephone number**.

p. Click the Save button on the Quick Access toolbar.

4. Add ZIP codes for the records in the Suppliers table by completing the following steps:

a. Click the View button to switch to Datasheet view.

b. Click in the field containing *LA* (immediately left of the new blank field below *ZipCode*) and then press the Tab key.

c. Type **303239089** and then press the Down Arrow key. (This moves the insertion point to the next blank field in the *ZipCode* column. The Input Mask automatically inserts a hyphen between 30323 and 9089.)

City	State	ZipCode	Telephone
Baton Rouge	LA	30323-9089	
Tampa	FL		
Atlanta	GA		
Atlanta	GA		
Little Rock	AR		

Step 4c

d. Type **303542487** and then press the Down Arrow key.

e. Type **303573652** and then press the Down Arrow key.

f. Type **303654311** and then press the Down Arrow key.

g. Type **303253499**.

5. Add telephone numbers for the records in the Suppliers table by completing the following steps:

a. Click in the field containing the ZIP code *30323-9089* and then press the Tab key.

b. Type **2255557454** and then press the Down Arrow key. (The Input Mask automatically inserts the parentheses, spaces, and hyphens in the telephone numbers.)

c. Type **8135553495** and then press the Down Arrow key.

d. Type **4045557732** and then press the Down Arrow key.

e. Type **4045550926** and then press the Down Arrow key.

f. Type **5015554509**.

6. Save, print, and then close the Suppliers table.

Using the Lookup Wizard

Like the Input Mask Wizard, you can use the Lookup Wizard to control the data entered in a field. Use the Lookup Wizard to confine the data entered into a field to a specific list of items. For example, in Project 1d you will use the Lookup Wizard to restrict the new *EmpCategory* field to one of three choices—*Salaried, Hourly,* and *Temporary*. When the user clicks in the field in the datasheet, a down-pointing arrow displays. The user clicks this down-pointing arrow to display a drop-down list of available entries and then clicks the desired item.

Use the Lookup Wizard when assigning a data type to a field. Click in the *Data Type* text box and then click the down-pointing arrow that displays at the right side of the box. At the drop-down list that displays, click *Lookup Wizard*. This displays the first Lookup Wizard dialog box as shown in Figure 3.4. At this dialog box, indicate that you want to enter the field choices by clicking the *I will type in the values that I want* option, and then click the Next button. At the second Lookup Wizard dialog box shown in Figure 3.5, click in the blank text box below *Col1* and then type the first choice. Press the Tab key and then type the second choice. Continue in this manner until all desired choices are entered and then click the Next button. At the third Lookup Wizard dialog box, make sure the proper name displays in the *What label would you like for your lookup column?* text box and then click the Finish button.

QUICK STEPS

Use Lookup Wizard
1. Open table in Design view.
2. Type text in *Field Name* column.
3. Press Tab key.
4. Click down-pointing arrow.
5. Click *Lookup Wizard*.
6. At first Lookup Wizard dialog box, make desired changes.
7. Click Next.
8. At second Lookup Wizard dialog box, click in blank text box.
9. Type desired text.
10. Press Tab key.
11. Continue typing text and pressing Tab until all desired text is entered.
12. Click Next.
13. Click Finish.

HINT
You can activate the Lookup Wizard by clicking the Lookup Column button in the Table Tools Datasheet tab.

Figure 3.4 First Lookup Wizard Dialog Box

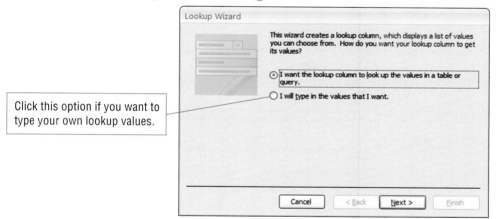

Click this option if you want to type your own lookup values.

Figure 3.5 Second Lookup Wizard Dialog Box

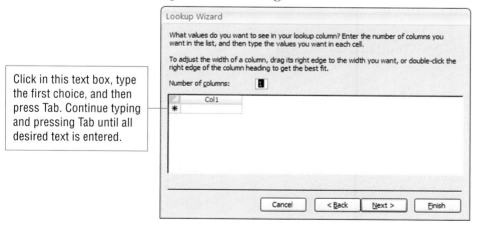

Click in this text box, type the first choice, and then press Tab. Continue typing and pressing Tab until all desired text is entered.

1. With the **MedSafeClinic.accdb** database open, open the Employees table.
2. Add the field *EmpCategory* and use the Lookup Wizard to specify field choices by completing the following steps:
   a. Click the View button to change to Design view.
   b. Click on any character in the *Ext* data in the *Field Name* column.
   c. Click the Insert Rows button in the Tools group.
   d. With the insertion point positioned in the new blank field in the *Field Name* column, type **EmpCategory**.
   e. Press the Tab key. (This moves the insertion point to the *Data Type* column.)
   f. Click the down-pointing arrow at the right side of the text box and then click *Lookup Wizard* at the drop-down list.
   g. At the first Lookup Wizard dialog box, click the *I will type in the values that I want* option and then click the Next button.

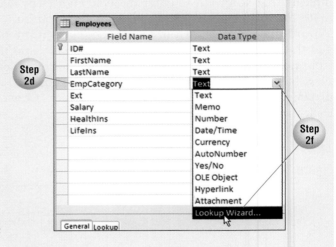

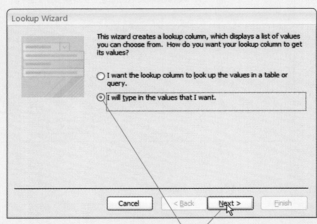

   h. At the second Lookup Wizard dialog box, click in the blank text box below *Col1*, type **Salaried**, and then press the Tab key.
   i. Type **Hourly** and then press the Tab key.
   j. Type **Temporary**.
   k. Click the Next button.
   l. At the third Lookup Wizard dialog box, click the Finish button.
   m. Press the Tab key and then type **Employee category** in the *Description* column.
3. Click the Save button on the Quick Access toolbar.

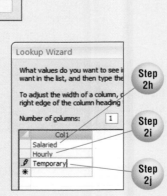

4. Insert information in the *EmpCategory* for the records by completing the following steps:
   a. Click the View button to switch to Datasheet view.
   b. Click in the first blank field below the new *EmpCategory* field.
   c. Click the down-pointing arrow at the right side of the field and then click *Hourly* at the drop-down list.
   d. Click in the next blank field in the *EmpCategory*, click the down-pointing arrow, and then click *Salaried* at the drop-down list.
   e. Continue entering information in the *EmpCategory* by completing similar steps. Type the following in the specified record:

Third record	Hourly
Fourth record	Salaried
Fifth record	Temporary
Sixth record	Hourly
Seventh record	Salaried
Eighth record	Temporary
Ninth record	Hourly

5. Save and then print the Employees table in landscape orientation.

Moving a Field

You can move a field in a table to a different location. To do this, open the table and then change to Design view. Click in the record selector bar at the left side of the row you want to move. With the row selected, position the arrow pointer in the record selector bar at the left side of the selected row until the pointer turns into the normal arrow pointer (white arrow pointing up and to the left). Hold down the left mouse button, drag the arrow pointer with the gray square attached until a thick black line displays in the desired position, and then release the mouse button.

QUICK STEPS

Move a Field
1. Open table in Design view.
2. Select row to be moved.
3. Drag selected row to new position.

Project 1e Moving Fields in Tables

1. With the Employees table open, click the View button to switch to Design view.
2. Move the *EmpCategory* field immediately below the *Ext* field by completing the following steps:
   a. Click in the record selector bar at the left side of the *EmpCategory* field to select the row.
   b. Position the arrow pointer in the record selector bar of the selected row until it turns into the normal arrow pointer (white arrow pointing up and to the left).
   c. Hold down the left mouse button, drag the arrow pointer with the gray square attached until a thick black line displays below the *Ext* field, and then release the mouse button.

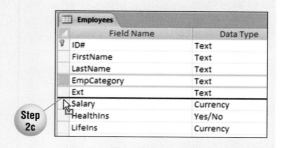

3. Click the Save button on the Quick Access toolbar.
4. Click the View button to switch to Datasheet view.
5. Print the table in landscape orientation.
6. Close the Employees table.
7. Open the Products table and then move the *ReorderLevel* field by completing the following steps:
   a. Click the View button to switch to Design view.
   b. Select the row containing the *ReorderLevel* field.
   c. Position the arrow pointer on the blue button at the left side of the selected row until the pointer turns into the normal arrow pointer (white arrow pointing up and to the left).
   d. Hold down the left mouse button, drag the arrow pointer above the *UnitsOnOrder* field, and then release the mouse button.

Products	
Field Name	**Data Type**
ProductID	AutoNumber
ProductName	Text
SupplierID	Text
UnitsInStock	Number
UnitsOnOrder	Number
UnitPrice	Currency
ReorderLevel	Number

Step 7d

8. Click the Save button on the Quick Access.
9. Click the View button to switch to Datasheet view.
10. Print the Products table in landscape orientation.
11. Close the Products table.

QUICK STEPS

Sort Records
1. Open table in Datasheet view.
2. Click in field in desired column.
3. Click Ascending button or Descending button.

Print Selected Records
1. Open table and select records.
2. Click Office button, *Print*.
3. Click *Selected Record(s)*.
4. Click OK.

Sort Ascending

Sort Descending

Sorting Records

The Sort & Filter group in the Home tab contains two buttons you can use to sort data in records. Click the Ascending button to sort from lowest to highest on the field where the insertion point is located or click the Descending button to sort from highest to lowest.

Printing Specific Records

If you click the Quick Print button on the Quick Access toolbar, all of the records in the selected or open table are printed. If you want to print specific records in a table, select the records and then display the Print dialog box by clicking the Office button and then clicking *Print* at the drop-down list. At the Print dialog box, click the *Selected Records* option in the *Print Range* section and then click OK. To select specific records, display the table in Datasheet view, click the record selector of the first record and then drag to select the desired records. The record selector is the light blue square that displays at the left side of the record. When you position the mouse pointer on the record selector, the pointer turns into a right-pointing black arrow.

1. With the **MedSafeClinic.accdb** database open, open the Employees table.
2. With the table in Datasheet view, sort records in ascending alphabetical order by completing the following steps:
   a. Click any last name in the table.
   b. Click the Ascending button in the Sort & Filter group in the Home tab.

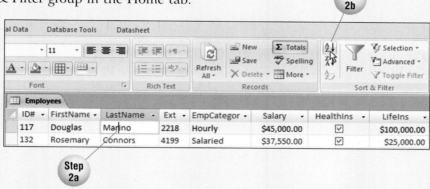

   c. Print the Employees table in landscape orientation.
3. Sort records in descending order (highest to lowest) by employee ID number by completing the following steps:
   a. Click on any number in the *ID#* field.
   b. Click the Descending button in the Sort & Filter group.

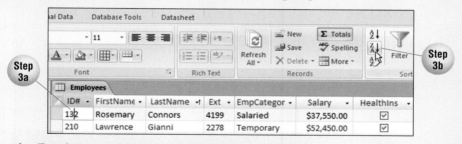

   c. Print the Employees table in landscape orientation.
4. Sort and print selected records of the salaried employees by completing the following steps:
   a. Click any entry in the *EmpCategory* field.
   b. Remove the Totals row by clicking the Totals button in the Records group in the Home tab.
   c. Click the Ascending button in the Sort & Filter group.
   d. Position the mouse pointer on the record selector of the first salaried employee, hold down the mouse button, and then drag to select the three records of salaried employees.
   e. Click the Office button and then click *Print* at the drop-down list.
   f. At the Print dialog box, click the *Selected Record(s)* option in the *Print Range* section.
   g. Click OK.
5. Click the Save button on the Quick Access toolbar.
6. Close the Employees table and then close the **MedSafeClinic.accdb** database.

Project 2 Check Spelling, Find and Replace Data, and Back Up, Compact, and Repair a Medical Clinic Database

You will complete a spelling check on data in tables and find data and replace it with other data in tables. You will also back up a database and compact and repair a database.

QUICK STEPS

Complete a Spelling Check
1. Open table in Datasheet view.
2. Click Spelling button.
3. Change or ignore spelling as needed.
4. Click OK.

HINT

You can also begin spell checking with the keyboard shortcut F7.

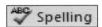

Completing a Spelling Check

The spelling checker feature in Access finds misspelled words and offers replacement words. It also finds duplicate words and irregular capitalizations. When you spell check an object in a database such as a table, the spelling checker compares the words in your table with the words in its dictionary. If a match is found, the word is passed over. If no match is found for the word, the spelling checker selects the word and offers replacement suggestions.

To complete a spelling check, open the desired table in Datasheet view and then click the Spelling button in the Records group in the Home tab. If the spelling checker does not find a match for a word in your table, the Spelling dialog box displays with replacement options. Figure 3.6 displays the Spelling dialog box with the word *Montain* selected and possible replacements displayed in the *Suggestions* list box. At the Spelling dialog box, you can choose to ignore the word (for example, if the spelling checker has selected a proper name), change to one of the replacement options, or add the word to the dictionary or AutoCorrect feature. You can also complete a spelling check on other objects in a database such as a query, form, or report. (You will learn about these objects in future chapters.)

Figure 3.6 Spelling Dialog Box

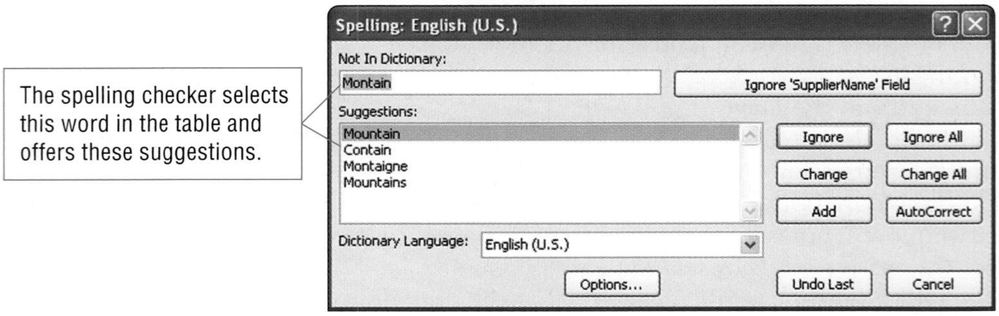

The spelling checker selects this word in the table and offers these suggestions.

Project 2a Checking Spelling in a Table

1. Open the **MedSafeClinic.accdb** database.
2. Open the Suppliers table.
3. In Datasheet view, add the following record at the end of the table. (Type the misspelled words as shown below. You will correct the spelling in a later step.)

SupplierID	=	6
SupplierName	=	Blue Montain Supplies
Address	=	9550 Unaversity Avenue
City	=	Little Rock
State	=	AR
ZipCode	=	322093412
Telephone	=	5015554400
Email	=	bluem@emcp.net

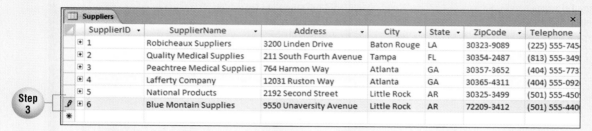

Step 3

SupplierID	SupplierName	Address	City	State	ZipCode	Telephone
1	Robicheaux Suppliers	3200 Linden Drive	Baton Rouge	LA	30323-9089	(225) 555-745
2	Quality Medical Supplies	211 South Fourth Avenue	Tampa	FL	30354-2487	(813) 555-349
3	Peachtree Medical Supplies	764 Harmon Way	Atlanta	GA	30357-3652	(404) 555-773
4	Lafferty Company	12031 Ruston Way	Atlanta	GA	30365-4311	(404) 555-092
5	National Products	2192 Second Street	Little Rock	AR	30325-3499	(501) 555-450
6	Blue Montain Supplies	9550 Unaversity Avenue	Little Rock	AR	72209-3412	(501) 555-440

4. Save the Suppliers table.
5. Click in the first entry in the *SupplierID* column.
6. Click the Spelling button in the Records group in the Home tab.
7. The spelling checker selects the name *Robicheaux*. This is a proper name, so click the Ignore button to tell the spelling checker to leave the name as written.
8. The spelling checker selects *Montain*. The proper spelling *(Mountain)* is selected in the *Suggestions* list box, so click the Change button.
9. The spelling checker selects *Unaversity*. The proper spelling *(University)* is selected in the *Suggestions* list box, so click the Change button.
10. At the message telling you that the spelling check is complete, click the OK button.

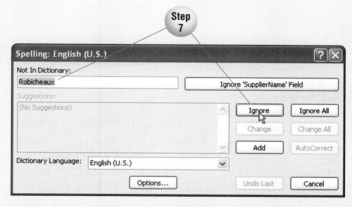

Step 7

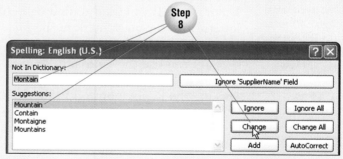

Step 8

Finding and Replacing Data

Find Data
1. Open table in Datasheet view.
2. Click Find button.
3. Type data in *Find What* text box.
4. Click Find Next button.
5. Continue clicking Find Next button until entire table is searched.

If you need to find a specific entry in a field in a table, consider using options at the Find and Replace dialog box with the Find tab selected as shown in Figure 3.7. Display this dialog box by clicking the Find button in the Find group in the Home tab. At the Find and Replace dialog box, enter the data for which you are searching in the *Find What* text box. By default, Access will look in the specific column where the insertion point is positioned. Click the Find Next button to find the next occurrence of the data or click the Cancel button to remove the Find and Replace dialog box.

HINT
Press Ctrl + F to display the Find and Replace dialog box with the Find tab selected.

Figure 3.7 Find and Replace Dialog Box with Find Tab Selected

Enter the data for which you are searching in this text box.

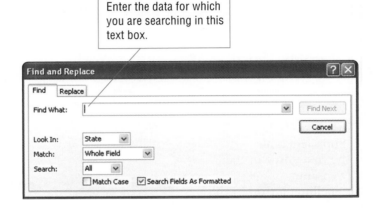

QUICK STEPS

Find and Replace Data
1. Open table in Datasheet view.
2. Click Replace button.
3. Type find data in *Find What* text box.
4. Type replace data in *Replace With* text box.
5. Click Find Next button.
6. Click Replace button or Find Next button.

The *Look In* option defaults to the column where the insertion point is positioned. You can choose to look in the entire table by clicking the down-pointing arrow at the right side of the option and then clicking the table name at the drop-down list. The *Match* option has a default setting of *Whole Field*. You can change this to *Any Part of Field* or *Start of Field*. The *Search* option has a default setting of *All*, which means that Access will search all data in a specific column. This can be changed to *Up* or *Down*. If you want to find data that contains specific uppercase and lowercase letters, insert a check mark in the *Match Case* check box. By default, Access will search fields as they are formatted.

You can use the Find and Replace dialog box with the Replace tab selected to search for specific data and replace with other data. Display this dialog box by clicking the Replace button in the Find group in the Home tab.

HINT
Press Ctrl + H to display the Find and Replace dialog box with the Replace tab selected.

1. With the Suppliers table open, find any records containing the two-letter state abbreviation *GA* by completing the following steps:

   a. Click in the first entry in the *State* column.

   b. Click the Find button in the Find group in the Home tab.

2. At the Find and Replace dialog box with the Find tab selected, type GA in the *Find What* text box.

   d. Click the Find Next button. (Access finds and selects the first occurrence of *GA*. If the Find and Replace dialog box covers the data, drag the dialog box to a different location on the screen.)

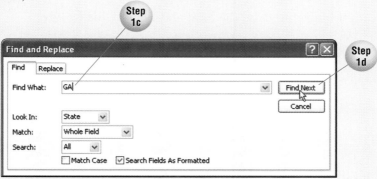

   e. Continue clicking the Find Next button until a message displays telling you that Access has finished searching the records. At this message, click OK.

   f. Click the Cancel button to close the Find and Replace dialog box.

2. Suppose Quality Medical Supplies has changed its telephone number. Complete the following steps to find the current telephone number and replace it with the new telephone number:

   a. Click in the first entry in the *Telephone* column.

   b. Click the Replace button in the Find group.

c. At the Find and Replace dialog box with the Replace tab selected, type (813) 555-3495 in the *Find What* text box.
d. Press the Tab key. (This moves the insertion point to the *Replace With* text box.)
e. Type (813) 555-9800 in the *Replace With* text box.
f. Click the Find Next button.
g. When Access selects the telephone number *(813) 555-3495*, click the Replace button.

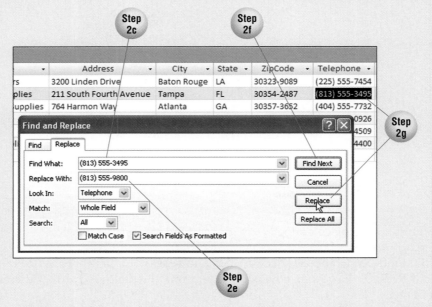

h. Click the Cancel button to close the Find and Replace dialog box.
3. Save the Suppliers table.
4. Display the table in Print Preview, change the page orientation to landscape, change the margins to *Normal*, and then print the table.
5. Close the Suppliers table.

QUICK STEPS

Back Up Database
1. Open database.
2. Click Office button, *Manage, Back Up Database.*
3. Navigate to desired folder or drive.
4. Type file name.
5. Click Save button.

Backing Up a Database

Back up a database on a consistent basis to protect the data in the database from accidental loss or from any hardware failure. To back up a database, click the Office button, point to *Manage*, and then click *Back Up Database*. At the Save As dialog box, navigate to the desired folder or drive, type a name for the database, and then press Enter or click the Save button.

Compacting and Repairing a Database

To optimize performance of your database, compact and repair the database on a consistent basis. As you work with a database, data in the database can become fragmented causing the amount of space the database takes on the storage medium or in the folder to be larger than necessary.

To compact and repair a database, open the database, click the Office button, point to *Manage*, and then click *Compact and Repair Database*. As the database is compacting and repairing, a message displays on the Status bar indicating the progress of the procedure. When the procedure is completed, close the database.

You can tell Access to compact and repair a database each time you close the database. To do this, click the Office button and then click the Access Options button located in the lower right corner of the drop-down list. At the Access Options dialog box, click *Current Database* in the left panel. This displays the Access Options dialog box as shown in Figure 3.8. Click the *Compact on Close* option to insert a check mark and then click OK to close the window.

Compact and Repair Database
1. Open database.
2. Click Office button, *Manage, Compact and Repair Database.*

HINT

Before compacting and repairing a database in a multi-user environment, make sure that no other user has the database open.

Figure 3.8 Access Options Dialog Box with *Current Database* Selected

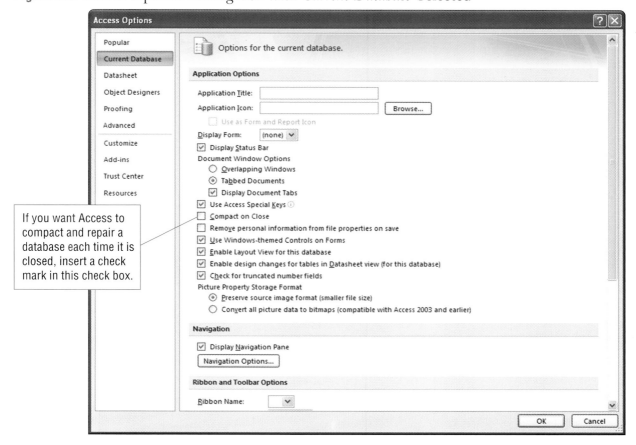

If you want Access to compact and repair a database each time it is closed, insert a check mark in this check box.

1. With the **MedSafeClinic,accdb** database open, create a backup of the database by completing the following steps:
   a. Click the Office button, point to *Manage*, and then click *Back Up Database*.
   b. At the Save As dialog box, type MSCBackup10-01-2010 in the *File name* text box. (This file name assumes that the date is October 1, 2010. You do not have to use the date in the file name but it does help when using the backup feature to archive databases.)
   c. Click the Save button.

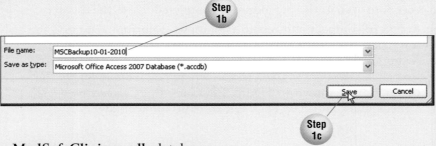

Step 1b

Step 1c

2. Close the **MedSafeClinic.accdb** database.
3. Determine the current size of the **MedSafeClinic.accdb** database (to compare to the size after compacting and repairing) by completing the following steps:
   a. Click the Open button on the Quick Access toolbar.
   b. At the Open dialog box, click the down-pointing arrow at the right side of the Views button and then click *Details* at the drop-down list.
   c. Display the drive (or folder) where your **MedSafeClinic.accdb** database is located and then check the size of the database.
   d. Close the Open dialog box.
4. Compact and repair the **MedSafeClinic.accdb** database by completing the following steps:
   a. Open the **MedSafeClinic.accdb** database.
   b. Click the Office button, point to *Manage*, and then click *Compact and Repair Database*.

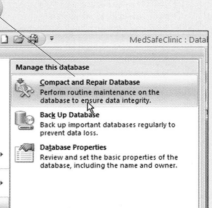

Step 3b

Step 4b

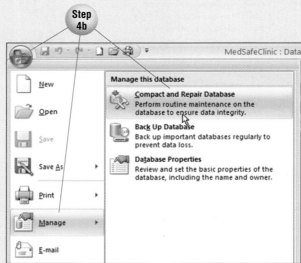

    c. When the compact and repair procedure is completed, close the **MedSafeClinic.accdb** database.

5. Determine the size of the compacted and repaired **MedSafeClinic.accdb** database by completing the following steps:

    a. Click the Open button on the Quick Access toolbar.

    b. At the Open dialog box, make sure the details display in the list box and then look at the size of the **MedSafeClinic.accdb** database and compare this size to the previous size. (Notice that the size of the compacted and repaired **MedSafeClinic.accdb** database is approximately the same size as the **MSCBackup10-01-2010.accdb** database. The backup database was automatically compacted and repaired when saved.)

    c. Return the display to a list by clicking the down-pointing arrow at the right side of the Views button and then clicking *List* at the drop-down list.

6. Close the Open dialog box.

Project ③ Use Access Help

You will use the Access Help feature to display information on creating an input mask and performing diagnostic tests.

Using Help

The Access Help feature is an on-screen reference manual containing information about all Access features and commands. The Access Help feature is similar to the Windows Help and the Help features in Word, PowerPoint, and Excel. Get help by clicking the Microsoft Office Access Help button located in the upper right corner of the screen (the button containing a question mark) or by pressing F1. This displays the Access Help window shown in Figure 3.9.

Use Help Feature
1. Click Microsoft Office Access Help button.
2. Type topic, feature, or question.
3. Press Enter.
4. Click desired topic.

Press F1 to display the Access Help window.

Help

Figure 3.9 Access Help Window

Type in this text box the word, topic, or phrase on which you want help.

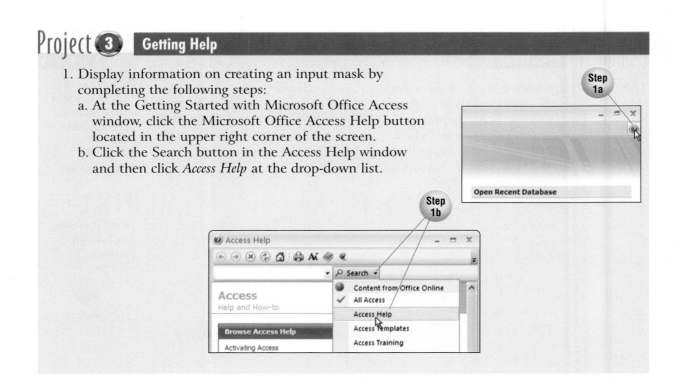

Project 3 Getting Help

1. Display information on creating an input mask by completing the following steps:
   a. At the Getting Started with Microsoft Office Access window, click the Microsoft Office Access Help button located in the upper right corner of the screen.
   b. Click the Search button in the Access Help window and then click *Access Help* at the drop-down list.

Step 1a

Step 1b

   c. Click in the *Search* text box.

   d. Type **input mask** and then press the Enter key.

   e. Click the *Create an input mask to enter field or control values in a specific format* option that displays in the Help window.

   f. Read the information on creating an input mask.

2. Find information on performing diagnostic tests by completing the following steps:

   a. Select the text *input mask* that displays in the *Search* text box.

   b. Type **diagnostic test** and then press Enter.

   c. Click the *Diagnose and repair crashing Office programs by using Office Diagnostics* option.

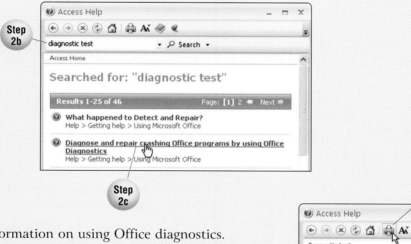

   d. Read the information on using Office diagnostics.

   e. Print the information by clicking the Print button on the toolbar located towards the top of the Help window.

   f. At the Print dialog box, click the Print button.

3. Close the Help window by clicking the Close button located in the upper right corner of the window.

CHAPTER summary

- Modifying a table can include adding, moving, or deleting a field.
- Add a new field in Datasheet or Design view. Type new records in a blank database or in the *Add New Field* column or add a row for a new field in Design view. Click the Insert Rows button in the Tools group to insert a new field.
- To delete a field, display the table in Design view, select the record you want deleted, and then click the Delete Rows button. Click Yes at the message.
- Select a row by clicking the record selector bar that displays at the left side of the row.
- Use the *Default Value* property in the *Field Properties* section to insert the most common field entry.
- Use the *Validation Rule* property to enter a statement containing a conditional test. Enter in the *Validation Text* property the error message you want to display if the data entered violates the validation rule.
- Click the Totals button in the Records group in the Home tab and Access inserts a row at the bottom of the datasheet with the label *Total* at the left. Click the down-pointing arrow in the Total row and then click the desired function at the drop-down list.
- Use the Input Mask Wizard to set a pattern for how data is entered in a field.
- Use the Lookup Wizard to confine data entered in a field to a specific list of items.
- Sort records in a table in ascending order with the Ascending button in the Sort & Filter group or in descending order with the Descending button.
- Use the spelling checker to find misspelled words in a table.
- The spelling checker compares the words in a table with words in its dictionary. If a match is found, the word is passed over. If no match is found, the spelling checker will select the word and offer possible replacements.
- Begin the spelling checker by clicking the Spelling button in the Records group in the Home tab.
- Use options at the Find and Replace dialog box with the Find tab selected to search for specific field entries in a table. Display this dialog box by clicking the Find button in the Find group in the Home tab.
- Use options at the Find and Replace dialog box with the Replace tab selected to search for specific data and replace with other data. Display this dialog box by clicking the Replace button in the Find group in the Home tab.
- Back up a database on a consistent basis to protect the data in the database from accidental loss or from any hardware failure. To back up a database, click the Office button, point to *Manage*, and then click *Back Up Database*.
- Compact and repair a database to optimize the performance of the database. Compact and repair a database by clicking the Office button, pointing to *Manage*, and then clicking *Compact and Repair Database*.
- Display the Access Help window by clicking the Microsoft Office Access Help button located in the upper right corner of the screen.

COMMANDS review

FEATURE	RIBBON TAB, GROUP	BUTTON, OPTION	KEYBOARD SHORTCUT
Add field	Table Tools Design, Tools	Insert Rows	
Delete field	Table Tools Design, Tools	Delete Rows	
Sort records ascending	Home, Sort & Filter	A↓Z	
Sort records descending	Home, Sort & Filter	Z↓A	
Spelling checker	Home, Records	Spelling	F7
Find and Replace dialog box with Find tab selected	Home, Find		Ctrl + F
Find and Replace dialog box with Replace tab selected	Home, Find	Replace	Ctrl + H
Back up database		, Manage, Back Up Database	
Compare and repair database		, Manage, Compact and Repair Database	
Access Help window			F1

CONCEPTS check

Test Your Knowledge

Completion: For each description, indicate the correct term, symbol, or character.

1. Select a row by clicking this bar that displays at the left side of the row.

   _____

2. If most records are likely to contain the same field value, use this property to insert the most common field entry.

   _____

3. Use this property to enter a statement containing a conditional test that is checked each time data is entered into a field.

   _____

4. Use this wizard to set a pattern for how data is entered in a field.

   _____

5. Use this wizard to confine data entered in a field to a specific list of items.

   _____

6. The Ascending and Descending sort buttons are located in this group in the Home tab.

   _____

7. The Spelling button is located in this group in the Home tab.

   _____

8. This is the keyboard shortcut to begin spell checking.

   _____

9. Use options at the Find and Replace dialog box with this tab selected to search for specific data and replace with other data.

   _____

10. To back up a database, click the Office button, point to this option, and then click *Back Up Database*.

    _____

11. Perform this action on a database to optimize the performance of the database.

    _____

12. This is the keyboard shortcut to display the Access Help window.

    _____

Demonstrate Your Proficiency

Assessment

1 CREATE TABLES AND RELATIONSHIPS BETWEEN TABLES IN A LAFFERTYCOMPANY DATABASE

1. Create a database named *LaffertyCompany* that contains two tables. Create the first table and name it *MarketingEmployees* and include the following fields (make sure the *EmpID* is identified as the primary key):

Field Name	Data Type
EmpID	Text (field size = 4)
FirstName	Text (field size = 20)
MiddleName	Text (field size = 20)
LastName	Text (field size = 30)
Status	Text (field size = 20; assign a default value of *Full-time*)
HireDate	Date/Time (use the Input Mask to control the date so it is entered as a short date)
Vacation	Text (field size = 10; use the Lookup Wizard to confine the field entry to one of three entries: *0 weeks*, *2 weeks*, or *3 weeks*

2. Type the following data or choose a field entry in the specified fields:

EmpID	1002		*EmpID*	3192
FirstName	Samantha		*FirstName*	Ralph
MiddleName	Lee		*MiddleName*	Edward
LastName	Murray		*LastName*	Sorrell
Status	Full-time		*Status*	Full-time
HireDate	06/15/2005		*HireDate*	11/04/2006
Vacation	3 weeks		*Vacation*	3 weeks
EmpID	1799		*EmpID*	2217
FirstName	Brandon		*FirstName*	Leland
MiddleName	Michael		*MiddleName*	John
LastName	Perrault		*LastName*	Nitsche
Status	Full-time		*Status*	Part-time
HireDate	03/12/2007		*HireDate*	09/05/2008
Vacation	2 weeks		*Vacation*	0 weeks
EmpID	1340		*EmpID*	1877
FirstName	Jack		*FirstName*	Immanuel
MiddleName	Ryan		*MiddleName*	Nolan
LastName	McCleary		*LastName*	Shandra
Status	Full-time		*Title*	Part-time
HireDate	07/01/2007		*HireDate*	08/01/2009
Vacation	2 weeks		*Vacation*	0 weeks

3. Complete a spelling check on the table. (Assume proper names are spelled correctly.)
4. Adjust the column widths.
5. Save the MarketingEmployees table.
6. Change the orientation to landscape and then print the table.
7. Close the MarketingEmployees table.
8. Create the second table and name it *Expenses* and include the following fields (make sure the *Item#* field is identified as the primary key):

Field Name	Data Type
Item#	AutoNumber
EmpID	Text (field size = 4)
Expense	Text (field size = 30)
Amount	Currency (Type a condition in the *Validation Rule* property that states the entry must be $500 or less. Type an error message in the *Validation Text* property box.)
DateSubmitted	Date/Time (Use the Input Mask to control the date so it is entered as a short date.)

9. Type the following data or choose a field entry in the specified fields (Access automatically inserts a number in the *Item#* field):

EmpID	3192	*EmpID*	1799
Expense	Brochures	*Expense*	Marketing Conference
Amount	$245.79	*Amount*	$500.00
DateSubmitted	02/01/2010	*DateSubmitted*	02/08/2010
EmpID	3192	*EmpID*	1340
Expense	Business Cards	*Expense*	Marketing Conference
Amount	$150.00	*Amount*	$500.00
DateSubmitted	02/10/2010	*DateSubmitted*	02/10/2010
EmpID	1799	*EmpID*	1340
Expense	Supplies	*Expense*	Reference Material
Amount	$487.25	*Amount*	$85.75
DateSubmitted	02/14/2010	*DateSubmitted*	02/15/2010

10. Complete a spelling check on the table.
11. Adjust the column widths.
12. Save, print, and then close the Expenses table.
13. Create a one-to-many relationship where *EmpID* in the MarketingEmployees table is the "one" and *EmpID* in the Expenses table is the "many."
14. Print the relationship and then close the relationships report window and the relationships window.

2 MODIFY A TABLE AND FIND AND REPLACE DATA IN A TABLE

1. With the **LaffertyCompany.accdb** database open, open the MarketingEmployees table and then make the following changes:
   a. Delete the *MiddleName* field.
   b. Insert a *Title* field between *LastName* and *Status*. (You determine the data type and description.)
   c. Move the *Status* field below the *HireDate* field.
   d. In Datasheet view, add the data to the *Title* field as specified below:

EmpID	Title
1002	Manager
3192	Assistant Manager
1799	Manager
2217	Assistant
1340	Assistant
1877	Assistant

2. Save the MarketingEmployees table.
3. Find all occurrences of *Manager* and replace with *Director*. **Hint: Position the insertion point in the first entry in the Title column and then display the Find and Replace dialog box. At the dialog box, change the Match option to Any Part of Field.**
4. Find all occurrences of *Assistant* and replace with *Associate*.
5. Save and then print the table in landscape orientation with *Normal* margins.
6. Close the MarketingEmployees table.
7. Open the Expenses table, insert a Total row in the table, and then calculate the sum of the expenses.
8. Save, print, and then close the Expenses table.
9. Close the **LaffertyCompany.accdb** database.

CASE study
Apply Your Skills

Part 1

You work for Sunrise Enterprises and your supervisor has asked you to create a database with information about clients and sales representatives. Create a database named *Sunrise* that contains two tables. Create a table named *Representatives* that includes fields for representative ID number, representative name, representative telephone number (use the Input Mask Wizard), insurance plan (use the Lookup Wizard and include four options: *Platinum, Premium, Standard,* and *None*) and yearly bonus (type a condition in the *Validation Rule* property that states the entry must be between $2,000 and $10,000 and type an error message in the *Validation Text* property box). Make sure the representative ID number is the primary key in the table. In Datasheet view, enter seven records in the table. Insert a total row and then sum the bonus amounts. Save, print, and then close the table.

Create a second table in the **Sunrise.accdb** database named *Clients* that includes fields for company ID number, representative ID number (the same field you created in the Representative table) company name, address, city, state, ZIP code (use the Input Mask Wizard and specify a nine digit ZIP code), telephone number (use the Input Wizard), and type of business (specify that *Wholesaler* is the default value). Make sure that the company ID number is identified as the primary key. In Datasheet view, enter at least five companies. Make sure you use representative ID numbers in the Clients table that match numbers in the Representative table. Identify that one of the clients is a "*Retailer*" rather than a "*Wholesaler*." Save, print, and then close the table.

Part 2

Create a one-to-many relationship with the representative ID number in the Representatives table as the "one" and the representative ID number in the Clients table as the "many." Save and then print the relationship.

Part 3

Open the Representatives table and then reverse the order of the yearly bonus and the insurance plan fields. Save, print, and then close the table. Open the Clients table and then reverse the order of the telephone number and type of business fields. Save, print, and then close the table.

Part 4

In Microsoft Word, create a document that describes three situations where you would use the Lookup Wizard, three situations where you would assign a default value to a field, and three situations where you would write a conditional statement for a field. Apply any formatting to the document to enhance the visual appeal and then save the document and name it **Access_C3_CS_P4**. Print and then close **Access_C3_CS_P4.docx**.

Performing Queries

CHAPTER

PERFORMANCE OBJECTIVES

Upon successful completion of Chapter 4, you will be able to:

- Design a query to extract specific data from a table
- Use the Simple Query Wizard to extract specific data from a table
- Modify a query
- Design queries with Or and And criteria
- Create a calculated field
- Use aggregate functions in queries
- Create crosstab, duplicate, and unmatched queries

access Chapter 4

One of the primary uses of a database is to extract specific information from the database. A company might need to know such information as: How much inventory is currently on hand? What products have been ordered? What accounts are past due? What customers live in a particular city? You can extract this type of information from a table by completing a query. You will learn how to perform a variety of queries on information in tables in this chapter.

Note: Before beginning computer projects, delete the Access2007L1C3 folder from your storage medium. Next, copy the Access2007L1C4 subfolder from the Access2007L1 folder on the CD that accompanies this textbook to your storage medium and make Access2007L1C4 the active folder.

Project 1 Design Queries

You will design and run a number of queries including queries with fields from one table and queries with fields from more than one table. You will also use the Simple Query Wizard to design queries.

Performing Queries

Being able to extract (pull out) specific data from a table is one of the most important functions of a database. Extracting data in Access is referred to as performing a query. The word *query* means to ask a question. Access provides

HINT

A query selects some of the fields from the table(s) to display or print rather than viewing all fields in a table.

HINT

The first step in building a query is to choose the fields that you wish to display in the query results datasheet.

several methods for performing a query. You can design your own query, use a simple query wizard, or use complex query wizards. In this chapter, you will learn to design your own query; use the Simple Query Wizard; use aggregate functions in a query; and use the Crosstab, Find Duplicates, and Unmatched Query Wizards.

Designing a Query

Designing a query consists of identifying the table from which you are gathering data, the field or fields from which the data will be drawn, and the criteria for selecting the data. To design a query and perform the query, open a database, click the Create tab, and then click the Query Design button in the Other group. This displays a query window in the work area and also displays the Show Table dialog box as shown in Figure 4.1.

Figure 4.1 Query Window with Show Table Dialog Box

Query design grid

Click the table you want included in the query and then click the Add button.

QUICK STEPS

Design a Query
1. Click Create tab.
2. Click Query Design button.
3. At Show Table dialog box, click desired table, click Add button.
4. Add any additional tables.
5. In query design grid, click down-pointing arrow in field text boxes and click desired field from drop-down list.
6. Click Run button.
7. Save query.

Click the table in the Show Table list box that you want included in the query and then click the Add button or double-click the desired table. Add any other tables required for the query. When all tables have been added, click the Close button. In the query window, click the down-pointing arrow at the right of the first *Field* text box in the query design grid and then click the desired field from the drop-down list. Figure 4.2 displays a sample query window.

Figure 4.2 Query Window

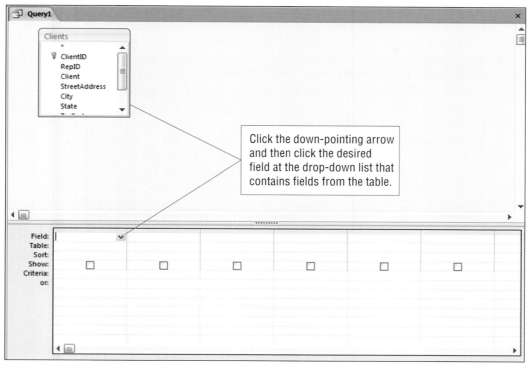

Click the down-pointing arrow and then click the desired field at the drop-down list that contains fields from the table.

To establish a criterion, click inside the *Criteria* text box in the column containing the desired field name in the query design grid and then type the criterion. With the fields and criteria established, click the Run button in the Results group in the Query Tools Design tab. Access searches the specified tables for records that match the criteria and then displays those records in the query results datasheet. If you plan to use the query in the future, save the query and name it. If you do not need the query again, close the query results datasheet without saving it.

You can click the down-pointing arrow at the right side of a *Field* text box and then click the desired field at the drop-down list. You can also double-click a field in a table and it is inserted in the first available *Field* text box in the query design grid. As an example, suppose you wanted to find out how many purchase orders were issued on a specific date. To do this, you would double-click *PurchaseOrderID* in the table (this inserts *PurchaseOrderID* in the first *Field* text box in the query design grid) and then double-click *OrderDate* in the table (this inserts *OrderDate* in the second *Field* text box in the query design grid). In this example, both fields are needed so the purchase order ID is displayed along with the specific order date. After inserting fields, you would then insert the criterion. The criterion for this example would be something like *#1/15/2010#*. After you insert the criterion, click the Run button in the Results group and the results of the query display in the query results datasheet.

A third method for inserting a field in the query design grid is to drag a field from the table to the desired field in the query design grid. To do this, position the mouse pointer on the desired field in the table, hold down the left mouse button, drag to the desired *Field* text box in the query design grid, and then release the mouse button.

HINT
Insert fields in the *Field* text boxes in the query design grid in the order in which you want the fields to display in the query results datasheet.

Run

Establishing Query Criteria

Establish Query Criterion
1. At query window, click in desired *Criteria* text box in query design grid.
2. Type criterion and then press Enter.
3. Click Run button.

A query does not require that specific criteria are established. In the example described on the previous page, if the criterion for the date was not included, the query would "return" (*return* is the term used for the results of the query) all Purchase Order numbers with the dates. While this information may be helpful, you could easily find this information in the table. The value of performing a query is to extract specific information from a table. To do this, you must insert a criterion like the one described in the example.

Access makes writing a criterion fairly simple because it inserts the necessary symbols in the criterion. If you type a city such as *Indianapolis* in the *Criteria* text box and then press Enter, Access changes the criterion to *"Indianapolis"*. The quotation marks are inserted by Access and are necessary for the query to run properly. You can either let Access put the proper symbols in the *Criteria* text box, or you can type the criterion with the symbols. Table 4.1 shows some criteria examples including what is typed and what is returned.

Table 4.1 Criteria Examples

Typing this criteria	*Returns this*
"Smith"	Field value matching *Smith*
"Smith" or "Larson"	Field value matching either *Smith* or *Larson*
Not "Smith"	Field value that is not *Smith* (the opposite of "Smith")
"S*"	Field value that begins with *S* and ends in anything
"*s"	Field value that begins with anything and ends in *s*
"[A-D]*"	Field value that begins with *A* through *D* and ends in anything
#01/01/2010#	Field value matching the date 01/01/2010
<#04/01/2010#	Field value less than (before) 04/01/2010
>#04/01/2010#	Field value greater than (after) 04/01/2010
Between #01/01/2010 And #03/31/2010	Any date between 01/01/2010 and 03/31/2010

HINT

Access inserts quotation marks around text criteria and the pound symbol around date criteria.

In Table 4.1, notice the quotation marks surrounding field values (such as "Smith"). If you do not type the quotation marks when typing the criterion, Access will automatically insert them. The same is true for the pound symbol (#). If you do not type the pound symbol around a date, Access will automatically insert the symbols. Access automatically inserts the correct symbol when you press the Enter key after typing the query criteria.

In the criteria examples, the asterisk was used as a wild card indicating any character. This is consistent with many other software applications where the asterisk is used as a wildcard character. Two of the criteria examples in Table 4.1 use the less than and greater than symbols. You can use these symbols for fields containing numbers, values, dates, amounts, and so forth. In the next several projects, you will be designing queries to extract specific information from different tables in databases.

Project 1a Performing Queries on Tables

1. Remove the read-only attribute from the **Deering.accdb** database located in the Access2007L1C4 folder.
2. Open the **Deering.accdb** database.
3. Create the following relationships:
   a. Create a one-to-one relationship where the *ClientID* field in the Clients table is the "one" and the *ClientID* field in the Sales table is the "one."
   b. Create a one-to-one relationship where the *RepID* field in the Representatives table is the "one" and the *RepID* field in the Benefits table is the "one."
   c. Create a one-to-many relationship where the *RepID* field in the Representatives table is the "one" and the *RepID* field in the Clients table is the "many."
   d. Create a one-to-many relationship where the *QuotaID* field in the Quotas table is the "one" and the *QuotaID* field in the Representatives table is the "many."
4. Save, print, and then close the relationships report and relationships window.
5. Extract records of those clients located in Indianapolis by completing the following steps:
   a. Click the Create tab.
   b. Click the Query Design button in the Other group.

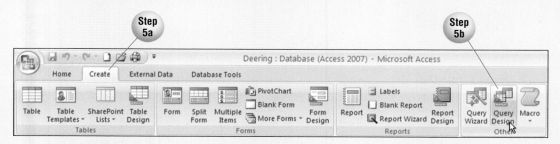

Step 5a

Step 5b

   c. At the Show Table dialog box with the Tables tab selected (see Figure 4.1), click *Clients* in the list box, click the Add button, and then click the Close button.
   d. Insert fields from the table to *Field* text boxes in the query design grid by completing the following steps:
      1) Click the down-pointing arrow located at the right of the first *Field* text box in the query design grid and then click *Client* in the drop-down list.

Step 5d1

2) Click inside the next *Field* text box (to the right of *Client*) in the query design grid, click the down-pointing arrow, and then click *StreetAddress* in the drop-down list.

3) Click inside the next *Field* box (to the right of *StreetAddress*), click the down-pointing arrow, and then click *City* in the drop-down list.

4) Click inside the next *Field* box (to the right of *City*), click the down-pointing arrow, and then click *State* in the drop-down list.

5) Click inside the next *Field* box (to the right of *State*), click the down-pointing arrow, and then select *ZipCode* in the drop-down list.

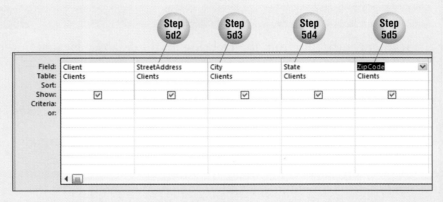

e. Insert the criterion text telling Access to display only those suppliers located in Indianapolis by completing the following steps:

1) Click in the *Criteria* text box in the *City* column in the query design grid. (This positions the insertion point inside the text box.)

2) Type **Indianapolis** and then press Enter. (This changes the criterion to "Indianapolis").

f. Return the results of the query by clicking the Run button in the Results group. (This displays the results in the query results datasheet.)

g. Save the results of the query by completing the following steps:

1) Click the Save button on the Quick Access toolbar.

2) At the Save As dialog box, type **IndianapolisQuery** and then press Enter or click OK.

h. Print the query results datasheet by clicking the Quick Print button on the Quick Access toolbar.

i. Close IndianapolisQuery.

6. Extract those records with quota identification numbers higher than 2 by completing the following steps:

a. Click the Create tab and then click the Query Design button in the Other group.

b. Double-click *Representatives* in the Show Table list box and then click the Close button.

c. In the query window, double-click *RepName* (this inserts the field in the first *Field* text box in the query design grid).

d. Double-click *QuotaID* (this inserts the field in the second *Field* text box in the query design grid).

e. Insert the query criterion by completing the following steps:
   1) Click in the *Criteria* text box in the *QuotaID* column in the query design grid.
   2) Type >2 and then press Enter. (Access will automatically insert quotation marks around 2 since the data type for the field is set at *Text* [rather than *Number*].)

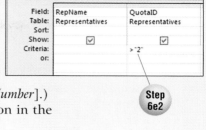

Step 6e2

f. Return the results of the query by clicking the Run button in the Results group.
g. Save the query and name it *QuotaIDGreaterThanTwoQuery*.
h. Print and then close the query.

7. Extract those 2009 sales greater than $99,999 by completing the following steps:
   a. Click the Create tab and then click the Query Design button.
   b. Double-click *Sales* in the Show Table dialog box and then click the Close button.
   c. At the query window, double-click *ClientID* (this inserts the field in the first *Field* text box in the query design grid).
   d. Insert the *Sales2009* field in the second *Field* text box.
   e. Insert the query criterion by completing the following steps:
      1) Click in the *Criteria* text box in the *Sales2009* column in the query design grid.
      2) Type >99999 and then press Enter. (Access will not insert quotation marks around *99999* since the field is identified as *Currency*.)

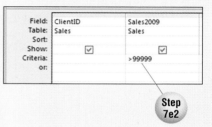

Step 7e2

   f. Return the results of the query by clicking the Run button in the Results group.
   g. Save the query and name it *2009SalesOver$99999Query*.
   h. Print and then close the query.

8. Extract records of those representatives with a telephone number that begins with the 765 area code by completing the following steps:
   a. Click the Create tab and then click the Query Design button.
   b. Double-click *Representatives* in the Show Table dialog box and then click the Close button.
   c. Insert the *RepName* field in the first *Field* text box.
   d. Insert the *Telephone* field in the second *Field* text box.
   e. Insert the query criterion by completing the following steps:
      1) Click in the *Criteria* text box in the *Telephone* column.
      2) Type *765* and then press Enter.

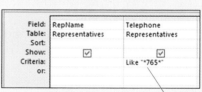

   f. Return the results of the query by clicking the Run button in the Results group.
   g. Save the query and name it *RepsWith765AreaCodeQuery*.
   h. Print and then close the query.

Step 8e2

In Project 1a, you performed several queries on specific tables. A query can also be performed on fields from more than one table. In Project 1b, you will be performing queries on related tables. As mentioned earlier, one method for inserting fields in the query design grid is to drag the field from the table to the desired *Field* text box.

1. With the **Deering.accdb** database open, extract information on representatives hired between March of 2006 and November of 2006 and include the representative's name by completing the following steps:

   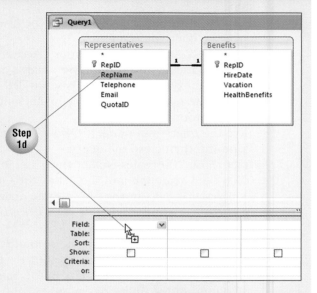

   Step 1d

   a. Click the Create tab and then click the Query Design button.
   b. Double-click *Representatives* in the Show Table dialog box.
   c. Double-click *Benefits* in the Show Table dialog box list box and then click the Close button.
   d. At the query window, position the mouse pointer on the *RepName* field in the Representatives table, hold down the left mouse button, drag to the first *Field* text box in the query design grid, and then release the mouse button. (This inserts the field in the *Field* text box.)
   e. Drag the *HireDate* field from the Benefits table to the second *Field* text box.
   f. Insert the query criterion by completing the following steps:
      1) Click in the *Criteria* text box in the *HireDate* column.
      2) Type **Between 3/1/2006 And 11/30/2006** and then press Enter. (Make sure you type zeros and not capital *O*s.)

   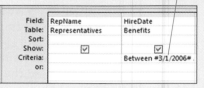

   Step 1f2

   g. Return the results of the query by clicking the Run button in the Results group.
   h. Save the query and name it *MarToNov2006HiresQuery*.
   i. Print and then close the query.

2. Extract records of those representatives who were hired in 2004 by completing the following steps:
   a. Click the Create tab and then click the Query Design button.
   b. Double-click *Representatives* in the Show Table dialog box.
   c. Double-click *Benefits* in the Show Table dialog box and then click the Close button.
   d. At the query window, drag the *RepID* field from the Representatives table to the first *Field* text box in the query design grid.
   e. Drag the *RepName* field from the Representatives table to the second *Field* text box.
   f. Drag the *HireDate* field from the Benefits table to the third *Field* text box.
   g. Insert the query criterion by completing the following steps:
      1) Click in the *Criteria* text box in the *HireDate* column.
      2) Type ***2004** and then press Enter.

   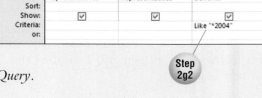

   Step 2g2

   h. Return the results of the query by clicking the Run button in the Results group.
   i. Save the query and name it *RepsHiredIn2004Query*.
   j. Print and then close the query.

3. Suppose you need to determine 2008 and 2009 sales for a company but you can only remember that the company name begins with *Blue*. Create a query that finds the company and identifies the sales by completing the following steps:
   a. Click the Create tab and then click the Query Design button.
   b. Double-click *Clients* in the Show Table dialog box.
   c. Double-click *Sales* in the Show Table dialog box and then click the Close button.
   d. At the query window, insert the *ClientID* field in the Clients table in the first *Field* text box in the query design grid.
   e. Insert the *Client* field in the Clients table in the second *Field* text box.
   f. Insert the *Sales2008* field from the Sales table in the third *Field* text box.
   g. Insert the *Sales2009* field from the Sales table in the fourth *Field* text box.
   h. Insert the query criterion by completing the following steps:
      1) Click in the *Criteria* text box in the *Client* column.
      2) Type **Blue*** and then press Enter.

Step
3h2

   i. Return the results of the query by clicking the Run button in the Results group.
   j. Save the query and name it *BlueRidgeSalesQuery*.
   k. Print and then close the query.
4. Close the **Deering.accdb** database.
5. Display the Open dialog box with Access2007L1C4 the active folder and then remove the read-only attribute from the **OutdoorOptions.accdb** database.
6. Open the **OutdoorOptions.accdb** database.
7. Extract information on products ordered between February 15 and February 28, 2010, and include the supplier's name by completing the following steps:
   a. Click the Create tab and then click the Query Design button.
   b. Double-click *Products* in the Show Table dialog box.
   c. Double-click *Orders* in the Show Table dialog box and then click the Close button.
   d. At the query window, insert the *Product#* field from the Products table in the first *Field* text box.
   e. Insert the *Product* field from the Products table in the second *Field* text box.
   g. Insert the *OrderDate* field from the Orders table in the third *Field* list box.
   h. Insert the query criterion by completing the following steps:
      1) Click in the *Criteria* text box in the *OrderDate* column.
      2) Type **Between 2/15/2010 And 2/28/2010** and then press Enter. (Make sure you type zeros and not capital *O*s.)

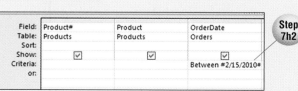

Step
7h2

   i. Return the results of the query by clicking the Run button in the Results group.
   j. Save the query and name it *Feb15-28OrdersQuery*.
   k. Print and then close the query.

Sort Fields in Query
1. At query window, click in *Sort* text box in query design grid.
2. Click down arrow in *Sort* text box.
3. Click *Ascending* or *Descending*.

Sorting Fields in a Query

When designing a query, you can specify the sort order of a field or fields. Click inside one of the columns in the *Sort* text box and a down-pointing arrow displays at the right of the field. Click this down-pointing arrow and a drop-down list displays with the choices *Ascending*, *Descending*, and *(not sorted)*. Click Ascending to sort from lowest to highest or click Descending to sort from highest to lowest.

Project 1G Performing a Query on Related Tables and Sorting in Ascending Order

1. With the **OutdoorOptions.accdb** database open, extract information on orders less than $1,500 by completing the following steps:
   a. Click the Create tab and then click the Query Design button.
   b. Double-click *Products* in the Show Table dialog box.
   c. Double-click *Orders* in the Show Table dialog box and then click the Close button.
   d. At the query window, insert the *Product#* field from the Products table in the first *Field* text box.
   e. Insert the *Supplier#* field from the Products table in the second *Field* text box.
   f. Insert the *UnitsOrdered* field from the Orders table in the third *Field* text box.
   g. Insert the *Amount* field from the Orders table in the fourth *Field* text box.
   h. Insert the query criterion by completing the following steps:
      1) Click in the *Criteria* text box in the *Amount* column.
      2) Type <1500 and then press Enter. (Make sure you type zeros and not capital *O*s.)

Field:	Product#	Supplier#	UnitsOrdered	Amount
Table:	Products	Products	Orders	Orders
Sort:				
Show:	☑	☑	☑	☑
Criteria:				<1500
or:				

Step 1h2

   i. Sort the *Amount* field values from lowest to highest by completing the following steps:
      1) Click in the *Sort* text box in the *Amount* column. (This causes a down-pointing arrow to display at the right side of the text box.)
      2) Click the down-pointing arrow at the right side of the *Sort* text box and then click *Ascending*.

Step 1i1

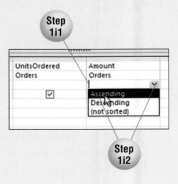

Step 1i2

   j. Return the results of the query by clicking the Run button in the Results group.
   k. Save the query and name it *OrdersLessThan$1500Query*.
   l. Print and then close the query.
2. Close the **OutdoorOptions.accdb** database.
3. Open the **Deering.accdb** database.

4. Extract information on sales below $100,000 for 2008 by completing the following steps:
   a. Click the Create tab and then click the Query Design button.
   b. Double-click *Clients* in the Show Table dialog box.
   c. Double-click *Sales* in the list Show Table dialog box.
   d. Double-click *Representatives* in the Show Table dialog box and then click the Close button.
   e. At the query window, insert the *Client* field from the Clients table in the first *Field* text box.
   f. Insert the *Sales2008* field from the Sales table in the second *Field* text box.
   g. Insert the *RepName* field from the Representatives table in the third *Field* text box.
   h. Insert the query criterion by completing the following steps:
      1) Click in the *Criteria* text box in the *Sales2008* column.
      2) Type <100000 and then press Enter. (Make sure you type zeros and not capital *O*s.)
   i. Sort the *Sales2008* field values from highest to lowest by completing the following steps:
      1) Click in the *Sort* text box in the *Sales2008* column. (This causes a down-pointing arrow to display at the right side of the text box.)
      2) Click the down-pointing arrow at the right side of the *Sort* text box and then click *Descending*.
   j. Return the results of the query by clicking the Run button in the Results group.
   k. Save the query and name it *2008SalesLessThan$100000Query*.
   l. Print and then close the query.

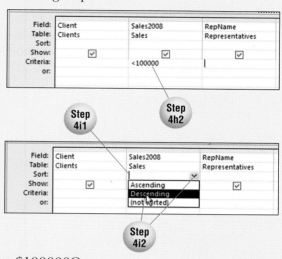

Modifying a Query

You can modify a saved query. For example, suppose after designing the query that displays the 2008 sales that are less than $100,000, you decide that you want to find sales for 2009 that are less than $100,000. Rather than designing a new query, open the existing query, make any needed changes, and then run the query.

To modify an existing query, double-click the query in the Navigation pane (this displays the query in Datasheet view). Click the View button to display the query in Design view. Make the desired changes and then click the Run button in the Results group. Click the Save button on the Quick Access toolbar to save the query with the same name. If you want to save the query with a new name, click the Office button and then click Save As. At the Save As dialog box, type a name for the query and then press Enter.

If your database contains a number of queries, you can group and display them in the Navigation pane. To do this, click the down-pointing arrow in the Navigation pane Menu bar (located in the upper right corner) and then click *Object Type* at the drop-down list. This displays objects grouped in categories such as *Tables* and *Queries*.

QUICK STEPS

Modify a Query
1. Double-click query in Navigation pane.
2. Click View button.
3. Make desired changes to query.
4. Click Run button.
5. Click Save button.

HINT
Save time designing a query by modifying an existing query.

1. With the **Deering.accdb** database open, find the sales less than $100,000 for 2009 by completing the following steps:
   a. Change the display of objects in the Navigation pane by clicking the down-pointing arrow in the Navigation pane Menu bar (located in the upper right corner of the pane) and then clicking *Object Type* at the drop-down list.
   b. Double-click the *2008SalesLessThan$100000Query* in the *Queries* section of the Navigation pane.
   c. Click the View button in the Views group to switch to Design view.
   d. Click in the *Field* text box containing the text *Sales2008*.
   e. Click the down-pointing arrow that displays at the right side of the *Field* text box and then click *Sales2009* at the drop-down list.

Step 1a

Step 1e

   f. Click the Run button in the Results group.
2. Save the query with a new name by completing the following steps:
   a. Click the Office button and then click Save As.
   b. At the Save As dialog box, type **2009SalesLessThan$100000Query** and then press Enter.
   c. Print and then close the query.
3. Modify an existing query and find employees with three weeks of vacation by completing the following steps:
   a. Double-click the *MarToNov2006HiresQuery*.
   b. Click the View button in the Views group to switch to Design view.
   c. Click in the *Field* text box containing the text *HireDate*.
   d. Click the down-pointing arrow that displays at the right side of the *Field* text box and then click *Vacation* at the drop-down list.
   e. Select the current text in the *Criteria* text box in the *Vacation* column, type **3 weeks**, and then press Enter.
   f. Click the Run button in the Results group.
4. Save the query with a new name by completing the following steps:
   a. Click the Office button and then click Save As.
   b. At the Save As dialog box, type **RepsWith3WeekVacationsQuery** and then press Enter.
   c. Print and then close the query.

Step 2b

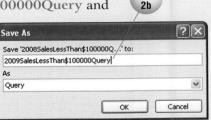

Step 3e

Designing Queries with *Or* and *And* Criteria

HINT

You can design a query that combines *And* and *Or* statements.

The query design grid contains an *Or* row you can use to design a query that instructs Access to display records that match either of the two criteria. For example, to display a list of employees with three weeks of vacation *or* four weeks of vacation, you would type 3 weeks in the *Criteria* text box for the *Vacation* field and then type 4 weeks in the field immediately below *3 weeks* in the *Or* row. Other examples include finding clients that live in *Muncie* or *Lafayette* or finding representatives with a quota of *1* or *2*.

You can also select records by entering criteria statements into more than one *Criteria* field. Multiple criteria all entered in the same row becomes an *And* statement where each criterion must be met for Access to select the record. For example, you could search for clients in the Indianapolis area with sales greater than $100,000.

Project 1e Designing Queries with *Or* and *And* Criteria

1. With the **Deering.accdb** database open, modify an existing query and find employees with three weeks or four weeks of vacation by completing the following steps:
   a. Double-click the *RepsWith3WeekVacationsQuery*.
   b. Click the View button in the Views group to switch to Design view.
   c. Click in the empty field below "*3 weeks*" in the *Or* row, type 4 weeks, and then press Enter.

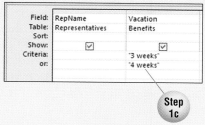

Step 1c

   d. Click the Run button in the Results group.
2. Save the query with a new name by completing the following steps:
   a. Click the Office button and then click Save As.
   b. At the Save As dialog box, type RepsWith3Or4WeekVacationsQuery and then press Enter.
   c. Print and then close the query.
3. Design a query that finds records of clients in the Indianapolis area with sales over $100,000 for 2008 and 2009 by completing the following steps:
   a. Click the Create tab and then click the Query Design button.
   b. Double-click *Clients* in the Show Table dialog box.
   c. Double-click *Sales* in the Show Table dialog box and then click the Close button.
   d. At the query window, insert the *Client* field from the Clients table in the first *Field* text box.
   e. Insert the *City* field from the Clients table in the second *Field* text box.
   f. Insert the *Sales2008* field from the Sales table in the third *Field* text box.
   g. Insert the *Sales2009* field from the Sales table in the fourth *Field* text box.

h. Insert the query criteria by completing the following steps:
   1) Click in the *Criteria* text box in the *City* column.
   2) Type Indianapolis and then press Enter.
   3) With the insertion point positioned in the *Criteria* text box in the *Sales2008* column, type >100000 and then press Enter.
   4) With the insertion point positioned in the *Criteria* text box in the *Sales2009* column, type >100000 and then press Enter.

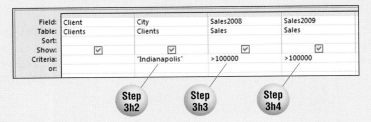

i. Click the Run button in the Results group.
j. Save the query and name it IndianapolisSalesOver$100000.
k. Print and then close the query.

Performing a Query with the Simple Query Wizard

The Simple Query Wizard provided by Access guides you through the steps for preparing a query. To use this wizard, open the database, click the Create tab, and then click the Query Wizard button in the Other group. At the New Query dialog box, make sure *Simple Query Wizard* is selected in the list box and then click the OK button. At the first Simple Query Wizard dialog box, shown in Figure 4.3, specify the table(s) in the *Tables/Queries* option box. After specifying the table, insert the fields you want included in the query in the *Selected Fields* list box, and then click the Next button.

Figure 4.3 First Simple Query Wizard Dialog Box

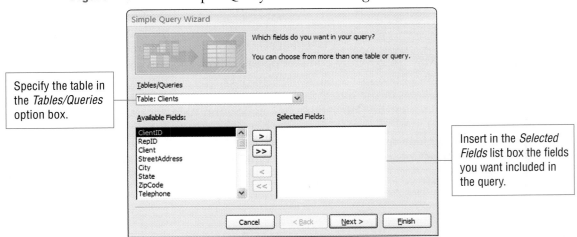

At the second Simple Query Wizard dialog box, specify whether you want a detail or summary query, and then click the Next button. At the third (and last) Simple Query Wizard dialog box, shown in Figure 4.4, type a name for the completed query or accept the name provided by the wizard. At this dialog box, you can also specify that you want to open the query to view the information or modify the query design. If you want to extract specific information, be sure to choose the *Modify the query design* option. After making any necessary changes, click the Finish button.

Create a Query with Simple Query Wizard
1. Click Create tab.
2. Click Query Wizard button.
3. Make sure *Simple Query Wizard* is selected in list box and then click OK.
4. Follow query steps.

Figure 4.4 Last Simple Query Wizard Dialog Box

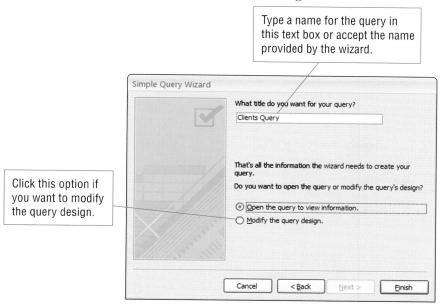

Type a name for the query in this text box or accept the name provided by the wizard.

Click this option if you want to modify the query design.

If you do not modify the query design in the last Simple Query Wizard dialog box, the query displays all records for the fields identified in the first Simple Query Wizard dialog box. In Project 1f you will perform a query without modifying the design, and in Project 1g you will modify the query design.

Project 1f Performing a Query with the Simple Query Wizard

1. With the **Deering.accdb** database open, click the Create tab and then click the Query Wizard button in the Other group.
2. At the New Query dialog box, make sure *Simple Query Wizard* is selected in the list box and then click OK.
3. At the first Simple Query Wizard dialog box, click the down-pointing arrow at the right of the *Tables/Queries* option box and then click *Table: Clients*. (You will need to scroll up the list to display this table.)

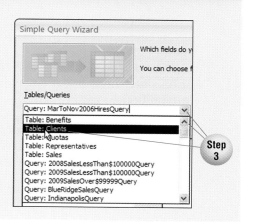

4. With *ClientID* selected in the *Available Fields* list box, click the button containing the greater than symbol. (This inserts the *ClientID* field in the *Selected Fields* list box.)

5. Click *Client* in the *Available Fields* list box and then click the button containing the greater than symbol.

6. Click the down-pointing arrow at the right of the *Tables/Queries* option box and then click *Table: Sales*.

7. Click *Sales2008* in the *Available Fields* list box and then click the button containing the greater than symbol.

8. With *Sales2009* selected in the *Available Fields* list box, click the button containing the greater than symbol.

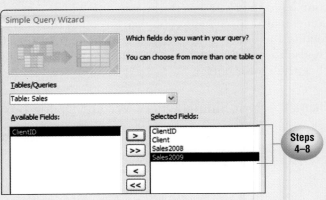

Steps
4–8

9. Click the Next button.

10. At the second Simple Query Wizard dialog box, click the Next button.

11. At the last Simple Query Wizard dialog box, click the Finish button.

12. When the results of the query display, print the results.

13. Close the Clients Query window.

14. Close the **Deering.accdb** database.

15. Open the **OutdoorOptions.accdb** database.

16. Click the Create tab and then click the Query Wizard button.

17. At the New Query dialog box, make sure *Simple Query Wizard* is selected in the list box and then click OK.

18. At the first Simple Query Wizard dialog box, click the down-pointing arrow at the right side of the *Tables/Queries* option box and then click *Table: Suppliers*.

19. With *Supplier#* selected in the *Available Fields* list box, click the button containing the greater than symbol. (This inserts the *Supplier#* field in the *Selected Fields* list box.)

20. With *SupplierName* selected in the *Available Fields* list box, click the button containing the greater than symbol.

21. Click the down-pointing arrow at the right of the *Tables/Queries* option box and then click *Table: Orders*.

22. Click *Product#* in the *Available Fields* list box and then click the button containing the greater than symbol.

23. Click *Amount* in the *Available Fields* list box and then click the button containing the greater than symbol.

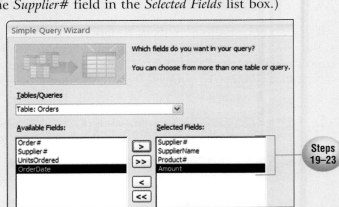

Steps
19–23

24. Click the Next button.

25. At the second Simple Query Wizard dialog box, click the Next button.

26. At the last Simple Query Wizard dialog box, click the Finish button.

27. When the results of the query display, print the results.

28. Close the query window.

To extract specific information when using the Simple Query Wizard, tell the wizard that you want to modify the query design. This displays the query window with the query design grid where you can insert query criteria.

Project 1g Performing and Modifying a Query with the Simple Query Wizard

1. With the **OutdoorOptions.accdb** database open, click the Create tab and then click the Query Wizard button.
2. At the New Query dialog box, make sure *Simply Query Wizard* is selected and then click OK.
3. At the first Simple Query Wizard dialog box, click the down-pointing arrow at the right side of the *Tables/Queries* option box and then click *Table: Suppliers*.
4. Insert the following fields in the *Selected Fields* list box:
    - SupplierName
    - StreetAddress
    - City
    - Province
    - PostalCode

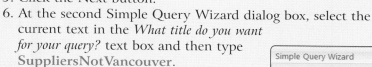

5. Click the Next button.
6. At the second Simple Query Wizard dialog box, select the current text in the *What title do you want for your query?* text box and then type **SuppliersNotVancouver**.
7. Click the *Modify the query design* option and then click the Finish button.
8. At the query window, complete the following steps:
    a. Click in the *Criteria* text box in the City column in the query design grid.
    b. Type **Not Vancouver** and then press Enter.
9. Specify that the fields are to be sorted in ascending order by postal code by completing the following steps:
    a. Click in the *Sort* text box in the PostalCode column. (You may need to scroll to see this column.)
    b. Click the down-pointing arrow that displays at the right side of the text box and then click *Ascending*.

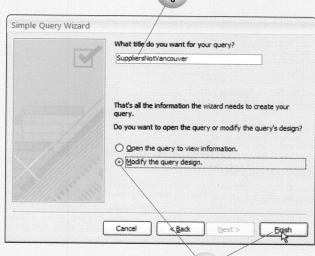

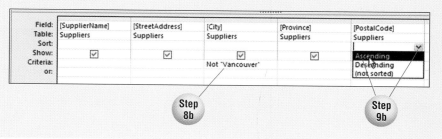

10. Click the Run button in the Results group. (This displays suppliers that are not located in Vancouver and displays the records sorted by PostalCode in ascending order.)
11. Save, print, and then close the query.
12. Close the **OutdoorOptions.accdb** database.
13. Open the **Deering.accdb** database.
14. Click the Create tab and then click the Query Wizard button.
15. At the New Query dialog box, make sure *Simply Query Wizard* is selected and then click OK.
16. At the first Simple Query Wizard dialog box, click the down-pointing arrow at the right of the *Tables/Queries* option box and then click *Table: Clients*. (You will need to scroll up the list to display this table.)
17. Insert the following fields in the *Selected Fields* list box:
    - Client
    - StreetAddress
    - City
    - State
    - ZipCode

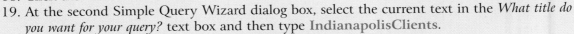

18. Click the Next button.
19. At the second Simple Query Wizard dialog box, select the current text in the *What title do you want for your query?* text box and then type **IndianapolisClients**.
20. Click the *Modify the query design* option and then click the Finish button.
21. At the query window, complete the following steps:
    a. Click in the *Criteria* text box in the *City* column.
    b. Type **Indianapolis** and then press Enter.
22. Click the Run button in the Results group. (This displays clients located in Indianapolis.)
23. Save, print, and then close the query.

Creating a Calculated Field

In Chapter 3, you learned how to insert a total row in a datasheet and then choose from a list of functions. You can also calculate values using a calculated control that uses a mathematical equation to determine the contents that display in the control object. In a query, you can insert a calculated field that performs mathematical equations by inserting a calculated field in the *Fields* text box. To insert a calculated field, click in the desired *Field* text box, type the desired field name followed by a colon, and then type the equation. For example, to add 2008 sales amounts with 2009 sales, you would type **Total:[Sales2008]+[Sales2009]** in the *Field* text box.

Project **1h** | **Creating a Calculated Field in a Query**

1. With the **Deering.accdb** database open, click the Create tab and then click the Query Wizard button in the Other group.
2. With *Simple Query Wizard* selected in the New Query dialog box, click OK.

3. At the first Simple Query Wizard dialog box, click the down-pointing arrow at the right of the *Tables/Queries* option box, and then click *Table: Clients*. (You will need to scroll up the list to display this table.)

4. Insert the *Client* field in the *Selected Fields* list box.

5. Click the down-pointing arrow at the right of the *Tables/Queries* option box, click *Table: Sales*, and then insert the following fields in the *Selected Fields* list box:
   Sales2008
   Sales2009

6. Click the Next button.

7. At the second Simple Query Wizard dialog box, click the Next button.

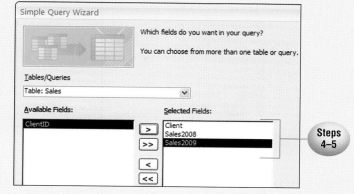

Steps 4–5

8. At the last Simple Query Wizard dialog box, select the current text in the *What title do you want for your query?* text box and then type **SalesTotals**.

9. Click the *Modify the query design* option and then click the Finish button.

10. At the query window, insert a calculated field that calculates the total sales for 2008 and 2009 for each client by completing the following steps:
    a. Click in the fourth *Field* text box.
    b. Type **Total:[Sales2008]+[Sales2009]** and then press Enter.

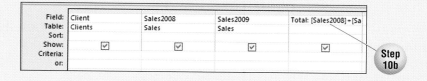

Step 10b

11. Click the Run button in the Results group. (All records will display with the total of the 2008 and 2009 sales.)

12. Save, print, and then close the query.

13. Close the **Deering.accdb** database.

14. Open the **OutdoorOptions.accdb** database.

15. Click the Create tab and then click the Query Wizard button in the Other group.

16. With the *Simple Query Wizard* option selected in the New Query dialog box, click OK.

17. At the first Simple Query Wizard dialog box, select *Table: Suppliers* in the *Tables/Queries* option box.

18. Insert the *SupplierName* field in the *Selected Fields* list box.

19. Click the down-pointing arrow at the right of the *Tables/Queries* option box, click *Table: Orders*, and then insert the following fields in the *Selected Fields* list box:
    Order#
    UnitsOrdered
    Amount

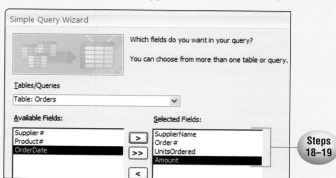

Steps 18–19

20. Click the Next button.

21. At the second Simple Query Wizard dialog box, click the Next button.
22. At the last Simple Query Wizard dialog box, select the current text in the *What title do you want for your query?* text box and then type UnitPrices.
23. Click the *Modify the query design* option and then click the Finish button.
24. At the query window, insert a calculated field that calculates the unit price by completing the following steps:
    a. Click in the fifth *Field* text box in the query design grid.
    b. Type UnitPrice:[Amount]*[UnitsOrdered] and then press Enter.

Field:	SupplierName	Order#	UnitsOrdered	Amount	UnitPrice: [Amount]*[U
Table:	Suppliers	Orders	Orders	Orders	
Sort:					
Show:	☑	☑	☑	☑	☑
Criteria:					
or:					

Step 24b

25. Click the Run button in the Results group. (All records will display with the unit price calculated for each order.)
26. Save, print, and then close the query.
27. Close the **OutdoorOptions.accdb** database.

Project 2 Create Aggregate Functions, Crosstab, Find Duplicates, and Find Unmatched Queries

You will create an aggregate functions query that determines the total, average, minimum, and maximum order amounts and determine total and average order amounts grouped by supplier. You will also use the Crosstab, Find Duplicates, and Find Unmatched query wizards to design queries.

Designing Queries with Aggregate Functions

You can include an aggregate function such as Sum, Avg, Min, Max, or Count in a query to calculate statistics from numeric field values of all the records in the table. When an aggregate function is used, Access displays one row in the query results datasheet with the formula result for the function used. For example, in a table with a numeric field containing the annual salary amounts, you could use the Sum function to calculate the total of all salary amount values.

To display the aggregate function list, click the Totals button in the Show/Hide group. Access adds a Total row to the design grid with a drop-down list from which you select the desired function. Access also inserts the words *Group By* in the list box. Click the down-pointing arrow and then click the desired aggregate function from the drop-down list. In Project 2a, you will create a query in Design view and use aggregate functions to find the total of all sales, the average sales amount, the maximum and the minimum sales, and the total number of sales. The completed query will display as shown in Figure 4.5. Access automatically chooses the column heading names.

Figure 4.5 Query Results for Project 2a

Access automatically determined the column heading names.

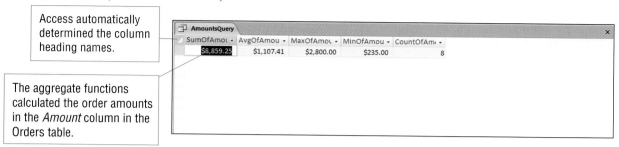

The aggregate functions calculated the order amounts in the *Amount* column in the Orders table.

Project 2a Using Aggregate Functions in a Query

1. Open the **OutdoorOptions.accdb** database.
2. Determine the total, average, minimum, and maximum order amounts as well as the total number of orders. To begin, click the Create tab and then click the Query Design button in the Other group.
3. At the Show Table dialog box, make sure *Orders* is selected in the list box, click the Add button, and then click the Close button.
4. Drag the *Amount* field to the first, second, third, fourth, and fifth *Field* text boxes.

Step 4

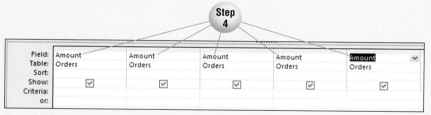

5. Click the Totals button in the Show/Hide group. (This adds a *Total* row to the design grid between *Table* and *Sort* with the default option of *Group By*.)
6. Specify a Sum function for the first *Group By* list box by completing the following steps:
   a. Click in the first *Group By* list box in the *Total* row.
   b. Click the down-pointing arrow that displays at the right side of the list box.
   c. Click *Sum* at the drop-down list.

Step 5

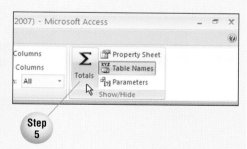

Step 6a   Step 6b

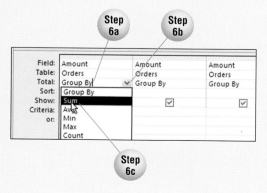

Step 6c

7. Complete steps similar to those in Step 6 to insert *Avg* in the second *Group By* list box in the *Total* row.
8. Complete steps similar to those in Step 6 to insert *Max* in the third *Group By* list box in the *Total* row.
9. Complete steps similar to those in Step 6 to insert *Min* in the fourth *Group By* list box in the *Total* row.
10. Complete steps similar to those in Step 6 to insert *Count* in the fifth *Group By* list box in the *Total* row.

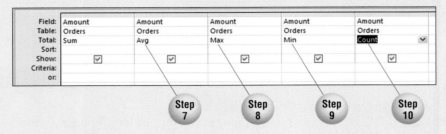

11. Click the Run button in the Results group. (Notice the headings that Access chooses for the columns.)
12. Save the query and name it *AmountsQuery*.
13. Automatically adjust the widths of the columns.
14. Print and then close the query.

Using the *Group By* option in the Total drop-down list you can add a field to the query upon which you want Access to group records for statistical calculations. For example, to calculate the total of all orders for a specific supplier, add the *Supplier#* field to the design grid with the Total set to *Group By*. In Project 2b, you will create a query in Design view and use aggregate functions to find the total of all order amounts and the average order amounts grouped by the supplier number.

Project 2b Using Aggregate Functions and Grouping Records

1. With the **OutdoorOptions.accdb** database open, determine the total and average order amounts for each supplier. To begin, click the Create tab and then click the Query Design button.
2. At the Show Table dialog box, make sure *Orders* is selected in the list box and then click the Add button.
3. Click *Suppliers* in the list box, click the Add button, and then click the Close button.
4. Insert the *Amount* field from the Orders table list box to the first *Field* text box.
5. Insert the *Amount* field from the Orders table list box to the second *Field* text box.
6. Insert the *Supplier#* field from the Orders table list box to the third *Field* text box.
7. Insert the *SupplierName* field from the Suppliers table to the fourth *Field* text box.

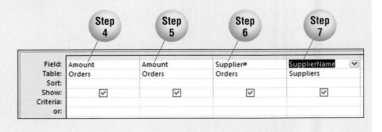

8. Click the Totals button in the Show/Hide group.
9. Click in the first *Group By* list box in the *Total* row, click the down-pointing arrow, and then click *Sum* at the drop-down list.
10. Click in the second *Group By* list box in the *Total* row, click the down-pointing arrow, and then click *Avg* at the drop-down list.
11. Make sure *Group By* displays in the third and fourth *Group By* list boxes.

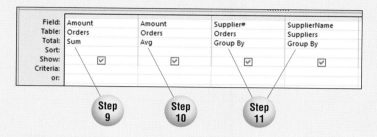

12. Click the Run button in the Results group.
13. Save the query and name it *SupplierAmountsQuery*.
14. Print and then close the query.

Creating a Crosstab Query

A crosstab query calculates aggregate functions such as Sum and Avg in which field values are grouped by two fields. A wizard is included that guides you through the steps to create the query. The first field selected causes one row to display in the query results datasheet for each group. The second field selected displays one column in the query results datasheet for each group. A third field is specified which is the numeric field to be summarized. The intersection of each row and column holds a value which is the result of the specified aggregate function for the designated row and column group.

Create a crosstab query from fields in one table. If you want to include fields from more than one table, you must first create a query containing the desired fields, and then create the crosstab query. For example, in Project 2c, you will create a new query that contains fields from each of the three tables in the OutdoorOptions.accdb database. Using this query, you will use the Crosstab Query Wizard to create a query that summarizes the order amounts by supplier name and by product ordered. Figure 4.6 displays the results of that crosstab query. The first column displays the supplier names, the second column displays the total of amounts for each supplier, and the remaining columns display the amounts by suppliers for specific items.

Create a Crosstab Query
1. Click Create tab.
2. Click Query Wizard button.
3. Double-click *Crosstab Query Wizard*.
4. Complete wizard steps.

Figure 4.6 Crosstab Query Results for Project 2c

In this query, the order amounts are grouped by supplier name and by individual product.

SupplierNam ▾	Total Of Amᵢ ▾	Backpack ▾	Ski goggles ▾	Snowboard ▾	Two-person ▾	Wool ski hat ▾
Freedom Corpᵢ	$1,787.50		$1,100.00			$687.50
KL Distribution	$3,043.75	$1,906.25			$1,137.50	
Rosewood, Inc	$2,800.00			$2,800.00		

OrdersBySupplierByProduct

Project 2c Creating a Crosstab Query

1. With the **OutdoorOptions.accdb** database open, create a query containing fields from the three tables by completing the following steps:
   a. Click the Create tab and then click the Query Design button.
   b. At the Show Table dialog box with *Orders* selected in the list box, click the Add button.
   c. Double-click *Products* in the Show Table dialog box.
   d. Double-click *Suppliers* in the list box and then click the Close button.
   e. Insert the following fields to the specified *Field* text boxes:
      1) From the Orders table, insert the *Product#* field to the first *Field* text box.
      2) From the Products table, insert the *Product* field to the second *Field* text box.
      3) From the Orders table, insert the *UnitsOrdered* field to the third *Field* text box.
      4) From the Orders table, insert the *Amount* field to the fourth *Field* text box.
      5) From the Suppliers table, insert the *SupplierName* field to the fifth *Field* text box.
      6) From the Orders table, insert the *OrderDate* field to the sixth *Field* text box.

Step 1e

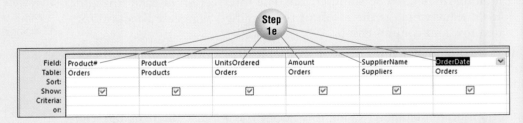

Field:	Product#	Product	UnitsOrdered	Amount	SupplierName	OrderDate	⌄
Table:	Orders	Products	Orders	Orders	Suppliers	Orders	
Sort:							
Show:	☑	☑	☑	☑	☑	☑	
Criteria:							
or:							

   f. Click the Run button to run the query.
   g. Save the query and name it *ItemsOrdered*.
   h. Close the query.
2. Create a crosstab query that summarizes the orders by supplier name and by product ordered by completing the following steps:
   a. Click the Create tab and then click the Query Wizard button.
   b. At the New Query dialog box, double-click *Crosstab Query Wizard* in the list box.

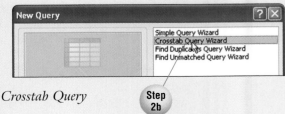

New Query

Simple Query Wizard
Crosstab Query Wizard
Find Duplicates Query Wizard
Find Unmatched Query Wizard

Step 2b

c. At the first Crosstab Query Wizard dialog box, click the *Queries* option in the *View* section and then click *Query: ItemsOrdered* in the list box.

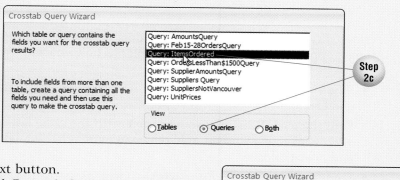

Step 2c

d. Click the Next button.
e. At the second Crosstab Query Wizard dialog box, click *SupplierName* in the *Available Fields* list box and then click the button containing the greater than (>) symbol. (This inserts *SupplierName* in the *Selected Fields* list box and specifies that you want *SupplierName* for the row headings.)

Step 2e

f. Click the Next button.
g. At the third Crosstab Query Wizard dialog box, click *Product* in the list box. (This specifies that you want *Product* for the column headings.)
h. Click the Next button.
i. At the fourth Crosstab Query Wizard dialog box, click *Amount* in the *Fields* list box and click *Sum* in the *Functions* list box.

Step 2g

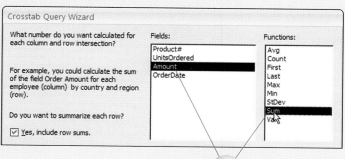

Step 2i

j. Click the Next button.
k. At the fifth Crosstab Query Wizard dialog box, select the current text in the *What do you want to name your query?* text box and then type **OrdersBySupplierByProduct**.

Step 2k

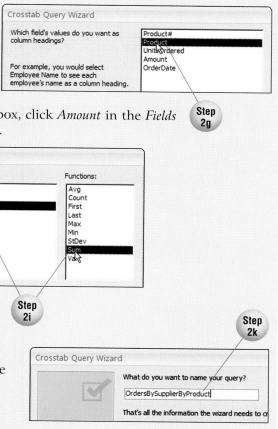

l. Click the Finish button.
3. Change the orientation to landscape and then print the query.
4. Close the OrdersBySupplierByProduct query.

Creating a Find Duplicates Query

Use the find duplicates query to search a specified table or query for duplicate field values within a designated field or fields. Create this type of query, for example, if you suspect a record, such as a product record has inadvertently been entered twice under two different product numbers. A find duplicates query has many applications. A few other examples of how you can use a find duplicates query include:

- Find the records in an Orders table with the same customer number so that you can identify your loyal customers.

- Find the records in a Customers table with the same last name and mailing address so that you send only one mailing to a household to save on printing and postage costs.

- Find the records in an EmployeeExpenses table with the same employee number so that you can see which employee is submitting the most claims.

Access provides the Find Duplicates Query Wizard that builds the select query based on the selections made in a series of dialog boxes. To use this wizard, open the desired table, click the Create tab, and then click the Query Wizard button. At the New Query dialog box, double-click *Find Duplicates Query Wizard* in the list box, and then complete the steps provided by the wizard.

In Project 2d, you will assume that you have been asked to update the address for a supplier in the OutdoorOptions.accdb database. Instead of updating the address, you create a new record. You will then use the Find Duplicates Query wizard to find duplicate field values in the Suppliers table.

Project 2d Creating a Find Duplicates Query

1. With the **OutdoorOptions.accdb** database open, double-click the *Suppliers: Table* option located in the *Suppliers* section of the Navigation pane.

2. Add the following record to the table:

Supplier#	29
SupplierName	Langley Corporation
StreetAddress	805 First Avenue
City	Burnaby
Province	BC
PostalCode	V5V 9K2
Email	lc@emcp.net

3. Close the Suppliers table.

4. Use the Find Duplicates Query wizard to find any duplicate supplier names by completing the following steps:

   a. Click the Create tab and then click the Query Wizard button.

   b. At the New Query dialog box, double-click *Find Duplicates Query Wizard*.

   c. At the first wizard dialog box, click *Table: Suppliers* in the list box.

   d. Click the Next button.

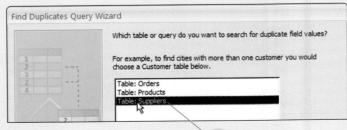

Step 4c

e. At the second wizard dialog box, click *SupplierName* in the *Available fields* list box and then click the button containing the greater than (>) symbol. (This moves the *SupplierName* field to the *Duplicate-value fields* list box.)

f. Click the Next button.

g. At the third wizard dialog box, click the button containing the two greater than (>>) symbols. (This moves all the fields to the *Additional query fields* list box. You are doing this because if you find a duplicate supplier name, you want to view all the fields to determine which record is accurate.)

h. Click the Next button.

i. At the fourth (and last) wizard dialog box, type **DuplicateSuppliers** in the *What do you want to name your query?* text box.

j. Click the Finish button.

k. Change the orientation to landscape and then print the DuplicateSuppliers query.

5. As you look at the query results, you realize that an inaccurate record was entered for Langley so you decide to delete one of the records. To do this, complete the following steps:

a. With the DuplicateSuppliers query open, click in the record selector bar next to the first record (the one with a Supplier# of *29*). (This selects the entire row.)

b. Click the Home tab and then click the Delete button in the Records group.

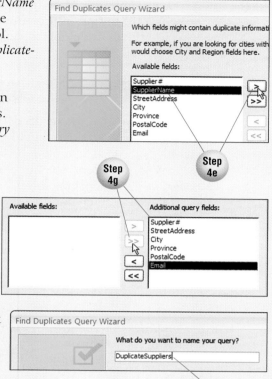

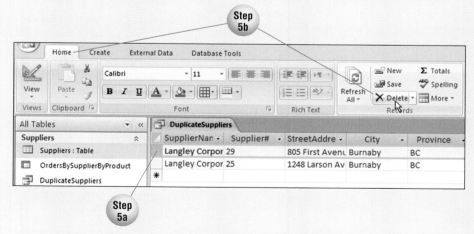

c. At the message asking you to confirm, click the Yes button.

d. Close the DuplicateSuppliers query.

6. Change the street address for Langley Corporation by completing the following steps:

a. Double-click the *Suppliers: Table* option located in the *Suppliers* section.

b. With the Suppliers table open in Datasheet view, change the address for Langley Corporation from *1248 Larson Avenue* to *805 First Avenue*. Leave the other fields as displayed.

c. Close the *Suppliers* table.

In Project 2d, you used the Find Duplicates Query Wizard to find records containing the same field. In Project 2e, you will use the Find Duplicates Query Wizard to find information on the suppliers you order from the most. You could use this information to negotiate for better prices or to ask for discounts.

Project 2e Finding Duplicate Orders

1. With the **OutdoorOptions.accdb** database open, create a query with the following fields (in the order shown) from the specified tables:

Order#	Orders table
Supplier#	Orders table
SupplierName	Suppliers table
Product#	Orders table
UnitsOrdered	Orders table
Amount	Orders table
OrderDate	Orders table

2. Run the query.
3. Save the query with the name *SupplierOrders* and then close the query.
4. Use the Find Duplicates Query Wizard to find the suppliers you order from the most by completing the following steps:

    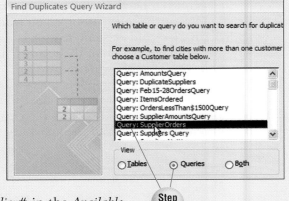

    a. Click the Create tab and then click the Query Wizard tab.
    b. At the New Query dialog box, double-click *Find Duplicates Query Wizard*.
    c. At the first wizard dialog box, click *Queries* in the *View* section, and then click *Query: SupplierOrders*. (You may need to scroll down the list to display this query.)
    d. Click the Next button.
    e. At the second wizard dialog box, click *Supplier#* in the *Available fields* list box and then click the button containing the greater than (>) symbol.
    f. Click the Next button.
    g. At the third wizard dialog box, click the button containing the two greater than (>>) symbols. (This moves all the fields to the *Additional query fields* list box.)
    h. Click the Next button.
    i. At the fourth (and last) wizard dialog box, type **DuplicateSupplierOrders** in the *What do you want to name your query?* text box.

    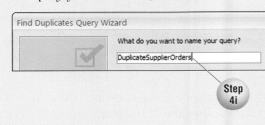

    j. Click the Finish button.
    k. Change the orientation to landscape and then print the DuplicateSupplierOrders query.
5. Close the query.

Creating an Unmatched Query

Create a find unmatched query to compare two tables and produce a list of the records in one table that have no matching record in the other related table. This type of query is useful to produce lists such as customers who have never placed an order or an invoice with no payment record. Access provides the Find Unmatched Query Wizard that builds the select query by guiding you through a series of dialog boxes.

In Project 2f, you will use the Find Unmatched Query Wizard to find all products that have no units on order. This information is helpful because it indicates which products are not selling and might need to be discontinued or returned. To use the Find Unmatched Query Wizard, click the Create tab and then click the Query Wizard button in the Other group. At the New Query dialog box, double-click *Find Unmatched Query Wizard* in the list box and then follow the wizard steps.

QUICK STEPS

Create an Unmatched Query
1. Click Create tab.
2. Click Query Wizard button.
3. Double-click *Find Unmatched Query Wizard*.
4. Complete wizard steps.

Project 2f Creating a Find Unmatched Query

1. With the **OutdoorOptions.accdb** database open, use the Find Unmatched Query Wizard to find all products that do not have any units on order by completing the following steps:
   a. Click the Create tab and then click the Query Wizard button.
   b. At the New Query dialog box, double-click *Find Unmatched Query Wizard*.
   c. At the first wizard dialog box, click *Table: Products* in the list box. (This is the table containing the fields you want to see in the query results.)
   d. Click the Next button.
   e. At the second wizard dialog box, make sure *Table: Orders* is selected in the list box. (This is the table containing the related records.)
   f. Click the Next button.
   g. At the third wizard dialog box, make sure *Product#* is selected in the *Fields in 'Products'* list box and in the *Fields in 'Orders'* list box.

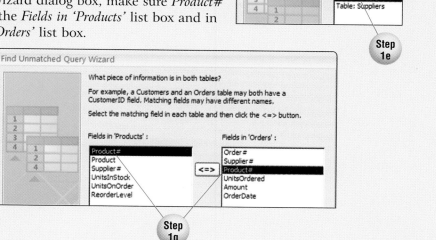

   h. Click the Next button.

i. At the fourth wizard dialog box, click the button containing the two greater than symbols (>>) to move all fields from the *Available fields* list box to the *Selected fields* list box.

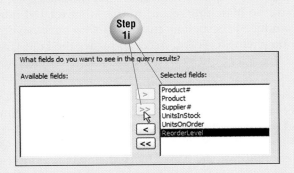

Step
1i

j. Click the Next button.
k. At the fifth wizard dialog box, click the Finish button. (Let the wizard determine the query name: *Products Without Matching Orders*.)
2. Print and then close the Products Without Matching Orders query.
3. Close the **OutdoorOptions.accdb** database.

CHAPTER summary

- Being able to extract specific information is one of the most important functions of a database. Data can be extracted from an Access database by performing a query, which can be accomplished by designing a query or using a query wizard.

- Designing a query consists of identifying the table, the field or fields from which the data will be drawn, and the criteria for selecting the data.

- During the designing of a query, write the criterion (or criteria) for extracting the specific data. Access inserts any necessary symbols in the criterion when the Enter key is pressed.

- In a criterion, quotation marks surround field values and pound symbols (#) surround dates. Use the asterisk (*) as a wildcard symbol.

- You can perform a query on fields within one table or on fields from related tables.

- When designing a query, you can specify the sort order of a field or fields.

- You can modify an existing query. To do this, double-click the query in the Navigation pane, click the View button to display the query in Design view, make the desired changes, and then click the Run button.

- Enter criterion in the *Or* row in the query design grid to instruct Access to display records that match either of the two criteria.

- Multiple criteria entered in the *Criteria* row in the query design grid become an *And* statement where each criterion must be met for Access to select the record.

- The Simple Query Wizard guides you through the steps for preparing a query. You can modify a query you create with the wizard.

- You can insert a calculated field in a *Field* text box when designing a query.

- Include an aggregate function such as Sum, Avg, Min, Max, or Count to calculate statistics from numeric field values. Click the Totals button in the Show/Hide group to display the aggregate function list.

- Use the *Group By* option in the Total drop-down list to add a field to a query upon which you want Access to group records for statistical calculations.

- Create a crosstab query to calculate aggregate functions such as Sum and Avg in which fields are grouped by two fields. Create a crosstab query from fields in one table. If you want to include fields from more than one table, create a query first, and then create the crosstab query.

- Use the find duplicates query to search a specified table or query for duplicate field values within a designated field or fields.

- Create a find unmatched query to compare two tables and produce a list of the records in one table that have no matching record in the other related table.

COMMANDS review

FEATURE	RIBBON TAB, GROUP	BUTTON, OPTION
Query design window	Create, Other	
Run query	Query Tools Design, Results	
New Query dialog box	Create, Other	
Simple Query Wizard	Create, Other	, Simple Query Wizard
Add Total row to query design	Query Tools Design, Show/Hide	Σ
Crosstab Query Wizard	Create, Other	, Crosstab Query Wizard
Find Duplicates Query Wizard	Create, Other	, Find Duplicates Query Wizard
Find Unmatched Query Wizard	Create, Other	, Find Unmatched Query Wizard

CONCEPTS check

Test Your Knowledge

Completion: For each description, indicate the correct term, symbol, or command.

1. The Query Design button is located in the Other group in this tab.

2. Click the Query Design button and the query window displays with this dialog box open.

3. To establish a criterion for the query, click in this text box in the column containing the desired field name and then type the criterion.

4. This is the term used for the results of the query.

5. This is the symbol Access automatically inserts around a date when writing a criterion for the query.

6. Use this symbol to indicate a wildcard character when writing a query criterion.

7. This is the criterion you would type to return field values greater than $500.

8. This is the criterion you would type to return field values that begin with the letter *L*.

_____

9. This is the criterion you would type to return field values that are not in Oregon.

_____

10. You can sort a field in a query in ascending order or this order.

_____

11. Enter a criterion in this row in the query design grid to instruct Access to display records that match either of the two criteria.

_____

12. This wizard guides you through the steps for preparing a query.

_____

13. This type of query calculates aggregate functions in which field values are grouped by two fields.

_____

14. Use this type of query to compare two tables and produce a list of the records in one table that have no matching record in the other related table.

_____

SKILLS check

Demonstrate Your Proficiency

Assessment

1 DESIGN QUERIES IN A LEGALSERVICES DATABASE

1. Display the Open dialog box with the Access2007L1C4 folder active, remove the read-only attribute from the **LegalServices.accdb** database, and then open **LegalServices.accdb**.
2. Design a query that extracts records from the Billing table with the following specifications:
   a. Include the fields *Billing#*, *ClientID*, and *Category* in the query.
   b. Extract those records with the *SE* category.
   c. Save the query and name it *SECategoryBillingQuery*.
   d. Print and then close the query.
3. Design a query that extracts records from the Billing table with the following specifications:
   a. Include the fields *Billing#*, *ClientID*, and *Date*.
   b. Extract those records in the *Date* field with dates between 6/8/2010 and 6/10/2010.
   c. Save the query and name it *June8-10BillingQuery*.
   d. Print and then close the query.

4. Design a query that extracts records from the Clients table with the following specifications:
   a. Include the fields *FirstName*, *LastName*, and *City*.
   b. Extract those records with any city other than Kent in the *City* field.
   c. Save the query and name it *ClientsNotInKentQuery*.
   d. Print and then close the query.
5. Design a query that extracts information from two tables with the following specifications:
   a. Include the fields *Billing#*, *ClientID*, *Date*, and *Rate#* from the Billing table.
   b. Include the field *Rate* from the Rates table.
   c. Extract those records with a rate number greater than 2.
   d. Save the query and name it *RateGreaterThan2Query*.
   e. Print and then close the query.
6. Design a query that extracts information from three tables with the following specifications:
   a. Include the field *Attorney* from the Attorneys table.
   b. Include the fields *FirstName* and *LastName* from the Clients table.
   c. Include the fields *AttorneyID*, *Date,* and *Hours* from the Billing table.
   d. Extract those records with an *AttorneyID* of 12.
   e. Save the query and name it *Attorney12Query*.
   f. Print and then close the query.
7. Design a query that extracts records from four tables with the following specifications:
   a. Add the Attorneys, Billing, Rates, and Clients tables to the query window.
   b. Insert the *Attorney* field from the Attorneys table to the first *Field* text box.
   c. Insert the *AttorneyID* field from the Billing table to the second *Field* text box.
   d. Insert the *Rate#* field from the Billing table to the third *Field* text box.
   e. Insert the *Rate* field from the Rates table to the fourth *Field* text box.
   f. Insert the *FirstName* field from the Clients table to the fifth *Field* text box.
   g. Insert the *LastName* field from the Clients table to the sixth *Field* text box.
   h. Extract those records with an *AttorneyID* of 17 and a *Rate#* of 4.
   i. Run the query.
   j. Save the query and name it *Attorney17Rate4*.
   k. Print and then close the query.

Assessment

2 USE THE SIMPLE QUERY WIZARD AND DESIGN QUERIES

1. With **LegalServices.accdb** database open, use the Simple Query Wizard to extract specific information from two tables with the following specifications:
   a. At the first Simple Query Wizard dialog box, include the following fields:
      From Attorneys table: *AttorneyID* and *Attorney*
      From Categories table: *CategoryName*
      From Billing table: *Hours*
   b. At the second Simple Query Wizard dialog box, click Next.
   c. At the third Simple Query Wizard dialog box, click the *Modify the query design* option, and then click the Finish button.
   d. At the query window, insert *14* in the *Criteria* text box in the *AttorneyID* column.
   e. Run the query.

x

f. Save the query with the default name.
g. Print and then close the query.
2. Create a query in Design view with the Billing table with the following specifications:
   a. Insert the *Hours* field from the Billing table to the first, second, third, and fourth *Field* text boxes.
   b. Click the Totals button in the Show/Hide group.
   c. Insert *Sum* in the first *Group By* list box in the *Total* row.
   d. Insert *Min* in the second *Group By* list box in the *Total* row.
   e. Insert *Max* in the third *Group By* list box in the *Total* row.
   f. Insert *Count* in the fourth *Group By* list box in the *Total* row.
   g. Run the query.
   h. Save the query and name it *HoursAmountQuery*.
   i. Automatically adjust the widths of the columns.
   j. Print and then close the query.
3. Create a query in Design view with the following specifications:
   a. Add the Attorneys table and the Billing table to the query window.
   b. Insert the *Attorney* field from the Attorneys table to the first *Field* text box.
   c. Insert the *AttorneyID* field from the Billing table to the second *Field* text box.
   d. Insert the *Hours* field from the Billing table to the third *Field* text box.
   e. Click the Totals button in the Show/Hide group.
   f. Insert *Sum* in the third *Group By* list box in the *Hours* column (in the *Total* row).
   g. Run the query.
   h. Save the query and name it *AttorneyHours*.
   i. Print and then close the query.
4. Create a query in Design view with the following specifications:
   a. Add the Attorneys, Clients, Categories, and Billing tables to the query window.
   b. Insert the *Attorney* field from the Attorneys table to the first *Field* text box.
   c. Insert the *ClientID* field from the Clients table to the second *Field* text box.
   d. Insert the *CategoryName* field from the Categories table to the third *Field* text box.
   e. Insert the *Hours* field from the Billing table to the fourth *Field* text box.
   f. Run the query.
   g. Save the query and name it *AttorneyClientHours*.
   h. Print and then close the query.

Assessment

3 CREATE A CROSSTAB QUERY AND USE THE FIND DUPLICATES AND FIND UNMATCHED QUERY WIZARDS

1. With the **LegalServices.accdb** database open, create a crosstab query that summarizes the hours by attorney by category with the following specifications:
   a. At the first Crosstab Query Wizard dialog box, click the *Queries* option in the *View* section, and then click *Query: AttorneyClientHours* in the list box.
   b. At the second Crosstab Query Wizard dialog box, click *Attorney* in the *Available Fields* list box and then click the button containing the greater than (>) symbol.
   c. At the third Crosstab Query Wizard dialog box, click *CategoryName* in the list box.
   d. At the fourth Crosstab Query Wizard dialog box, click *Hours* in the *Fields* list box and click *Sum* in the *Functions* list box.

e. At the fifth Crosstab Query Wizard dialog box, type **HoursByAttorneyByCategory** in the *What do you want to name your query?* text box.

f. Print the query in landscape orientation and then close the query.

2. Use the Find Duplicates Query Wizard to find those clients with the same last name with the following specifications:

a. At the first wizard dialog box, click *Table: Clients* in the list box.

b. At the second wizard dialog box, click *LastName* in the *Available fields* list box and then click the button containing the greater than (>) symbol.

c. At the third wizard dialog box, click the button containing the two greater than (>>) symbols.

d. At the fourth wizard dialog box, name the query *DuplicateLastNames*.

e. Print the query in landscape orientation and then close the query.

3. Use the Find Unmatched Query Wizard to find all clients who do not have any billing hours with the following specifications:

a. At the first wizard dialog box, click *Table: Clients* in the list box.

b. At the second wizard dialog box, click *Table: Billing* in the list box.

c. At the third wizard dialog box, make sure *ClientID* is selected in the *Fields in 'Products'* list box and in the *Fields in 'Orders'* list box.

d. At the fourth wizard dialog box, click the button containing the two greater than symbols (>>) to move all fields from the *Available fields* list box to the *Selected fields* list box.

e. At the fifth wizard dialog box, click the Finish button. (Let the wizard determine the query name: *Clients Without Matching Billing*.)

4. Print the query in landscape orientation and then close the Clients Without Matching Billing query.

5. Close the **LegalServices.accdb** database.

Assessment

DESIGN AND HIDE FIELDS IN A QUERY

1. You can use the check boxes in the query design grid *Show* row to show or hide fields in the query. Experiment with these check boxes and then open the **LegalServices.accdb** database and design the following query:

a. At the Show Table dialog box, add the Billing table, the Clients table, and the Rates table.

b. At the query window, insert the following fields to *Field* text boxes:

> Clients table:
> > *FirstName*
> > *LastName*
> Billing table:
> > *Hours*
> Rates table:
> > *Rate*

c. Insert in the fifth *Field* text box the calculated field *Total:*[Hours]*[Rate].

d. Hide the *Hours* and the *Rate* fields.

e. Run the query.

f. Save the query and name it *ClientBillingQuery*.

g. Print and then close the query.

2. Close the **LegalServices.accdb** database.

CASE study

Apply Your Skills

You work for the Skyline Restaurant in Fort Myers, Florida. Your supervisor is reviewing the restaurant operations and has asked for a number of query reports. Before running queries, you realize that the tables in the restaurant database, **Skyline.accdb**, are not related. Open the **Skyline.accdb** database and then create the following relationships:

Field Name	"One" Table	"Many" Table
EmployeeID	Employees	Banquets
Item#	Inventory	Orders
SupplierID	Suppliers	Orders
EventID	Events	Banquets

Save and then print the relationships.

As part of the review of the restaurant records, your supervisor has asked you for the following information. Create a separate query for each bulleted item listed below and save, name, and print the queries (you determine the name).

- Suppliers in Fort Myers (include supplier identification number, supplier name, and telephone number)
- Suppliers that are not located in Fort Myers (include supplier identification number, supplier name, and telephone number)
- Employees hired in 2007 (include employee identification number, first and last names, and hire date)
- Wedding receptions booked in the banquet room (include the reservation identification number; reservation date; and last name, first name, and telephone number of the person making the reservation)
- Banquet reservations booked between 6/15/2010 and 6/30/2010 (include reservation identification number; reservation date; and last name, first name, and telephone number of the person making the reservation)
- Banquet reservations that have not been confirmed (include reservation identification number and first name, last name, and telephone number)
- Names of employees that are signed up for health insurance (include employee first and last names)
- Items ordered from supplier number 4 (include the item number, item, supplier name, and supplier telephone number)
- Banquet room reserved by someone whose last name begins with "Wie" (include the first and last names of the employee who booked the reservation and the first and last names and telephone number of the person making the reservation)
- A query that inserts a calculated field that calculates the total of the number of units ordered by the unit price (information located in the Orders table) for all orders for supplier number 2

Design at least three additional queries that require fields from at least two tables. Run the queries and then save and print the queries. In Microsoft Word, write the query information and include specific information about each query and format the document to enhance the visual appeal. Save the document and name it **Access_C4_CS_P3**. Print and then close **Access_C4_CS_P3.docx**.

Creating Tables and Queries

ASSESSING proficiency

In this unit, you have learned to design, create, and modify tables and to create one-to-many relationships and one-to-one relationships between tables. You also learned how to perform queries on data in tables.

Note: Before beginning unit assessments, delete the Access2007L1C4 folder from your storage medium. Next, copy to your storage medium the Access2007L1U1 subfolder from the Access2007L1 folder on the CD that accompanies this textbook and then make Access2007L1U1 the active folder.

Assessment 1 Create Tables in a Cornerstone Catering Database

1. Use Access to create tables for Cornerstone Catering. Name the database **Cornerstone**. Create a table named *Employees* that includes the following fields (you determine the field name, data type, field size, and description):
   Employee# (primary key)
   FirstName
   LastName
   CellPhone (Consider using the Input Mask Wizard for this field.)
2. After creating the table, switch to Datasheet view and then enter the following data in the appropriate fields:

   Employee#: 10   *Employee#*: 14
   FirstName: Erin   *FirstName*: Mikio
   LastName: Jergens   *LastName*: Ogami
   CellPhone: (505) 555-3193   *CellPhone*: (505) 555-1087

   Employee#: 19   *Employee#*: 21
   FirstName: Martin   *FirstName*: Isabelle
   LastName: Vaughn   *LastName*: Baptista
   CellPhone: (505) 555-4461   *CellPhone*: (505) 555-4425

   Employee#: 24   *Employee#*: 26
   FirstName: Shawn   *FirstName*: Madison
   LastName: Kettering   *LastName*: Harris
   CellPhone: (505) 555-3885   *CellPhone*: (505) 555-2256

3. Automatically adjust the column widths.
4. Save, print, and then close the Employees table.

5. Create a table named *Plans* that includes the following fields:
   PlanCode (primary key)
   Plan
6. After creating the table, switch to Datasheet view and then enter the following data in the appropriate fields:

   PlanCode: A
   Plan: Sandwich Buffet

   PlanCode: B
   Plan: Cold Luncheon Buffet

   PlanCode: C
   Plan: Hot Luncheon Buffet

   PlanCode: D
   Plan: Combination Dinner

7. Automatically adjust the column widths.
8. Save, print, and then close the Plans table.
9. Create a table named *Prices* that includes the following fields:
   PriceCode (primary key)
   PricePerPerson (identify this data type as Currency)
10. After creating the table, switch to Datasheet view and then enter the following data in the appropriate fields:

    PriceCode: 1
    PricePerPerson: $11.50

    PriceCode: 2
    PricePerPerson: $12.75

    PriceCode: 3
    PricePerPerson: $14.50

    PriceCode: 4
    PricePerPerson: $16.00

    PriceCode: 5
    PricePerPerson: $18.50

11. Automatically adjust the column widths.
12. Save, print, and then close the Prices table.
13. Create a table named *Clients* that includes the following fields:
    Client# (primary key)
    ClientName
    StreetAddress
    City
    State
    ZipCode
    Telephone (Consider using the Input Mask Wizard for this field.)
14. After creating the table, switch to Datasheet view and then enter the following data in the appropriate fields:

    Client#: 104
    ClientName: Sarco Corporation
    StreetAddress: 340 Cordova Road
    City: Santa Fe
    State: NM
    ZipCode: 87510
    Telephone: (505) 555-3880

    Client#: 155
    ClientName: Creative Concepts
    StreetAddress: 1026 Market Street
    City: Los Alamos
    State: NM
    ZipCode: 87547
    Telephone: (505) 555-1200

Client#: 218	*Client#:* 286
ClientName: Allenmore Systems	*ClientName:* Sol Enterprises
StreetAddress: 7866 Second Street	*StreetAddress:* 120 Cerrillos Road
City: Espanola	*City:* Santa Fe
State: NM	*State:* NM
ZipCode: 87535	*ZipCode:* 87560
Telephone: (505) 555-3455	*Telephone:* (505) 555-7700

15. Automatically adjust the column widths and change the orientation to landscape.
16. Save, print, and then close the Clients table.
17. Create a table named *Events* that includes the following fields:
    Event# (primary key; identify this data type as AutoNumber)
    Client#
    Employee#
    DateOfEvent (identify this data type as Date/Time)
    PlanCode
    PriceCode
    NumberOfPeople (identify this data type as Number)
18. After creating the table, switch to Datasheet view and then enter the following data in the appropriate fields:

Event#: (AutoNumber)	*Event#:* (AutoNumber)
Client#: 218	*Client#:* 104
Employee#: 14	*Employee#:* 19
DateOfEvent: 7/1/2010	*DateOfEvent:* 7/2/2010
PlanCode: B	*PlanCode:* D
PriceCode: 3	*PriceCode:* 5
NumberOfPeople: 250	*NumberOfPeople:* 120
Event#: (AutoNumber)	*Event#:* (AutoNumber)
Client#: 155	*Client#:* 286
Employee#: 24	*Employee#:* 10
DateOfEvent: 7/8/2010	*DateOfEvent:* 7/9/2010
PlanCode: A	*PlanCode:* C
PriceCode: 1	*PriceCode:* 4
NumberOfPeople: 300	*NumberOfPeople:* 75
Event#: (AutoNumber)	*Event#:* (AutoNumber)
Client#: 218	*Client#:* 104
Employee#: 14	*Employee#:* 10
DateOfEvent: 7/10/2010	*DateOfEvent:* 7/12/2010
PlanCode: C	PlanCode: B
PriceCode: 4	*PriceCode:* 3
NumberOfPeople: 50	*NumberOfPeople:* 30

19. Automatically adjust the column widths and change the orientation to landscape.
20. Save, print, and then close the Events table.

Assessment 2 Create Relationships between Tables

1. With the **Cornerstone.accdb** database open, create the following one-to-many relationships:
   a. *Client#* in the Clients table is the "one" and *Client#* in the Events table is the "many."
   b. *Employee#* in the Employees table is the "one" and *Employee#* in the Events table is the "many."
   c. *PlanCode* in the Plans table is the "one" and *PlanCode* in the Events table is the "many."
   d. *PriceCode* in the Prices table is the "one" and *PriceCode* in the Events table is the "many."
2. Save and then print the relationships.

Assessment 3 Modify Tables

1. With the **Cornerstone.accdb** database open, open the Plans table in Datasheet view and then add the following record at the end of the table:
   PlanCode: E
   Plan: Hawaiian Luau Buffet
2. Save, print, and then close the Plans table.
3. Open the Events table in Datasheet view and then add the following record at the end of the table:
   Event#: (AutoNumber)
   Client#: 104
   Employee#: 21
   Date: 7/16/2010
   PlanCode: E
   PriceCode: 5
   NumberOfPeople: 125
4. Save, print (in landscape orientation), and then close the Events table.

Assessment 4 Design Queries

1. With the **Cornerstone.accdb** database open, create a query to extract records from the Events table with the following specifications:
   a. Include the fields *Client#*, *DateOfEvent*, and *PlanCode*.
   b. Extract those records with a PlanCode of C.
   c. Save the query and name it *PlanCodeC*.
   d. Print and then close the query.
2. Extract records from the Clients table with the following specifications:
   a. Include the fields *ClientName*, *City*, and *Telephone*.
   b. Extract those records with a city of Santa Fe.
   c. Save the query and name it *SantaFeClients*.
   d. Print and then close the query.
3. Extract information from two tables with the following specifications:
   a. From the Clients table, include the fields *ClientName* and *Telephone*.
   b. From the Events table, include the fields *DateOfEvent*, *PlanCode*, and *NumberOfPeople*.
   c. Extract those records with a date between July 10 and July 25, 2010.
   d. Save the query and name it *July10-25Events*.
   e. Print and then close the query.

Assessment 5 Design a Query with a Calculated Field Entry

1. With the **Cornerstone.accdb** database open, create a query in Design view with the Events table and the Prices table and insert the following fields to the specified locations:
   a. Insert *Event#* from the Events table to the first *Field* text box.
   b. Insert *DateOfEvent* from the Events table to the second *Field* text box.
   c. Insert *NumberOfPeople* from the Events table to the third *Field* text box.
   d. Insert *PricePerPerson* from the Prices table to the fourth *Field* text box.
2. Insert the following calculated field entry in the fifth *Field* text box: *Amount:[NumberOfPeople]*[PricePerPerson]*.
3. Run the query.
4. Save the query and name it *EventAmounts*.
5. Print and then close the query.

Assessment 6 Design a Query with Aggregate Functions

1. With the **Cornerstone.accdb** database open, create a query in Design view using the EventAmounts query with the following specifications:
   a. At the Cornerstone : Database window, click the Create tab and then click the Query Design button.
   b. At the Show Tables dialog box, click the Queries tab.
   c. Double-click *EventAmounts* in the list box and then click the Close button.
   d. Insert the *Amount* field to the first, second, third, and fourth *Field* text boxes.
   e. Click the Totals button in the Show/Hide group.
   f. Insert *Sum* in the first *Group By* list box in the *Total* row.
   g. Insert *Avg* in the second *Group By* list box in the *Total* row.
   h. Insert *Min* in the third *Group By* list box in the *Total* row.
   i. Insert *Max* in the fourth *Group By* list box in the *Total* row.
2. Run the query.
3. Automatically adjust the column widths.
4. Save the query and name it *AmountTotals*.
5. Print and then close the query.

Assessment 7 Design a Query Using Fields from Tables and a Query

1. With the **Cornerstone.accdb** database open, create a query in Design view using the Employees table, the Clients table, the Events table, and the EventAmounts query with the following specifications:
   a. At the Cornerstone : Database window, click the Create tab and then click the Query Design tab.
   b. At the Show Tables dialog box, double-click *Employees*.
   c. Double-click *Clients*.
   d. Double-click *Events*.
   e. Click the Queries tab, double-click *EventAmounts* in the list box, and then click the Close button.
   f. Insert the *LastName* field from the Employees table to the first *Field* text box.
   g. Insert the *ClientName* field from the Clients table to the second *Field* text box.
   h. Insert the *Amount* field from the EventAmounts query to the third *Field* text box.

i. Insert the *DateOfEvent* field from the Events table to the fourth *Field* text box.
2. Run the query.
3. Save the query and name it *EmployeeEvents*.
4. Close the query.
5. Using the Crosstab Query Wizard, create a query that summarizes the total amount of events by employee by client using the following specifications:
   a. At the first Crosstab Query Wizard dialog box, click the *Queries* option in the *View* section, and then click *Query: EmployeeEvents* in the list box.
   b. At the second Crosstab Query Wizard dialog box, click *Last Name* in the *Available Fields* list box and then click the button containing the greater than (>) symbol.
   c. At the third Crosstab Query Wizard dialog box, make sure *ClientName* is selected in the list box.
   d. At the fourth Crosstab Query Wizard dialog box, make sure *Amount* is selected in the *Fields* list box, and then click *Sum* in the *Functions* list box.
   e. At the fifth Crosstab Query Wizard dialog box, type AmountsByEmployeeByClient in the *What do you want to name your query?* text box.
6. Automatically adjust the column widths and change the orientation to landscape.
7. Print and then close the AmountsByEmployeeByClient query.

Assessment 8 Use the Find Duplicates Query Wizard

1. With the **Cornerstone.accdb** database open, use the Find Duplicates Query Wizard to find employees who are responsible for at least two events with the following specifications:
   a. At the first wizard dialog box, double-click *Table: Events* in the list box.
   b. At the second wizard dialog box, click *Employee#* in the *Available fields* list box and then click the button containing the greater than (>) symbol.
   c. At the third wizard dialog box, move the *DateOfEvent* field and the *NumberOfPeople* field from the *Available fields* list box to the *Additional query fields* list box.
   d. At the fourth wizard dialog box, name the query *DuplicateEvents*.
2. Print and then close the DuplicateEvents query.

Assessment 9 Use the Find Unmatched Query Wizard

1. With the **Cornerstone.accdb** database open, use the Find Unmatched Query Wizard to find any employees who do not have an upcoming event scheduled with the following specifications:
   a. At the first wizard dialog box, click *Table: Employees* in the list box.
   b. At the second wizard dialog box, click *Table: Events* in the list box.
   c. At the third wizard dialog box, make sure *Employee#* is selected in the *Fields in 'Employees'* list box and in the *Fields in 'Events'* list box.
   d. At the fourth wizard dialog box, click the button containing the two greater than symbols (>>) to move all fields from the *Available fields* list box to the *Selected fields* list box.
   e. At the fifth wizard dialog box, click the Finish button. (Let the wizard determine the query name: *Employees Without Matching Events*.)
2. Print and then close the *Employees Without Matching Events* query.

WRITING activities

The following activities give you the opportunity to practice your writing skills along with demonstrating an understanding of some of the important Access features you have mastered in this unit. Use correct grammar, appropriate word choices, and clear sentence constructions.

Create a Payroll Table and Word Report

The manager of Cornerstone Catering has asked you to add information to the **Cornerstone.accdb** database on employee payroll. You need to create another table that will contain information on payroll. The manager wants the table to include the following (you determine the appropriate field name, data type, field size, and description):

Employee Number: 10
Status: Full-time
Monthly Salary: $2,850

Employee Number: 14
Status: Part-time
Monthly Salary: $1,500

Employee Number: 19
Status: Part-time
Monthly Salary: $1,400

Employee Number: 21
Status: Full-time
Monthly Salary: $2,500

Employee Number: 24
Status: Part-time
Monthly Salary: $1,250

Employee Number: 26
Status: Part-time
Monthly Salary: $1,000

Print and then close the payroll table. Open Word and then write a report to the manager detailing how you created the table. Include a title for the report, steps on how the table was created, and any other pertinent information. Save the completed report and name it **Access_U01_Act01**. Print and then close **Access_U01_Act01.docx**.

INTERNET research

Vehicle Search

In this activity you will search the Internet for information on different vehicles before doing actual test drives. Learning about a major product, such as a vehicle, can increase your chances of finding a good buy, can potentially guide you away from a poor purchase, and can help speed up the process of narrowing the search to the type of vehicle that will meet your needs. Before you begin, list the top five criteria you would look for in a vehicle. For example, it must be a four-door vehicle, needs to be four-wheel drive, etc.

Using key search words, find at least two Web sites that list vehicle reviews. Use the search engines provided within the different review sites to find vehicles that fulfill the criteria you listed to meet your particular needs. Create a database in Access and create a table in that database that will contain the results from your vehicle search. Design the table keeping in mind what type of data you need to record for each vehicle that meets your requirements. Include at least the make, model, year, price, description, and special problems in the table. Also, include the ability to rate the vehicle as poor, fair, good, or excellent. You will decide on the rating of each vehicle depending on your findings.

Microsoft®

access

Unit 2:   Creating Forms and Reports

➤ Creating Forms

➤ Creating Reports and Mailing Labels

➤ Modifying, Filtering, and Viewing Data

➤ Importing and Exporting Data

Benchmark Microsoft® Access 2007 Level 1

Microsoft Certified Application Specialist Skills—Unit 2

Reference No.	Skill	Pages
2	**Creating and Formatting Database Elements**	
2.5	Create forms	
2.5.3	Create multiple item forms	168-169
2.5.4	Create split forms	166-167
2.5.6	Create PivotTable forms	229-231
2.5.7	Create forms using Layout view	154-166
2.5.8	Create simple forms	147-152
2.6	Create reports	
2.6.1	Create reports as a simple report	183-185
2.6.2	Create reports using the Report Wizard	198-203
2.6.6	Set the print layout	185-186
2.6.7	Create labels using the Label Wizard	203-206
2.7	Modify the design of reports and forms	
2.7.7	Apply AutoFormats to forms and reports	164-166, 194, 196-198
3	**Entering and Modifying Data**	
3.2	Navigate among records	149-150
3.5	Import data	
3.5.1	Import data from a specific source	260-261
3.5.2	Link to external data sources	262-263

Note: The Level 1 and Level 2 texts each address approximately half of the Microsoft Certified Application Specialist skills. Complete coverage of the skills is offered in the combined Level 1 and Level 2 text titled *Benchmark Series Microsoft® Access 2007: Levels 1 and 2,* which has been approved as certified courseware and which displays the Microsoft Certified Application Specialist logo on the cover.

Creating Forms

PERFORMANCE OBJECTIVES

Upon successful completion of Chapter 5, you will be able to:

- Create a form using the Form button
- Change views in a form
- Print and navigate in a form
- Add records to and delete records from a form
- Customize a form with options at the Form Layout Tools Format tab
- Create a form using the Simple Form button
- Create a form using the Multiple Items button
- Create a form using the Form Wizard

access Chapter 5

In this chapter, you will learn to create forms from database tables, improving the data display and making data entry easier. Access offers several methods for presenting data on the screen for easier data entry. You will create a form using the Form, Split Form, and Multiple Items buttons as well as the Form Wizard. You will also learn how to customize control objects in a form.

Note: Before beginning computer projects, delete the Access2007L1U1 folder from your storage medium. Next, copy to your storage medium the Access2007L1C5 subfolder from the Access2007L1 folder on the CD that accompanies this textbook and make Access2007L1C5 the active folder.

Project 1 Create Forms with the Form Button

You will use the Form button to create forms with fields in the Clients, Representatives, and Sales tables. You will also add, delete, and print records and use buttons in the Form Layout Tools Format tab to apply formatting to control objects in the forms.

Create a Form with Form Button
1. Click desired table.
2. Click Create tab.
3. Click Form button.

HINT
A form allows you to focus on a single record at a time.

HINT
Save a form before making changes or applying formatting to the form.

Form

Creating a Form

Access offers a variety of options for presenting data in a more easily read and attractive format. When entering data in a table in Datasheet view, multiple records display at the same time. If a record contains several fields, you may not be able to view all fields within a record at the same time. If you create a form, generally all fields for a record are visible on the screen. Several methods are available for creating a form. In this section, you will learn how to create a form using the Form, Split Form, and Multiple Items buttons as well as the Form Wizard.

Creating a Form with the Form Button

You can view, add, or edit data in a table in Datasheet view. You can also perform these functions on data inserted in a form. A form is an object you can use to enter and edit data in a table or query and is a user-friendly interface for viewing, adding, editing, and deleting records. A form is also useful in helping prevent incorrect data from being entered and it can be used to control access to specific data.

You can use a variety of methods to create a form. The simplest method to create a form is to click the Create tab and then click the Form button in the Forms groups. Figure 5.1 displays the form you will create in Project 1a with the Clients table in the Deering.accdb database. Access creates the form using all fields in the table in a vertical layout and displays the form in Layout view with the Form Layout Tools Format tab active.

Figure 5.1 Form Created from Data in the Clients Table

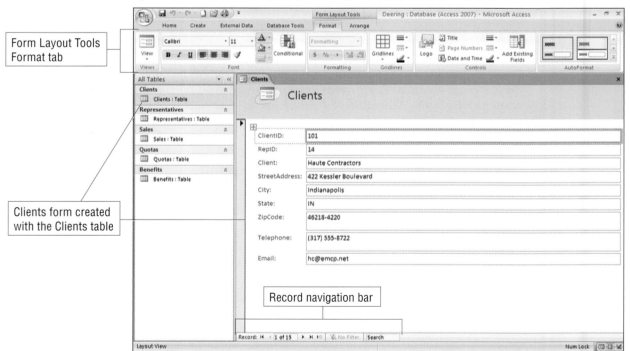

Changing Views

When you click the Form button to create a form, the form displays in Layout view. This is one of three views you can use when working with forms. Use the Form view to enter and manage records. Use the Layout view to view the data as well as modify the appearance and contents of the form and use the Design view to view the structure of the form and modify the form. Change views with the View button in the Views group in the Form Layout Tools Format tab or with buttons in the view area located at the right side of the Status bar.

Printing a Form

Print all records in the form by clicking the Quick Print button on the Quick Access toolbar or by displaying the Print dialog box with *All* selected in the *Print Range* section and then clicking OK. If you want to print a specific record, display the desired record and then display the Print dialog box. At the Print dialog box, click the *Selected Record(s)* option and then click OK. You can also print a range of records by clicking the *Pages* option in the *Print Range* section of the Print dialog box and then entering the beginning record number in the *From* text box and the ending record number in the *To* text box.

Print Specific Record
1. Display form.
2. Click Office button, *Print.*
3. Click *Selected Record(s).*
4. Click OK.

Navigating in a Form

When a form displays in either Form view or Layout view, navigation buttons display along the bottom of the form in the Record navigation bar as identified in Figure 5.1. Using these navigation buttons, you can display the first record in the form, the previous record, the next record, the last record, and a new record.

Along with the Record navigation bar, you can display records in a form using the keyboard. Press the Page Down key to move forward a single record or press the Page Up key to move back a single record. Press Ctrl + Home to display the first record or Press Ctrl + End to display the last record.

First record   Previous record

Next record   Last record

Project 1a   Creating a Form with the Clients Table

1. Remove the read-only attribute from the **Deering.accdb** database located in the Access2007L1C5 folder.
2. Open the **Deering.accdb** database.
3. Create a form with the Clients table by completing the following steps:
   a. Click the Clients table in the Navigation pane.
   b. Click the Create tab.
   c. Click the Form button in the Forms group.

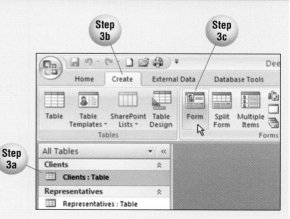

4. Switch to the Form view by clicking the View button in the Views group in the Form Layout Tools Format tab.

5. Navigate in the form by completing the following steps:
   a. Click the Next record button in the Record navigation bar to display the next record.
   b. Click the Last record button in the Record navigation bar to display the last record.
   c. Click the First record button in the Record navigation bar to display the first record.

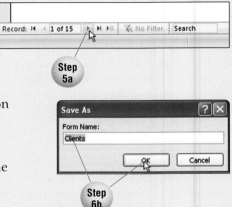

6. Save the form by completing the following steps:
   a. Click the Save button on the Quick Access toolbar.
   b. At the Save As dialog box, with *Clients* inserted in the *Form Name* text box, click OK.

7. Change orientation and print the current record in the form by completing the following steps:
   a. Display Print Preview, change the orientation to landscape, and then close Print Preview.
   b. Click the Office button and then click *Print* at the drop-down menu.
   c. At the Print dialog box, click the *Select Record(s)* option in the *Print Range* section and then click OK.

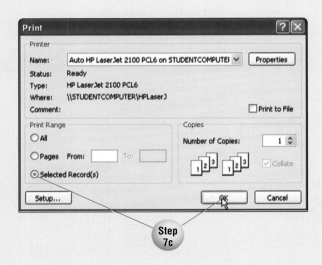

Adding and Deleting Records

Add a new record to the form by clicking the New (blank) record button (contains a right arrow followed by a yellow asterisk) that displays in the Record navigation bar along the bottom of the form. You can also add a new record to a form by clicking the Home tab and then clicking the New button in the Records group. To delete a record, display the record, click the Home tab, click the Delete button arrow in the Records group, and then click *Delete Record* at the drop-down list. At the message telling you that the record will be deleted permanently, click Yes.

Sorting Records

You can sort data in a form by clicking in the field containing data on which you want to sort and then clicking the Ascending button or Descending button in the Sort & Filter group in the Home tab. Click the Ascending button to sort text in alphabetic order from A to Z or numbers from lowest to highest or click the Descending button to sort text in alphabetic order from Z to A or numbers from highest to lowest.

Add a Record
Click New (blank) record button.
OR
1. Click Home tab.
2. Click New button.

Delete a Record
1. Click Home tab.
2. Click Delete button arrow.
3. Click *Delete Record*.
4. Click Yes.

New record

Project 1b   Adding and Deleting Records in a Form

1. With the Clients form open and the first record displayed, add a new record by completing the following steps:
   a. Click the New (blank) record button located in the Record navigation bar.
   b. At the new blank record, type the following information in the specified fields (move to the next field by pressing Tab or Enter; move to the previous field by pressing Shift + Tab):

ClientID	=	116
RepID	=	14
Client	=	Gen-Erin Productions
StreetAddress	=	1099 15th Street
City	=	Muncie
State	=	IN
ZipCode	=	473067963
Telephone	=	7655553120
Email	=	gep@emcp.net

2. Print the current record in the form by completing the following steps:
   a. Click the Office button and then click *Print* at the drop-down menu.
   b. At the Print dialog box, click the *Select Record(s)* option in the *Print Range* section and then click OK.

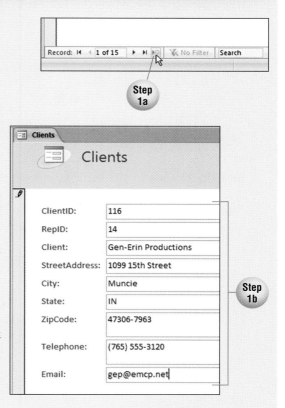

3. Delete the second record (ClientID 102) by completing the following steps:
   a. Click the First record button in the Record navigation bar.
   b. Click the Next record button in the Record navigation bar.
   c. With Record 2 active, click the Home tab.
   d. Click the Delete button arrow and then click *Delete Record* at the drop-down list.

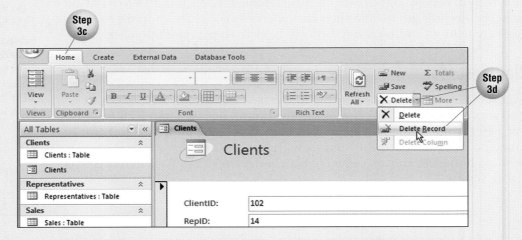

   e. At the message telling you that you will not be able to undo the delete operation, click Yes.
4. Click the New (blank) record button in the Record navigation bar and then type the following information in the specified fields.

ClientID	=	102
RepID	=	11
Client	=	Sunrise Corporation
StreetAddress	=	14432 Center Avenue
City	=	Indianapolis
State	=	IN
ZipCode	=	462381744
Telephone	=	3175555640
Email	=	sc@emcp.net

5. Sort the records in the form by completing the following steps:
   a. Click in the field containing the data *Sunrise Corporation* and then click the Ascending button in the Sort & Filter group in the Home tab.
   b. Click in the field containing the data *Indianapolis* and then click the Descending button in the Sort & Filter group.
   c. Click in the field containing the data *47306-4839* and then click the Ascending button in the Sort & Filter group.
   d. Click in the field containing the data *114* and then click the Ascending button in the Sort & Filter group.
6. Click the Save button on the Quick Access toolbar.
7. Close the Clients form by clicking the Close button located in the upper right corner of the forms window.

Creating a Form with a Related Table

When you created the form with the Clients table, only the Clients table fields displayed in the form. If you create a form with a table that has a one-to-many relationship established, Access adds a datasheet to the form that is based on the related table. For example, in Project 1c, you will create a one-to-many relationship between the Clients table and the Representatives table and then create a form with the Representatives table. Since it is related to the Clients table by a one-to-many relationship, Access inserts a datasheet at the bottom of the form containing all of the records in the Clients table. Figure 5.2 displays the form you will create in Project 1c. Notice the datasheet that displays at the bottom of the form.

If you have created only a single one-to-many relationship, the datasheet for the related table displays in the form. If you have created more than one relationship in a table, Access will not display any datasheets when you create a form with the table.

Figure 5.2 Representatives Form with Clients Datasheet

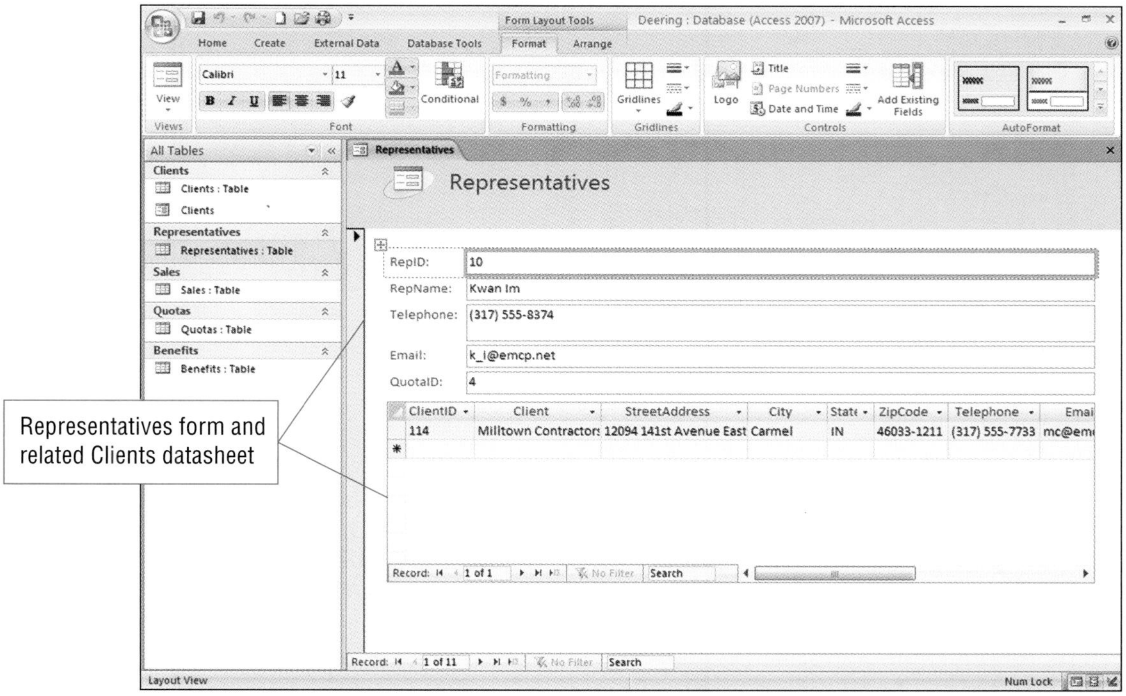

Representatives form and related Clients datasheet

Project 1c   Creating a Form with a Related Table

1. With the **Deering.accdb** database open, create a one-to-many relationship where the *RepID* field in the Representatives table is the "one" and the *RepID* field in the Clients table is the "many." Save and then close the relationships window.
2. Create a form with the Representatives table by completing the following steps:
   a. Click the Representatives table in the Navigation pane.
   b. Click the Create tab.
   c. Click the Form button in the Forms group.

3. Insert a new record in the Clients table for representative 12 (Catherine Singleton) by completing the following steps:
   a. Click twice on the Next record button in the Record navigation bar at the bottom of the form window (not the Record navigation bar in the Clients datasheet) to display the record for Catherine Singleton.
   b. Click in the cell immediately below *113* in the *ClientID* field in the Clients datasheet.
   c. Type the following information in the specified fields:

ClientID	=	117
Client	=	Dan-Built Construction
StreetAddress	=	903 James Street
City	=	Carmel
State	=	IN
ZipCode	=	46033-9050
Telephone	=	(317) 555-1122
Email	=	dc@emcp.net

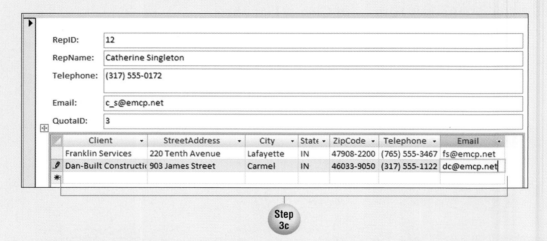

Step 3c

4. Click the Save button on the Quick Access toolbar and at the Save As dialog box with *Representatives* in the *Form Name* text box, click OK.
5. Print the current record in the form by completing the following steps:
   a. Click the Office button and then click *Print* at the drop-down menu.
   b. At the Print dialog box, click the *Select Record(s)* option in the *Print range* section and then click OK.
6. Close the Representatives form.

Customizing a Form

A form is comprised of a series of control objects, which are objects that display titles or descriptions, accept data, or perform actions. You can customize control objects with buttons in the Form Layout Tools Format tab. This tab is active when you display a form in Layout view and contains buttons for changing the font, alignment, and formatting of text; applying gridlines; and inserting controls such as a logo, title, and the date and time.

To customize an individual control object, click the object to select it. A selected control object displays with an orange border. To apply formatting to multiple objects, hold down the Shift key while clicking each object. To select all objects in a column, click the first object, position the mouse pointer at the top of the selected object until the pointer turns into a black, down-pointing arrow, and then click the left mouse button.

Changing the Font

With buttons in the Font group, you can change the font, font style, font size, and font color. You can also change the alignment of text in a field and apply fill to fields. The Font group also contains a Format Painter button to copy formatting and apply it to other data.

Project 1d   Applying Font Formatting to a Form

1. With the **Deering.accdb** database open, open the Clients form by completing the following steps:
   a. Click the Navigation pane Menu bar.
   b. Click *Object Type* at the drop-down list. (This option displays the objects grouped by type—Tables, Queries, Forms, and Reports. The **Deering.accdb** database only contains tables and forms, so you will see only those two types in the Navigation pane.)
   c. Double-click *Clients* in the *Forms* section of the Navigation pane.
2. Click the Layout View button located at the right side of the Status bar. (The form must display in Layout view to display the Form Layout Tools Format tab.)
3. Change the font and alignment formatting of form elements by completing the following steps:
   a. Click the *ClientID* control object.
   b. Hold down the Shift key.
   c. Click each of the field names through *Email*.
   d. With the nine control objects selected, click the Font button arrow in the Font group and then click *Candara* at the drop-down list.
   e. Click the Bold button and then click the Italic button in the Font group.
   f. Click the Align Text Right button in the Font group.
   g. Click the Font Color button arrow and then click *Maroon 5* at the drop-down color palette. (See image at the right.)
4. Change the font and width of control objects by completing the following steps:
   a. Click the control object containing the text *101*.
   b. Position the mouse pointer at the top of the selected object until the mouse pointer displays as a black, down-pointing arrow and then click the left mouse button.

c. With the nine control objects selected, position the mouse pointer on the right edge of any of the selected control objects until the pointer changes to a left- and right-pointing arrow, drag the right border left to the approximate width shown in the image below, and then release the mouse button.

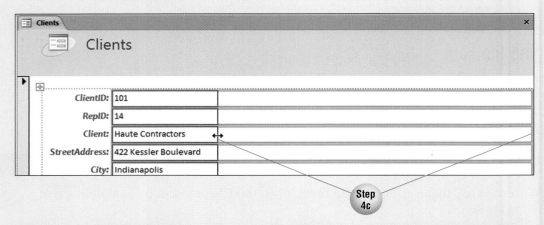

d. Click the Font Color button arrow and then click *Dark Blue* at the drop-down color palette (second color from the *right* in the bottom row of the *Standard Colors* section).

e. Click the Fill/Back Color button arrow and then click *Maroon 1* at the drop-down color palette.

f. Click outside the selected control objects to deselect them.

5. Click the Save button on the Quick Access toolbar.

6. Click the Next record button in the Record navigation bar to display the next record. Continue navigating through the records to view the records with the font formatting applied.

7. Click the First record button in the Record navigation bar.

Applying Conditional Formatting

Conditional

Click the Conditional button in the Font group in the Form Layout Tools Format tab and the Conditional Formatting dialog box displays as shown in Figure 5.3. In the *Default Formatting* section, specify the type of formatting you want applied to the control object if the condition (or conditions) is not met. A preview box displays in the *Default Formatting* section showing you how the control object will display if the condition is not met. Use options in the *Condition 1* section of the dialog box to specify a criterion and choose the formatting you want applied to data in a control object that meet the criterion. For example, in Project 1e you will specify that you want any *Indianapolis* entries in the *City* field to display in red.

Click the down-pointing arrow at the right side of the second option box in a condition section and a drop-down list displays with the options *between, not between, equal to, not equal to, greater than, less than, greater than or equal to,* and *less than or equal to.* Use these options when creating conditional formatting.

Figure 5.3 Conditional Formatting Dialog Box

Use options in this dialog box to apply conditions to text in a form.

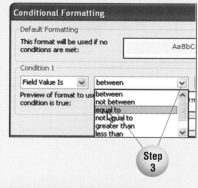

Click the Add button to insert up to two additional conditions.

Project 1e Applying Conditional Formatting

1. With the **Deering.accdb** database open, the Clients form open, and the first record displayed, click the control object containing the word *Indianapolis*.
2. Click the Conditional button in the Font group in the Form Layout Tools Format tab.
3. At the Conditional Formatting dialog box, click the down-pointing arrow in the second list box in the *Condition 1* section (the list box containing the word *between*) and then click *equal to* at the drop-down list.
4. Click in the text box immediately right of the option box containing *equal to* and then type Indianapolis.
5. Click the Fill/Back Color button in the *Condition 1* section (this inserts light maroon fill in the preview cell).
6. Click the Font/Fore Color button arrow in the *Condition 1* section and then click the red color at the drop-down color palette (second color from the left in the bottom row).
7. Click OK to close the dialog box.
8. Navigate through the records and notice that *Indianapolis* in the *City* field displays in red while the other cities display in the dark blue color your chose in the previous project.
9. Save the Clients form.
10. Click the First record button in the Record navigation bar and then print the record.
11. Close the Clients form.

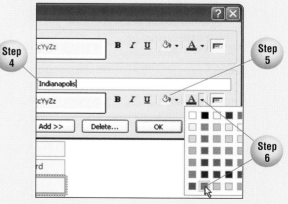

HINT

You can apply up to three conditions on a field.

Adding Additional Conditions

In Project 1e you created one condition for the *City* field—if the field is equal to *Indianapolis* then the font color changes to red. At the Conditional Formatting dialog box, you can create up to three conditions. Click the Add button in the dialog box to insert additional conditions. For example, in Project 1f you will create two conditions specifying that if an amount is greater than $99,999 then the font color changes to green and if an amount is less than $100,000 then the font color changes to red.

Formatting Numbers and Applying Gridlines

Use options in the Formatting group of the Form Layout Tools Format tab to apply Currency, Percentage, or Comma formatting to numbers and choose a number style from the Format option drop-down list. With options in the Gridlines group, you can apply gridlines to control objects and then change the width, style, and color of the lines. To apply gridlines, you must select at least one control object to make active the buttons in the Gridline group. By default, Access applies formatting to all control objects in the form.

Project **1f** **Formatting Numbers and Applying Gridlines and Conditional Formatting**

1. With the **Deering.accdb** database open, create a form with the Sales table by completing the following steps:
   a. Click the Sales table in the Navigation pane.
   b. Click the Create tab.
   c. Click the Form button in the Forms group.
2. Decrease the number of decimals in the *Sales2008* and *Sales2009* fields by completing the following steps:
   a. Make sure the form displays in Layout view.
   b. Click in the control object containing the number *$289,563.00*.
   c. Click twice on the Decrease Decimals button in the Formatting group in the Form Layout Tools Format tab.
   d. Click in the control object containing the number *$327,541.00*.
   e. Click twice on the Decrease Decimals button in the Formatting group in the Form Layout Tools Form tab.
3. Change the width of form control objects by completing the following steps:
   a. Click the control object containing the text *101*.
   b. Hold down the Shift key and then click each of the two remaining control objects containing money amounts.

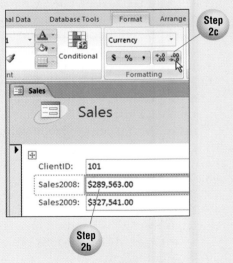

c. With the three control objects selected, position the mouse pointer on the right edge of any of the selected control objects until the pointer changes to a left- and right-pointing arrow, drag the right border left to the approximate width shown in the image below, and then release the mouse button.

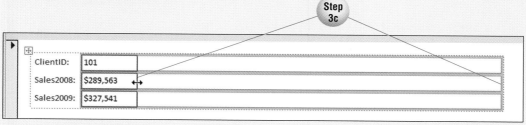

Step 3c

ClientID: 101
Sales2008: $289,563
Sales2009: $327,541

d. Click the Font Color button arrow and then click *Dark Blue* at the drop-down color palette (second color from the *right* in the bottom row of the *Standard Colors* section).
e. Click the Fill/Back Color button arrow and then click *Maroon 1* at the drop-down color palette.
f. Click outside the selected control objects to deselect them.
4. Format the three field name control objects by completing the following steps:
  a. Select the *ClientID*, *Sales2008*, and *Sales2009* control objects.
  b. Click the Font Color button arrow and then click *Maroon 5* at the drop-down color palette.
  c. Click the Bold button and the Italic button in the Font group.
  d. Click the Align Text Right button in the Font group.
  e. Click outside the selected control objects to deselect them.
5. Apply and format gridlines by completing the following steps:
  a. Click the *ClientID* control object.
  b. Click the Gridlines button in the Gridlines group and then click *Horizontal* at the drop-down list.

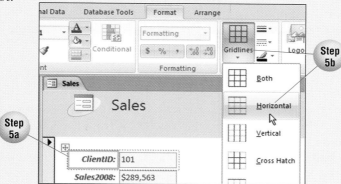

Step 5b

Step 5a

Step 5c

  c. Click the Width button in the Gridlines group and then click the *Hairline* option (top option in the drop-down list).
  d. Click the Style button in the Gridlines group and then click the *Dashes* option (third option from the top of the drop-down list).
  e. Click the Color button arrow in the Gridlines group and then click *Dark Blue* at the drop-down color gallery.
  f. After looking at the gridlines, you decide to change them by clicking the Gridlines button and then clicking *Cross Hatch* at the drop-down list.
6. Scroll through the records and notice the formatting you applied to the control objects.
7. Click the Save button on the Quick Access toolbar and at the Save As dialog box with *Sales* in the *Form Name* text box, click OK.

8. Apply conditional formatting by completing the following steps:
   a. Click the First record button in the Record navigation bar.
   b. Click the control object containing the amount *$289,563*.
   c. Click the Conditional button in the Font group in the Form Layout Tools Format tab.
   d. At the Conditional Formatting dialog box, click the down-pointing arrow in the second list box in the *Condition 1* section (the list box containing the word *between*) and then click *greater than* at the drop-down list.

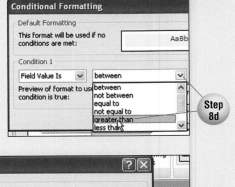

Step 8d

   e. Click in the text box immediately right of the option box containing *greater than* and then type 99999.
   f. Click the Bold button
   g. Click the Fill/Back Color button in the *Condition 1* section (this inserts light maroon fill in the preview cell).
   h. Click the Font/Fore Color button arrow in the *Condition 1* section and then click the green color at the drop-down color palette (sixth color from the left in the bottom row).

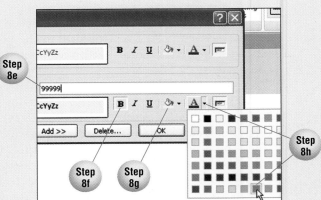

Step 8e

Step 8f   Step 8g

Step 8h

   i. Click the Add button. (This inserts a *Condition 2* section toward the bottom of the dialog box.)
   j. Click the down-pointing arrow in the second list box in the *Condition 2* section and then click *less than* at the drop-down list.
   k. Click in the text box immediately right of the option box containing *less than* and then type 100000.
   l. Click the Bold button.
   m. Click the Fill/Back Color button in the *Condition 2* section (this inserts light maroon fill in the preview cell).
   n. Click the Font/Fore Color button arrow in the *Condition 2* section and then click the red color at the drop-down color palette (second color from the left in the bottom row).
   o. Click OK to close the dialog box.
9. Complete steps similar to those in Step 8 to apply the same conditional formatting to the field containing the *Sales2009* amount *$327,541*.
10. Scroll through the records and notice the conditional formatting applied to amounts in the *Sales2008* and *Sales2009* fields.
11. Click the First record button and then print the current record.
12. Save and then close the *Sales* form.

Formatting Controls

With options in the Controls group in the Form Layout Tools Format tab, you can insert a logo, form title, page numbers, and date and time. You can also apply lines to control objects and then change the line thickness, type, and color.

Click the Add Existing Fields button in the Controls group and the Field List window opens and displays at the right side of the screen. This window displays the fields available in the current view, fields available in related tables, and fields available in other tables. Figure 5.4 presents the Field List window you display in Project 1g. You can add fields to the form by double-clicking a field or by dragging the field from the Field List window into the form.

Figure 5.4 Field List Window

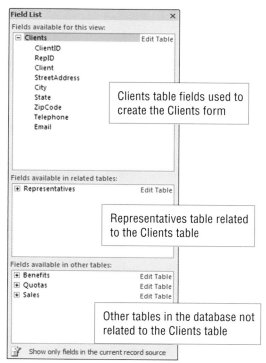

In the *Fields available for this view* section, Access displays all fields in any tables used to create the form. So far, you have been creating a form with all fields in one table. In the *Fields available in related tables*, Access displays tables that are related to the table(s) used to create the form. To display the fields in the related table, click the plus symbol that displays before the table name in the Field List window and the list expands to display all field names. To add a field to the form, double-click the desired field in the Field List window. This inserts the field below the existing fields in the form.

You can also drag a field from the Field List window into the form. To do this, position the mouse pointer on the desired field in the Field List window, hold down the left mouse button, drag into the form window, and then release the mouse button. A horizontal gold bar displays as you drag the field in the existing fields in the form. When the gold bar is positioned in the desired location, release the mouse button. You can insert multiple fields in a form from the Field List window. To do this, hold down the Ctrl key while clicking the desired fields and then drag the fields into the form.

If you try to drag a field from a table in the *Fields available in other tables* section, the Specify Relationship dialog box will display. To move a field from the Field List window to the form, the field must be located in a table that is related to the table(s) used to create the form.

Changing Field Order

When you drag a field from the Field List window into the form window, a horizontal gold bar displays as you drag in the existing fields in the form. Position the gold bar at the location where you want the field inserted and then release the mouse button. You can also change the order of existing fields by clicking the field control object and then dragging the field to the desired position.

Sizing a Control Object

You can change the size of a selected control object. To do this, select the object and then position the mouse pointer on the object border until the mouse pointer displays as a double-headed arrow pointing in the desired direction. Drag in or out to decrease or increase the size of the object.

Moving a Control Object in the Form Header

A form contains a form header that is the top portion of the form containing the logo container control object and the form title. You can move control objects in a form header to different locations within the header. To move a control object in a header, click the object to select it and then drag it with the mouse to the desired position.

Project 1g Formatting Controls in a Form

1. With the **Deering.accdb** database open, right-click the Clients form in the Navigation pane and then click *Layout View* at the shortcut menu. (Make sure you right-click the Clients form and not the Clients table.)
2. Insert a logo image by completing the following steps:
   a. Click the logo container control object that displays in the upper left corner of the form (in the form header).
   b. Click the Logo button in the Controls group in the Form Layout Tools Format tab.

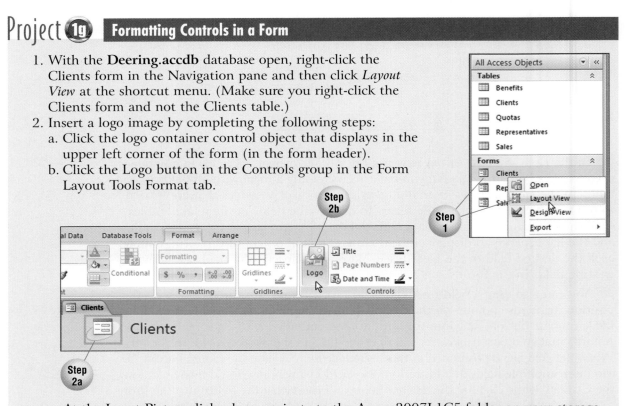

   c. At the Insert Picture dialog box, navigate to the Access2007L1C5 folder on your storage medium and then double-click *Mountain.jpg*.

---

3. Increase the size of the logo control object by completing the following steps:
   a. With the logo control object selected, position the mouse pointer on the bottom right corner of the object until the mouse pointer displays as a diagonally-pointing two-headed arrow.
   b. Drag down and to the right until the logo control object is approximately the size shown at the right and then release the mouse button.

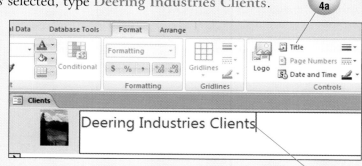

4. Change the form title and format the title by completing the following steps:
   a. Click the Title button in the Controls group.
   b. With *Clients* selected, type **Deering Industries Clients**.

Step 3b

Step 4a

Step 4b

c. Click the Font Color button arrow in the Font group and then click the *Maroon 5* color at the drop-down color palette.
   d. Click the Bold button in the Font group.
   e. Click the Line Thickness button in the Controls group and then click the *2 pt* option (third option from the top).
   f. Click the Line Type button in the Controls group and then click the *Dashes* option (third option from the top).
   g. Click the Line Color button arrow and then click *Dark Blue* at the color palette.
   h. Drag the title control object so it is centered vertically in the form header.

Step 4h

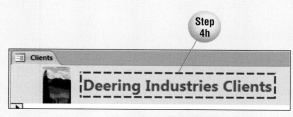

5. Insert and format the date and time by completing the following steps:
   a. Click the Date and Time button in the Controls group.
   b. At the Date and Time dialog box, click the bottom option in the *Include Date* section.
   c. Click the middle option in the *Include Time* section.
   d. Click OK to close the dialog box.
   e. Click the date control object, hold down the Shift key, and then click the time control object.
   f. Click the Font color button in the Font group. (This applies the *Maroon 5* color you choose in Step 4c.)
   g. Click the Bold button in the Font group.
   h. Click outside the control objects to deselect them.

Step 5b

Step 5c

Step 5d

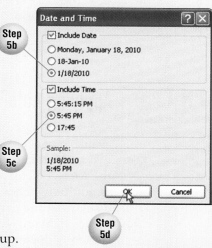

6. Insert an additional field into the Clients form from the Representatives table by completing the following steps:
   a. Click the Add Existing Fields button in the Controls group.

b. Click the plus symbol that displays immediately left of the Representatives table name located in the *Fields available in related tables* section of the Field List window. (If this section does not display, click the <u>Show all tables</u> hyperlink that displays at the bottom of the Field List window.)

c. Position the mouse pointer on the *RepName* field, hold down the left mouse button, drag into the form until the gold horizontal bar displays immediately below the *RepID* field in the form, and then release the mouse button. (This inserts the field with a down-pointing arrow at the right side. Access inserts the field as a Lookup field.)

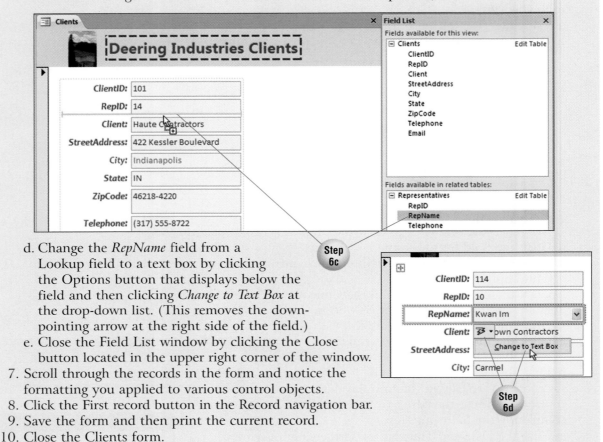

d. Change the *RepName* field from a Lookup field to a text box by clicking the Options button that displays below the field and then clicking *Change to Text Box* at the drop-down list. (This removes the down-pointing arrow at the right side of the field.)

e. Close the Field List window by clicking the Close button located in the upper right corner of the window.

7. Scroll through the records in the form and notice the formatting you applied to various control objects.

8. Click the First record button in the Record navigation bar.

9. Save the form and then print the current record.

10. Close the Clients form.

HINT

Applying AutoFormats

Access includes autoformats you can apply to a form. These autoformats are available in the AutoFormat group of the Form Layout Tools Format tab. Generally, two autoformats display—the Access 2003 and the Access 2007 autoformats. Click the More button at the right side of the autoformats to display a drop-down list of additional choices. Hover the mouse pointer over an autoformat and the name displays in the ScreenTip. The names of the autoformats align with the theme names in Word, Excel, and PowerPoint. To maintain a consistent appearance in company documents, you can apply the same autoformat to a form that matches the theme you apply to a Word document, Excel spreadsheet, or PowerPoint presentation.

1. With the **Deering.accdb** database open, *right-click* the Representatives form and then click *Layout View* at the shortcut menu. (Make sure you right-click the Representatives form and not the Representatives table.)

2. Apply an autoformat by clicking the More button located at the right side of the AutoFormat group and then clicking the *Urban* autoformat at the drop-down list.

3. After looking at the formatting, you decide that you want to change the autoformat. To do this, click the More button at the right side of the AutoFormat group and then click *Equity* at the drop-down list.

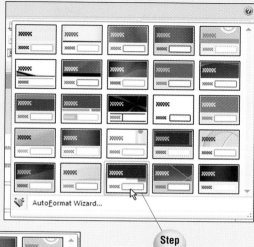

Step 2

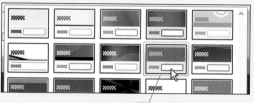

Step 3

4. Apply conditional formatting to the numbers in the *QuotaID* field by completing the following steps:

   a. Click the First record button in the Record navigation bar.
   b. Click the *QuotaID* control object containing the number *4*.
   c. Click the Conditional button in the Font group in the Form Layout Tools Format tab.
   d. At the Conditional Formatting dialog box, click the down-pointing arrow in the second list box in the *Condition 1* section (the list box containing the word *between*) and then click *equal to* at the drop-down list.
   e. Click in the text box immediately right of the option box containing *equal to* and then type 2.
   f. Click the Font/Fore Color button arrow in the *Condition 1* section and then click the purple color at the drop-down color palette (last color in the bottom row).

Step 4d   Step 4e   Step 4f

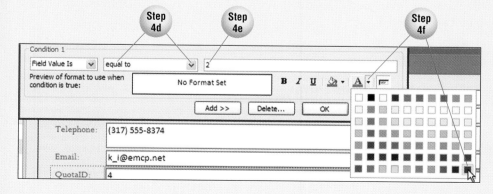

   g. Click the Add button. (This inserts a *Condition 2* section toward the bottom of the dialog box.)

h. Click the down-pointing arrow in the second list box in the *Condition 2* section and then click *equal to* at the drop-down list.

i. Click in the text box immediately right of the option box containing *equal to* and then type 3.

j. Click the Font/Fore Color button arrow in the *Condition 2* section and then click the green color at the drop-down color palette (sixth color from the left in the bottom row).

k. Click the Add button. (This inserts a *Condition 3* section toward the bottom of the dialog box.)

l. Click the down-pointing arrow in the second list box in the *Condition 3* section and then click *equal to* at the drop-down list.

m. Click in the text box immediately right of the option box containing *equal to* and then type 4.

n. Click the Font/Fore Color button arrow in the *Condition 3* section and then click the red color at the drop-down color palette (second color from the left in the bottom row).

o. Click OK to close the dialog box.

5. Scroll through the records and notice the coloring of the quote ID number.

6. Save the Representatives form.

7. Click the First record button in the Record navigation bar and then print the record.

8. Close the Representatives form.

9. Open the Clients form by right-clicking the Clients form name in the Navigation pane and then clicking *Layout View* at the shortcut menu.

10. Apply the Equity format by clicking the More button located at the right side of the AutoFormat group and then clicking *Equity* option at the drop-down list. (Position the date and time on the orange background.)

11. Make the first record active and then print the current record.

12. Save and then close the Clients form.

13. Open the Sales form in Layout view, apply the Equity autoformat, and then save the form.

14. Print the first record in the form and then close the form.

15. Close the **Deering.accdb** database.

Project 2 Create Forms with the Split Form and Multiple Items Buttons and the Form Wizard

You will create a form with the Split Form button, the Multiple Form button, and the Form Wizard.

QUICK STEPS

Create a Split Form
1. Click desired table.
2. Click Create tab.
3. Click Split Form button.

Creating a Split Form

You can create a form with the Split Form button in the Forms group in the Create tab. When you use this button to create a form, Access splits the screen in the work area and provides two views for the form. The top half of the work area displays the form in Layout view and the bottom half of the work area displays the form in Datasheet view. The two views are connected and are synchronous, which means that displaying or modifying a specific field in the Form view portion will cause the same action to occur in the field in the Datasheet view portion. Figure 5.5 displays the split form you will create for Project 2a.

Figure 5.5 Split Form

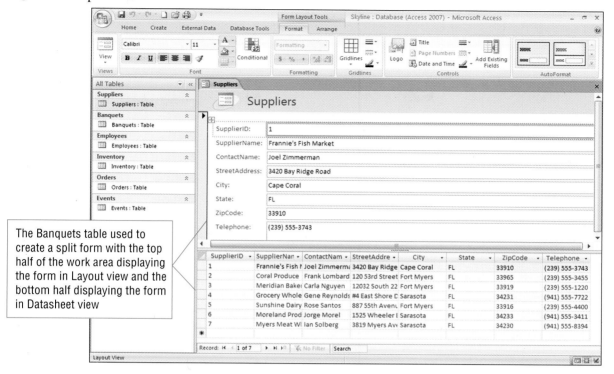

The Banquets table used to create a split form with the top half of the work area displaying the form in Layout view and the bottom half displaying the form in Datasheet view

Project 2a Creating a Split Form

1. Remove the read-only attribute from the **Skyline.accdb** database located in the Access2007L1C5 folder.
2. Open the **Skyline.accdb** database.
3. Create a split form with the Suppliers table by completing the following steps:
   a. Click the Suppliers table in the Navigation pane.
   b. Click the Create tab.
   c. Click the Split Form button in the Forms group.
   d. Click several times on the Next record button in the Record navigation bar. (Notice that as you scroll through records, the current record in Form view in the top portion of the window is the same record selected in Datasheet view in the lower portion of the window.)
4. Apply an autoformat by completing the following steps:
   a. Make sure the form displays in Layout view.
   b. Click the More button located at the right side of the AutoFormat group.
   c. Click the *Flow* autoformat at the drop-down list.

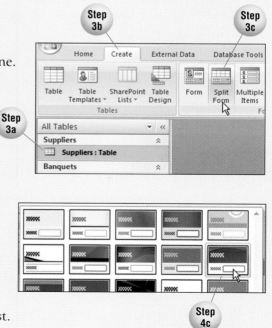

Step 3b

Step 3c

Step 3a

Step 4c

5. Insert a logo image by completing the following steps:
   a. Click the logo container control object that displays in the upper left corner of the form.
   b. Click the Logo button in the Controls group in the Form Layout Tools Format tab.
   c. At the Insert Picture dialog box, navigate to the Access2007L1C5 folder on your storage medium and then double-click *Cityscape.jpg*.
6. Increase the size of the logo so it displays as shown in the image at the right.

Step 6

Suppliers

Suppliers

SupplierID: 1

7. Change the form title and format the title by completing the following steps:
   a. Click the Title button in the Controls group.
   b. With *Suppliers* selected, type Skyline Suppliers.
   c. Click the Font Color button arrow in the Font group and then click the *White* color at the drop-down color palette (first color from the left in the first row of the *Standard Colors* section).
   d. Click the Bold button in the Font group.
   e. Click the Font Size button arrow and then click *24* at the drop-down list.
8. Insert a new record in the Suppliers form by completing the following steps:
   a. Click the Form View button located in the lower right corner of the Status bar.
   b. Click the New (blank) record button in the Record navigation bar.
   c. Click in the *SupplierID* field in the Form view portion of the window and then type the following information in the specified fields:

Supplier10	=	8
SupplierName	=	Jackson Produce
ContactName	=	Marshall Jackson
StreetAddress	=	5790 Cypress Avenue
City	=	Fort Myers
State	=	FL
ZipCode	=	33917
Telephone	=	2395555002

9. Click the Save button on the Quick Access toolbar and save the form with the name *Suppliers*.
10. Print the current form by completing the following steps:
    a. Display the Print dialog box.
    b. At the Print dialog box, click the Setup button.
    c. At the Page Setup dialog box, click Print Form Only and then click OK.
    d. At the Print dialog box, click the Selected Record(s) option and then click OK.
11. Close the *Suppliers* form.

Creating a Multiple Item Form

When you create a form with the Form button, a single record displays. You can use the Multiple Items button in the Forms group in the Create tab to create a form that displays multiple records. The advantage to creating a multiple item form over displaying the table in Datasheet view is that you can customize the form using options in the Form Layout Tools Format tab.

Multiple Items

Project 2h   Creating a Multiple Item Form

1. With the **Skyline.accdb** database open, create a multiple item form by completing the following steps:
   a. Click the Orders table in the Navigation pane.
   b. Click the Create tab.
   c. Click the Multiple Items button in the Forms group.
2. Apply the Flow autoformat to the form.
3. Insert the **Cityscape.jpg** image as the logo.
4. Insert the title *Skyline Orders* and turn on bold.
5. Insert the date and time in the form header. Change the font color of the date and time to white, turn on bold, and then drag the date and time so they are right-aligned with the SupplierID heading.
6. Save the form with the name *Orders*.
7. Print the first record in the form by completing the following steps:
   a. Display the Print dialog box.
   b. Click the *Pages* option in the *Print Range* section.
   c. Type 1 in the *From* text box, press the Tab key, and then type 1 in the *To* text box.
   d. Click OK.
   e. At the message that displays, click OK.
8. Close the Orders form.

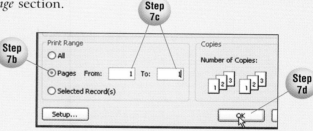

Creating a Form Using the Form Wizard

Access offers a Form Wizard that will guide you through the creation of a form. To create a form using the Form Wizard, click the Create tab, click the More Forms button in the Forms group, and then click *Form Wizard* at the drop-down list. At the first Form Wizard dialog box, shown in Figure 5.6, specify the table and then the fields you want included in the form. To select the table, click the down-pointing arrow at the right side of the *Tables/Queries* option box and then click the desired table. Select the desired field in the *Available Fields* list box and then click the button containing the greater than symbol (>). This inserts the field in the *Selected Fields* list box. Continue in this manner until you have inserted all desired fields in the *Selected Fields* list box. If you want to insert all fields into the *Selected Fields* list box at one time, click the button containing the two greater than symbols (>>). After specifying fields, click the Next button.

QUICK STEPS

Create a Form Using Form Wizard
1. Click Create tab.
2. Click More Forms button.
3. Click *Form Wizard* at drop-down list.
4. Choose desired options at each of the Form Wizard dialog boxes.

HINT
Using the Form Wizard, you can be more selective about what fields you insert in a form.

Figure 5.6 First Form Wizard Dialog Box

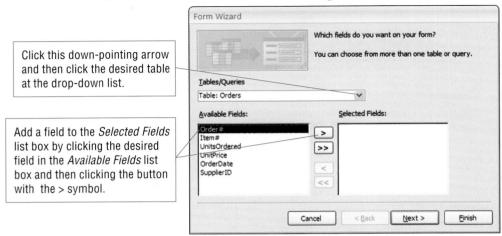

Click this down-pointing arrow and then click the desired table at the drop-down list.

Add a field to the *Selected Fields* list box by clicking the desired field in the *Available Fields* list box and then clicking the button with the > symbol.

At the second Form Wizard dialog box, shown in Figure 5.7, specify the layout for the records. You can choose from *Columnar*, *Tabular*, *Datasheet*, and *Justified* (with *Columnar* the default). After choosing the layout, click the Next button.

Figure 5.7 Second Form Wizard Dialog Box

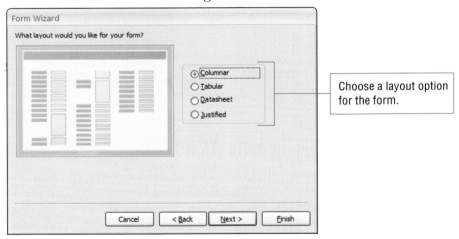

Choose a layout option for the form.

At the third Form Wizard dialog box, shown in Figure 5.8, choose an autoformat style. These are the same autoformats that are available in the AutoFormat group in the Form Layout Tools Format tab. Click a format style and the results of the style display in the preview box. After selecting the desired format style, click the Next button.

Figure 5.8 Third Form Wizard Dialog Box

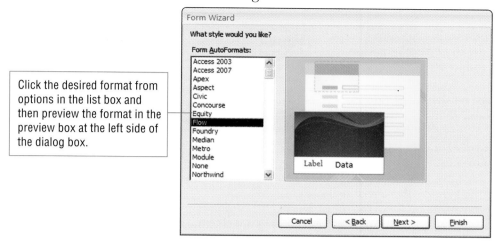

Click the desired format from options in the list box and then preview the format in the preview box at the left side of the dialog box.

At the final Form Wizard dialog box, shown in Figure 5.9, the Form Wizard offers a title for the form and also provides the option *Open the form to view or enter information*. Make any necessary changes in this dialog box and then click the Finish button.

Figure 5.9 Fourth Form Wizard Dialog Box

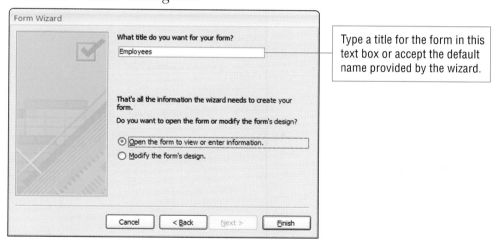

Type a title for the form in this text box or accept the default name provided by the wizard.

Project 2c Creating a Form Using the Form Wizard

1. With the **Skyline.accdb** database open, create a form with the Form Wizard by completing the following steps:

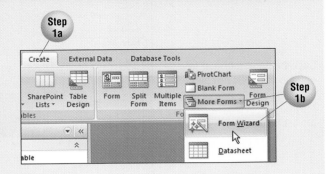

Step 1a

Step 1b

a. Click the Create tab.
b. Click the More Forms button in the Forms group and then click *Form Wizard* at the drop-down list.
c. At the first Form Wizard dialog box, click the down-pointing arrow at the right side of the *Tables/Queries* option box and then click *Table: Employees* at the drop-down list.
d. Specify that you want all fields included in the form by clicking the button containing the two greater than symbols (>>).
e. Click the Next button.

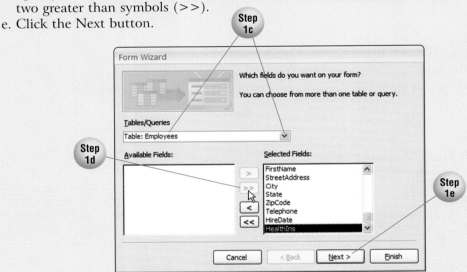

Step 1c

Step 1d

Step 1e

f. At the second Form Wizard dialog box, click the Next button. (This leaves the layout at the default of *Columnar*.)
g. At the third Form Wizard dialog box, make sure the Flow autoformat is selected in the list box and then click the Next button.
h. At the fourth Form Wizard dialog box, leave the options at the default, and then click the Finish button.

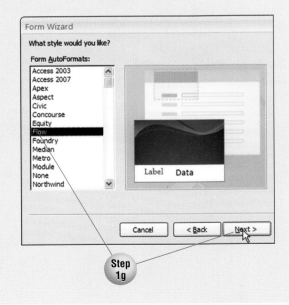

Step 1g

2. When the first record displays, click the New (blank) record button and then add the following records:

EmployeeID	=	11
LastName	=	Thompson
FirstName	=	Carol
StreetAddress	=	6554 Willow Drive, Apt. B
City	=	Fort Myers
State	=	FL
ZipCode	=	33915
Telephone	=	2395553719
HireDate	=	12/1/2007
HealthIns	=	*(Click in the check box to insert a check mark.)*

EmployeeID	=	12
LastName	=	Hahn
FirstName	=	Eric
StreetAddress	=	331 South 152nd Street
City	=	Cape Coral
State	=	FL
ZipCode	=	33906
Telephone	=	2395558107
HireDate	=	12/1/2007
HealthIns	=	*(Leave blank.)*

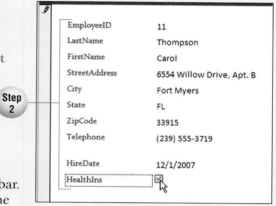

Step 2

3. Click the Save button on the Quick Access toolbar.
4. Print the record for Eric Hahn and then print the record for Carol Thompson.
5. Close the Employees form.

Creating a Form with Fields from Related Tables

In Project 2c you used the Form Wizard to create a form with all of the fields in one table. If tables are related, you can create a form using fields from related tables. At the first Form Wizard dialog box (see Figure 5.6), choose fields from the selected table and then choose fields from a related table. To change to the related table, click the down-pointing arrow at the right of the *Tables/Queries* option box and then click the name of the desired table.

Project **2d** **Creating a Form with Related Tables**

1. With the **Skyline.accdb** database open, create the following relationships:

Field Name	"One" Table	"Many" Table
EmployeeID	Employees	Banquets
EventID	Events	Banquets

2. Create a form with fields from related tables by completing the following steps:
   a. Click the Create tab.
   b. Click the More Forms button in the Forms group and then click *Form Wizard* at the drop-down list.
   c. At the first Form Wizard dialog box, click the down-pointing arrow at the right of the *Tables/Queries* option box and then click *Table: Banquets*.
   d. Click *ResDate* in the *Available Fields* list box and then click the button containing the greater than symbol (>). (This inserts *ResDate* in the *Selected Fields* list box.)
   e. Click *AmountTotal* in the *Available Fields* list box and then click the button containing the greater than symbol.
   f. Click *AmountPaid* in the *Available Fields* list box and then click the button containing the greater than symbol.
   g. Click the down-pointing arrow at the right side of the *Tables/Queries* option box and then click *Table: Events* at the drop-down list.
   h. Click *Event* in the *Available Fields* list box and then click the button containing the greater than symbol.
   i. Click the down-pointing arrow at the right side of the *Tables/Queries* option box and then click *Table: Employees* at the drop-down list.
   j. Click *LastName* in the *Available Fields* list box and then click the button containing the greater than symbol.
   k. Click the Next button.
   l. At the second Form Wizard dialog box, click the Next button.
   m. At the third Form Wizard dialog box, click the Next button.
   n. At the fourth Form Wizard dialog box, make sure *Flow* is selected in the list box and then click the Next button.

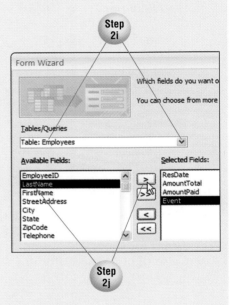

   o. At the fifth Form Wizard dialog box, select the text in the *What title do you want for your form?* text box, type **Upcoming Banquets**, and then click the Finish button.

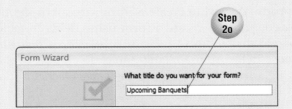

3. When the first record displays, print the record.
4. Save and then close the form.
5. Close the **Skyline.accdb** database.

CHAPTER summary

- A form generally improves the ease with which data is entered into a table. Some methods for creating a form include using the Form, Split Form, or Multiple Items buttons or the Form Wizard.

- A form is an object you can use to enter and edit data in a table or query and to help prevent incorrect data from being entered in a database.

- The simplest method for creating a form is to click a table in the Navigation pane, click the Create button, and then click the Form button in the Forms group.

- When you create a form, it displays in Layout view. Use this view to display data as well as modify the appearance and contents of the form. Other form views include Form view and Design view. Use Form view to enter and manage records and use Design view to view the structure of the form and modify the form.

- Print a form with options at the Print dialog box or by clicking the Quick Print button. To print an individual record, display the Print dialog box, click the *Select Record(s)* option, and then click OK.

- Navigate in a form with buttons in the Record navigation bar.

- Add a new record to a form by clicking the New Record button in the Record navigation bar or by clicking the Home tab and then clicking the New button in the Records group.

- Delete a record from a form by displaying the record, clicking the Home tab, clicking the Delete button arrow, and then clicking *Delete Record* at the drop-down list.

- If you create a form with a table that has a one-to-many relationship established, Access adds a datasheet at the bottom of the form.

- A form is comprised of a series of control objects and you can customize these control objects with buttons in the Form Layout Tools Format tab, which is active when you display a form in Layout view.

- Use options in the Font group in the Form Layout Tools Format tab to change the font, font style, font size, and font color. Use the Conditional button to apply specific formatting to data that matches a specific criterion.

- Format numbers and apply and customize gridlines with buttons in the Formatting group in the Form Layout Tools Format tab.

- With options in the Controls group in the Form Layout Tools Format tab, you can insert a logo, form title, page numbers, and date and time; apply lines to control objects; and customize the lines.

- Click the Add Existing Fields button in the Controls group to display the Field List window. Add fields to the form by double-clicking on or dragging the field from the window.

- Change the order of fields in a form by dragging the field to the desired position.

- Change the size of a selected control object by dragging a border of the object with the mouse.

- Move a selected control object by dragging the object with the mouse.

- Apply an autoformat to a form by clicking one of the two autoformats that display in the Form Layout Tools Form tab or by clicking the More button at the right side of the autoformats and then clicking the desired autoformat at the drop-down list.
- Create a split form by clicking the Split Form button in the Forms group in the Create tab. Access displays the form in Form view in the top portion of the work area and the form in Datasheet view in the bottom of the work area. The two views are connected and are synchronous.
- Create a form with the Multiple Items button and the form displays multiple records.
- The Form Wizard walks you through the steps for creating a form and lets you specify the fields you want included in the form, a layout for the records, the desired formatting, and a name for the form.
- You can create a form with the Form Wizard that contains fields from tables connected by a one-to-many relationship.

COMMANDS review

FEATURE	RIBBON TAB, GROUP	BUTTON, OPTION
Form	Create, Forms	
Conditional Formatting dialog box	Form Layout Tools Format, Font	
Field List window	Form Layout Tools Format, Controls	
Split Form	Create, Forms	
Multiple Items form	Create, Forms	
Form Wizard	Create, Forms	More Forms ▼ , Form Wizard

CONCEPTS check
Test Your Knowledge

Completion: In the space provided at the right, indicate the correct term, symbol, or command.

1. The simplest method to create a form is to click this tab and then click the Form button.

   _____

2. When you click the Form button to create a form, the form displays in this view.

   _____

3. To print the current record in a form, click this option at the Print dialog box and then click OK.

   _____

4. Navigate in a form using buttons in this bar.

   _____

5. Click this button to add a new record to a form.

   _____

6. The Form Layout Tools Format tab is active when a form displays in this view.

   _____

7. The Conditional button is located in this group in the Form Layout Tools Format tab.

   _____

8. Click the Add Existing Fields button in the Controls group in the Form Layout Tools Format tab and this window displays.

   _____

9. The top portion of the form containing the logo container control object and the form title is referred to as this.

   _____

10. When you create a form with the Split Form button, the form displays in this view in the top half of the work area.

    _____

11. Click this button in the Forms group in the Create tab to create a form that displays multiple records.

    _____

12. Click this button in the Forms group in the Create tab to display a drop-down list containing the option *Form Wizard*.

    _____

SKILLS check
Demonstrate Your Proficiency

1 CREATE AND CUSTOMIZE A SALES FORM

1. Remove the read-only attribute from the **OutdoorOptions.accdb** database located in the Access2007L1C5 folder.
2. Open the **OutdoorOptions.accdb** database.
3. Use the Form button in the Forms group in the Create tab to create a form with the Suppliers table.
4. Switch to Form view and then add the following records to the Suppliers form:

Supplier#	=	12
SupplierName	=	Seaside Suppliers
StreetAddress	=	4120 Shoreline Drive
City	=	Vancouver
Province	=	BC
PostalCode	=	V2V 8K4
Email	=	ss@emcp.net

Supplier#	=	34
SupplierName	=	Carson Company
StreetAddress	=	120 Plaza Center
City	=	Vancouver
Province	=	BC
PostalCode	=	V2V 1K6
Email	=	cc@emcp.net

5. Delete the record containing information on Manning, Inc.
6. Switch to Layout view and then apply the Civic autoformat to the form.
7. Select the seven field names (from *Supplier#* through *Email*) and then change the font color to Aqua Blue 5, alignment to Align Text Right, and turn on bold.
8. Click in the *City* field entry and then apply conditional formatting that changes the font color to red and turns on bold for any *City* field that contains the name *Calgary*.
9. Insert the image named **River.jpg** in the logo container control object.
10. Change the name of the form title to *Company Suppliers*. Change the font color of the title to Aqua Blue 5 and turn on bold.
11. Insert the date and time in the form header. Change the font color of the date and time to Aqua Blue 5 and turn on bold.
12. Save the form with the name *Suppliers*.
13. Print the first record in the form in landscape orientation and then close the Suppliers form.

2 CREATE AND CUSTOMIZE AN ORDERS FORM AND A PRODUCTS FORM

1. With the **OutdoorOptions.accdb** database open, create a form with the Orders table using the Form button in the Create tab.
2. Make the following changes to the form:
    a. Display the Field List window and then, if necessary, click the <u>Show all tables</u> hyperlink (located toward the bottom of the window). Expand the Suppliers table in the *Fields available in related tables* section and then drag the field named *SupplierName* into the form and position it between *Supplier#* and *Product#*.
    b. Apply the Civic autoformat to the form.
    c. Apply horizontal gridlines to the form.
    d. Select the seven field names (from *Order#* through *OrderDate*) and then change the font color to Aqua Blue 5, the alignment to Align Text Right, and turn on bold.
    e. Apply conditional formatting that changes the font color to green for any *Amount* field entry that contains an amount greater than $999 and changes the font color to blue for any amount less than $1000. (Do not use the dollar sign when specifying the conditions.)
    f. Insert the image named **River.jpg** in the logo container control object.
3. Save the form with the name *Orders*.
4. Print the first record in the form and then close the Orders form.
5. Create a form with the Products table using the Split Form button in the Create tab with the following specifications:
    a. Apply the Civic autoformat to the form.
    b. Apply horizontal gridlines to the form.
    c. Select the six field names (from *Product#* through *ReorderLevel*) and then change the font color to Aqua Blue 5, the alignment to Align Text Right, and turn on bold.
    d. Change to Form view, create a new record, and then enter the following information in the specified fields:

Product#	=	303
Product	=	Ski helmet
Supplier#	=	68
UnitsInStock	=	12
UnitsOnOrder	=	0
ReorderLevel	=	10

6. Save the form with the name *Products*.
7. Print the current record (the record you just typed). (Hint: Display the Print dialog box, click the Setup button, and then click the *Print Form Only* option. Click *Selected Record(s)* at the Print dialog box.)
8. Close the Products form.

3 CREATE A FORM USING THE FORM WIZARD

1. With the **OutdoorOptions.accdb** database open, create a form from two related database tables using the Form Wizard with the following specifications:
   a. At the first Form Wizard dialog box, insert the following fields in the *Selected Fields* list box:

   From the Products table:
   > *Product#*
   > *Product*
   > *UnitsOnOrder*

   From the Suppliers table:
   > *Supplier#*
   > *SupplierName*
   > *StreetAddress*
   > *City*
   > *Province*
   > *PostalCode*

   b. Do not make any changes at the second Form Wizard dialog box.
   c. Do not make any changes at the third Form Wizard dialog box.
   d. Do not make any changes at the fourth Form Wizard dialog box.
   e. At the fifth Form Wizard dialog box, select the text in the *What title do you want for your form?* text box, type the name Units On Order, and then click the Finish button.
   f. Switch to the Layout view and then apply the Civic autoformat.
2. Print only the first record.
3. Close the Units On Order form.
4. Create a form with the Suppliers table using the Form Wizard with the following specifications:
   a. At the first Form Wizard dialog box, insert all of the Suppliers table fields in the *Selected fields* list box.
   b. At the second Form Wizard dialog box, specify that you want the layout of the form to be *Tabular*.
   c. At the third Form Wizard dialog box, make sure *Civic* is selected.
   d. At the fourth Form Wizard dialog box, select the text in the *What title do you want for your form?* text box, type the name Company Suppliers, and then click the Finish button.
5. Print the form.
6. Close the Company Suppliers form and then close the **OutdoorOptions.accdb** database.

CASE study

Apply Your Skills

Part 1

You are the office manager at the Lewis Vision Care Center and your center is switching over to Access to manage files. You have already created four basic tables and now need to create relationships and enter data. Open the **LewisCenter.accdb** database and then create the following relationships between tables:

Field Name	"One" Table	"Many" Table
Patient#	Patients	Billing
ServiceID	Services	Billing
Doctor#	Doctors	Billing

Save and then print the relationships.

Part 2

Before entering data in the tables, create a form for each table and apply the same autoformat to each form. Apply any additional formatting to enhance the visual appeal of each form. Using the forms, insert the information on the next page in the correct fields in the specified forms. After entering the information in the forms, print the first record of each form.

Part 3

Apply the following conditions to fields in forms:

- In the Patients form, apply the condition that the city *Tulsa* displays in red and the city *Broken Arrow* displays in blue in the *City* field.
- In the Billing form, apply the condition that amounts in the *Fee* field over $99 display in green.

Print the first record of the form. Close the Patients form and then close the **LewisCenter.accdb** database.

Part 4

Your center has a procedures manual that describes processes and procedures in the center. Open Word and then create a document for the procedures manual that describes the formatting and conditions you applied to the forms in the **LewisCenter.accdb** database. Save the completed document and name it **Access_C5_CS_P4**. Print and then close **Access_C5_CS_P4.docx**.

Patients form

Patient number 030
Rhonda J. Mahler
130 East 41st Street
Tulsa, OK 74155
(918) 555-3107

Patient number 076
Patrick S. Robbins
3281 Aspen Avenue
Tulsa, OK 74108
(918) 555-9672

Patient number 092
Oren L. Vargas
21320 Tenth Street
Broken Arrow, OK 74012
(918) 555-1188

Patient number 085
Michael A. Dempsey
506 Houston Street
Tulsa, OK 74142
(918) 555-5541

Patient number 074
Wendy L. Holloway
23849 22nd Street
Broken Arrow, OK 74009
(918) 555-8842

Patient number 023
Maggie M. Winters
4422 South 121st
Tulsa, OK 74142
(918) 555-8833

Doctors form

Doctor number 1
Carolyn Joswick
(918) 555-4772

Doctor number 2
Gerald Ingram
(918) 555-9890

Doctor number 3
Kay Feather
(918) 555-7762

Doctor number 4
Sean Granger
(918) 555-1039

Doctor number 5
Jerome Deltoro
(918) 555-8021

Services form

Co = Consultation

V = Vision Screening

G = Glaucoma Testing

C = Cataract Testing

S = Surgery

E = Emergency

Billing form

Patient number 076
Doctor number 2
Date of visit = 04/01/2010
Service ID = C
Fee = $85

Patient number 076
Doctor number 3
Date of visit = 04/01/2010
Service ID = V
Fee = $150

Patient number 085
Doctor number 1
Date of visit = 04/01/2010
Service ID = Co
Fee = $0

Patient number 074
Doctor number 3
Date of visit = 4/1/2010
Service ID = V
Fee = $150

Patient number 023
Doctor number 5
Date of visit = 04/01/2010
Service ID = S
Fee = $750

Patient number 092
Doctor number 1
Date of visit = 04/01/2010
Service ID = G
Fee = $85

CHAPTER 6

Creating Reports and Mailing Labels

PERFORMANCE OBJECTIVES

Upon successful completion of Chapter 6, you will be able to:

- Create a report using the Report button
- Display a report in Print Preview
- Create a report with a query
- Format and customize a report
- Group and sort records in a report
- Create a report using the Report Wizard
- Create mailing labels using the Label Wizard

access Chapter 6

In this chapter, you will learn how to prepare reports from data in a table using the Report button in the Reports group in the Create tab and with the Report Wizard. You will also learn how to format and customize a report with options in the Report Layout Tools Format tab and create mailing labels using the Label Wizard.

Note: Before beginning computer projects, delete the Access2007L1C5 folder from your storage medium. Next, copy to your storage medium the Access2007L1C6 subfolder from the Access2007L1 folder on the CD that accompanies this textbook and make Access2007L1C6 the active folder.

Project 1 Create and Customize Reports Using Tables and Queries

You will create reports with the Report button using tables and queries. You will change the report views; select, move, and resize control objects; sort records; customize reports; apply conditional formatting; and group and sort fields in a report.

Creating a Report

The primary purpose for inserting data in a form is to improve the display of the data and to make data entry easier. You can also insert data in a report. The purpose for this is to control what data appears on the page when printed. Reports generally answer specific questions (queries). For example, a report could answer the question

Create a Report
1. Click Create tab.
2. Click desired table or query in Navigation pane.
3. Click Report button.

What customers have submitted claims? or *What products do we currently have on order?* You can use the Report button in the Reports group in the Create tab to create a report based on a table or query. You can also use the Report Wizard that walks you through the process of creating a report.

Creating a Report with the Report Button

To create a report with the Report button, click the desired table or query in the Navigation pane, click the Create tab, and then click the Report button in the Reports group. This displays the report in columnar style in Layout view with the Report Layout Tools Format tab active as shown in Figure 6.1. Access creates the report using all of the fields in the table.

HINT

Create a report to control what data appears on the page when printed.

Figure 6.1 Report Created with Sales Table

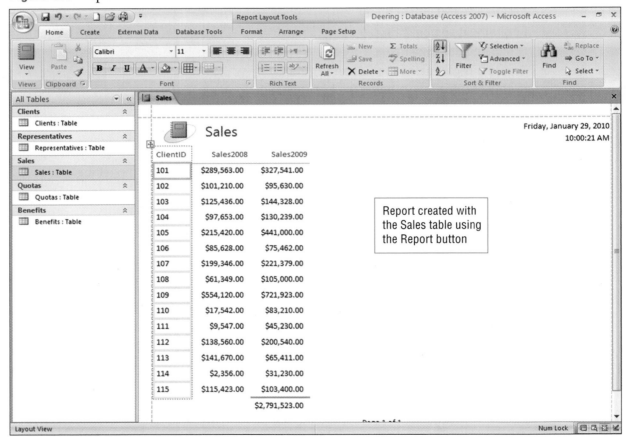

Project 1a Creating a Report with the Report Button

1. Remove the read-only attribute from the **Deering.accdb** database located in the Access2007L1C6 folder.
2. Open the **Deering.accdb** database.
3. Create a report by completing the following steps:
   a. Click the Sales table in the Navigation pane.
   b. Click the Create tab.
   c. Click the Report button in the Reports group.

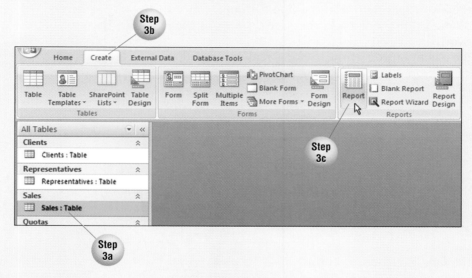

4. Print the report by clicking the Quick Print button on the Quick Access toolbar.
5. Save the report by clicking the Save button on the Quick Access toolbar, making sure *Sales* displays in the *Report Name* text box in the Save As dialog box, and then clicking OK.

Displaying a Report in Print Preview

When you create a report, the report displays in the work area in Layout view. This is one of four views available including Report view, Print Preview, and Design view. Use Print Preview to display the report as it will appear when printed. To change to Print Preview, click the Print Preview button in the view area located at the right side of the Status bar. You can also click the View button arrow in the Views group in either the Home tab or the Report Layout Tools Format tab and then click *Print Preview* at the drop-down list.

Print Preview

View

Print

At the Print Preview tab, send the report to the printer by clicking the Print button. Use options in the Page Layout group to specify the size, orientation, and margins of the printed report. Click the Size button and a drop-down list of size choices displays. By default, a report prints in portrait orientation. Click the Landscape button if you want the report printed in landscape orientation. Change margins with the Margins button in the Page Layout group and click the Page Setup button to display a dialog box with page layout options. If you want to print only the report data and not the column headings or report title, click the *Print Data Only* check box to insert a check mark. Use options in the Zoom group to display specific

Size

Landscape

Margins

Page Setup

locations in the report. The Print Preview tab also contains options for exporting a report to Word or to a text format. You will learn more about exporting data in Chapter 8.

Project 1b Displaying a Report in Print Preview

1. With the Sales report open, click the Print Preview button in the view area at the right side of the Status bar.
2. Click the Two Pages button in the Zoom group. (Since this report contains only one page, the page displays at the left side of the work area.)
3. Click the Zoom button arrow in the Zoom group and then click *50%* at the drop-down list.

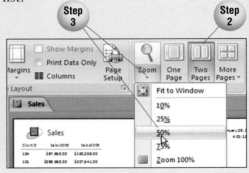

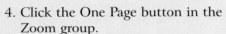

4. Click the One Page button in the Zoom group.
5. Click the Landscape button in the Page Layout group.
6. Click the Margins button in the Page Layout group and then click the *Wide* option at the drop-down list.
7. Print the report by clicking the Print button in the Print Preview tab and then clicking OK at the Print dialog box.
8. Close Print Preview by clicking the Close Print Preview button located at the right side of the Print Preview tab.
9. Close the Sales report.

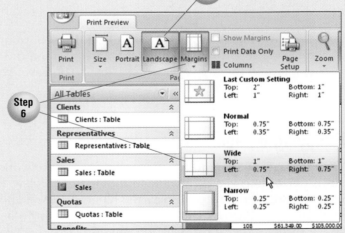

10. Create a report with the Clients table by completing the following steps:
    a. Click the Clients table in the Navigation pane.
    b. Click the Create tab.
    c. Click the Report button in the Reports group.
11. Click the Print Preview button in the view area at the right side of the Status bar.
12. Click the Two Pages button in the Zoom group.
13. Change the setup of the report by completing the following steps:
    a. Click the Page Setup button in the Page Layout group.

b. At the Page Setup dialog box with the Print Options tab selected, change the *Top*, *Bottom*, *Left*, and *Right* measurements to 1.

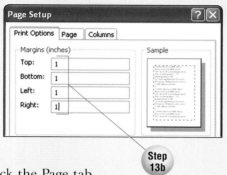

Step 13b

Step 13c

Step 13d

Step 13e

c. Click the Page tab.
d. At the Page Setup dialog box with the Page tab selected, click the *Landscape* option.
e. Click OK to close the dialog box.

14. After looking at the report, you decide to return to portrait orientation by clicking the Portrait button in the Page Layout group.
15. Print the report by clicking the Print button in the Print Preview tab and then clicking OK at the Print dialog box.
16. Close Print Preview by clicking the Close Print Preview button.
17. Save the report with the name *Clients*.
18. Close the Clients report.

Creating a Report with a Query

Since one of the purposes of a report is to answer specific questions, design and run a query and then create a report based on that query. Create a report from a query in the same manner as creating a report from a table.

Project **1c**   **Creating a Report with a Query**

1. With the **Deering.accdb** database open, create the following one-to-many relationships:

Field Name	"One" Table	"Many" Table
RepID	Representatives	Clients
RepID	Benefits	Clients
QuotaID	Quotas	Representatives

2. Create a one-to-one relationship between the *ClientID* field in the Clients table and the Sales table.
3. Save and then close the relationships window.
4. Design a query that extracts records from two tables with the following specifications:
   a. Add the Clients and Sales tables to the query window.
   b. Insert the *Client* field from the Clients table to the first *Field* text box.
   c. Insert the *StreetAddress* field from the Clients table to the second *Field* text box.

d. Insert the *City* field from the Clients table to the third *Field* text box.
e. Insert the *State* field from the Clients table to the fourth *Field* text box.
f. Insert the *ZipCode* field from the Clients table to the fifth *Field* text box.
g. Insert the *Sales2008* field from the Sales table to the sixth *Field* text box.
h. Insert the criterion *Indianapolis Or Muncie* in the *Criteria* text box in the *City* column.
i. Insert the criterion *>75000* in the *Criteria* text box in the *Sales2008* column.

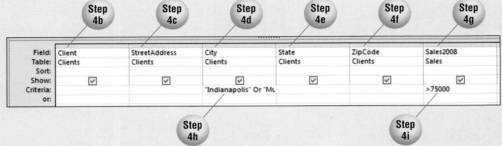

j. Run the query.
k. Save the query and name it *IndianapolisMuncieSalesOver$75000*.
l. Close the query.
5. Create a report with the query by completing the following steps:
a. Click the IndianapolisMuncieSalesOver$75000 query in the Navigation pane.
b. Click the Create tab.
c. Click the Report button in the Reports group.
d. Click the View button arrow in the Views group at the left side of the Report Layout Tools Format tab and then click *Print Preview* at the drop-down list.
e. Click the Landscape button in the Page Layout group.
f. Click the Margins button in the Page Layout group and then click the *Wide* option at the drop-down list.
g. Close Print Preview by clicking the Close Print Preview button.
6. Save the report and name it *IndianapolisMuncieSales*.
7. Print and then close the report.

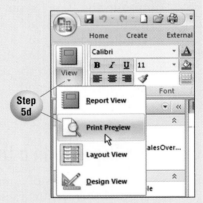

Selecting Control Objects

To apply formatting to specific control objects in a report, click the object to select it. If you click a data field in the report, Access selects all data in the column except the column heading. To select all control objects in a report, press Ctrl + A. You can also select multiple objects in a report by holding down the Shift key as you click each object.

Sizing and Moving a Control Object

Change the size of a selected control object by positioning the mouse pointer on the object border until the mouse pointer displays as a double-headed arrow and then drag in or out to decrease or increase the size of the object. A report, like a form, contains a report header that is the top portion of the report containing the logo container control object, the report title, and the current date and time. You can move a control object in a report header by clicking the object to select it and then dragging with the mouse to the desired location.

Changing the Width and Order of a Column

You can change the width of columns in a report. To do this, click in any data field in the column, position the mouse pointer on the right border of the column until the mouse pointer displays as a two-headed arrow pointing left and right, hold down the left mouse button, drag in or out to decrease or increase the width of the column, and then release the mouse button.

You can change the order of columns in a report. To do this, click the desired column heading, position the mouse pointer in the column heading until the pointer displays with a four-headed arrow attached, and then drag the column left or right to the desired position. As you drag the column, a vertical orange bar displays indicating the location at which the column will be placed when you release the mouse button.

Sorting Records

You can sort data in a report by clicking in the field containing data on which you want to sort and then clicking the Ascending button or Descending button in the Sort & Filter group in the Home tab. Click the Ascending button to sort text in alphabetic order from A to Z or numbers from lowest to highest, or click the Descending button to sort text in alphabetic order from Z to A or numbers from highest to lowest.

Sort Records
1. Click in field containing data.
2. Click Ascending or click Descending button.

Ascending

Descending

Project 1d   Sizing, Moving, and Sorting Control Objects

1. With the **Deering.accdb** database open, open the Sales report by right-clicking the Sales report in the Navigation pane and then clicking *Layout View* at the shortcut menu.
2. Close the Navigation pane by clicking the Shutter Bar Open/Close Button located in the upper right corner of the pane.

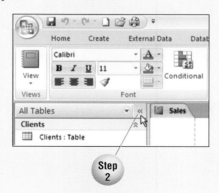

Step 2

3. Move the date control object by completing the following steps:
   a. Click the current date that displays in the upper right corner of the report.
   b. Position the mouse pointer inside the selected object (mouse displays with a four-headed arrow attached), drag to the left to the approximate location shown in the image below, and then release the mouse button.
4. Complete steps similar to those in Step 3 to move the time control object so it is right-aligned with the date (see image below).

5. Change the width of the *ClientID* column by completing the following steps:
   a. Click the *ClientID* column heading.
   b. Position the mouse pointer on the right border of the *ClientID* column until the mouse pointer displays as a double-headed arrow pointing left and right.
   c. Hold down the left mouse button, drag to the right the approximate distance shown in the image at the right, and then release the mouse button.
6. Reverse the order of the *Sales2008* and *Sales2009* columns by completing the following steps:
   a. Click the *Sales2009* column heading.
   b. Position the mouse pointer inside the *Sales2009* column heading until the pointer displays with a four-headed arrow attached.
   c. Hold down the left mouse button, drag to the left until the vertical orange bar displays between *ClientID* and *Sales2008*, and then release the mouse button.
7. Sort the records in the report by completing the following steps:
   a. Click in the field containing the amount *$289,563.00* (located below the *Sales2008* column heading).
   b. Click the Home tab.
   c. Click the Ascending button in the Sort & Filter group.

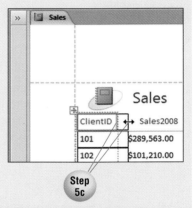

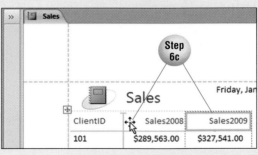

Customizing a Report

HINT
Customize the formatting of control objects with options at the Report Layout Tools Format tab.

A report, like a form, is comprised of a series of control objects, which are objects that display titles or descriptions, accept data, or perform actions. You can customize control objects with buttons in the Report Layout Tools Format tab.

Changing the Font

Use options in the Font group to change the font, font style, font size, and font color of the selected control object in the report. You can also change the alignment of text and apply fill to fields in the report.

Applying Conditional Formatting

Click the Conditional button in the Font group in the Report Layout Tools Format tab and the Conditional Formatting dialog box displays. This is the same dialog box that displays when you click the Conditional button in the Font group in the Form Layout Tools Format tab. With the options at this dialog box, specify the formatting you want applied to control objects that meet a specific criterion (condition).

Totaling Numbers

You can use the Totals button in the Grouping & Totals group in the Report Layout Tools Format tab to perform functions such as finding the sum, average, maximum, or minimum of the numbers in a column. To use the Totals button, click the column heading of the column containing data you want to total, click the Totals button in the Grouping & Totals group, and then click the desired function at the drop-down list.

Formatting Numbers and Applying Gridlines

The Report Layout Tools Format tab contains numbering and gridline options similar to those in the Form Layout Tools Format tab. Use options in the Formatting group to apply Currency, Percent, or Comma Number formatting to numbers and choose a number style from the Format option drop-down list. Use options in the Gridlines group to apply and customize gridlines to control objects.

Formatting Controls

Use options in the Controls group in the Report Layout Tools Format tab to insert a logo, title, or date and time. The group also contains buttons for applying lines to control objects and then changing the line thickness, type, and color. Click the

Add Existing Fields button in the Controls group and the Field List window displays. This window displays the fields available in the current view, fields available in related tables, and fields available in other tables.

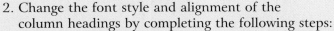

Project 1e — Applying Fonts and Conditional Formatting to a Report

1. With the Sales report open, change the font for all control objects in the report by completing the following steps:
   a. Press Ctrl + A to select all control objects in the report (an orange border displays around objects).
   b. Click the Font button arrow in the Font group in the Report Layout Tools Format tab and then click *Cambria* at the drop-down list. (You will need to scroll down the list to display *Cambria*.)

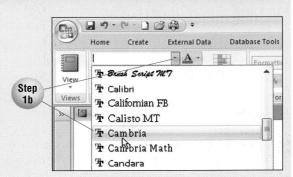

2. Change the font style and alignment of the column headings by completing the following steps:
   a. Click *ClientID* to select the control object (orange border surrounds the object).
   b. Hold down the Shift key, click *Sales2009*, and then click *Sales2008*.
   c. Click the Center button in the Font group.
   d. Click the Bold button in the Font group.

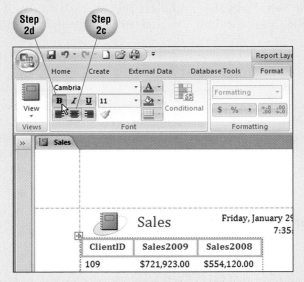

3. Change the alignment of data in the *ClientID* column by clicking *109* (below the *ClientID* column heading) and then clicking the Center button in the Font group.
4. Format amounts and apply conditional formatting to the amounts in the report by completing the following steps:
   a. Click the control object containing the amount *$721,923.00*. (This selects all of the amounts in the column.)
   b. Hold down the Shift key and then click the control object containing the amount *$554,120.00*.

c. Click twice on the Decrease Decimals button in the Formatting group in the Report Layout Tools Format tab.

d. Click the Conditional button in the Font group.

e. At the Conditional Formatting dialog box, click the down-pointing arrow in the second list box in the *Condition 1* section and then click *greater than* at the drop-down list.

f. Click in the text box immediately right of the option box containing *greater than* and then type 199999.

g. Click the Fill/Back Color button arrow and then click the seventh color option from the left in the third row (light green).

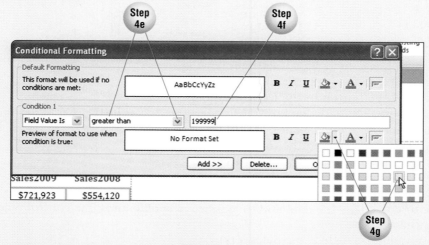

h. Click the Add button. (This inserts a *Condition 2* section toward the bottom of the dialog box.)

i. Click the down-pointing arrow in the second list box in the *Condition 2* section and then click *less than* at the drop-down list.

j. Click in the text box immediately right of the option containing *less than* and then type 200000.

k. Click the Fill/Back Color button arrow and then click the sixth color from the left in the second row (light red).

l. Click OK to close the dialog box.

5. Apply and format gridlines by completing the following steps:

a. Click the *ClientID* column heading, hold down the Shift key, click *Sales2009*, and then click *Sales2008*.

b. Click the Gridlines button in the Gridlines group in the Report Layout Tools Format tab and then click *Cross Hatch* at the drop-down list.

c. Click the Color button arrow in the Gridlines group and then click the purple color at the drop-down list (last color in the bottom row in the *Standard Colors* section).

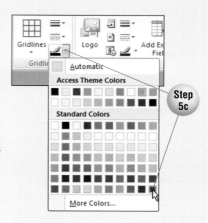

d. Click in the control object containing the number *109*, hold down the Shift key, click the amount *$721,923*, and then click the amount *$554,120*.

e. Click the Gridlines button in the Gridlines group and then click *Cross Hatch* at the drop-down list.

f. Click the Color button. (This applies the purple color to the line.)

6. Sum the totals in the *Sales2008* column by completing the following steps:
   a. Click in the *Sales2008* column heading.
   b. Click the Totals button and then click *Sum* at the drop-down list.

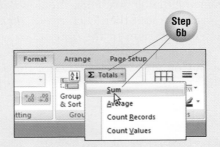

7. Insert a logo image by completing the following steps:
   a. Click the logo container content control object.
   b. Click the Logo button in the Controls group.
   c. At the Insert Picture dialog box, navigate to the Access2007L1C6 folder on your storage medium and then double-click **Mountain.jpg**.
8. Insert a title by completing the following steps:
   a. Click the Title button in the Controls group.
   b. Type **2008-2009 Sales**.
   c. Click the Bold button in the Font group.
   d. If the title overlaps the date and time, select the date and time control objects and then move them to the right.
9. Save, print, and then close the Sales report.
10. Display the Navigation pane by clicking the Shutter Bar Open/Close Button.

Apply AutoFormat
1. Click Report Layout Tools Format tab.
2. Click AutoFormat button.
3. Click desired autoformat at drop-down list.

Applying AutoFormats

Click the AutoFormat button in the Report Layout Tools Format tab to display a list of autoformats. These are the same autoformats available in the Form Layout Tools Format tab. The names of the autoformats align with the theme names in Word, Excel, and PowerPoint. Apply an autoformat by clicking the AutoFormat button and then clicking the desired autoformat at the drop-down list.

HINT

Autoformats apply formatting similar to themes in Word, Excel, and PowerPoint.

Changing Page Setup

The Print Preview tab contains options for changing page setup options such as margins, orientation, and size. Many of these options are also available in the Report Layout Tools Page Setup tab. Display this tab by opening a report in Layout view and then clicking the Page Setup tab in the Report Layout Tools tab.

Grouping and Sorting Records

A report presents database information in a printed form and generally displays data that answers a specific question. To make the data in a report easy to understand you can divide the data into groups. For example, you can divide data in a report by region, sales, dates, or any other division that helps identify the data to the reader. Access contains a powerful group and sort feature you can use in a report. In this section you will complete basic group and sort functions. For more detailed information on grouping and sorting, please refer to the Access help files.

Click the Group & Sort button in the Grouping & Totals group in the Report Layout Tools Format tab and the Group, Sort, and Total pane displays at the bottom of the work area as shown in Figure 6.2. Click the Add a group button in the Group, Sort, and Total pane and Access adds a new grouping level row to the pane along with a list of available fields. Click the field on which you want to group data in the report and Access adds the grouping level in the report. With options in the grouping level row, you can change the group, specify the sort order, and expand the row to display additional options.

QUICK STEPS

Group and Sort Records
1. Open desired report in layout view.
2. Click Report Layout Tools Format tab.
3. Click Group & Sort button.
4. Click Add a group button.
5. Click desired group field.

HINT
Grouping allows you to separate groups of records visually.

Figure 6.2 Group, Sort, and Total Pane

Group records by a specific field by clicking this button and then clicking the desired field.

Sort records by a specific field by clicking this button and then clicking the desired field.

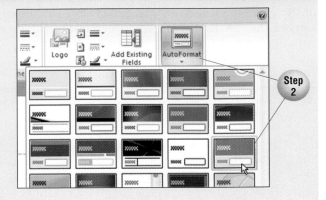

When you specify a grouping level, Access automatically sorts that level in ascending order (from A to Z or from lowest to highest). You can then sort additional data within the report by clicking the Add a sort button in the Group, Sort, and Total pane. This inserts a sorting row in the pane below the grouping level row along with a list of available fields. At this list, click the field on which you want to sort. For example, in Project 1f you will specify that a report is grouped by city (which will display in ascending order) and then specify that the client names display in alphabetical order within the city.

To delete a grouping or sorting level in the Group, Sort, and Total pane, click the Delete button that displays at the right side of the level row. After specifying the grouping and sorting levels, close the Group, Sort, and Total pane by clicking the close button located in the upper right corner of the pane.

Project 1f Applying an AutoFormat and Grouping and Sorting Data

1. With the **Deering.accdb** database open, open the Clients report in Layout view.
2. Click the AutoFormat button in the AutoFormat group in the Report Layout Tools Format tab and then click *Northwind* at the drop-down list.
3. Click each of the column headings individually and then decrease the size of each column so the right border of the column is just right of the longest entry in each column.
4. Change the orientation to landscape by completing the following steps:
   a. Click the Report Layout Tools Page Setup tab.
   b. Click the Landscape button in the Page Setup group.
5. Group the report by RepID and then sort by clients by completing the following steps:
   a. Click the Report Layout Tools Format tab.
   b. Click the Group & Sort button in the Grouping & Tools group.
   c. Click the Add a group button in the Group, Sort, and Total pane.
   d. Click the *RepID* field in the list box.
   e. Scroll through the report and notice that the records are grouped by the *RepID* field. Also, notice that the client names within each RepID group are not in alphabetic order.
   f. Click the Add a sort button in the Group, Sort, and Total pane.
   g. Click the *Client* field in the list box.
   h. Scroll through the report and notice that client names are now alphabetized within RepID groups.

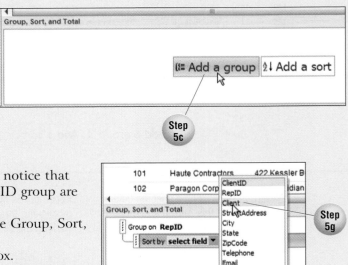

i. Close the Group, Sort, and Total pane by clicking the Close button located in the upper right corner of the pane.

6. Save, print, and then close the Clients report.
7. Open the IndianapolisMuncieSales report in Layout view.
8. Click the AutoFormat button in the AutoFormat group in the Report Layout Tools Format tab and then click *Northwind* at the drop-down list.
9. Click each of the column headings individually and then decrease the size of each column so the right border of the column is near the longest entry in each column.
10. Group the report by city and then sort by clients by completing the following steps:
   a. Click the Group & Sort button in the Grouping & Tools group in the Report Layout Tools Format tab.
   b. Click the Add a group button in the Group, Sort, and Total pane.
   c. Click the *City* field in the list box.
   d. Click the Add a sort button in the Group, Sort, and Total pane and then click the *Client* field in the list box.
   e. Close the Group, Sort, and Total pane by clicking the Close button located in the upper right corner of the pane.
11. Save, print, and then close the IndianapolisMuncieSales report.
12. Close the **Deering.accdb** database.
13. Remove the read-only attribute from the **LegalServices.accdb** database located in the Access2007L1C6 folder.
14. Open the **LegalServices.accdb** database.
15. Design a query that extracts records from three tables with the following specifications:
   a. Add the Billing, Clients, and Rates tables to the query window.
   b. Insert the *LastName* field from the Clients table to the first *Field* text box.
   c. Insert the *Date* field from the Billings table to the second *Field* text box.
   d. Insert the *Hours* field from the Billings table to the third *Field* text box.
   e. Insert the *Rate* field from the Rates table to the fourth *Field* text box.
   f. Click in the fifth *Field* text box, type **Total: [Hours]*[Rate]**, and then press Enter.

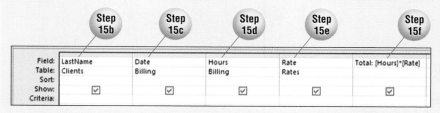

	Step 15b	Step 15c	Step 15d	Step 15e	Step 15f
Field:	LastName	Date	Hours	Rate	Total: [Hours]*[Rate]
Table:	Clients	Billing	Billing	Rates	
Sort:					
Show:	☑	☑	☑	☑	☑
Criteria:					

   g. Run the query.
   h. Save the query and name it *ClientBilling*.
   i. Close the query.
16. Create a report with the query by completing the following steps:
   a. Click the ClientBilling query in the Navigation pane.
   b. Click the Create tab.
   c. Click the Report button in the Reports group.
17. Click the AutoFormat button in the Report Layout Tools Format tab and then click *Median* at the drop-down list.

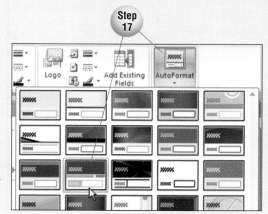

18. Click each of the column headings individually and then decrease the size of each column so the right border of the column is near the longest entry.

19. Click in the first field below the *Total* column (the field containing the data *262.5*) and then click the Apply Currency Format button in the Formatting group. If necessary, increase the column width to display all amounts.

20. Group the report by last name by completing the following steps:
    a. Click the Group & Sort button in the Grouping & Tools group.
    b. Click the Add a group button in the Group, Sort, and Total pane.
    c. Click the *LastName* field in the list box.
    d. Click the Add a sort button in the Group, Sort, and Total pane.
    e. Click the *Date* field in the list box.
    f. Close the Group, Sort, and Total pane by clicking the Close button located in the upper right corner of the pane.

21. Save the report and name it *ClientBillingReport*.

22. Print and then close the report.

23. Close the **LegalServices.accdb** database.

Step 19

LastName	Date	Hours	Rate	Total
Czubek	6/1/2010	1.75	$150.00	262.5
Czubek	6/3/2010	0.50	$150.00	75

ClientBilling

Project ② Use Wizards to Create Reports and Labels

You will create reports using the Report Wizard and prepare mailing labels using the Label Wizard.

QUICK STEPS

Creating a Report Using the Report Wizard

Create a Report Using Report Wizard
1. Click Create tab.
2. Click Report Wizard button.
3. Choose desired options at each of the Report Wizard dialog boxes.

HINT
Use the Report Wizard to select specific fields and specify how data is grouped and sorted.

Report Wizard

Access offers a Report Wizard that will guide you through the steps for creating a report. To create a report using the wizard, click the Create tab and then click the Report Wizard button in the Reports group. At the first wizard dialog box, shown in Figure 6.3, choose the desired table with options from the *Tables/Queries* option box. Specify the fields you want included in the report by inserting them in the *Selected Fields* list box and then clicking the Next button.

Figure 6.3 First Form Wizard Dialog Box

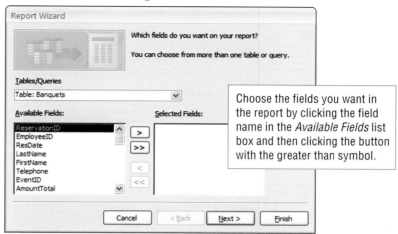

At the second Report Wizard dialog box, shown in Figure 6.4, you can specify the grouping level of data in the report. To group data by a specific field, click the field in the list box at the left side of the dialog box and then click the button containing the greater than symbol. Use the button containing the left-pointing arrow to remove an option as a grouping level. Use the up-pointing and down-pointing arrows to change the priority of the field.

Figure 6.4 Second Report Wizard Dialog Box

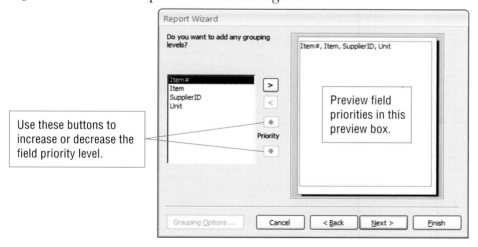

Specify a sort order with options at the third Report Wizard dialog box shown in Figure 6.5. To specify a sort order, click the down-pointing arrow at the right of the option box preceded by a number 1 and then click the field name. The default sort is done in ascending order. You can change this to descending by clicking the button that displays at the right side of the text box. After identifying the sort order, click the Next button.

Figure 6.5 Third Report Wizard Dialog Box

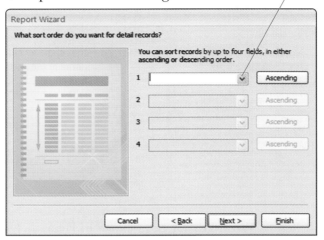

Specify a sort order by clicking this down-pointing arrow and then clicking the desired field name.

Use options at the fourth Report Wizard dialog box as shown in Figure 6.6 to specify the layout and orientation of the report. The *Layout* option has a default setting of *Stepped*. You can change this to *Block* or *Outline*. By default the report will print in *Portrait* orientation. You can change this to *Landscape* in the *Orientation* section of the dialog box. Access will adjust field widths in the report so all fields fit on one page. If you do not want Access to make the adjustment, remove the check mark from the *Adjust the field width so all fields fit on a page* option.

Figure 6.6 Fourth Report Wizard Dialog Box

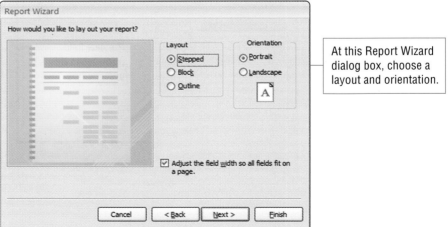

At this Report Wizard dialog box, choose a layout and orientation.

Choose an autoformat for the report at the fifth Report Wizard dialog box. By default, Access selects the autoformat that was previously applied to a report. Click the desired autoformat and then click the Next button. At the final Report Wizard dialog box, type a name for the report and then click the Finish button.

1. Remove the read-only attribute from the **Skyline.accdb** database located in the Access2007L1C6 folder.
2. Open the **Skyline.accdb** database.
3. Create a report using the Report Wizard by completing the following steps:
   a. Click the Create tab.
   b. Click the Report Wizard button in the Reports group.
   c. At the first Report Wizard dialog box, click the down-pointing arrow at the right side of the *Tables/Queries* option box and then click *Table: Inventory* at the drop-down list.
   d. Click the button containing the two greater than symbols to insert all Inventory fields in the *Selected Fields* list box.
   e. Click the Next button.

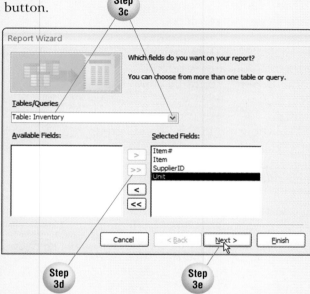

f. At the second Report Wizard dialog box, click the *SupplierID* field in the list box at the left side of the dialog box and then click the button containing the greater than symbol. (This tells Access that you want data in the report grouped by the supplier identification number.)

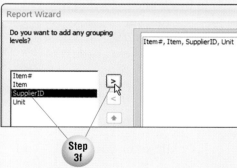

g. Click the Next button.
h. At the third Report Wizard dialog box, click the Next button. (You want to use the sorting defaults.)
i. At the fourth Report Wizard dialog box, click the *Block* option in the *Layout* section and then click the Next button.
j. At the fifth Report Wizard dialog box, click *Concourse* in the style list box and then click the Next button.
k. At the sixth Report Wizard dialog box, make sure *Inventory* displays in the *What title do you want for your report?* text box and then click the Finish button.
4. Change to Layout view. (If the *Field List* option box displays, close it.)
5. Decrease the column width for the *Item* and *Unit* columns so the right border of the column is just right of the longest entry.
6. Save, print, and then close the Inventory report.

If you create a report with fields from only one table, you will choose options from six Report Wizard dialog boxes. If you create a report with fields from more than one table, you will choose options from seven Report Wizard dialog boxes. After choosing the tables and fields at the first dialog box, the second dialog box that displays asks how you want to view the data. For example, if you specify fields from a Suppliers table and fields from an Orders table, the second Report Wizard dialog box will ask you if you want to view data "by Suppliers" or "by Orders."

Project 2b   Creating a Report with Fields from Multiple Tables

1. With the **Skyline.accdb** database open, create the following one-to-many relationships:

Field Name	"One" Table	"Many" Table
SupplierID	Suppliers	Orders
EmployeeID	Employees	Banquets
EventID	Events	Banquets

2. Save and then close the relationships window.
3. Create a report with the Report Wizard by completing the following steps:
   a. Click the Create tab.
   b. Click the Report Wizard button in the Reports group.
   c. At the first Report Wizard dialog box, click the down-pointing arrow at the right side of the *Tables/Queries* option box and then click *Table: Events* at the drop-down list.

   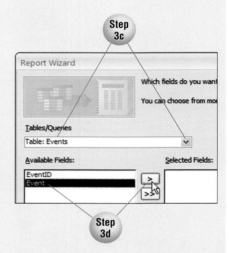

   d. Click the *Event* field in the *Available Fields* list box and then click the button containing the greater than (>) symbol.
   e. Click the down-pointing arrow at the right side of the *Tables/Queries* option box and then click *Table: Banquets* at the drop-down list.
   f. Insert the following fields in the *Selected Fields* list box:
      ResDate
      LastName
      FirstName
      Telephone
      AmountTotal
      AmountPaid
   g. After inserting the fields, click the Next button.
   h. At the second Report Wizard dialog box, make sure *by Events* is selected and then click the Next button.
   i. At the third Report Wizard dialog box, click the Next button. (The report preview shows that the report will be grouped by event.)

   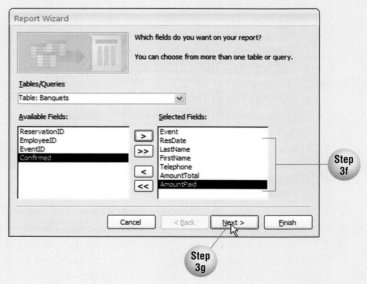

j. At the fourth Report Wizard dialog box, click the Next button. (You want to use the sorting defaults.)

k. At the fifth Report Wizard dialog box, click the *Block* option in the *Layout* section, click *Landscape* in the *Orientation* section, and then click the Next button.

l. At the sixth Report Wizard dialog box, make sure *Concourse* is selected in the style list box and then click the Next button.

m. At the seventh Report Wizard dialog box, select the current name in the *What title do you want for your report?* text box, type BanquetEvents, and then click the Finish button.

4. Change to Layout view.

5. Increase and/or decrease the size of each column to display the longest entry in each column.

6. Save, print, and then close the BanquetEvents report.

7. Close the **Skyline.accdb** database.

Preparing Mailing Labels

Access includes a mailing label wizard that walks you through the steps for creating mailing labels with fields in a table. To create mailing labels, click the Create tab and then click the Labels button in the Reports group. At the first Label Wizard dialog box shown in Figure 6.7, specify the label size, units of measure, and the label type, and then click the Next button.

QUICK STEPS

Create Mailing Labels Using Label Wizard
1. Click Create tab.
2. Click Labels button.
3. Choose desired options at each of the Label Wizard dialog boxes.

Figure 6.7 First Label Wizard Dialog Box

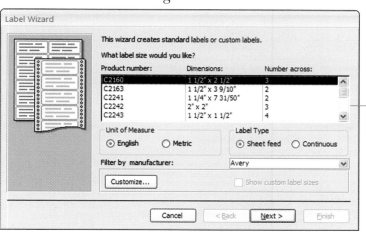

Scroll through this list box and choose the desired label.

At the second Label Wizard dialog box shown in Figure 6.8, specify the font name, size, weight, and color, and then click the Next button.

Figure 6.8 Second Label Wizard Dialog Box

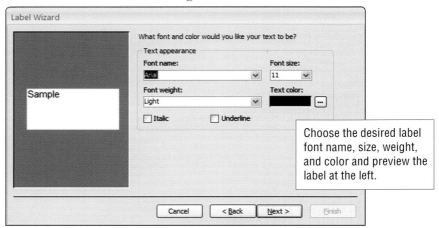

Specify the fields you want included in the mailing labels at the third Label Wizard dialog box shown in Figure 6.9. To do this, click the field in the *Available fields* list box, and then click the button containing the greater than symbol (>). This moves the field to the *Prototype label* box. Insert the fields in the *Prototype label* box as you want the text to display on the label. After inserting the fields in the *Prototype label* box, click the Next button.

Figure 6.9 Third Label Wizard Dialog Box

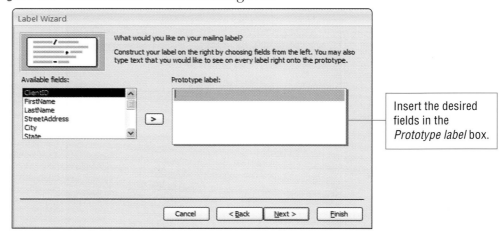

At the fourth Label Wizard dialog box, shown in Figure 6.10, you can specify a field from the database by which the labels are sorted. If you want the labels sorted (for example, by last name, postal code, etc.), insert the field by which you want the fields sorted in the *Sort by* list box and then click the Next button.

Figure 6.10 Fourth Label Wizard Dialog Box

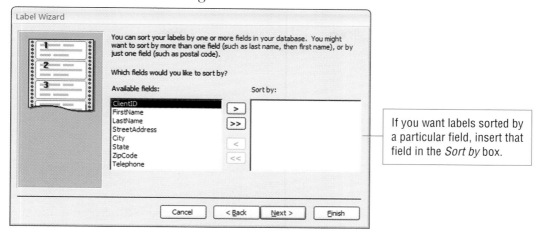

If you want labels sorted by a particular field, insert that field in the *Sort by* box.

At the last Label Wizard dialog box, type a name for the label file, and then click the Finish button. After a few moments, the labels display on the screen in Print Preview. Print the labels and/or close Print Preview.

Project 2c   Preparing Mailing Labels

1. Open the **LegalServices.accdb** database.
2. Click the Clients table in the Navigation pane.
3. Click the Create tab and then click the Labels button in the Reports group.
4. At the first Label Wizard dialog box, make sure *English* is selected in the *Unit of Measure* section, *Avery* is selected in the *Filter by manufacturer* list box, *Sheet feed* is selected in the *Label Type* section, *C2160* is selected in the *Product number* list box, and then click the Next button.

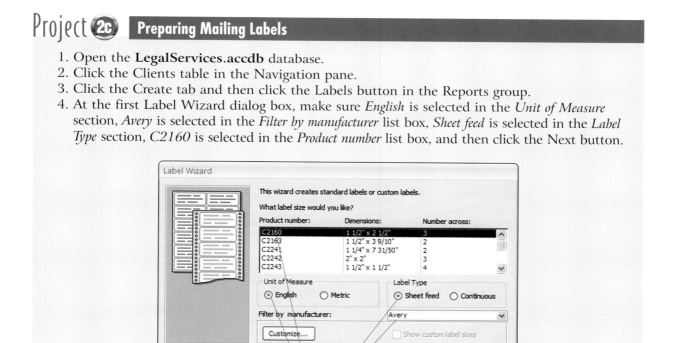

5. At the second Label Wizard dialog box, if necessary, change the font size to 11, and then click the Next button.
6. At the third Label Wizard dialog box, complete the following steps to insert the fields in the *Prototype label* box:
   a. Click *FirstName* in the *Available fields* list box and then click the button containing the greater than symbol (>).
   b. Press the spacebar, make sure *LastName* is selected in the *Available fields* list box, and then click the button containing the greater than symbol (>).
   c. Press the Enter key (this moves the insertion point down to the next line in the *Prototype label* box).
   d. With *StreetAddress* selected in the *Available fields* list box, click the button containing the greater than symbol (>).
   e. Press the Enter key.
   f. With *City* selected in the *Available fields* list box, click the button containing the greater than symbol (>).
   g. Type a comma (,) and then press the spacebar.
   h. With *State* selected in the *Available fields* list box, click the button containing the greater than symbol (>).
   i. Press the spacebar.
   j. With *ZipCode* selected in the *Available fields* list box, click the button containing the greater than symbol (>).

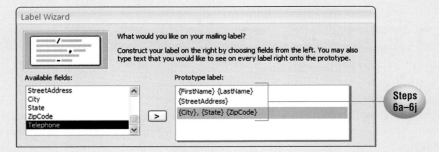

Steps 6a–6j

   k. Click the Next button.
7. At the fourth Label Wizard dialog box, sort by ZIP code. To do this, click *ZipCode* in the *Available fields* list box and then click the button containing the greater than symbol (>).
8. Click the Next button.
9. At the last Label Wizard dialog box, click the Finish button. (The Label Wizard automatically names the label report *Labels Clients*.)
10. Print the labels by clicking the Quick Print button on the Quick Access toolbar.
11. Close the labels report and then close the **LegalServices.accdb** database.

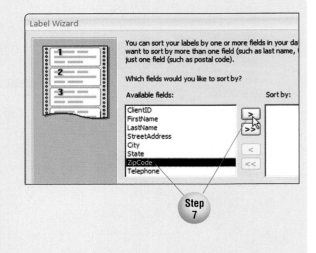

Step 7

CHAPTER summary

- You can create a report with data in a table or query to control how data appears on the page when printed.

- Create a report with the Report button in the Reports group in the Create tab.

- Four views are available for viewing a report—Report view, Print Preview, Layout view, and Design view.

- Use options in the Print Preview tab to specify how a report prints.

- In Layout view, you can select a report control object and then size or move the object. You can also change column width by clicking a column heading and then dragging the border to the desired width.

- Sort data in a record using the Ascending or Descending buttons in the Sort & Filter group in the Home tab.

- Customize a report with options in the Report Layout Tools Format tab.

- Apply font formatting to a report with options in the Font group in the Report Layout Tools Format tab.

- Apply conditional formatting to a report with options at the Conditional Formatting dialog box. Display this dialog box by clicking the Conditional button in the Font group in the Report Layout Tools Format tab.

- Use the Totals button in the Grouping & Totals group in the Report Layout Tools Format tab to perform functions such as finding the sum, average, maximum, or minimum of the numbers in a column.

- Apply formatting to numbers with options in the Formatting group in the Report Layout Tools Format tab and apply gridline formatting with options in the Gridlines group.

- Use options in the Controls group in the Report Layout Tools Format tab to insert a logo, title, or the date and time. Click the Add Existing Fields button in the Controls group to display the Field List window.

- Click the AutoFormat button in the Report Layout Tools Format tab to display a list of autoformats.

- Use options in the Report Layout Tools Page Setup tab to change the page setup for a report.

- To make data in a report easier to understand, divide the data into groups using the Group, Sort, and Total pane. Display this pane by clicking the Group & Sort button in the Grouping & Totals group in the Report Layout Tools Format tab.

- Use the Report Wizard to guide you through the steps for creating a report. Begin the wizard by clicking the Create tab and then clicking the Report Wizard button in the Reports group.

- Create mailing labels with data in a table using the Label Wizard. Begin the wizard by clicking the Create tab and then clicking the Labels button in the Reports group.

COMMANDS review

FEATURE	RIBBON TAB, GROUP	BUTTON, OPTION
Report	Create, Reports	
Conditional Formatting dialog box	Report Layout Tools Format, Font	
Field List window	Report Layout Tools Format, Controls	
Group, Sort, and Total pane	Report Layout Tools Format, Grouping & Totals	
Report Wizard	Create, Reports	Report Wizard
Labels Wizard	Create, Reports	Labels

CONCEPTS check

Test Your Knowledge

Completion: In the space provided at the right, indicate the correct term, symbol, or command.

1. Create a report with the Report button in the Create tab and the report displays in the work area in this view.

2. Layout view is one of four views available in a report including Report view, Design view, and this.

3. Press these keys to select all control objects in a report in Layout view.

4. The Ascending button is located in this group in the Home tab.

5. Click the Conditional button in the Font group in the Report Layout Tools Format tab and this dialog box displays.

6. Click this button in the Grouping & Totals group in the Report Layout Tools Format tab to perform functions such as finding the sum, average, maximum, or minimum of the numbers in a column.

7. Click the Add Existing Fields button in the Controls group in the Report Layout Tools Format tab and this displays.

8. The Group & Sort button is located in this group in the Report Layout Tools Format tab.

_____

9. Click the Group & Sort button and this pane displays.

_____

10. Use this to guide you through the steps for creating a report.

_____

SKILLS check

Demonstrate Your Proficiency

Assessment

1

CREATE AND FORMAT REPORTS IN THE HILLTOP DATABASE

1. Open the **Hilltop.accdb** database.
2. Create a report with the Inventory table.
3. With the report in Layout view, apply the following formatting:
   a. Center the data below each of the following column headings: *Equipment#*, *AvailableHours*, *ServiceHours*, and *RepairHours*.
   b. Select all of the control objects and then change the font to Constantia.
   c. Select the date control object and then move the object so the right side aligns with the right side of the *RepairHours* column.
   d. Select the time control object and then move the object so the right side aligns with the right side of the date.
   e. Select the money amounts below the *PurchasePrice* column heading and then decrease the decimal so the money amounts display without a decimal point.
   f. Click in the *$473,260.00* amount and then decrease the decimal so the amount displays without a decimal.
   g. Apply horizontal gridlines to the column headings and the data below each column heading (except the amount *$473,260*).
   h. Change the title of the report to *Inventory Report*.
4. Save the report and name it *Inventory Report*.
5. Print and then close Inventory Report.
6. Create a query in Design view with the following specifications:
   a. Add the Customers, Equipment, Invoices, and Rates tables to the query window.
   b. Insert the *Customer* field from the Customers table in the first *Field* text box.
   c. Insert the *Equipment* field from the Equipment table in the second *Field* text box.
   d. Insert the *Hours* field from the Invoices table in the third *Field* text box.
   e. Insert the *Rate* field from the Rates table in the fourth *Field* text box.
   f. Click in the fifth *Field* text box, type Total: [Hours]*[Rate], and then press Enter.
   g. Run the query.
   h. Save the query and name it *CustomerRentals* and then close the query.
7. Create a report with the CustomerRentals query using the Report button.

8. With the report in Layout view, apply the following formatting:
   a. Decrease the width of columns so the right border of each column displays near the right side of the longest entry.
   b. Select the money amounts and then decrease the decimal so the amounts display with no decimal point.
   c. Click in the 8305 amount (located at the bottom of the Total column), click the Apply Currency Format button, and then decrease the decimal so the amount displays without a decimal point.
   d. Display the Group, Sort, and Total pane, group the records by *Customer*, sort by *Equipment*, and then close the pane.
   e. Apply the Apex autoformat.
   f. Select the date control object and the time control object, change the font color to black, and then drag the objects to the left so the right border of the objects aligns with the right side of the *Total* column.
   g. Select the five column headings and then change the font color to white and turn on bold.
   h. Change the title to *Rentals*.
   i. Make sure the margins are set to *Narrow*.
   j. Display the report in Print Preview and make sure the data will print on one page, and then change to Layout view.
9. Save the report and name it *Rental Report*.
10. Print and then close Rental Report.

Figure out!

GO BACK AND DO AFTER!

Assessment

2 / CREATE REPORTS USING THE REPORT WIZARD

1. With the **Hilltop.accdb** database open, create a report using the Report Wizard with the following specifications:
   a. At the first Report Wizard dialog box, insert the following fields in the *Selected Fields* list box:
      From the Equipment table:
        Equipment
      From the Inventory table:
        Purchase Date
        Purchase Price
        Available Hours
   b. Do not make any changes at the second Report Wizard dialog box.
   c. Do not make any changes at the third Report Wizard dialog box.
   d. At the fourth Report Wizard dialog box, choose the *Columnar* option.
   e. At the fifth Report Wizard dialog box, make sure the Apex autoformat is selected.
   f. At the last Report Wizard dialog box, click the Finish button. (This accepts the default report name of *Equipment*.)
2. Print and then close the report.
3. Create a report using the Report Wizard with the following specifications:
   a. At the first Report Wizard dialog box, insert the following fields in the *Selected Fields* list box:
      From the Customers table:
        Customer

From the Invoices table:
    BillingDate
    Hours
From the Equipment table:
    Equipment
From the Rates table:
    Rate

  b. Do not make any changes at the second Report Wizard dialog box.
  c. Do not make any changes at the third Report Wizard dialog box.
  d. Do not make any changes at the fourth Report Wizard dialog box.
  e. At the fifth Report Wizard dialog box, choose the *Block* option.
  f. At the sixth Report Wizard dialog box, make sure the Apex autoformat is selected.
  g. At the last Report Wizard dialog box, name the report *Rentals*.
4. Increase or decrease column widths to display column data.
5. Print and then close the report.

Assessment

3 CREATE MAILING LABELS

1. With the **Hilltop.accdb** database open, click the Customers table in the Navigation pane.
2. Use the Label Wizard to create mailing labels (you determine the label type) with the customer names and addresses and sorted by customer names. Name the mailing label report *Customer Mailing Labels*.
3. Print the mailing labels.
4. Close the mailing labels.

Assessment

4 ADD A FIELD TO A REPORT

1. In Chapter 5, you added a field list to an existing form using the Field List window. Experiment with adding a field to an existing report and then complete the following:
  a. Open the report named Rental Report (created in Assessment 1).
  b. Display the Field List window and display all tables.
  c. Drag the *BillingDate* field from the Invoices table so the field is positioned between the *Equipment* column and the *Hours* column.
  d. At the message indicating that Access will modify the RecordSource property and asking if you want to continue, click Yes.
2. Decrease the widths of the columns to ensure that all columns will fit on one page.
3. Save, print, and then close the report.
4. Close the **Hilltop.accdb** database.

CASE study
Apply Your Skills

As the office manager at Millstone Legal Services, you need to enter records for three new clients in the **MillstoneLegal.accdb** database. Using the following information, enter the data in the appropriate tables:

Patient number 42
Martin Costanzo
1002 Thomas Drive
Casper, WY 82602
(307) 555-5001
Mr. Costanzo saw Douglas Sheehan regarding divorce proceedings on 3/14/2010 with a fee of $150.

Patient number 43
Susan Nordyke
23193 Ridge Circle East
Mills, WY 82644
(307) 555-2719
Ms. Nordyke saw Loretta Ryder regarding support enforcement on 3/14/2010 with a fee of $75.

Patient number 44
Monica Sommers
1105 Riddell Avenue
Casper, WY 82609
(307) 555-1188
Ms. Sommers saw Anita Leland regarding a guardianship on 3/15/2010 for a fee of $150.

Part 2

Create the following queries, reports, and labels:

- Create a report with the Clients table. Apply formatting to enhance the visual appeal of the report.
- Create a query that displays the client ID, first name, and last name; attorney last name; date of visit; and fee. Name the query *ClientBilling*.
- Create a report with the ClientBilling query. Group the records in the report by attorney last name (the second *LastName* field in the drop-down list) and sort alphabetically in ascending order by client last name (the first *LastName* field in the drop-down list). Apply formatting to enhance the visual appeal of the report.
- Create a telephone directory by creating a report that includes client last names, first names, and telephone numbers. Sort the records in the report alphabetically by last name and in ascending order.
- Edit the ClientBilling query so it includes a criterion that displays only visits between 3/01/2010 and 3/05/2010. Save the query with Save As and name it *ClientBilling01-05*.
- Create a report with the ClientBilling01-05 query. Apply formatting to enhance the visual appeal of the report.
- Create mailing labels for the clients.

Part 3

Apply the following conditions to fields in reports:

- In the Clients report, apply the condition that the city *Casper* displays in red and the city *Mills* displays in blue in the *City* field.
- In the ClientBilling report, apply the condition that amounts over $99 display in green and amounts less than $100 display in blue.

Your center has a procedures manual that describes processes and procedures in the center. Open Word and then create a document for the procedures manual that describes the process for creating a report using the Report button, the Report Wizard, and the process for preparing mailing labels using the Label Wizard. Save the completed document and name it **Access_C6_CS_P4**. Print and then close **Access_C6_CS_P4.docx**.

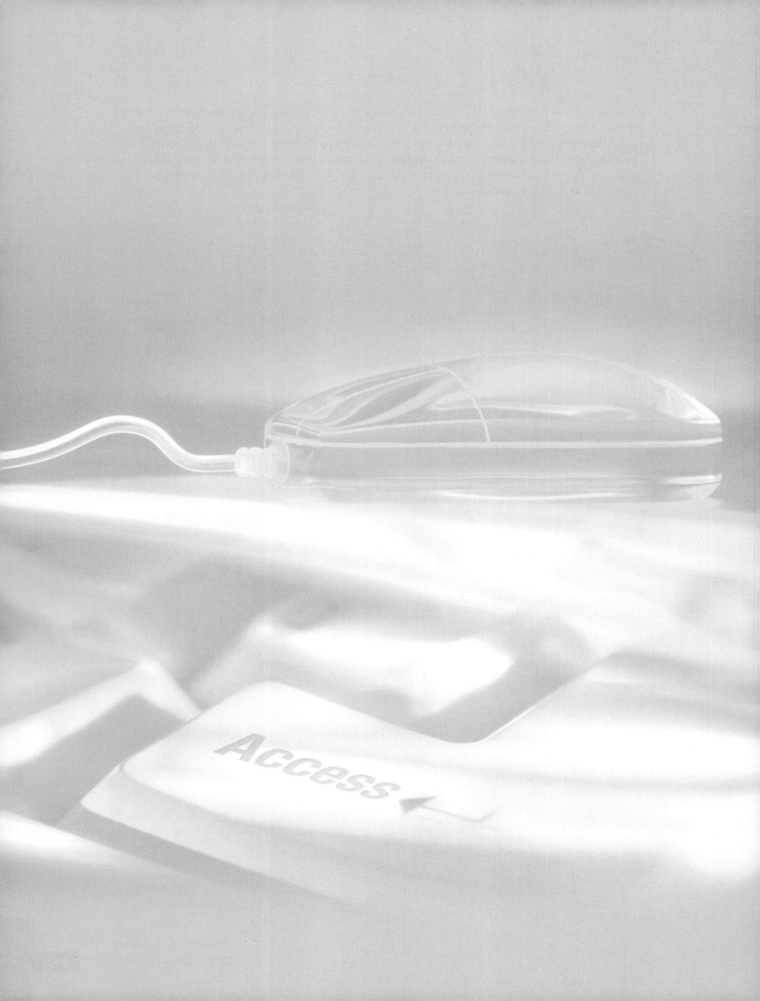

Modifying, Filtering, and Viewing Data

PERFORMANCE OBJECTIVES

Upon successful completion of Chapter 7, you will be able to:

- **Filter data by selection and by form**
- **Remove a filter**
- **Summarize and analyze data in PivotTable view**
- **Summarize and analyze data in a PivotTable form**
- **Summarize and analyze data in PivotChart view**
- **View and customize document properties**
- **View object dependencies**

access Chapter 7

You can filter data in a database object to view specific records without having to change the design of the object. In this chapter, you will learn how to filter data, filter by selection, and filter by form. You will also learn how to summarize and analyze data in an object in PivotTable and PivotChart view and view document properties and object dependencies.

Note: Before beginning computer projects, delete the Access2007L1C6 folder from your storage medium. Next, copy to your storage medium the Access2007L1C7 subfolder from the Access2007L1 folder on the CD that accompanies this textbook and make Access2007L1C7 the active folder.

Project ① Filter Records

You will filter records in a table, query, and report in the Skyline database using the Filter button, Selection button, Toggle Filter button, and shortcut menu. You will also remove filters and filter by form.

Filtering Data

You can place a set of restrictions, called a *filter*, on records in a table, query, form, or report to isolate temporarily specific records. A filter, like a query, lets you view specific records without having to change the design of the table, query, form, or report. Access provides a number of buttons and options for filtering data. You can filter data using the Filter button in the Sort & Filter group in the Home tab, right-click specific data in a record and then specify a filter, and use the Selection and Advanced buttons in the Sort & Filter group.

Filtering Using the Filter Button

You can use the Filter button in the Sort & Filter group in the Home tab to filter records in an object (table, query, form or report). To use this button, open the desired object, click in any entry in the field column on which you want to filter and then click the Filter button. This displays a drop-down list with sorting options and a listing of all of the field entries. Figure 7.1 displays the drop-down list that displays when you click in the *City* field and then click the Filter button. To sort on a specific criterion, click the *(Select All)* check box to move all check marks from the list of field entries. Click the item in the list box on which you want to sort and then click OK.

Figure 7.1 City Field Drop-down List

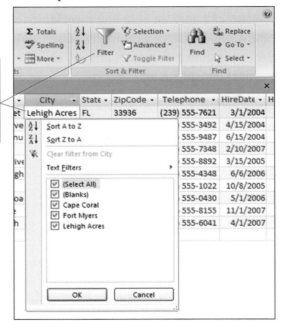

To filter on the *City* field, click in any entry in the field column and then click the Filter button. This displays a drop-down list with sorting options and a listing of all field entries.

When you open a table, query, or form, the Record navigation bar contains the dimmed words *No Filter* preceded by a filter icon with a delete symbol (an X). If you filter records in one of these objects, *Filtered* displays in place of *No Filter*, the delete symbol is removed, and the text and filter icon display with an orange background. In a report, the word *Filtered* displays at the right side of the Status bar if you apply a filter to records.

Removing a Filter

When you filter data, the underlying data in the object is not deleted. You can switch back and forth between the data and the filtered data by clicking the Toggle Filter button in the Sort & Filter group in the Home tab. If you click the Toggle Filter button and turn off the filter, all of the data in a table, query, or form displays and the message *Filtered* in the Record navigation bar changes to *Unfiltered*.

Clicking the Toggle Filter button may redisplay all data in an object but it does not remove the filter. To remove the filter, click in the field column containing the filter and then click the Filter button in the Sort & Filter group in the Home tab. At the drop-down list that displays, click the *Clear filter from xxx* (where *xxx* is the name of the field). You can remove all filters from an object by clicking the Advanced button in the Sort & Filter group and then clicking the *Clear All Filters* option.

QUICK STEPS

Remove a Filter
1. Click in field column containing filter.
2. Click Filter button.
3. Click *Clear filter from xxx.*

OR
1. Click Advanced button.
2. Click *Clear All Filters* at drop-down list.

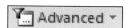

Project 1a   Filtering Records in a Table, Form, and Report

1. Remove the read-only attribute from the **Skyline.accdb** database located in the Access2007L1C7 folder.
2. Open the **Skyline.accdb** database.
3. Filter records in the Employees table by completing the following steps:
   a. Open the Employees table.
   b. Click in any entry in the *City* field.
   c. Click the Filter button in the Sort & Filter group in the Home tab. (This displays a drop-down list in the *City* field.)
   d. Click the *(Select All)* check box in the filter drop-down list box. (This removes all check marks from the list options.)
   e. Click the *Fort Myers* check box in the list box. (This inserts a check mark in the check box.)

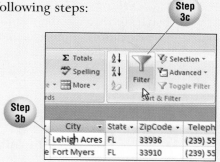

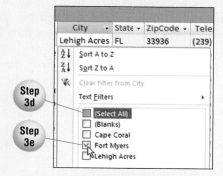

   f. Click OK. (Access displays only those records with a city field of *Fort Myers* and also displays *Filtered* and the filter icon with an orange background in the Record navigation bar.)
   g. Click the Quick Print button on the Quick Access toolbar.
4. Toggle the display of filtered data by clicking the Toggle Filter button in the Sort & Filter group in the Home tab. (This redisplays all data in the table.)

5. Remove the filter by completing the following steps:
   a. Click in any entry in the *City* field.
   b. Click the Filter button in the Sort & Filter group.
   c. Click the *Clear filter from City* option at the drop-down list. (Notice that the message on the Record navigation bar changes to *No Filter* and dims the words.)
6. Save and then close the Employees table.
7. Create a form by completing the following steps:
   a. Click the Orders table in the Navigation pane.
   b. Click the Create tab and then click the Form button in the Forms group.
   c. Click the Form View button in the view area at the right side of the Status bar.
   d. Save the form and name it Orders.
8. Filter the records and display only those records with a supplier identification number of 2 by completing the following steps:
   a. Click in the *SupplierID* field containing the text *2*.
   b. Click the Filter button in the Sort & Filter group.
   c. At the filter drop-down list, click *(Select All)* to remove all of the check marks from the list options.
   d. Click the *2* option to insert a check mark.
   e. Click OK.
   f. Navigate through the records and notice that only the records with a supplier identification number of 2 display.
   g. Close the Orders form.

Step 5b

Step 5c

Filtering on Specific Values

When you filter on a specific field, you can display a list of unique values for that field. If you click the Filter button for a field containing text, the drop-down list for the specific field will contain a *Text Filters* option. Click this option and a values list displays next to the drop-down list. The options in the values list will vary depending on the type of data in the field. If you click the Filter button for a field containing number values, the option in the drop-down list displays as *Number Filters* and if you are filtering dates, the option at the drop-down list displays as *Date Filters*. Use options in the values list to refine further a filter for a specific field. For example, you can use the values list to display money amounts within a specific range or order dates between certain dates. You can use the values list to find fields that are "equal to" or "not equal to" text in the current field.

Project 1b   Filtering Records in a Query and a Report

1. With the **Skyline.accdb** database open, create the following one-to-many relationships:

Field Name	"One" Table	"Many" Table
EmployeeID	Employees	Banquets
Item#	Inventory	Orders
SupplierID	Suppliers	Orders
EventID	Events	Banquets

2. Create a query in Design view with the following specifications:
    a. Add the Banquets and Events tables to the query window.
    b. Insert the *ResDate* field from the Banquets table to the first *Field* text box.
    c. Insert the *LastName* field from the Banquets table to the second *Field* text box.
    d. Insert the *FirstName* field from the Banquets table to the third *Field* text box.
    e. Insert the *Telephone* field from the Banquets table to the fourth *Field* text box.
    f. Insert the *Event* field from the Events table to the fifth *Field* text box.
    g. Insert the *EmployeeID* field from the Banquets table to the sixth *Field* text box.
    h. Run the query.
    i. Save the query and name it *BanquetReservations*.

3. Filter records of reservations before July 15, 2010, in the query by completing the following steps:
    a. With the BanquetReservations query open, make sure the first entry is selected in the *ResDate* field.
    b. Click the Filter button in the Sort & Filter group in the Home tab.
    c. Point to the *Date Filters* option in the drop-down list box.
    d. Click *Before* in the values list.

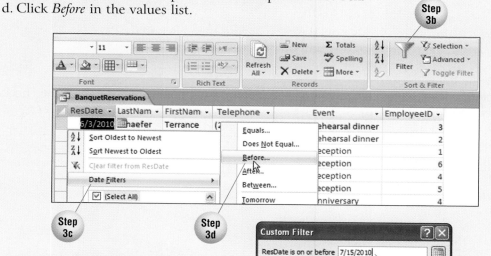

Step 3b

Step 3c

Step 3d

Step 3e

Step 4

Custom Filter

ResDate is on or before 7/15/2010

e. At the Custom Filter dialog box, type 7/15/2010 and then click OK.
    f. Print the filtered query by clicking the Quick Print button on the Quick Access toolbar.

4. Remove the filter by clicking the filter icon that displays at the right side of the *ResDate* column heading and then clicking *Clear filter from ResDate* at the drop-down list.

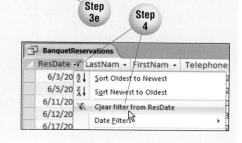

5. Save and then close the BanquetReservations query.

6. Create a report by completing the following steps:
   a. Click the BanquetReservations query in the Navigation pane.
   b. Click the Create tab and then click the Report button in the Reports group.
   c. With the report in Layout view, decrease the column widths so the right column border displays near the longest entry in each column.
   d. Click the Report View button in the view area at the right side of the Status bar.
   e. Save the report and name it *BanquetReport*.
7. Filter the records and display all records of events except *Other* events by completing the following steps:
   a. Click in the first entry in the *Event* field.
   b. Click the Filter button in the Sort & Filter group.
   c. Point to the *Text Filters* option in the drop-down list box and then click *Does Not Equal* at the values list.

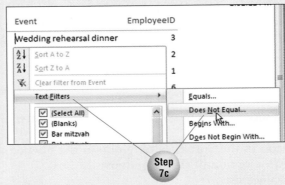

Step 7c

   d. At the Custom Filter dialog box, type **Other** and then click OK.
8. Further refine the filter by completing the following steps:
   a. Click in the first entry in the *EmployeeID* field.
   b. Click the Filter button.
   c. At the filter drop-down list, click the *(Select All)* check box to remove all of the check marks from the list options.
   d. Click the *3* check box to insert a check mark.
   e. Click OK.
9. Click the Quick Print button on the Quick Access toolbar.
10. Save and then close the BanquetReport report.

Filtering by Selection

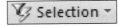

If you click in a field in an object and then click the Selection button in the Sort & Filter group in the Home tab, a drop-down list displays below the button with options for filtering on the data in the field. For example, if you click in a field containing the city name *Fort Myers*, clicking the Selection button will cause a drop-down list to display as shown in Figure 7.2. Click one of the options at the drop-down list to filter records. You can select specific text in a field entry and then filter based on the specific text. For example, in Project 1c you will select the word *peppers* in the entry *Green peppers* and then filter records containing the word *peppers*.

Figure 7.2 Selection Button Drop-down List

To filter by selection, click in a field containing the text on which to filter and then click the Selection button. This displays a drop-down list of filtering options.

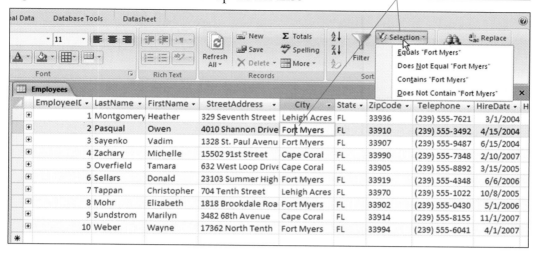

Filtering by Shortcut Menu

If you right-click on a field entry, a shortcut menu displays with options to sort the text, display a values list, or filter on a specific value. For example, if you right-click the field entry *Schaefer* in the *LastName* field, a shortcut menu displays as shown in Figure 7.3. Click a sort option to sort text in the field in ascending or descending order, point to the *Text Filters* option to display a values list, or click one of the values filters located toward the bottom of the menu. You can also select specific text within a field entry and then right-click the selection to display the shortcut menu.

Figure 7.3 Filtering Shortcut Menu

Right-click a field entry and a shortcut menu displays with sorting and filtering options.

1. Open the Inventory table.
2. Filter only those records with a supplier number of 6 by completing the following steps:
   a. Click in the first entry containing *6* in the *SupplierID* field.
   b. Click the Selection button and then click *Equals "6"* at the drop-down list.
   c. Click the Quick Print button on the Quick Access toolbar.
   d. Click the Toggle Filter button in the Sort & Filter group.

3. Filter any records in the *Item* field containing the word "pepper" by completing the following steps:
   a. Click in the entry in the *Item* field containing the entry *Green peppers*.
   b. Using the mouse, select the word *peppers*.
   c. Click the Selection button and then click *Contains "peppers"* at the drop-down list.

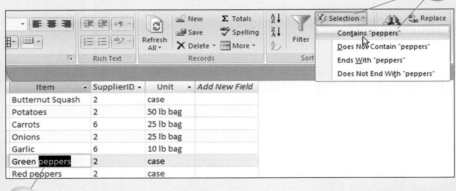

   d. Click the Quick Print button on the Quick Access toolbar.
4. Close the Inventory table without saving the changes.
5. Open the BanquetReservations query.
6. Filter records in the *Event* field except *Wedding reception* by completing the following steps:
   a. Right-click in the first *Wedding reception* entry in the *Event* field.
   b. Click *Does Not Equal "Wedding reception"* at the shortcut menu.
   c. Click the Quick Print button on the Quick Access toolbar.
   d. Click the Toggle Filter button in the Sort & Filter group.

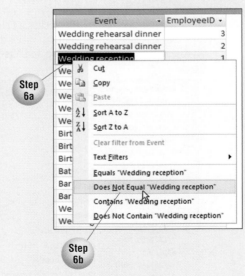

7. Filter any records in the *Event* field containing the word *mitzvah* by completing the following steps:
   a. Click in the entry in the *Event* field containing the entry *Bar mitzvah*.
   b. Using the mouse, select the word *mitzvah*.
   c. Right-click on the selected word and then click *Contains "mitzvah"* at the shortcut menu.
   d. Click the Quick Print button on the Quick Access toolbar.
8. Close the BanquetReservations query without saving the changes.

Using Filter By Form

One of the options from the Advanced button drop-down list is *Filter By Form*. Click this option and a blank record displays in a Filter by Form window in the work area. In the Filter by Form window, the *Look for* and *Or* tabs display toward the bottom of the form. The *Look for* tab is active by default and tells Access to look for whatever data you insert in a field. Click in the empty field below the desired column and a down-pointing arrow displays at the right side of the field. Click the down-pointing arrow and then click the item on which you want to filter. Click the Toggle Filter button to display the desired records. Add an additional value to a filter by clicking the *Or* tab at the bottom of the form.

Use Filter By Form
1. Click Advanced button.
2. Click *Filter By Form* at drop-down list.
3. Click in empty field below desired column to filter.
4. Click down-pointing arrow.
5. Click on item to filter.

Project 1d Using Filter By Form to Display Specific Records

1. With the **Skyline.accdb** database open, open the Banquets table.
2. Filter records for a specific employee identification number by completing the following steps:
   a. Click the Advanced button in the Sort & Filter group in the Home tab and then click *Filter By Form* at the drop-down list.
   b. At the Filter by Form window, click in the blank record below the *EmployeeID* field.
   c. Click the down-pointing arrow at the right side of the field and then click *3* at the drop-down list.
   d. Click the Toggle Filter button in the Sort & Filter group.
3. Print the filtered table by completing the following steps:
   a. Click the Office button, point to *Print*, and then click *Print Preview* at the side menu.
   b. Click the Landscape button in the Page Layout group.
   c. Click the Print button and then click OK at the Print dialog box.
   d. Click the Close Print Preview button.
4. Close the Banquets table without saving the changes.
5. Open the Inventory table.
6. Filter records for supplier numbers 2 or 7 by completing the following steps:
   a. Click the Advanced button in the Sort & Filter group in the Home tab and then click *Filter By Form* at the drop-down list.

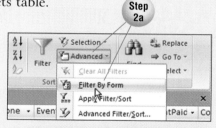

Step 2a

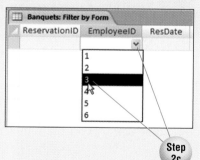

Step 2c

b. At the Filter by Form window, click in the blank record below the *SupplierID* field.

c. Click the down-pointing arrow at the right side of the field and then click *2* at the drop-down list.

d. Click the *Or* tab located toward the bottom of the form.

e. If necessary, click in the blank record below the *SupplierID* field.

f. Click the down-pointing arrow at the right side of the field and then click *7* at the drop-down list.

g. Click the Toggle Filter button in the Sort & Filter group.

h. Click the Quick Print button on the Quick Print toolbar.

i. Click the Toggle Filter button to redisplay all records in the table.

j. Click the Advanced button and then click *Clear All Filters* from the drop-down list.

7. Close the Inventory table without saving the changes.

8. Close the **Skyline.accdb** database.

Project ② Summarize and Analyze Data in PivotTable and PivotChart Views

You will view and analyze data in the OutdoorOptions database in PivotTable view and create a PivotTable form. You will also save an object as a different object and with a new name and view and analyze data in PivotChart view.

Summarizing Data by Changing Views

PivotTable View

Access provides additional views in a table and query that you can use to summarize data. Change to the PivotTable view to create a PivotTable, which is an interactive table that organizes and summarizes data. Use the PivotChart view to create a PivotChart that summarizes data in a graph.

Summarizing Data Using PivotTable View

A PivotTable is an interactive table that organizes and summarizes data based on the fields you designate for row headings, column headings, and source record filtering. In PivotTable view, you can easily add aggregate functions to the table such as sum, avg, and count. A PivotTable provides more options for viewing data than a Crosstab query because you can easily change the results by filtering data by an item in a row, a column, or for all source records. This interactivity allows you to analyze the data for numerous scenarios.

To create a PivotTable, open a table or query in Datasheet view and then click the PivotTable View button in the view area at the right side of the Status bar. You can also display a table or query in PivotTable view by clicking the View button arrow in the Views group in the Home tab and then clicking *PivotTable View* at the drop-down list. This displays the datasheet in PivotTable layout with four sections along with a *PivotTable Field List* box as shown in Figure 7.4. Dimmed text in each section describes the types of fields you should drag and drop.

Figure 7.4 PivotTable Layout

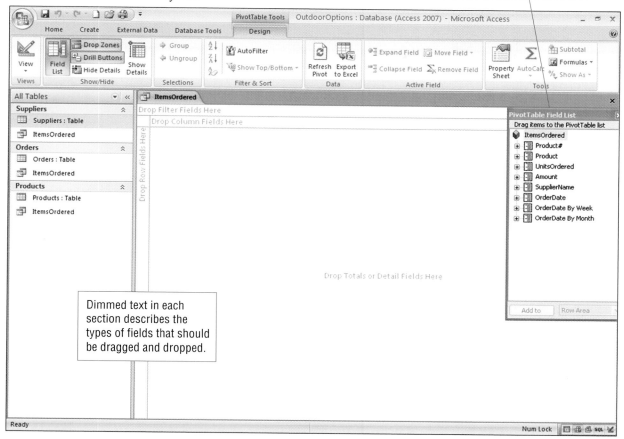

Drag the desired item from this list box and drop it in the appropriate location.

Dimmed text in each section describes the types of fields that should be dragged and dropped.

Drag the fields from the *PivotTable Field List* box to the desired locations in the PivotTable layout. The dimmed text in the PivotTable layout identifies the field you should drop in the location. In Project 2a, you will drag the *SupplierName* field to the Row field section, the *Product* field to the Column field section, the *Amount* field to the Totals or Details field section, and the *OrderDate* to the Filter section. The PivotTable will then display as shown in Figure 7.5.

Figure 7.5 PivotTable for Project 2a

OrderDate ▾							
All							
		Product ▾					
		Backpack	Ski goggles	Snowboard	Two-person tent	Wool ski hats	Grand Total
		+ –	+ –	+ –	+ –	+ –	+ –
SupplierName	▾	Amount ▾	Amount ▾	Amount ▾	Amount ▾	Amount ▾	No Totals
Freedom Corporation			$1,100.00			$687.50	
KL Distributions		$1,906.25			$1,137.50		
Rosewood, Inc.				$2,800.00			
Grand Total							

1. Remove the read-only attribute from the **OutdoorOptions.accdb** database located in the Access2007L1C7 folder.
2. Open the **OutdoorOptions.accdb** database.
3. Create a new query in Design view with the following specifications:
   a. Add the Orders, Products, and Suppliers tables to the design grid.
   b. Add the following fields from the specified tables:

Product#	=	Orders table
Product	=	Products table
UnitsOrdered	=	Orders table
Amount	=	Orders table
SupplierName	=	Suppliers table
OrderDate	=	Orders table

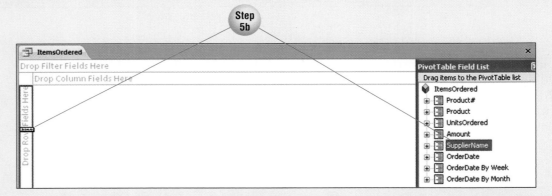

Field:	Product#	Product	UnitsOrdered	Amount	SupplierName	OrderDate	
Table:	Orders	Products	Orders	Orders	Suppliers	Orders	
Sort:							
Show:	☑	☑	☑	☑	☑	☑	
Criteria:							
or:							

   c. Run the query.
   d. Save the query and name it *ItemsOrdered*.
4. Click the PivotTable View button in the view area at the right side of the Status bar.

Step 4

5. At the PivotTable layout, drag and drop the *SupplierName* field to the Row field section by completing the following steps:
   a. Position the mouse pointer on the *SupplierName* field in the *PivotTable Field List* box.
   b. Hold down the left mouse button, drag to the dimmed text *Drop Row Fields Here* located at the left side of the query window, and then release the mouse button.

Step 5b

6. Complete steps similar to those in Step 5 to drag and drop the following fields:
   a. Drag the *Product* field from the *PivotTable Field List* box and drop it on the dimmed text *Drop Column Fields Here*.
   b. Drag the *Amount* field from the *PivotTable Field List* box and drop it on the dimmed text *Drop Totals or Detail Fields Here*.
   c. Drag the *OrderDate* field from the *PivotTable Field List* box and drop it on the dimmed text *Drop Filter Fields Here*.

7. Remove the *PivotTable Field List* box from the screen by clicking the Field List button in the Show/Hide group in the PivotTable Tools Design tab. (Your PivotTable should look like the one shown in Figure 7.5.)
8. Click the Quick Print button on the Quick Access toolbar to print the query in PivotTable view.
9. Click the View button arrow in the Views group in the Home tab and then click *Datasheet View* at the drop-down list.
10. Save and then close the query.

When you create a PivotTable in a query or table, it becomes a part of and is saved with the table or query. The next time you open the table or query, display the PivotTable by clicking the PivotTable View button in the view area on the Status bar or by clicking the View button arrow in the Views group in the Home tab and then clicking *PivotTable View* at the drop-down list. If you make changes to data in fields that are part of the table or query (and PivotTable), the data is automatically updated in the table or query.

The power of a PivotTable is the ability to analyze data for numerous scenarios. For example, in the PivotTable you created in Project 2a, you can display orders for a specific date or isolate a specific supplier. Use the plus and minus symbols that display in a row or column heading to show (plus symbol) or hide (minus symbol) data. Use the down-pointing arrow (called the *filter arrow*) that displays in a field to display specific data in the field. You can also use buttons in the PivotTable Tools Design tab to perform actions such as filtering data and performing calculations on data.

Project 2b Analyzing Data in PivotTable View

1. With the **OutdoorOptions.accdb** database open, open the Orders table.
2. Add the following records to the table:

Order#	=	(AutoNumber)
Supplier#	=	68
Product#	=	558
UnitsOrdered	=	25
Amount	=	$550
OrderDate	=	2/26/2010

Order#	=	(AutoNumber)
Supplier#	=	70
Product#	=	897
UnitsOrdered	=	10
Amount	=	$1,120
OrderDate	=	2/26/2010

3. Close the Orders table.
4. Double-click the ItemsOrdered query in the *Orders* list box.

5. With the query open, click the View button arrow in the Views group in the Home tab and then click *PivotTable View* at the drop-down list. (Notice the PivotTable reflects the two new order records you inserted in the Orders table.)

6. Display only items ordered on February 26 by completing the following steps:

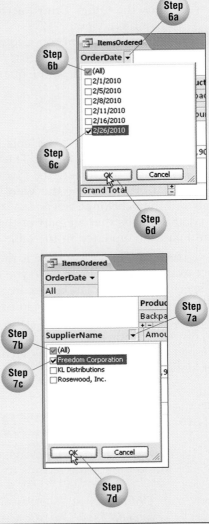

Step 6a

Step 6b

Step 6c

Step 6d

   a. Click the filter arrow (down-pointing arrow) at the right of the *OrderDate* field (located in the upper left corner of the query window).
   b. At the drop-down list that displays, click the *(All)* check box to remove the check mark before each date.
   c. Click the check box to the left of *2/26/2010*.
   d. Click the OK button.
   e. Click the Quick Print button on the Quick Access toolbar.
   f. Redisplay all items by clicking the filter arrow at the right of the *OrderDate* field, clicking the check box to the left of *(All)*, and then clicking OK.

7. Display only those order amounts for Freedom Corporation by completing the following steps:
   a. Click the filter arrow at the right of the *SupplierName* field.
   b. At the drop-down list, click the *(All)* check box to remove the check mark before each supplier name.
   c. Click the check box to the left of *Freedom Corporation*.
   d. Click the OK button.
   e. Click the Quick Print button on the Quick Access toolbar.
   f. Redisplay all supplier names by clicking the filter arrow at the right of the *SupplierName* field, clicking the check box to the left of *(All)*, and then clicking OK.

Step 7a

Step 7b

Step 7c

Step 7d

8. Display subtotals and totals of order amounts by completing the following steps:
   a. Position the mouse pointer on any *Amount* column heading until the pointer displays with a four-headed arrow attached and then click the left mouse button. (This displays all the *Amount* column headings and amounts with a light blue background.)
   b. Click the AutoCalc button in the Tools group in the PivotTable Tools Design tab and then click *Sum* at the drop-down list. (This inserts subtotals and totals in the PivotTable.)

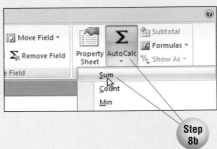

Step 8b

9. Save, print, and then close the PivotTable.

Summarizing and Analyzing Data in a PivotTable Form

When you create a PivotTable in a query or table, the PivotTable settings are saved and become part of the table or query. When you open a table or query in which you have created a PivotTable and then switch to PivotTable view, the table or query displays with the PivotTable settings you created. If you want to view different fields or perform other functions in PivotTable view, you have to edit the last settings. For example, if you created a PivotTable in an Employees query that summed the salary field by department by year of hire, and then wanted to sum by month, you would have to edit the previous PivotTable. If you want to view data by year and month or other date, consider creating a PivotTable form. A PivotTable form is a separate object from the query or table, so you could create one showing the sum by year and another showing the sum by month.

To create a PivotTable form, click the desired object in the Navigation pane and then click the Create tab. Click the More Forms button in the Forms group and then click *PivotTable* at the drop-down list. This displays the object in PivotTable layout. Click the Field List button in the Show/Hide group to display the *PivotTable Field List* box. (You may need to click the button twice to display the list box.)

Field List

Saving Objects

If you want to create an object that is similar to another object in the database, use the *Save As* option from the Office button drop-down list. For example, if you want to save a query as a form, open the query, click the Office button, and then click *Save As*. At the Save As dialog box, type a name for the new object, click the down-pointing arrow at the right side of the *As* list box, click the desired object type, and then click OK. If you want to save an open object with a new name, click the Office button, and then click *Save As*. At the Save As dialog box, type a new name for the object, leave the *As* list box as the default, and then click OK.

Project 2c **Creating a PivotTable Form**

1. With the **OutdoorOptions.accdb** database open, save the ItemsOrdered query as a form by completing the following steps:
   a. Click the ItemsOrdered query in the Navigation pane.
   b. Click the Office button and then click *Save As* at the drop-down list.
   c. At the Save As dialog box, type ItemsOrdered in the *Save 'ItemsOrdered' to* text box.
   d. Click the down-pointing arrow at the right side of the *As* list box and then click *Form* at the drop-down list.
   e. Click OK.
   f. Close the ItemsOrdered form.

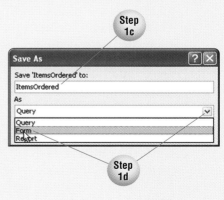

2. Create a PivotTable form by completing the following steps:
   a. Click the ItemsOrdered form in the Navigation pane.
   b. Click the Create tab.
   c. Click the More Forms button in the Forms group and then click *PivotTable* at the drop-down list.

Step 2b

Step 2a

Step 2c

   d. At the PivotTable form, click twice on the Field List button in the Show/Hide group in the PivotTable Tools Design tab.
   e. Drag the *SupplierName* field in the *PivotTable Field List* box and drop it on the dimmed text *Drop Row Fields Here*.
   f. Drag the *Product* field from the *PivotTable Field List* box and drop it on the dimmed text *Drop Column Fields Here*.
   g. Drag the *Amount* field from the *PivotTable Field List* box and drop it on the dimmed text *Drop Totals or Detail Fields Here*.
   h. Drag the *OrderDate* field from the *PivotTable Field List* box and drop it on the dimmed text *Drop Filter Fields Here*.
   i. Close the PivotTable Field List box.
3. Display subtotals and totals of order amounts by completing the following steps:
   a. Position the mouse pointer on any *Amount* column heading until the pointer displays with a four-headed arrow attached and then click the left mouse button. (This displays all the *Amount* column headings and amounts with a light blue background.)
   b. Click the AutoCalc button in the Tools group in the PivotTable Tools Design tab and then click *Sum* at the drop-down list. (This inserts subtotals and totals in the PivotTable.)
4. Display only the order amounts for Freedom Corporation by completing the following steps:
   a. Click the filter arrow at the right of the *SupplierName* field.
   b. At the drop-down list, click the *(All)* check box to remove the check mark before each supplier name.
   c. Click the check box to the left of *Freedom Corporation*.
   d. Click the OK button.
5. Save the PivotTable form by completing the following steps:
   a. Click the Save button on the Quick Access toolbar.
   b. At the Save As dialog box, type **FreedomOrders** and then click OK.

6. Display only the order amounts for KL Distributions by completing the following steps:
   a. Click the filter arrow at the right of the *SupplierName* field.
   b. At the drop-down list, click the *Freedom Corporation* check box to remove the check mark.
   c. Click the check box to the left of *KL Distributions*.
   d. Click the OK button.

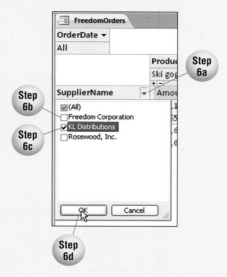

7. Save and print the PivotTable form by completing the following steps:
   a. Click the Office button and then click *Save As* at the drop-down list.
   b. At the Save As dialog box, type **KLOrders** and then click OK.
   c. Click the Quick Print button on the Quick Access toolbar.
8. Complete steps similar to those in Steps 6 and 7 to save and print a PivotTable form that displays order amounts for Rosewood, Inc. and name the form *RosewoodOrders*.
9. Close the RosewoodOrders PivotTable form.

Summarizing Data Using PivotChart View

A PivotChart performs the same function as a PivotTable with the exception that Access displays the source data in a graph instead of a table or query. You create a chart by dragging fields from the *Chart Field List* box to the Filter, Data, Category, and Series sections of the chart. As with a PivotTable, you can easily alter the PivotChart using the filter arrows.

To create a PivotChart, open a table or query in Datasheet view, click the PivotChart View button in the view area at the right side of the Status bar or click the View button arrow in the Views group in the Home tab, and then click PivotChart View at the drop-down list. This changes the datasheet to PivotChart layout, which contains four sections, and displays the *Chart Field List* box. Dimmed text in each section describes the types of fields that you should drag and drop. Figure 7.6 displays the PivotChart layout you will be using in Project 2d.

Display PivotChart View
1. Open table or query.
2. Click PivotChart View button in view area at right side of Status bar.
OR
1. Open table or query.
2. Click View button arrow.
3. Click PivotChart View at drop-down list.

PivotChart View

Figure 7.6 PivotChart Layout

Drag the desired item from this list box and drop it in the appropriate location.

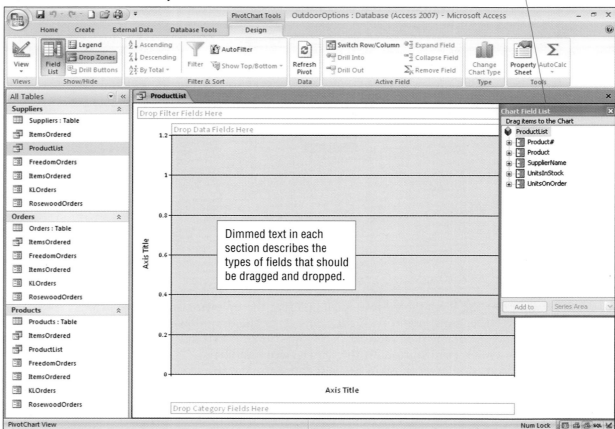

Dimmed text in each section describes the types of fields that should be dragged and dropped.

HINT

A PivotTable is linked dynamically to a PivotChart. Changes made to the filter settings in PivotChart view are also updated in PivotTable view.

Drag the fields from the *Chart Field List* box to the desired locations in the PivotChart layout. The dimmed text in the PivotChart layout identifies the field you should drop in the location. In Project 2d, you will drag the *SupplierName* field to the Row field section, the *Product* field to the Column field section, the *Amount* field to the Totals or Details field section, and the *OrderDate* to the Filter section. The PivotChart will then display as shown in Figure 7.7. When you create a PivotChart, Access automatically creates a PivotTable. View a PivotTable based on a PivotChart by changing to PivotTable view.

Figure 7.7 PivotChart for Project 2d

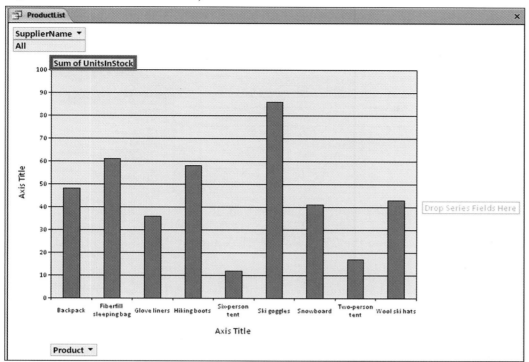

Project 2d Summarizing Data Using PivotChart View

1. With the **OutdoorOptions.accdb** database open, create a new query in Design view with the following specifications:
   a. Add the Products and Suppliers tables to the design grid.
   b. Add the following fields from the specified tables:

Product#	=	Products table
Product	=	Products table
SupplierName	=	Suppliers table
UnitsInStock	=	Products table
UnitsOnOrder	=	Products table

   c. Run the query.
   d. Save the query and name it *ProductList*.
2. Click the View button arrow in the Views group in the Home tab and then click *PivotChart View* at the drop-down list.

3. At the PivotChart layout, drag and drop the following fields:
   a. Drag the *SupplierName* field from the *Chart Field List* box and drop it on the dimmed text *Drop Filter Fields Here*.

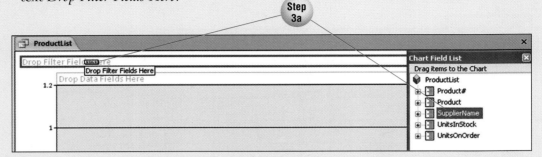

Step 3a

   b. Drag the *Product* field from the *Chart Field List* box and drop it on the dimmed text *Drop Category Fields Here*.
   c. Drag the *UnitsInStock* field from the *Chart Field List* box and drop it on the dimmed text *Drop Data Fields Here*.
4. Remove the *Chart Field List* box from the screen by clicking the Field List button in the Show/Hide group. (Your PivotChart should look like the PivotChart shown in Figure 7.7.)
5. Click the Quick Print button on the Quick Access toolbar to print the query in PivotChart view.
6. Display specific items on order by completing the following steps:
   a. Click the filter arrow at the right of the *Product* field (located in the lower left corner of the query window).
   b. At the pop-up list that displays, click the *(All)* check box to remove the check mark before each date.
   c. Click the check box to the left of *Ski goggles*.
   d. Click the check box to the left of *Snowboard*.
   e. Click the check box to the left of *Wool ski hats*.
   f. Click the OK button.

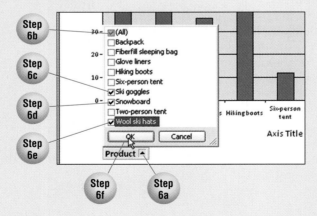

Step 6b

Step 6c

Step 6d

Step 6e

Step 6f

Step 6a

   g. Click the Quick Print button on the Quick Access toolbar.
   h. Redisplay all items by clicking the filter arrow at the right of the *Product* field, clicking the check box to the left of *(All)*, and then clicking OK.

7. Display only those products ordered from KL Distributions by completing the following steps:
   a. Click the filter arrow at the right of the *SupplierName* field.
   b. At the drop-down list, click the *(All)* check box to remove the check mark before each supplier name.
   c. Click the check box to the left of *KL Distributions*.
   d. Click the OK button.
   e. Click the Quick Print button in the Quick Access toolbar.
   f. Redisplay all supplier names by clicking the filter arrow at the right of the *SupplierName* field, clicking the check box to the left of *(All)*, and then clicking OK.
8. Click the View button arrow in the Views group and then click *PivotTable View* at the drop-down list. (This displays the chart in PivotTable view.)
9. Click the Quick Print button in the Quick Access toolbar.
10. Click the View button arrow in the Views group and then click *Datasheet View* at the drop-down list. (This returns the query to the Datasheet view.)
11. Save and then close the query.
12. Close the **OutdoorOptions.accdb** database.

Project ③ View Document Properties and Object Dependencies

You will view and customize document properties for the OutdoorOptions database and view object dependencies in the Hilltop database.

Viewing and Customizing Document Properties

The Properties dialog box contains **metadata**, which is data that describes other data. Data in the Properties dialog box describes details about the database such as title, author name, and subject, and contains options you can use to further describe or identify the database. You can display properties for the current database or display properties for a database at the Open dialog box.

Viewing Properties at the Open Dialog Box

View properties for a database at the Open dialog box by clicking the Tools button located in the lower left corner of the Open dialog box and then clicking *Properties* at the drop-down list. This displays the Properties dialog box similar to what you see in Figure 7.8. The Properties dialog box with the General tab selected displays information about the document type, size, and location.

Figure 7.8 OutdoorOptions.accdb Properties Dialog Box

Click the **OutdoorOptions.accdb** database in the Open dialog box list box, click the Tools button, and then click *Properties*, and this dialog box displays.

If you display the properties for a database saved on the hard drive, the Properties dialog box will display the Summary tab along with the General tab. The Summary tab contains fields where you can enter the title, subject, category, keywords, and comments about the database. Move the insertion point to a field by clicking in the field or by pressing the Tab key until the insertion point is positioned in the desired field.

Project 3a — Viewing Database Properties

1. At the *Getting Started with Microsoft Office Access* window, click the Open button on the Quick Access toolbar.
2. At the Open dialog box, make sure the Access2007L1C7 folder on your storage medium is active and then click **OutdoorOptions.accdb** in the list box.
3. Click the Tools button located in the lower left corner of the dialog box and then click *Properties* at the drop-down list.

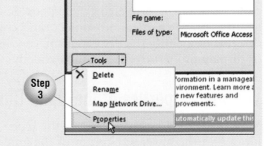

4. At the Properties dialog box, read the information that displays in the dialog box with the General tab selected and then click the Cancel button.
5. Click **Skyline.accdb** in the list box, click the Tools button, and then click *Properties*.
6. Read the information that displays and then click the Cancel button.
7. Close the Open dialog box.

Viewing and Customizing Properties for the Current Database

To view properties for the currently open database, click the Office button, point to *Manage*, and then click *Database Properties*. This displays the Properties dialog box similar to what you see in Figure 7.9. The Properties dialog box for an open database contains additional tabs with information on the database. The General tab contains the same options as the Properties dialog box that displays when you click the Tools button in the Open dialog box and then click *Properties*. Click the Summary tab and fields display such as title, subject, author, category, keywords, and comments. Some fields may contain data and others may be blank. You can insert, edit, or delete text in the fields. Move the insertion point to a field by clicking in the field or by pressing the Tab key until the insertion point is positioned in the desired field.

Click the Statistics tab and information displays such as dates for when the database was created, modified, accessed, and printed. You can view the objects in the database by clicking the Contents tab. The *Document contents* section displays the objects in the database including tables, queries, form, reports, macros, and modules.

Figure 7.9 Current Database Properties Dialog Box

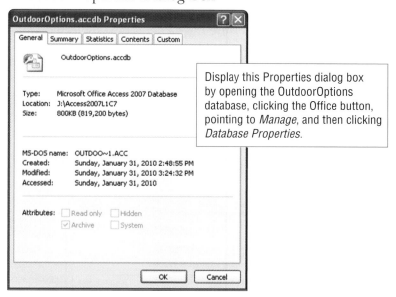

Use options at the Properties dialog box with the Custom tab selected to add custom properties to the database. For example, you can add a property that displays the date the database was completed, information on the department in which the database was created, and much more. The list box below the *Name* option box displays the predesigned properties provided by Access. You can choose a predesigned property or create your own.

To choose a predesigned property, select the desired property in the list box, specify what type of property it is (value, date, number, yes/no), and then type a value. For example, to specify the department in which the database was created, you would click *Department* in the list box, make sure the *Type* displays as *Text*, click in the *Value* text box, and then type the name of the department.

1. Open the **OutdoorOptions.accdb** database.
2. Display database properties by clicking the Office button, pointing to *Manage*, and then clicking *Database Properties*.

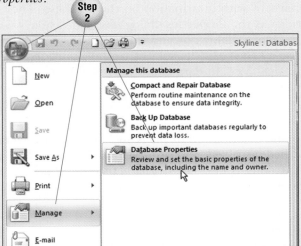

3. At the Properties dialog box, make sure the General tab is selected and then read the information that displays in the dialog box.
4. Click the Summary tab and then type the following text in the specified text boxes:

    Title = **OutdoorOptions database**
    Subject = **Outdoor equipment and supplies**
    Author = *(type your first and last names)*
    Category = **Retail store**
    Keywords = **retail, equipment, products, suppliers**
    Comments = **This database contains information on Outdoor Options suppliers, products, and orders.**

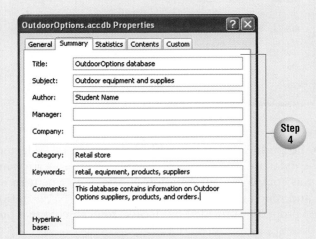

5. Click the Statistics tab and read the information that displays in the dialog box.
6. Click the Contents tab and notice that the *Document contents* section of the dialog box displays the objects in the database.

7. Click the Custom tab and then create custom properties by completing the following steps:
   a. Click the *Date completed* option in the *Name* list box.
   b. Click the down-pointing arrow at the right of the *Type* option box and then click *Date* at the drop-down list.
   c. Click in the *Value* text box and then type the current date in this format: *##/##/####*.
   d. Click the Add button.

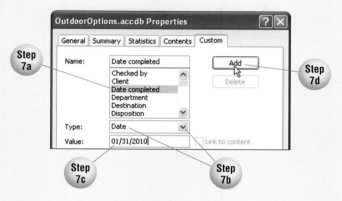

   e. With the insertion point positioned in the *Name* text box, type Course.
   f. Click the down-pointing arrow at the right of the *Type* option box and then click *Text* at the drop-down list.
   g. Click in the *Value* text box, type your current course number, and then press Enter.
   h. Click OK to close the dialog box.
8. Close the **OutdoorOptions.accdb** database.

Viewing Object Dependencies

The structure of a database is comprised of table, query, form, and report objects. Tables are related to other tables by creating relationships. Queries, forms, and reports draw the source data from records in the tables to which they have been associated and forms and reports can include subforms and subreports which further expand the associations between objects. A database with a large number of interdependent objects is more complex to work with. Viewing a list of the objects within a database and viewing the dependencies between objects can be beneficial to ensure an object is not deleted or otherwise modified causing an unforeseen effect on another object.

Display the structure of a database, including tables, queries, forms, and reports as well as relationships, at the Object Dependencies task pane. Display this task pane by opening the database, clicking the Database Tools tab, and then clicking the Object Dependencies button in the Show/Hide group. The Object Dependencies task pane in Figure 7.10 displays the objects for the Hilltop database.

QUICK STEPS

View Object Dependencies
1. Open desired database.
2. Click Database Tools tab.
3. Click Object Dependencies button.

Figure 7.10 Object Dependencies Task Pane

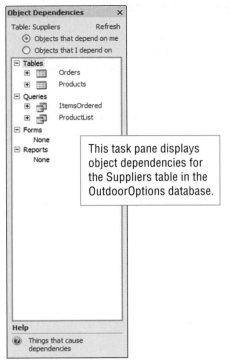

This task pane displays object dependencies for the Suppliers table in the OutdoorOptions database.

By default, *Objects that depend on me* is selected in the Object Dependencies task pane and the list box displays the names of objects for which the Employee Dates and Salaries table is the source. Next to each object in the task pane list is an expand button (plus symbol). Clicking the expand button will show objects dependent at the next level. For example, if a query is based upon the Employee Dates and Salaries table and the query is used to generate a report, clicking the expand button next to the query name would show the report name.

Clicking an object name in the Object Dependencies task pane opens the object in Design view so that you can remove the dependency by deleting bound fields, controls, or otherwise changing the source from which the data is obtained. Relationships between tables are deleted by opening the Relationships window (as you learned in Chapter 2).

Project 3c   Viewing Object Dependencies

1. With the **OutdoorOptions.accdb** database open, display the structure of the database by completing the following steps:

   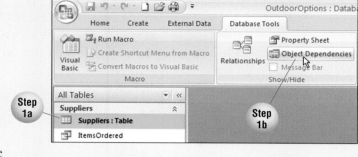

   a. Click the Suppliers table in the Navigation pane.
   b. Click the Database Tools tab and then click Object Dependencies in the Show/Hide group. (This displays the Object Dependencies task pane. By default, *Objects that depend on me* is selected and the task pane lists the names of objects for which the Suppliers table is the source.)

   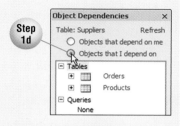

   c. Click the expand button (plus symbol) to the left of *Orders* in the Tables section. (This displays all objects that are dependent on the Orders table.)
   d. Click the *Objects that I depend on* option located toward the top of the Object Dependencies task pane.
   e. Click the Products table in the Navigation pane.
   f. Click the Refresh hyperlink located in the upper right corner of the Object Dependencies task pane.

   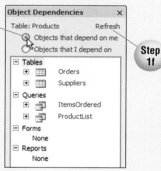

   g. Click the *Objects that depend on me* option located toward the top of the Object Dependencies task pane. Notice the objects that are dependent on the Products table.
   h. Close the Object Dependencies task pane.
2. Delete the relationship between the Orders table and the Products table by completing the following steps:
   a. Click the Relationships button in the Show/Hide group with the Database Tools tab selected.
   b. Right-click the black join line between the Orders and Products tables.
   c. At the shortcut menu that displays, click *Delete*.
   d. At the message asking if you are sure you want to permanently delete the relationship, click Yes.
   e. Close the Relationships window.

   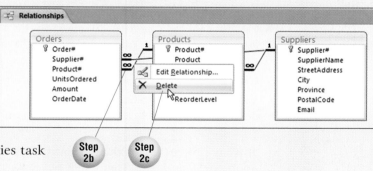

3. Display the Object Dependencies task pane for the Invoices table by completing the following steps:
   a. Click the Orders table in the Navigation pane.
   b. Click the Database Tools tab and then click Object Dependencies in the Show/Hide group. (Notice that the Products table is not listed in the Tables section of the Object Dependencies task pane.)
4. Close the Object Dependencies task pane.
5. Close the **OutdoorOptions.accdb** database.

CHAPTER summary

- A set of restrictions, called a filter, can be set on records in a table or form. A filter lets you select specific field values.
- You can filter records with the Filter button in the Sort & Filter group in the Home tab.
- Click the Toggle Filter button in the Sort & Filter group to switch back and forth between data and filtered data.
- Remove a filter by clicking the Filter button in the Sort & Filter group and then clicking the *Clear filter from xxx* (where *xxx* is the name of the field).
- Another method for removing a filter is to click the Advanced button in the Sort & Filter group and then click *Clear All Filters*.
- Display a list of filter values by clicking the Filter button and then pointing to *Text Filters* (if the data is text), *Number Filters* (if the data is numbers), or *Date Filters* (if the data is a date).
- Filter by selection by clicking the Selection button in the Sort & Filter group.
- Right-click a field entry to display a shortcut menu with filtering options.
- Filter by form by clicking the Advanced button in the Sort & Filter group and then clicking *Filter By Form* at the drop-down list. This displays a blank record with the two tabs *Look for* and *Or*.
- A PivotTable is an interactive table that organizes and summarizes data. Create a PivotTable for an object to analyze data for numerous scenarios. Change to the PivotTable view to create a PivotTable.
- A PivotTable you create in a query or table is saved with the object. You can also create a PivotTable form that is saved as a separate object from the table or query.
- You can save an open object as a different object with the *As* option at the Save As dialog box. Display this dialog box by clicking the Office button and then clicking *Save As* at the drop-down list.
- Create a PivotTable form by clicking the More Forms button in the Forms group in the Create tab and then clicking *PivotTable* at the drop-down list.
- Create a PivotChart to analyze data in a chart rather than a table or query. Change to the PivotChart view to create a PivotChart.
- View database properties by displaying the Open dialog box, clicking the desired database, clicking the Tools button, and then clicking *Properties* at the drop-down list.
- To view properties for the currently open database, click the Office button, point to *Manage*, and then click *Database Properties*.
- Customize database properties with options at the Properties dialog box with the Custom tab selected.
- Display the structure of a database and the relationship between objects at the Object Dependencies task pane. Display this task pane by clicking the Database Tools tab and then clicking the Object Dependencies button in the Show/Hide group.

COMMANDS review

FEATURE	RIBBON TAB, GROUP	BUTTON, OPTION
Filter	Home, Sort & Filter	[Filter icon]
Toggle filter	Home, Sort & Filter	Toggle Filter
Remove filter	Home, Sort & Filter	[Filter icon], Clear filter from *xxx*, OR
		Advanced ▾, Clear All Filters
Filter by selection	Home, Sort & Filter	Selection ▾
Filter by form	Home, Sort & Filter	Advanced ▾, Filter By Form
PivotTable view	Home, Views	[icon], PivotTable View
PivotTable form	Create, Forms	More Forms ▾, PivotTable
PivotChart	Home, Views	[icon], PivotChart View
Object Dependencies task pane	Database Tools, Show/Hide	Object Dependencies

CONCEPTS check

Test Your Knowledge

Completion: In the space provided at the right, indicate the correct term, symbol, or command.

1. The Filter button is located in this group in the Home tab.

2. If you filter data, you can switch between the data and the filtered data by clicking this button.

3. Remove filtering from an object with the Filter button or by clicking this button and then clicking *Clear All Filters*.

4. In the Filter By Form window, these two tabs display toward the bottom of the form.

5. Display a table or query in this view to summarize data based on the fields you designate for row headings, column headings, and source record filtering.

6. To create a PivotTable form, click this button in the Forms group and then click *PivotTable* at the drop-down list.

7. Click this button in the Show/Hide group in the PivotTable Tools Design tab to display the *PivotTable Field List* box.

8. Use this view to display data in a graph.

9. View properties for a database at the Open dialog box by clicking this button located in the lower left corner of the dialog box and then clicking *Properties*.

10. Display the structure of a database at this task pane.

SKILLS check
Demonstrate Your Proficiency

1 FILTER RECORDS IN TABLES

1. Remove the read-only attribute from the **LegalServices.accdb** database located in the Access2007L1C7 folder.
2. Open the **LegalServices.accdb** database.
3. Open the Clients table and then filter the records to display the following records:
   a. Display only those records of clients who live in Renton. When the records of clients in Renton display, print the results and then remove the filter.
   b. Display only those records of clients with the Postal Code of 98033. When the records of clients with the ZIP code 98033 display, print the results in landscape orientation and then remove the filter. (Hint: Change to landscape orientation in Print Preview.)
4. Close the Clients table without saving the changes.
5. Open the Billing table and then filter records by selection to display the following records:
   a. Display only those records with a Category of CC. Print the CC records and then remove the filter.
   b. Display only those records with an Attorney ID of 12. Print the records and then remove the filter.
   c. Display only those records between the dates 6/1/2010 and 6/10/2010. Print the records and then remove the filter.
6. Close the Billing table without saving the changes.
7. Open the Clients table and then use Filter By Form to display clients in Auburn or Renton. (Be sure to use the Or tab at the very bottom of the table.) Print the table in landscape orientation and then remove the filter.
8. Close the Clients table without saving the changes.
9. Open the Billing table and then use Filter By Form to display categories G or P. Print the table and then remove the filter.
10. Close the Billing table without saving the changes.
11. Close the **LegalServices.accdb** database.

2 VIEW AND ANALYZE DATA IN PIVOTTABLE AND PIVOTCHART VIEW

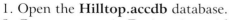

1. Open the **Hilltop.accdb** database.
2. Create a query in Design view with the following specifications:
   a. Add the Invoices, Customers, Equipment, and Rates tables to the design grid.
   b. Add the following fields from the specified tables:
BillingDate	=	Invoices table
Customer	=	Customers table
Equipment	=	Equipment table
Hours	=	Invoices table
Rate	=	Rates table

c. Click in the sixth *Field* text and then insert a calculation to total the rental hour amounts by typing Total: [Hours]*[Rate]. (Press the Tab key to move to the next field.)

    d. Run the query.

    e. Save the query and name it *RentalTotals*.

3. Display the query in PivotTable view.

4. At the PivotTable layout, drag and drop the fields as follows:

    a. Drag the *Equipment* field to the *Drop Row Fields Here* section.

    b. Drag the *Customer* field to the *Drop Column Fields Here* section.

    c. Drag the *Total* field to the *Drop Totals or Detail Fields Here* section.

    d. Drag the *BillingDate* field to the *Drop Filter Fields Here* section.

5. Remove the *PivotTable Field List* box from the screen.

6. Click the Quick Print button on the Quick Access toolbar to print the query in PivotTable view. (If the total amounts in the Cascade Enterprises and Country Electrical columns print as number symbols instead of amounts, increase the size of the Total column by dragging to the right the border at the right side of the Total heading below Cascade Enterprises.)

7. In the *BillingDate* field, display only equipment rentals for May 1, 2010.

8. Print the PivotTable and then redisplay all rental dates.

9. In the *Equipment* field, display records only for the Hydraulic Pump and Pressure Sprayer.

10. Print the PivotTable and then redisplay all equipment.

11. Switch to Datasheet view, save the query, and then close the query.

12. Create a query in Design view with the following specifications:

    a. Add the Equipment, Customers, and Invoices tables to the design grid.

    b. Add the following fields from the specified tables:

Equipment	=	Equipment table
Customer	=	Customers table
Hours	=	Invoices table

    c. Run the query.

    d. Save the query and name it *CustomerHours*.

13. Click the View button arrow in the Views group in the Home tab and then click *PivotChart View* at the drop-down list.

14. At the PivotChart layout, drag and drop the following fields:

    a. Drag the *Equipment* field to the *Drop Filter Fields Here* section.

    b. Drag the *Customer* field to the *Drop Category Fields Here* section.

    c. Drag the *Hours* field to the *Drop Data Fields Here* section.

15. Remove the *Chart Field List* box from the screen.

16. Click the Quick Print button on the Quick Access toolbar to print the query in PivotChart view.

17. In the *Equipment* field, display only records for Backhoe, print the PivotChart, and then redisplay all equipment.

18. In the *Customer* field, display only the customers Allied Builders and Cascade Enterprises, print the PivotChart, and then redisplay all customers.

19. Save the PivotChart, switch to Datasheet view, and then close the query.

20. Create a PivotTable form with the RentalTotals query and drag and drop the following fields in the PivotTable layout:

    a. Drag the *Equipment* field to the *Drop Row Fields Here* section.

    b. Drag the *Customer* field to the *Drop Column Fields Here* section.

    c. Drag the *Total* field to the *Drop Totals or Detail Fields Here* section.

    d. Drag the *BillingDate* field to the *Drop Filter Fields Here* section.

21. Save the PivotTable form and name it *CustomerRentals*.
22. Display only those records for Able Construction. Save the PivotTable form with Save As and name it *AbleConstruction*. Print the form.
23. Display only those records for Cascade Enterprises. Save the PivotTable form with Save As and name it *CascadeEnterprises*. Print and then close the form.

Assessment

3

DELETE AND RENAME OBJECTS

1. With the **Hilltop.accdb** database open, experiment with the options in the shortcut menu that displays when you right-click an object and then complete the following:
   a. Delete the AbleConstruction form.
   b. Rename the CascadeEnterprises form to *CascadeHours*.
   c. Rename the RentalTotals query to *RentalHoursTotals*.
2. Close the **Hilltop.accdb** database.

CASE study
Apply Your Skills

Part 1

As the office manager at the Summit View Medical Services, you are responsible for maintaining clinic records. Open the **SummitView.accdb** database and then insert the following additional services into the appropriate table:

- Edit the *Doctor visit* entry in the Services table so it displays as *Clinic visit*.
- Add the entry *X-ray* with a service identification of *X*.
- Add the entry *Cholesterol screening* with a service identification of *CS*.

Add the following new patient information in the database in the appropriate tables or forms:

Patient number 118
Brian M. Gould
2887 Nelson Street
Helena, MT 59604
(406) 555-3121
Mr. Gould saw Dr. Wallace for a clinic visit on 4/5/2010, which has a fee of $75.

Patient number 119
Ellen L. Augustine
12990 148th Street
East Helena, MT 59635
(406) 555-0722
Ms. Augustine saw Dr. Kennedy for cholesterol screening on 4/5/2010, which has a fee of $90.

Patient number 120
Jeff J. Masura
3218 Eldridge Avenue
Helena, MT 59624
(406) 555-6212
Mr. Masura saw Dr. Rowe for an x-ray on 4/5/2010, which has a fee of $75.

Add the following information to the Billing form:

- Patient 109 came for cholesterol screening with Dr. Kennedy on 4/5/2010 with a $90 fee.
- Patient 106 came for immunizations with Dr. Pena on 4/5/2010 with a $100 fee.
- Patient 114 came for an x-ray with Dr. Kennedy on 4/5/2010 with a $75 fee.

Part 2

Create the following filters, queries, PivotTable, and PivotChart:

- Open the Billing table and then filter and print the records for the date 04/01/2010. Clear the filter and then filter and then print the records with a doctor number of 18. Save and then close the table.
- Create a report that displays the patient's first name, last name, street address, city, state, and ZIP code. Apply formatting to enhance the visual appeal of the report. Filter and print the records of those patients living in Helena and then filter and print those patients living in East Helena. Close the report.
- Design a query that includes the doctor number, doctor last name, patient number, date of visit, and fee. Save the query with the name *DoctorBillingFees* and then print the query.
- Create a PivotTable with the DoctorBillingFees query with the following specifications: Drop the *DateOfVisit* field in the Filter Fields section, the *Patient#* field in the Column Fields section, the *LastName* field in the Row Fields, and the *Fee* field in the Totals or Detail Fields. Save and then print the PivotTable.
- Filter records in the PivotTable for Dr. Kennedy and Dr. Pena. Print the filtered PivotTable.
- Remove the filter and then filter records for the dates 4/1/2010 and 4/2/2010. Print the filtered table. Save and then close the query.

Part 3

Using the PivotTable layout you designed in the DoctorBillingFees query in Part 2, create a PivotTable form in the same layout. Save the PivotTable form and name it *BillingFees* and then print the PivotTable form. Decide on two different filters you can apply to the data in the PivotTable form. Complete each filter and save the filtered PivotTable form with a new name and print the form.

Part 4

Your clinic has a procedures manual that describes processes and procedures in the center. Open Word and then create a document for the procedures manual that describes the process for creating the PivotTable form you created in Part 3. Save the completed document and name it **Access_C7_CS_P4**. Print and then close **Access_C7_CS_P4.docx**.

Importing and Exporting Data

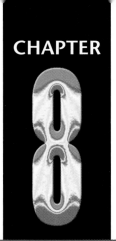

PERFORMANCE OBJECTIVES

Upon successful completion of Chapter 8, you will be able to:

- Export Access data to Excel
- Export Access data to Word
- Merge Access data with a Word document
- Import data to a new table
- Link data to a new table
- Use the Office Clipboard
- Save a database in an earlier version of Access

access Chapter 8

Microsoft Office 2007 is a suite of programs that allows easy data exchange between programs. In this chapter you will learn how to export data from Access to Excel and Word, merge Access data with a Word document, import and link data to a new table, and copy and paste data between programs. You will also learn how to copy and paste data between applications and save a database in an earlier version of Access.

Note: Before beginning computer projects, delete the Access2007L1C7 folder from your storage medium. Next, copy to your storage medium the Access2007L1C8 subfolder from the Access2007L1 folder on the CD that accompanies this textbook and make Access2007L1C8 the active folder.

Project ① Export Data to Excel and Export and Merge Data to Word

You will export a table and query to Excel and export a table and report to Word. You will also merge data in an Access table and query with a Word document.

Exporting Data

One of the advantages of a suite like Microsoft Office is the ability to exchange data between one program and another. Access, like other programs in the suite, offers a feature to export data from Access into Excel and/or Word. The Export group in the External Data tab contains buttons for exporting a table, query, form, or report to other programs such as Excel and Word.

QUICK STEPS

Export Data to Excel
1. Click the desired table, query, form, or report.
2. Click the External Data tab.
3. Click Excel button in Export group.
4. Make desired changes at Export - Excel Spreadsheet dialog box.
5. Click OK.

Exporting Data to Excel

Use the Excel button in the Export group in the External Data tab to export data in a table, query, or form to an Excel worksheet. Click the object containing data you want to export to Excel, click the External Data tab, click the Excel button in the Export group and the first Export - Excel Spreadsheet wizard dialog box displays as shown in Figure 8.1.

Click the Browse button and then navigate to the desired folder and file.

Figure 8.1 Export - Excel Spreadsheet Dialog Box

Insert a check mark in this check box to open the file in the destination program.

Insert a check mark in this check box to export all object formatting and layout.

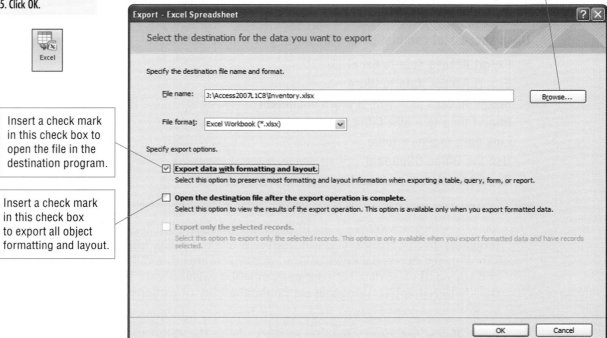

HINT

Data exported from Access to Excel is saved as an Excel workbook with the .xlsx extension.

HINT

You can export only one database object at a time, and you cannot export reports to Excel.

At the first wizard dialog box, Access uses the name of the object as the Excel workbook name. You can change this by selecting the current name and then typing a new name and you can specify the file format with the *File format* option. Click the *Export data with formatting and layout* check box to insert a check mark. This exports all data formatting to the Excel workbook. If you want Excel to open with the exported data, click the *Open the destination file after the export operation is complete* option to insert a check mark. When you have made all desired changes, click the OK button. This opens Excel with the data in a workbook. Make any desired changes to the workbook and then save, print, and close the workbook. Exit Excel and Access displays with a second wizard dialog box asking if you want to save the export steps. At this dialog box, insert a check mark in the *Save export steps* if you want to save the export steps, or leave the option blank and then click the Close button.

1. Remove the read-only attribute from the **Hilltop.accdb** database located in the Access2007L1C8 folder.
2. Open the **Hilltop.accdb** database.
3. Save the Inventory table as an Excel worksheet by completing the following steps:
   a. Click the Inventory table in the Navigation pane.
   b. Click the External Data tab and then click the Excel button in the Export group.

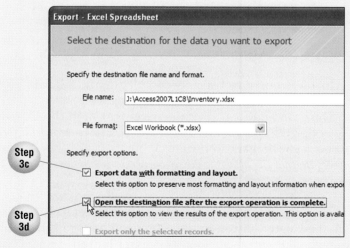

   c. At the Export - Excel Spreadsheet dialog box, click the *Export data with formatting and layout* option to insert a check mark in the check box.
   d. Click the *Open the destination file after the export operation is complete* option to insert a check mark in the check box.

   e. Click OK.

f. When the data displays on the screen in Excel as a
   worksheet, select cells A2 through A11 and then click
   the Center button in the Alignment
   group in the Home tab.
g. Select cells D2 through F11 and then
   click the Center button.
h. Click the Save button on the Quick
   Access toolbar.
i. Click the Quick Print button on the
   Quick Access toolbar.
j. Close the worksheet and then exit Excel.
4. In Access, click the Close button to close
   the second wizard dialog box.
5. Design a query that extracts records from
   three tables with the following
   specifications:
   a. Add the Invoices, Customers, and Rates
      tables to the query window.
   b. Insert the *BillingDate* field from the
      Invoices table to the first *Field* text box.
   c. Insert the *Customer* field from the Customers table to the second *Field* text box.
   d. Insert the *Hours* field from the Invoices table to the third *Field* text box.
   e. Insert the *Rate* field from the Rates table to the fourth *Field* text box.
   f. Click in the fifth *Field* text box, type **Total: [Hours]*[Rate]** and then press Enter.

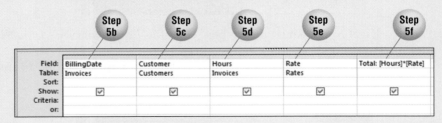

g. Run the query.
h. Save the query and name it *CustomerInvoices*.
i. Close the query.
6. Export the CustomerInvoices query to Excel by completing the following steps:
   a. Click the CustomerInvoices query in the Navigation pane.
   b. Click the External Data tab and then click the Excel button in the Export group.
   c. At the Export - Excel Spreadsheet dialog box, click the *Export data with formatting and layout* option to insert a check mark in the check box.
   d. Click the *Open the destination file after the export operation is complete* option to insert a check mark in the check box.
   e. Click OK.
   f. When the data displays on the screen in Excel as a worksheet, select cells A2 through A20 and then click the Center button in the Alignment group in the Home tab.
   g. Select cells C2 through C20 and then click the Center button.
   h. Click the Save button on the Quick Access toolbar.
   i. Click the Quick Print button on the Quick Access toolbar.
   j. Close the worksheet and then exit Excel.
7. In Access, click the Close button to close the second wizard dialog box.

Exporting Data to Word

Export data from Access to Word in the same manner as exporting to Excel. To export data to Word, select the desired object in the Navigation pane, click the External Data tab, and then click the Word button in the Export group. At the Export - RTF File dialog box, make desired changes and then click OK. Word automatically opens and the data displays in a Word document that is saved automatically with the same name as the database object. The difference is that the file extension .rtf is added to the name. An RTF file is saved in "rich-text format," which preserves formatting such as fonts and styles. You can export a document saved with the .rtf extension in Word and other Windows word processing or desktop publishing programs.

QUICK STEPS

Export Data to Word
1. Click the desired table, query, form, or report.
2. Click External Data tab.
3. Click Word button in Export group.
4. Make desired changes at Export - RTF File dialog box.
5. Click OK.

HINT
Data exported from Access to Word is saved with the .rtf file extension.

Project 1b Exporting a Table and Report to Word

1. Click the Invoices table in the Navigation pane.
2. Click the External Data tab and then click the Word button in the Export group.

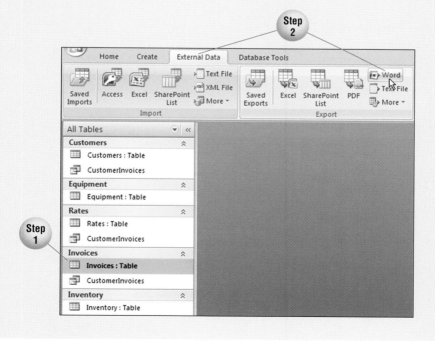

3. At the Export - RTF File wizard dialog box, click the Browse button.
4. At the File Save dialog box, navigate to the Access2007L1C8 folder on your storage medium and then click the Save button.
5. At the Export - RTF File wizard dialog box, click the *Open the destination file after the export operation is complete* check box.

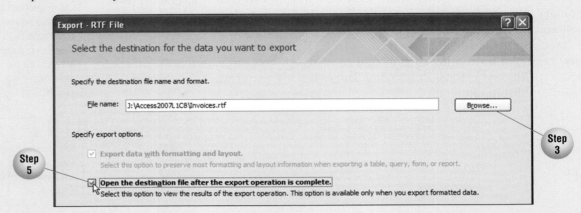

6. Click OK.
7. With the **Invoices.rtf** file open in Word, click the Quick Print button on the Quick Access toolbar.
8. Close the **Invoices.rtf** file and then exit Word.
9. Click the Close button to close the wizard dialog box.
10. Create a report with the Report Wizard by completing the following steps:
    a. Click the Create tab and then click the Report Wizard button in the Reports group.
    b. At the first Report Wizard dialog box, insert the following fields in the *Selected Fields* list box:

    From the Customers table:
        Customer
    From the Equipment table:
        Equipment
    From the Invoices table:
        BillingDate
        Hours

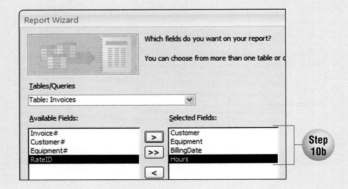

c. After inserting the fields, click the Next button.

d. At the second Report Wizard dialog box, make sure *by Customers* is selected in the list box in the upper left corner and then click the Next button.

e. At the third Report Wizard dialog box, click the Next button.

f. At the fourth Report Wizard dialog box, click the Next button.

g. At the fifth Report Wizard dialog box, click *Block* in the *Layout* section and then click the Next button.

h. At the sixth Report Wizard dialog box, click *Solstice* in the list box and then click the Next button.

i. At the seventh Report Wizard dialog box, select the current name in the *File name* text box, type CustomerReport, and then click the Finish button.

j. When the report displays in Print Preview, click the Layout View button located in the view area at the right side of the Status bar.

k. Click the *Customer* column heading and then increase the width of the column so all of the customer names display in the fields.

l. Click the Quick Print button on the Quick Access toolbar.

m. Save and then close the CustomerReport report.

11. Export the CustomerReport report to Word by completing the following steps:

a. Click the CustomerReport report in the Navigation pane.

b. Click the External Data tab and then click the Word button in the Export group.

c. At the Export - RTF File wizard dialog box, click the *Open the destination file after export operation is complete* option to insert a check mark in the check box and then click OK.

d. When the data displays on the screen in Word, click the Quick Print button on the Quick Access toolbar.

e. Save and then close the CustomerReport document.

f. Exit Word.

12. In Access, click the Close button to close the second wizard dialog box.

Merging Access Data with a Word Document

You can merge data from an Access table with a Word document. When merging data, the data in the Access table is considered the data source and the Word document is considered the main document. When the merge is completed, the merged documents display in Word. To merge data, click the desired table in the Navigation pane and then click the External Data tab. Click the More button in the Export group and then click the *Merge it with Microsoft Office Word* option at the drop-down list. When merging Access data, you can either type the text in the main document or merge Access data with an existing Word document.

Merge Data with Word

1. Click the desired table or query.
2. Click External Data tab.
3. Click More button, *Merge it with Microsoft Office Word*.
4. Make desired choices at each wizard dialog box.

1. Click the Customers table in the Navigation pane.
2. Click the External Data tab.
3. Click the More button in the Export group and then click the *Merge it with Microsoft Office Word* option at the drop-down list.

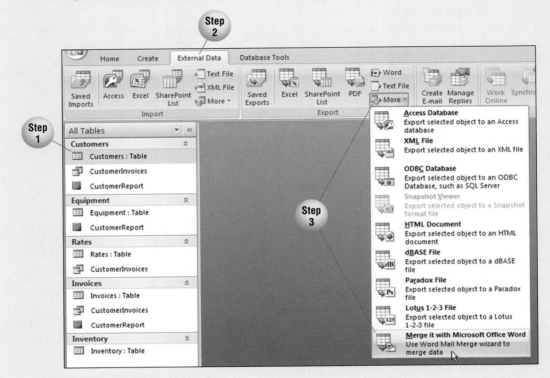

4. At the Microsoft Word Mail Merge Wizard dialog box, make sure *Link your data to an existing Microsoft Word document* is selected and then click OK.
5. At the Select Microsoft Word Document dialog box, make the Access2007L1C8 folder on your storage medium the active folder and then double-click the document named **HilltopLetter.docx**.
6. Click the Maximize button located at the right side of the HilltopLetter.docx title bar and then close the Mail Merge task pane.
7. Press the down arrow key six times (not the Enter key) and then type the current date.
8. Press the down arrow key five times and then insert fields for merging from the Customers table by completing the following steps:
   a. Click the Insert Merge Field button arrow located in the Write & Insert Fields group and then click *Customer1* in the drop-down list. (This inserts the «*Customer1*» field in the document. The drop-down list contains a *Customer* and a *Customer1* option. The first *Customer* option is actually the *Customer#* field. Word dropped the # symbol from the field name and added the *1* to the second *Customer* field to differentiate the two fields.)

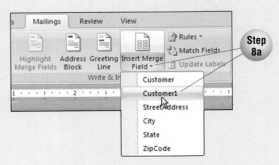

b. Press Enter, click the Insert Merge Field button arrow, and then click *StreetAddress* in the drop-down list.

c. Press Enter, click the Insert Merge Field button arrow, and then click *City* in the drop-down list.

d. Type a comma (,) and then press the spacebar.

e. Click the Insert Merge Field button arrow and then click *State* in the drop-down list.

f. Press the spacebar, click the Insert Merge Field button arrow, and then click *ZipCode* in the drop-down list.

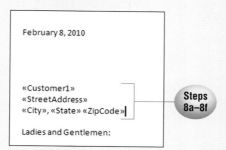

g. Replace the letters *XX* that display toward the bottom of the letter with your initials.

h. Click the Finish & Merge button in the Finish group and then click *Edit Individual Documents* in the drop-down list.

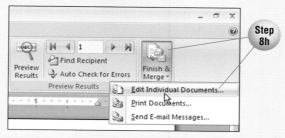

i. At the Merge to New Document dialog box, make sure *All* is selected and then click OK.

j. When the merge is completed, save the new document and name it **AccessL1_C8_P1a** in the Access2007L1C8 folder on your storage medium.

9. Print just the first two pages (two letters) of **AccessL1_C8_P1a.docx**.

10. Close **AccessL1_C8_P1a.docx** and then close **HilltopLetter.docx** without saving the changes.

11. Exit Word.

Merging Query Data with a Word Document

You can perform a query in a database and then use the query to merge with a Word document. In Project 1d you merged a table with an existing Word document. You can also merge a table or query and then type the Word document. You will create a query in Project 1e and then merge data in the query with a new document in Word.

Project 1d   Performing a Query and Then Merging with a Word Document

1. Perform a query with the Query Wizard and modify the query by completing the following steps:
   a. Click the Create tab and then click the Query Wizard button in the Other group.
   b. At the New Query dialog box, make sure Simple Query Wizard is selected and then click OK.
   c. At the first Simple Query Wizard dialog box, click the down-pointing arrow at the right of the *Tables/Queries* option box and then click *Table: Customers*.
   d. Click the button containing the two greater than symbols (>>) to insert all of the fields in the *Selected Fields* list box.
   e. Click the Next button.
   f. At the second Simple Query Wizard dialog box, make the following changes:
      1) Select the current name in the *What title do you want for your query?* text box and then type **DenverCustomersQuery**.
      2) Click the *Modify the query design* option.
      3) Click the Finish button.
   g. At the query window, click in the *Criteria* text box in the *City* column, type **Denver**, and then press Enter.

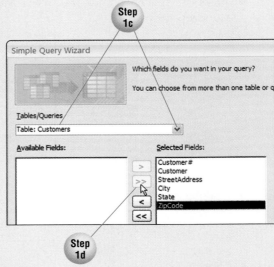

Field:	[Customer#]	[Customer]	[StreetAddress]	[City]	[State]	[ZipCode]
Table:	Customers	Customers	Customers	Customers	Customers	Customers
Sort:						
Show:	☑	☑	☑	☑	☑	☑
Criteria:				"Denver"		
or:						

h. Click the Run button in the Results group. (Those customers located in Denver will display.)
   i. Save and then close the DenverCustomersQuery query.
2. Click the DenverCustomersQuery query in the Navigation pane.
3. Click the External Data tab, click the More button in the Export group, and then click the *Merge it with Microsoft Office Word* option at the drop-down list.
4. At the Microsoft Word Mail Merge Wizard dialog box, click the *Create a new document and then link the data to it.* option and then click OK.

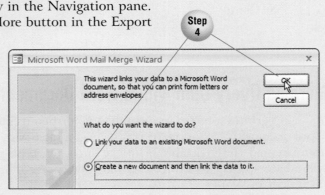

5. Click the Maximize button located at the right side of the Document1 title bar and then close the Mail Merge task pane.
6. Complete the following steps to type text and insert fields in the blank Word document:
   a. Click the Home tab and then click the No Spacing style in the Styles group.
   b. Press Enter six times.

c. Type the current date.
d. Press Enter five times.
e. Click the Mailings tab.
f. Insert the following fields at the left margin in the order shown below (start by clicking the Insert Merge Field button arrow in the Write & Insert Fields group):
   «Customer1»
   «StreetAddress»
   «City», «State» «ZipCode»
g. Press Enter twice and then type the salutation Ladies and Gentlemen:.
h. Press Enter twice and then type the following paragraphs of text:

To provide quality service to our customers, we have opened a new branch office in downtown Denver. The branch office hours are 7:30 a.m. to 7:00 p.m. Monday through Friday, 8:00 a.m. to 5:00 p.m. Saturday, and 9:00 a.m. to 3:30 p.m. Sunday.

Our new branch is located at 7500 Alameda Avenue. Stop by during the next two weeks and receive a 10% discount on your next equipment rental.

i. Press Enter twice and then type the following complimentary close (at the left margin):

Sincerely,

Lou Galloway
Manager

XX:AccessL1_C8_P1b.docx

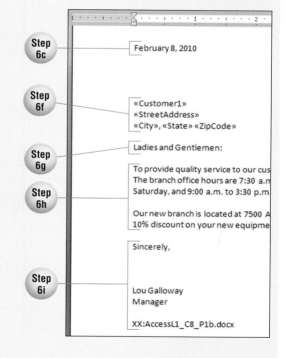

Step 6c

Step 6f

Step 6g

Step 6h

Step 6i

j. Click the Finish & Merge button in the Finish group and then click *Edit Individual Documents* in the drop-down menu.
k. At the Merge to New Document dialog box, make sure *All* is selected, and then click OK.
l. When the merge is complete, save the new document as **AccessL1_C8_P1b** in the Access2007L1C8 folder on your storage medium.
7. Print the first two pages (two letters) of **AccessL1_C8_P1b.docx**.
8. Close **AccessL1_C8_P1b.docx**.
9. Save the main document as **AccessHilltopLetter** in the Access2007L1C8 folder on your storage medium and then close the document.
10. Exit Word.
11. Close the **Hilltop.accdb** database.

Project 2 Import and Link Excel Worksheets with an Access Table

You will import an Excel worksheet into an Access table. You will also link an Excel worksheet into an Access table and then add a new record to the Access table.

QUICK STEPS

Import Data to a New Table
1. Click External Data tab.
2. Click desired application in Import group.
3. Click Browse button.
4. Double-click desired file name.
5. Make desired choices at each wizard dialog box.

Importing and Linking Data to a New Table

In this chapter, you learned how to export Access data to Excel and Word. You can also import data from other programs into an Access table. For example, you can import data from an Excel worksheet and create a new table in a database using data from the worksheet. Data in the original program is not connected to the data imported into an Access table. If you make changes to the data in the original program, those changes are not reflected in the Access table. If you want the imported data connected to the original program, link the data.

Importing Data to a New Table

To import data, click the External Data tab and then determine where you would like to retrieve data with options in the Import group. At the Import dialog box that displays, click Browse and then double-click the desired file name. This activates the Import Wizard and displays the first wizard dialog box. The appearance of the dialog box varies depending on the file selected. Complete the steps of the Import Wizard specifying information such as the range of data, whether or not the first row contains column headings, whether you want to store the data in a new table or store it in an existing table, the primary key, and the name of the table.

HINT
Store data in Access and use Excel to analyze data.

HINT
You can import and link data between Access databases.

Project 2a Importing an Excel Worksheet into an Access Table

1. Remove the read-only attribute from the **SouthwestInsurance.accdb** database located in the Access2007L1C8 folder.
2. Open the **SouthwestInsurance.accdb** database.
3. Import an Excel worksheet into a new table in the **SouthwestInsurance.accdb** database by completing the following steps:
   a. Click the External Data tab and then click the Excel button in the Import group.
   b. At the Get External Data - Excel Spreadsheet dialog box, click Browse and then make the Access2007L1C8 folder on your storage medium the active folder.
   c. Double-click *ExcelC08_01.xlsx* in the list box.
   d. Click OK at the Get External Data - Excel Spreadsheet dialog box.

Step 3a

e. At the first Import Spreadsheet Wizard dialog box, click the Next button.
f. At the second Import Spreadsheet Wizard dialog box, make sure the *First Row Contains Column Headings* option contains a check mark and then click the Next button.
g. At the third Import Spreadsheet Wizard dialog box, click the Next button.
h. At the fourth Import Spreadsheet Wizard dialog box, click the *Choose my own primary key* option (this inserts *Policy#* in the text box located to the right of the option) and then click the Next button.

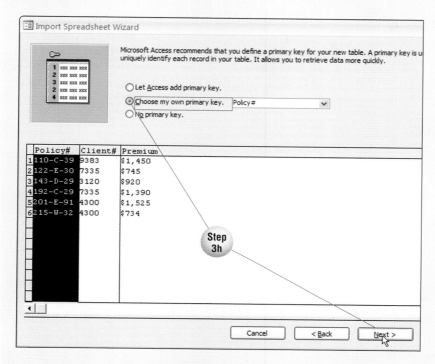

i. At the fifth Import Spreadsheet Wizard dialog box, type **Policies** in the *Import to Table* text box and then click the Finish button.

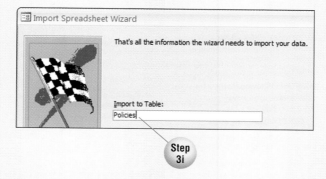

j. At the Get External Data - Excel Spreadsheet dialog box, click the Close button.
4. Open the new Policies table in Datasheet view.
5. Print and then close the Policies table.

QUICK STEPS

Link Data to Excel Worksheet
1. Click External Data tab.
2. Click Excel button in Import group.
3. Click Browse button.
4. Double-click desired file name.
5. Click *Link to a data source by creating a linked table.*
6. Make desired choices at each wizard dialog box.

Linking Data to an Excel Worksheet

Imported data is not connected to the source program. If you know that you will use your data only in Access, import it. However, if you want to update data in a program other than Access, link the data. Changes made to linked data in the source program file are reflected in the destination program file. For example, you can link an Excel worksheet with an Access table and when you make changes in the Excel worksheet, the changes are reflected in the Access table.

To link data to a new table, click the External Data tab and then click the Excel button in the Import group. At the Get External Data - Excel Spreadsheet dialog box, click the Browse button, double-click the desired file name, and then click the *Link to a data source by creating a linked table* option. This activates the Link Wizard and displays the first wizard dialog box. Complete the steps of the Link Wizard, specifying the same basic information as the Import Wizard.

Excel

Project 2b Linking an Excel Worksheet with an Access Table

1. With the **SouthwestInsurance.accdb** database open, click the External Data tab and then click the Excel button in the Import group.
2. At the Get External Data - Excel Spreadsheet dialog box, click the Browse button, navigate to the Access2007L1C8 folder on your storage medium, and then double-click **ExcelC08_01.xlsx**.
3. At the Get External Data - Excel Spreadsheet dialog box, click the *Link to the data source by creating a linked table* option and then click OK.

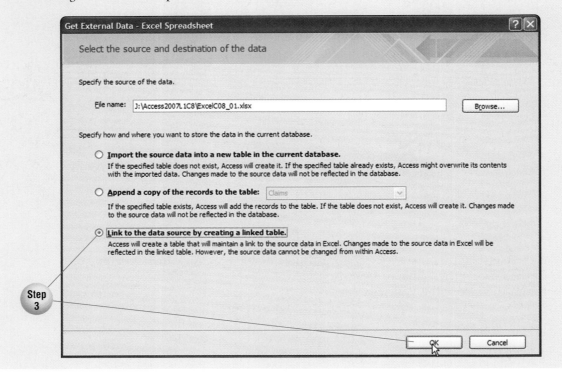

4. At the first Link Spreadsheet Wizard dialog box, make sure *Show Worksheets* and *Sheet 1* are selected in the list box and then click the Next button.
5. At the second Link Spreadsheet Wizard dialog box, make sure the *First Row Contains Column Headings* option contains a check mark and then click the Next button.
6. At the third Link Spreadsheet Wizard dialog box, type LinkedPolicies in the *Linked Table Name* text box and then click the Finish button.
7. At the message stating the linking is finished, click OK.
8. Open the new LinkedPolicies table in Datasheet view.
9. Close the LinkedPolicies table.
10. Open Excel, open the **ExcelC08_01.xlsx** workbook and then make the following changes:
    a. Change the amount *$745* in cell C3 to *$850*.
    b. Add the following information in the specified cells:
        A8 = 227-C-28
        B8 = 3120
        C8 = $685

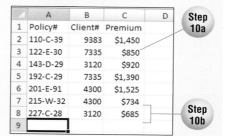

11. Save, print, and then close **ExcelC08_01.xlsx**.
12. Exit Excel.
13. With Access the active program and the **SouthwestInsurance.accdb** database open, open the LinkedPolicies table. Notice the changes you made in Excel are reflected in the table.
14. Close the LinkedPolicies table and then close the **SouthwestInsurance.accdb** database.

Project ③ Collect Data in Word and Paste in an Access Table

You will open a Word document containing Hilltop customer names and addresses and then copy the data and paste it into an Access table.

Using the Office Clipboard

Use the Office Clipboard to collect and paste multiple items. You can collect up to 24 different items in Access or other programs in the Office suite and then paste the items in various locations. To copy and paste multiple items, display the Clipboard task pane shown in Figure 8.2 by clicking the Clipboard group dialog box launcher.

Select data or an object you want to copy and then click the Copy button in the Clipboard group in the Home tab. Continue selecting text or items and clicking the Copy button. To insert an item from the Clipboard task pane to a field in an Access table, make the desired field active and then click the button in the task pane representing the item. If the copied item is text, the first 50 characters display. When all desired items are inserted, click the Clear All button to remove any remaining items from the Clipboard task pane.

You can copy data from one object to another in an Access database or from a file in another program to an Access database. In Project 3a, you will copy data from a Word document and paste it into a table. You can also collect data from other programs such as PowerPoint and Excel.

Figure 8.2 Office Clipboard Task Pane

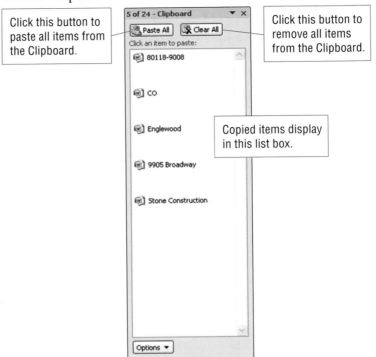

Click this button to paste all items from the Clipboard.

Click this button to remove all items from the Clipboard.

Copied items display in this list box.

Project 3a Collecting Data in Word and Pasting it in an Access Table

1. Open the **Hilltop.accdb** database.
2. Open the Customers table.
3. Copy data from Word and paste it into the Customers table by completing the following steps:
    a. Open Word, make the Access2007L1C8 folder active, and then open **HilltopCustomers.docx**.
    b. Make sure the Home tab is active.
    c. Click the Clipboard group dialog box launcher to display the Clipboard task pane.
    d. Select the first company name, *Stone Construction*, and then click the Copy button in the Clipboard group.
    e. Select the street address, *9905 Broadway*, and then click the Copy button.

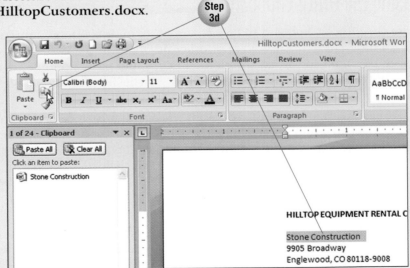

f. Select the city, *Englewood*, and then click the Copy button.
g. Select the state, *CO* (select only the two letters and not the space after the letters), and then click the Copy button.
h. Select the ZIP code, *80118-9008*, and then click the Copy button.
i. Click the button on the Taskbar representing Access. (Make sure the Customer table is open and displays in Datasheet view.)
j. Click in the first empty cell in the *Customer#* field and then type 178.
k. Display the Clipboard task pane by clicking the Clipboard group dialog box launcher.
l. Close the Navigation pane by clicking the Shutter Bar Open/Close Button.
m. Click in the first empty cell in the *Customer* field and then click *Stone Construction* in the Clipboard task pane.

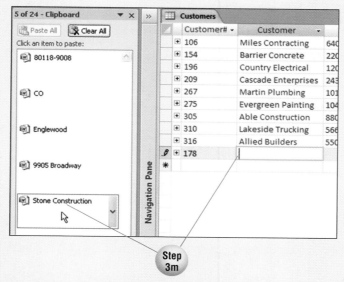

Step 3m

n. Click in the *StreetAddress* field and then click *9905 Broadway* in the Clipboard task pane.
o. Click in the *City* field and then click *Englewood* in the Clipboard task pane.
p. Click in the *State* field and then click *CO* in the Clipboard task pane.
q. Click in the *ZipCode* field, make sure the insertion point is positioned at the left side of the field, and then click *80118-9008* in the Clipboard task pane.

Step 3r

r. Click the Clear All button in the Clipboard task pane. (This removes all entries from the Clipboard.)
4. Complete steps similar to those in 3c through 3q to copy the information for Laughlin Products and paste it into the Customers table. (The Customer# is 225.)
5. Click the Clear All button in the Clipboard task pane.
6. Close the Clipboard task pane by clicking the Close button (contains an *X*) located in the upper right corner of the task pane.
7. Save, print, and then close the Customers table.
8. Open the Navigation pane by clicking the Shutter Bar Open/Close Button.
9. Make Word the active program, close **HilltopCustomers.docx** without saving changes, and then exit Word.

Saving a Database in a Previous Version Format

Save a Database in a Previous Version Format
1. Click Office button.
2. Point to *Save As*.
3. Click desired version.

If you need to share an Access 2007 database with someone who is using an earlier version of Access, you will need to save the database in a different format. An Access 2007 database is saved with the .accdb file extension. Earlier versions of Access such as versions 2003, 2002, or 2000 save a database with the .mdb file extension. To save an Access 2007 database in an earlier version, open the database, click the Office button, point to *Save As*, and then click the desired version at the side menu shown in Figure 8.3.

Figure 8.3 Save As Side Menu

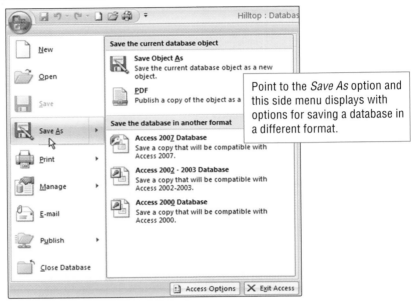

Point to the *Save As* option and this side menu displays with options for saving a database in a different format.

HINT
An Access 2007 database cannot be opened with an earlier version of Access

If you want to create a database in an earlier version, change the *Default file format* at the Access Options dialog box with the *Popular* option selected. To display this dialog box, click the Office button and then click the Access Options button located toward the bottom right side of the drop-down list. At the Access Options dialog box with *Popular* selected, click the down-pointing arrow at the right side of the *Default file format* option and then click *Access 2000* or *Access 2002 - 2003* at the drop-down list. This default format change remains in effect even if you exit and then open Access.

1. With the **Hilltop.accdb** database open, save the database in a previous version of Access by completing the following steps:

   a. Click the Office button, point to *Save As*, and then click *Access 2002 - 2003 Database* at the side menu.

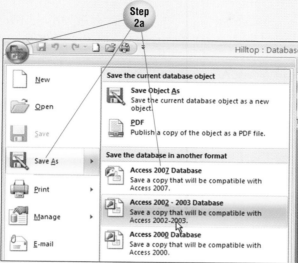

   b. At the Save As dialog box, type Hilltop2003Format.

   c. Notice that the *Save as type* option displays as *Microsoft Access Database (2002-2003) (*.mdb)*.

   d. Click the Save button.

2. Notice the Title bar displays the database file name *Hilltop2003Format : Database (Access 2002 - 2003 file format)*.

3. Close **Hilltop.mdb**.

CHAPTER summary

- Use the Excel button in the Export group in the External Data tab to export data in a table, query, or form to an Excel worksheet.
- Use the Word button in the Export group in the External Data tab to export data in a table, query, form, or report to a Word document. Access exports the data to an RTF (rich-text format) file.
- You can merge Access data with a Word document. The Access data is the data source and the Word document is the main document. To merge data, click the desired table or query and then click the External Data tab. Click the More button in the Export group and then click *Merge it with Microsoft Office Word* at the drop-down list.
- Use the Excel button in the Import group in the External Data tab to import Excel data to an Access table.
- You can link imported data. Changes made to the data in the source program file are reflected in the destination source file.
- If you want to link imported data, click the *Link to the data source by creating a linked table* option at the Get External Data dialog box.
- Use the Clipboard task pane to collect up to 24 different items in Access or other programs and paste them in various locations.
- Display the Clipboard task pane by clicking the Clipboard group dialog box launcher.
- Save an Access database in an earlier version of Access by clicking the Office button, pointing to *Save As*, and then clicking *Access 2002 - 2003 Database* or *Access 2000 Database* at the side menu.

COMMANDS review

FEATURE	RIBBON TAB, GROUP	BUTTON, OPTION
Export object to Excel	External Data, Export	
Export object to Word	External Data, Export	Word
Merge Access data with Word	External Data, Export	More , Merge it with Microsoft Office Word
Import Excel data	External Data, Import	
Clipboard task pane	Home, Clipboard	
Save as 2002 - 2003 database		, Save As, Access 2002 - 2003 Database
Save as 2000 Database		, Save As, Access 2000 Database

CONCEPTS check

Test Your Knowledge

Completion: In the space provided at the right, indicate the correct term, symbol, or command.

1. Click this tab to display the Export group.

2. Click this button in the Export group to display the Export - Excel Spreadsheet wizard dialog box.

3. At the first Export - Excel Spreadsheet wizard dialog box, click this option if you want Excel to open with the exported data.

4. When you export Access data to Word, the document is saved with this file format.

5. When merging data, the data in the Access table is considered this.

6. To merge data, click the More button in the Export group and then click this option.

7. If you want imported data connected to the original program, do this to the data.

8. Use this task pane to collect and paste multiple items.

9. To save a database in the 2003 format, click the Office button, point to *Save As*, and then click this option at the side menu.

10. To create a database in an earlier version, change the *Default file format* option at this dialog box with the *Popular* option selected.

SKILLS check
Demonstrate Your Proficiency

Assessment

1 EXPORT A FORM TO EXCEL AND A REPORT TO WORD

1. Remove the read-only attribute from the **LegalServices.accdb** database located in the Access2007L1C8 folder.
2. Open the **LegalServices.accdb** database.
3. Create a form named *Billing* using the Form Wizard with the following fields:

    From the Billing table:

    > *Billing#*
    > *ClientID*
    > *Date*
    > *Hours*

    From the Rates table:

    > *Rate*

4. When the form displays, close it.
5. Create an Excel worksheet with the Billing form.
6. Make the following changes to the Excel Billing worksheet:
    a. Select columns A through E and then autofit the column widths.
    b. Select cells A2 through B28 and then click the Center button in the Alignment group in the Home tab.
    c. Save the Billing worksheet.
    d. Print and then close the Billing worksheet.
    e. Exit Excel.
7. In Access, close the Export Wizard.
8. Create a report named *ClientBilling* using the Report Wizard with the following fields:

    From the Clients table:

    > *FirstName*
    > *LastName*

    From the Billing table:

    > *Date*
    > *Hours*

    From the Rates table:

    > *Rate*

9. Apply the Foundry autoformat to the report.
10. When the report displays, change to Layout view and then decrease the size of the columns so the right border of the column displays just right of the longest entry in the column.
11. Save and then close the report.
12. Create a Word document with the ClientBilling report and save it to the Access2007L1C8 folder on your storage medium with the default name. In the Word document, make the following changes:
    a. Press Ctrl + A to select the entire document, change the font color to black, and then deselect the text.
    b. Insert a space between *Client* and *Billing* in the title.
    c. Position the insertion point immediately right of the word *Billing*, press the spacebar, and then type of Legal Services.

13. Save and then print **ClientBilling.rtf**.
14. Close the document and then exit Word.
15. In Access, close the wizard dialog box.

Assessment

2 MERGE TABLE AND QUERY DATA WITH A WORD DOCUMENT

1. With the **LegalServices.accdb** database open, merge data in the Clients table to a new Word document using the *Merge it with Microsoft Office Word* option.
2. Maximize the Word document, close the Mail Merge task pane, and then compose a letter with the following elements:
   a. Click the Home tab and then click the No Spacing style in the Styles group.
   b. Press Enter six times, type the current date, and then press Enter five times.
   c. Click the Mailings tab and then insert the proper field names for the recipient's name and address. **Hint: Use the Insert Merge Field button in the Write & Insert Fields group.**
   d. Insert a proper salutation.
   e. Compose a letter to clients that includes the following information:

   The last time you visited our offices, you may have noticed how crowded we were. To alleviate the overcrowding, we are leasing new offices in the Meridian Building and will be moving in at the beginning of next month.

   Stop by and see our new offices at our open house planned for the second Friday of next month. Drop by any time between 2:00 and 5:30 p.m. We look forward to seeing you.

   f. Include an appropriate complimentary close for the letter. Use the name and title *Marjorie Shaw, Senior Partner* for the signature and add your reference initials and the document name (**AccessL1_C8_A2a.docx**).
3. Merge to a new document and then save the document with the name **AccessL1_C8_A2a**.
4. Print only the first two letters in the document and then close **AccessL1_C8_A2a.docx**.
5. Save the main document and name it **AccessL1_C8_A2_MD1**, close the document, and then exit Word.
6. At the LegalServices database, extract the records from the Clients table of those clients located in Kent and then name the query *KentQuery*.
7. Merge the KentQuery to a new Word document using the *Merge it with Microsoft Office Word* option.
8. Maximize the Word document, close the Mail Merge task pane, and then compose a letter with the following elements:
   a. Click the Home tab and then click the No Spacing style in the Styles group.
   b. Press Enter six times, type the current date, and then press Enter five times.
   c. Click the Mailings tab and then insert the proper field names for the inside address.
   d. Insert a proper salutation.

e. Compose a letter to clients that includes the following information:
The City of Kent Municipal Court has moved from 1024 Meeker Street to a new building located at 3201 James Avenue. All court hearings after the end of this month will be held at the new address. If you need directions to the new building, please call our office.

f. Include an appropriate complimentary close for the letter. Use the name *Thomas Zeiger* and the title *Attorney* in the complimentary close and add your reference initials and the document name (**AccessL1_C8_A2b.docx**).

9. Merge the letter to a new document and then save the document with the name **AccessL1_C8_A2b**.

10. Print only the first two letters in the document and then close **AccessL1_C8_A2b.docx**.

11. Save the main document and name it **AccessL1_C8_A2_MD2**, close the document, and then exit Word.

Assessment

3 IMPORT AND LINK AN EXCEL WORKBOOK

1. At the **LegalServices.accdb** database, import and link **ExcelC8_02.xlsx** into a new table named *Cases*.

2. Open the Cases table in Datasheet view.

3. Print and then close the Cases table.

4. Open Excel, open the **ExcelC08_02.xlsx** workbook and then add the following data in the specified cell:

A8	=	57-D
B8	=	130
C8	=	$1,100
A9	=	42-A
B9	=	144
C9	=	$3,250
A10	=	29-C
B10	=	125
C10	=	$900

5. Save, print, and then close **ExcelC08_02.xlsx**.

6. Exit Excel.

7. In Access, open the Cases table in Datasheet view. (Notice the changes you made in Excel are reflected in the table.)

8. Print and then close the Cases table.

CASE study
Apply Your Skills

Part 1

As the office manager at Woodland Dermatology Center, you are responsible for managing the center database. In preparation for an upcoming meeting, open the **Woodland.accdb** database and prepare the following with data in the database:

- Create a query that displays the patient number, first name, and last name; doctor last name; date of visit; and fee. Name the query *PatientBilling*.
- Export the PatientBilling query to an Excel worksheet. Apply formatting to enhance the appearance of the worksheet and then print the worksheet.
- Create mailing labels for the patients.
- Export the patient labels to a Word (.rtf) document and then print the document.
- Import and link the **WoodlandPayroll.xlsx** Excel worksheet to a new table named *WeeklyPayroll*. Print the WeeklyPayroll table.

You have been given some updated information about the weekly payroll and need to make the following changes to the **WoodlandPayroll.xlsx** worksheet: Change the hours for Irene Vaughn to *30*, change the wage for Monica Saunders to *$10.50*, and change the hours for Dale Jorgensen to *20*. After making the changes, open, print, and then close the WeeklyPayroll table.

Part 2

The center is expanding and will be offering cosmetic dermatology services at the beginning of next month to residents in the Altoona area. Design a query that extracts records of patients living in the city of Altoona and then merge the query with Word. At the Word document, write a letter describing the new services which include microdermabrasion, chemical peels, laser resurfacing, sclerotherapy, and photorejuvenation as well as an offer for a free facial and consultation. Insert the appropriate fields in the document and then complete the merge. Save the merged document and name it **Access_C8_CS_P2**. Print the first two letters of the document and then close the document. Close the main document without saving it and then exit Word.

Part 3

You need to save objects in the Woodland database in a format that can be read by employees that do not have Access available. You have researched the various file formats available and have determined that the PDF format is the most universal. Use the Access Help feature to learn how to save a database object in PDF format. (You may need to download an add-in to save an object in PDF format.) Save the Patients table in PDF format and then print the PDF file. Save the Doctors table in PDF format and then print the PDF file.

Part 4

Since you are responsible for updating the clinic procedures manual, you decide to create a Word document that describes the steps for saving an object in PDF format. Save the completed document and name it **Access_C8_CS_P4**. Print and then close **Access_C8_CS_P4.docx**.

Creating Forms and Reports

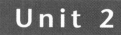
ASSESSING proficiency

In this unit, you have learned to create forms, reports, and mailing labels; filter data; and summarize and analyze data in PivotTable and PivotChart view as well as create a PivotTable form. You also learned how to modify document properties; view object dependencies; and export, import, and link data between programs.

Note: Before beginning unit assessments, delete the Access2007L1C8 folder from your storage medium. Next, copy to your storage medium the Access2007L1U2 subfolder from the Access2007L1 folder on the CD that accompanies this textbook and then make Access2007L1U2 the active folder.

Assessment 1 Create Tables in a Clinic Database

1. Use Access to create a database for clients of a mental health clinic. Name the database **LancasterClinic**. Create a table named *Clients* that includes the following fields (you determine the field name, data type, field size, and description):
   ClientNumber (primary key)
   ClientName
   StreetAddress
   City
   State
   ZipCode
   Telephone
   DateOfBirth
   DiagnosisID

2. After creating the table, switch to Datasheet view and then enter the following data in the appropriate fields:

   ClientNumber: 1831
   George Charoni
   3980 Broad Street
   Philadelphia, PA 19149
   (215) 555-3482
   DateOfBirth: 4/12/1958
   DiagnosisID: SC

   ClientNumber: 3219
   Marian Wilke
   12032 South 39th
   Jenkintown, PA 19209
   (215) 555-9083
   DateOfBirth: 10/23/1981
   DiagnosisID: OCD

   ClientNumber: 2874
   Arthur Shroeder
   3618 Fourth Avenue

   ClientNumber: 5831
   Roshawn Collins
   12110 52nd Court East

Philadelphia, PA 19176
(215) 555-8311
DateOfBirth: 3/23/1958
DiagnosisID: OCD

Cheltenham, PA 19210
(215) 555-4779
DateOfBirth: 11/3/1965
DiagnosisID: SC

ClientNumber: 4419
Lorena Hearron
3112 96th Street East
Philadelphia, PA 19132
(215) 555-3281
DateOfBirth: 7/2/1984
DiagnosisID: AD

ClientNumber: 1103
Raymond Mandato
631 Garden Boulevard
Jenkintown, PA 19209
(215) 555-0957
DateOfBirth: 9/20/1979
DiagnosisID: MDD

3. Save, print, and then close the Clients table.
4. Create a table named *Diagnoses* that includes the following fields:
   DiagnosisID (primary key)
   Diagnosis
5. After creating the table, switch to Datasheet view and then enter the following data in the appropriate fields:

DiagnosisID	=	AD
Diagnosis	=	Adjustment Disorder
DiagnosisID	=	MDD
Diagnosis	=	Manic-Depressive Disorder
DiagnosisID	=	OCD
Diagnosis	=	Obsessive-Compulsive Disorder
DiagnosisID	=	SC
Diagnosis	=	Schizophrenia

6. Save, print, and then close the Diagnoses table.
7. Create a table named *Fees* that includes the following fields (you determine the field name, data type, field size, and description):
   FeeCode (primary key)
   HourlyFee
8. After creating the table, switch to Datasheet view and then enter the following data in the appropriate fields:

FeeCode	=	A
HourlyFee	=	$75.00
FeeCode	=	B
HourlyFee	=	$80.00
FeeCode	=	C
HourlyFee	=	$85.00
FeeCode	=	D
HourlyFee	=	$90.00

```
FeeCode      =  E
HourlyFee    =  $95.00

FeeCode      =  F
HourlyFee    =  $100.00

FeeCode      =  G
HourlyFee    =  $105.00

FeeCode      =  H
HourlyFee    =  $110.00
```

9. Save, print, and then close the Fees table.
10. Create a table named *Employees* that includes the following fields (you determine the field name, data type, field size, and description):
    ProviderNumber (primary key)
    ProviderName
    Title
    Extension
11. After creating the table, switch to Datasheet view and then enter the following data in the appropriate fields:

ProviderNumber: 29	*ProviderNumber:* 15
ProviderName: James Schouten	*ProviderName:* Lynn Yee
Title: Psychologist	*Title:* Child Psychologist
Extension: 399	*Extension:* 102
ProviderNumber: **33**	*ProviderNumber:* 18
ProviderName: Janice Grisham	*ProviderName:* Craig Chilton
Title: Psychiatrist	*Title:* Psychologist
Extension: 11	*Extension:* 20

12. Save, print, and then close the Employees table.
13. Create a table named *Billing* that includes the following fields (you determine the field name, data type, field size, and description):
    BillingNumber (primary key; identify the data type as *AutoNumber*)
    ClientNumber
    DateOfService (apply the Date/Time data type)
    Insurer
    ProviderNumber
    Hours
    FeeCode
14. After creating the table, switch to Datasheet view and then enter the following data in the appropriate fields:

ClientNumber: 4419	*ClientNumber:* 1831
DateOfService: 3/1/2010	*DateOfService:* 3/1/2010
Insurer: Health Plus	*Insurer:* Self
ProviderNumber: 15	*ProviderNumber:* 33
Hours: 2	*Hours:* 1
FeeCode: B	*FeeCode:* H

ClientNumber: 3219
DateOfService: 3/2/2010
Insurer: Health Plus
ProviderNumber: 15
Hours: 1
FeeCode: D

ClientNumber: 5831
DateOfService: 3/2/2010
Insurer: Penn-State Health
ProviderNumber: 18
Hours: 2
FeeCode: C

ClientNumber: 4419
DateOfService: 3/3/2010
Insurer: Health Plus
ProviderNumber: 15
Hours: 1
FeeCode: A

ClientNumber: 1103
DateOfService: 3/3/2010
Insurer: Penn-State Health
ProviderNumber: 18
Hours: 0.5
FeeCode: A

ClientNumber: 1831
DateOfService: 3/4/2010
Insurer: Self
ProviderNumber: 33
Hours: 1
FeeCode: H

ClientNumber: 5831
DateOfService: 3/4/2010
Insurer: Penn-State Health
ProviderNumber: 18
Hours: 0.5
FeeCode: C

15. Save, print, and then close the Billing table.

Assessment 2 Relate Tables and Create Forms in a Clinic Database

1. With the **LancasterClinic.accdb** database open, create the following one-to-many relationships:
   a. *ClientNumber* in the Clients table is the "one" and *ClientNumber* in the Billing table is the "many."
   b. *DiagnosisID* in the Diagnoses table is the "one" and *DiagnosisID* in the Clients table is the "many."
   c. *ProviderNumber* in the Employees table is the "one" and *ProviderNumber* in the Billing table is the "many."
   d. *FeeCode* in the Fees table is the "one" and *FeeCode* in the Billing table is the "many."
2. Create a form with the data in the Clients table.
3. After creating the form, add the following record to the Clients form:
   ClientNumber: 1179
   Timothy Fierro
   1133 Tenth Southwest
   Philadelphia, PA 19178
   (215) 555-5594
   DateOfBirth: 12/7/1987
   DiagnosisID: AD
4. Save the form as Clients, print the form, and then close the form.
5. Add the following records to the Billing table:

ClientNumber: 1179
DateOfService: 3/8/2010
Insurer: Health Plus
ProviderNumber: 15
Hours: 0.5
FeeCode: C

ClientNumber: 1831
DateOfService: 3/8/2010
Insurer: Self
ProviderNumber: 33
Hours: 1
FeeCode: H

6. Save and then print the Billing table.
7. Close the Billing table.

Assessment 3 Create Forms Using the Form Wizard

1. With the **LancasterClinic.accdb** database open, create a form with fields from related tables using the Form Wizard with the following specifications:
   a. At the first Form Wizard dialog box, insert the following fields in the Selected Fields list box:
      From the Clients table:
         ClientNumber
         DateOfBirth
         DiagnosisID
      From the Billing table:
         Insurer
         ProviderNumber
   b. Do not make any changes at the second Form Wizard dialog box.
   c. Do not make any changes at the third Form Wizard dialog box.
   d. You determine the format style at the fourth Form Wizard dialog box.
   e. At the fifth Form Wizard dialog box, type the name ProviderInformation in the *Form* text box.
2. When the first record displays, print the first record.
3. Close the form.

Assessment 4 Create Labels with the Label Wizard

1. With the **LancasterClinic.accdb** database open, use the Label Wizard to create mailing labels with the client names and addresses and sorted by ZIP code. Name the mailing label file **ClientMailingLabels**.
2. Print the mailing labels.
3. Close the mailing labels file.

Assessment 5 Filter Records in Tables

1. With the **LancasterClinic.accdb** database open, open the Billing table and then filter the records to display the following records:
   a. Display only those records with the Health Plus insurer. Print the results and then remove the filter.
   b. Display only those records with the 4419 client number. Print the results and then remove the filter.
2. Filter records by selection to display the following records:
   a. Display only those records with a C fee code. Print the results and then remove the filter.
   b. Display only those records between the dates of 3/1/2010 and 3/3/2010. Print the results and then remove the filter.
3. Close the Billing table without saving the changes.
4. Open the Clients table and then use Filter By Form to display clients in Jenkintown or Cheltenham. Print the results and then remove the filter.
5. Close the Clients table without saving the changes.

Assessment 6 View and Analyze Data in PivotTable View

1. With the **LancasterClinic.accdb** database open, create a query in Design view with the following specifications:
   a. Add the Billing, Employees, and Clients tables to the design grid.
   b. Add the following fields from the specified tables:

DateOfService	=	Billing table
ProviderNumber	=	Employees table
ClientNumber	=	Clients table
Hours	=	Billing table

  c. Run the query.
  d. Save the query and name it *ProviderHours*.
 2. Display the query in PivotTable view.
 3. At the PivotTable layout, drag and drop the fields as follows:
  a. Drag the *ProviderNumber* field to the *Drop Row Fields Here* section.
  b. Drag the *ClientNumber* field to the *Drop Column Fields Here* section.
  c. Drag the *Hours* field to the *Drop Totals or Detail Fields Here* section.
  d. Drag the *DateOfService* field to the *Drop Filter Fields Here* section.
 4. Remove the *PivotTable Field List* box from the screen.
 5. Click the Quick Print button to print the query in PivotTable view.
 6. In the *ProviderNumber* field, display only the hours for provider number 15.
 7. Print the PivotTable and then redisplay all providers.
 8. In the *DateOfService* field, display only hours for March 2, 2010.
 9. Print the PivotTable and then redisplay all rental dates.
 10. Switch to Datasheet view, save the query, and then close the query.

Assessment 7 Export a Table to Excel

 1. With the **LancasterClinic.accdb** database open, export the Billing table to an Excel workbook.
 2. Apply formatting to the cells in the Excel workbook to enhance the appearance of the data.
 3. Change the page orientation to landscape.
 4. Save, print, and then close the workbook.
 5. Exit Excel.

Assessment 8 Merge Records to Create Letters in Word

 1. With the **LancasterClinic.accdb** database open, merge data in the Clients table to a blank Word document. ***Hint: Use the* Merge it with Microsoft Office Word *option from the More button in the Export group in the External Data tab.*** You determine the fields to use in the inside address and an appropriate salutation. Type March 10, 2010 as the date of the letter and type the following text in the body of the document:

> The building of a new wing for the Lancaster Clinic will begin April 1, 2010. We are excited about this new addition to our clinic. With the new facilities, we will be able to offer additional community and group services along with enhanced child-play therapy treatment.
>
> During the construction, the main entrance will be moved to the north end of the building. Please use this entrance until the construction of the wing is completed. We apologize in advance for any inconvenience this causes you.

Include an appropriate complimentary close for the letter. Use the name and title *Marianne Lambert, Clinic Director* for the signature and add your reference initials and the document name (**AccessL1_U2_A8.docx**).

2. Merge to a new document and then save the document with the name **AccessL1_U2_A8**.
3. Print the first two letters of the document and then close **AccessL1_U2_A8.docx**.
4. Save the main document as **ConstructionLetter** and then close **ConstructionLetter.docx**.
5. Exit Word.

Assessment 9 Import and Link Excel Data to an Access Table

1. With the **LancasterClinic.accdb** database open, import and link **ExcelU02_01.xlsx** into a new table named *StaffHours*.
2. Open the StaffHours table in Datasheet view.
3. Print and then close the StaffHours table.
4. Open **ExcelU02_01.xlsx** in Excel.
5. Insert a formula in cell D2 that multiplies B2 with C2 and then copy the formula down to cells D3 through D7.
6. Save and then close **ExcelU02_01.xlsx**.
7. Exit Excel.
8. In Access with the **LancasterClinic.accdb** database open, open the StaffHours table.
9. Print and then close the StaffHours table.

WRITING activities

The following activities give you the opportunity to practice your writing skills along with demonstrating an understanding of some of the important Access features you have mastered in this unit. Use correct grammar, appropriate word choices, and clear sentence constructions.

Activity 1 Add a Table to the Clinic Database

The director at Lancaster Clinic has asked you to add information to the **LancasterClinic.accdb** database on insurance companies contracted by the clinic. You need to create a table that will contain information on insurance companies. The director wants the table to include the insurance company name, address, city, state, and ZIP code along with a telephone number and the name of a representative. You determine the field names, data types, field sizes, and description for the table and then include the following information (in the appropriate fields):

Health Plus
4102 22nd Street
Philadelphia, PA 19166
(212) 555-0990
Representative: Byron Tolleson

Penn-State Health
5933 Lehigh Avenue
Philadelphia, PA 19148
(212) 555-3477
Representative: Tracey Pavone

Quality Medical
51 Cecil B. Moore Avenue
Philadelphia, PA 19168
(212) 555-4600
Representative: Lee Stafford

Delaware Health
4418 Front Street
Philadelphia, PA 19132
(212) 555-6770
Representative: Melanie Chon

Save, print, and then close the insurance company table. Open Word and then write a report to the clinic director detailing how you created the table. Include a title for the report, steps on how you created the table, and any other pertinent information. Save the completed report and name it **AccessL1_U2_Act1**. Print and then close **AccessL1_U2_Act1.docx**.

Activity 2 Merge Records to Create Letters to Insurance Companies

Merge data in the insurance company database to a blank Word document. You determine the fields to use in the inside address and an appropriate salutation. Compose a letter to the insurance companies informing them that Lancaster Clinic is providing mental health counseling services to people with health insurance through their company. You are sending an informational brochure about Lancaster Clinic and are requesting information from the insurance companies on services and service limitations. Include an appropriate complimentary close for the letter. Use the name and title *Marianne Lambert, Clinic Director* for the signature and add your reference initials. When the merge is completed, name the document containing the merged letters **AccessL1_U2_Act2**. Print the first two letters in the merged document and then close **AccessL1_U2_Act2.docx**. Close the main document without saving it and then exit Word. Close the **LancasterClinic.accdb** database.

Health Information Search

In this activity, you will search the Internet for information on a health concern or disease that interests you. You will be looking for specific organizations, interest groups, or individuals who are somehow connected to the topic you have chosen. Your topic may be an organization that raises money to support research, it may be a support group that posts information or answers questions, or you may find information about clinics or doctors who specialize in your topic. Try to find at least ten different groups that support the health concern you are researching.

Create a database in Access and create a table that includes information from your search. Design the table so that you can store the name, address, phone number, and Web address of the organizations you find. You will also want to identify the connection the group has to your topic (supports research, interest group, treats patients, etc.). Create a report to summarize your findings. In Microsoft Word, create a letter that you can use to write for further information about the organization. Use the names and addresses in your database to merge with the letter. Select and then print the first two letters that result from the merge. Finally, write a paragraph describing information you learned about the health concern that you previously did not know.

City Improvement Projects

In this activity, you are working with the city council in your area to keep the public informed of the progress being made on improvement projects throughout the city. These projects are paid for through tax dollars voted on by the public, and the city council feels that an informed public leads to a good voter turnout when it is time to make more improvements.

Your job is to create a database and a table in the database that will store the following information for each project: a project ID number, a description of the project, the budgeted dollar amount to be spent, the amount spent so far, the amount of time allocated to the project, and the amount of time spent so far. Enter five city improvement projects into the table (sample data created by you). Create a query based on the table that calculates the percent of budgeted dollars spent so far and the percent of budgeted time spent so far. Print the table and the query.

P

Page Down key: navigating in forms with, 149
Page layout
changing, 25–26
changing, in table, 23–24
Page Layout group, 29, 185
in Print Preview, 23
Page margins: changing, 23
Page orientation
changing, 25, 29
changing, in reports, 194
Page setup: changing in reports, 194, 207
Page Setup button, 23, 25, 185, 186
Page Setup dialog box, 23, 29, 30, 187
with Page tab selected, 24
with Print Options tab selected, 24
Page Up key: navigating in forms with, 149
Paper size: changing, 29
Percent formatting: applying to numbers in reports, 191
Performing queries, 99–100
on related tables and sorting in ascending order, 108–109
with Simple Query Wizard, 112–115
on tables, 103–105
and then merging with a Word document, 258–259
Performing queries: on related database tables, 106–107
Period (.): exclusion of, from field names, 13
PivotChart, 233, 243
creating, 224, 231, 242
PivotChart layout, 232
PivotChart view, 215, 224
data summarized in, 231–235
PivotChart View button, 231
PivotTable
creating, 224, 242
power of, 227
viewing those based on PivotChart, 231, 232
PivotTable form
creating, 229–231
summarizing and analyzing data in, 229
PivotTable layout, 225
displaying, 229
PivotTable Tools Design tab, 227
PivotTable view, 215, 243
data analysis in, 227–228
summarizing data in, 224–227
PivotTable View button, 224, 227
Plus symbol
as expand button, 240
as expand indicator, 54, 58
showing data in PivotTable and, 227
Portrait orientation, 23, 30
reports printed in, 185, 200

Pound symbol (#): query criteria and, 102, 129
PowerPoint: collecting data from, 263
Predesigned properties: choosing, 237
Premium:Database window, 18
Previous record button, 149
Previous versions: saving databases in, 266–267, 268
Primary field: creating, 37
Primary Key button, 37, 58
Primary key field: defining, 58
Primary keys, 35, 37, 58
defining, 38–40
Primary table, 41
Print button, 43, 58, 185
Print dialog box, 149, 150, 175
Print group, 43
Printing
employees table, 25–26
forms, 149, 175
mailing labels, 205
records, specific, 80
relationships, 43, 58
reports, 207
tables, 22, 29, 30
Print Preview, 22, 23, 207
reports displayed in, 185–187
tables displayed in, 25
Print Preview button, 185, 186
Print Preview tab, 29, 194
Properties
customizing, for current database, 238–239
predesigned, choosing, 237
viewing and customizing, for current database, 237
Properties dialog box, 235, 236, 238
for open database, 237

Q

Queries, 8, 10, 37
aggregate functions used in, 119–120
completing spelling check on, 82
creating calculated field in, 116–118
creating PivotTable in, 227
crosstab, 120–123
defined, 99
designing, 100–101, 129
designing, with aggregate functions, 118
designing, with Or and And criteria, 111–112
exporting data in, to Excel worksheet, 268
exporting to Excel, 251–252
exporting to other programs, 249
fields sorted in, 108
filtering records in, 219–220
find duplicates, 124–125, 129
modifying, 109–110, 129
performing, 99–100
performing, and then merging with a Word document, 258–259

reports created with, 187–188
returning, 102
unmatched, 127–128, 129
viewing object dependencies and, 239
Query criteria: establishing, 102–103
Query data: merging with a Word document, 257
Query Design button, 100, 108, 122
Query design grids, 101
Query design window, 130
Query Tools Design tab, 101
Query window, 101
with Show Table dialog box, 100
Query Wizard button, 124, 127
Quick Access toolbar, 9, 10, 16, 22, 109
Quick Print arrow, 228
Quick Print button, 22, 149, 175, 222

R

Record navigation bar, 149, 151, 156, 164, 168, 216
Records, 29
adding and deleting in forms, 151–152
adding and deleting in tables, 26–28
adding and/or deleting, 29, 30
adding and/or deleting, in related database tables, 49–50
deleting from forms, 175
filtering by selection, 222–223
filtering in a query and a report, 219–220
filtering in a table, form, and report, 217–218
filters applied to, 216
grouping, using aggregate functions and, 120–121
grouping and sorting, 195–198
printing specific, 80
related, displaying in subdatasheets, 54–55
sorting, 80, 93
sorting, in ascending and descending order, 92
sorting, in employees table, 81
sorting, in forms, 151
sorting, in reports, 189
sorting, in tables, 92
using Filter by Form for display of, 223–224
Record selector bar, 26, 92
Records group, 70, 82, 151, 175
Redundancies
eliminating, 36
eliminating, in database tables, 58
Referential integrity, 41
specifying, 43

Related database tables, 41
creating, 35–36
creating forms with, 153–154, 173–174
performing queries on, 106–107
updating fields and adding/deleting records in, 49–50
Relational database management system, 35, 36
Relational databases, 13, 35
power of, 18
Relational database software program, 58
Relationship Report button, 43
Relationships
determining, 36–37
editing and deleting, 51
printing, 43, 58
Relationships button, 41, 46, 51, 53
Relationships window, 41, 42, 45, 240
Remove filter, 243
Replace button, 84, 92, 93
Report button, 183
reports created with, 184–185, 207
Report Layout Tools Format tab, 183, 191, 194, 207
Report Layout Tools Page Setup tab, 194
Report objects: viewing object dependencies and, 239
Reports, 8, 10, 37
applying autoformats and grouping and sorting data in, 196–198
autoformats applied to, 194
changing width and order of columns in, 189
completing spelling check on, 82
conditional formatting applied to, 191, 207
control objects sized and moved in, 188–191
controls formatted in, 191–192
creating, 183–184, 207, 208
creating with fields from multiple tables, 202–203
creating with Report button, 184–185
creating with Report Wizard, 207
creation of, with queries, 187–188
creation of, with Report Wizard, 198–201
creation of, with sales table, 184
customizing, 191–192, 207
displaying in Print Preview, 185–187
exporting to Word, 253–255
filtering records in, 217–218, 219–220
fonts and conditional formatting applied to, 192–194

Access 2007 Feature	Ribbon Tab, Group	Button, Option	Keyboard Shortcut
Access Help window			F1
Add existing fields in a form	Form Design Tools Design, Tools		
Add existing fields in a report	Report Design Tools Design, Tools		
Add field	Table Tools Design, Tools	Insert Rows	
Add record	Home, Records	New	Ctrl + Shift + +
Add Total row to query design	Query Tools Design, Show/Hide	Σ	
Advanced Filter Options	Home, Sort & Filter	Advanced	
Align multiple controls at same position	Form Design Tools Arrange, Control Alignment	Left Right	
Append query	Query Tools Design, Query Type		
AutoFormat	Report Design Tools Arrange, AutoFormat		
Back up database		, Manage, Back Up Database	
Change tab order of fields	Form Design Tools Arrange, Control Layout	Tab Order	
Clipboard task pane	Home, Clipboard		
Close database		, Close Database	
Compact and repair database		, Manage, Compact and Repair Database	
Conditional Formatting dialog box	Report Layout Tools Format, Font		
Create ACCDE file	Database Tools, Database Tools		
Create command button	Form Design Tools Design, Controls		
Create datasheet form	Create, Forms	More Forms	
Create macro	Create, Other		
Create query in Design view	Create, Other		
Create table in Design view	Create, Table		
Crosstab Query Wizard	Create, Other	, Crosstab Query Wizard	
Customize Access options		, Access Options	
Datasheet view	Home, Views	, Datasheet View OR	
Date and Time	Report Design Tools Design, Controls	Date and Time	
Delete field	Table Tools Design, Tools	Delete Rows	
Delete query	Query Tools Design, Query Type		
Delete record	Home, Records	X Delete	
Design view	Home, Views	, Design View OR	
Documenter	Database Tools, Analyze	Database Documenter	
Edit relationships	Relationship Tools Design, Tools		
Encrypt database	Database Tools, Database Tools	Encrypt with Password	
Export data as Text file	External Data, Export	Text File	
Export object	External Data, Export	Word OR	
Field List window	Report Layout Tools Format, Controls		
Filter	Home, Sort & Filter		
Filter by form	Home, Sort & Filter	Advanced, Filter By Form	
Filter by selection	Home, Sort & Filter	Selection	
Find and Replace	Home, Find	/ Replace	Ctrl + F, Ctrl + H
Find Duplicates Query Wizard	Create, Other	, Find Duplicates Query Wizard	
Find Unmatched Query Wizard	Create, Other	, Find Unmatched Query Wizard	
Form	Create, Forms		
Form view	Form Design Tools Design, Views		
Form Wizard	Create, Forms	More Forms, Form Wizard	
Group & Sort	Report Design Tools Design, Grouping & Totals OR Report Layout Tools Format, Grouping & Totals	Group & Sort OR	
Group selected controls	Form Design Tools Arrange, Control Layout		
Image	Form Design Tools Design, Controls		
Import data from text file	External Data, Import	Text File	
Import Excel data	External Data, Import		
Import or link data from Access database	External Data, Import		
Indexes	Table Tools Design, Show/Hide		
Insert a chart	Report Design Tools Design, Controls		
Insert page in tab control	Form Design Tools Design, Controls		
Insert Subdatasheet dialog box	Home, Records	, Subdatasheet, Subdatasheet	
Label control object	Form Design Tools Design, Controls	Aa	

Access 2007 Feature	Ribbon Tab, Group	Button, Option	Keyboard Shortcut
Labels Wizard	Create, Reports	Labels	
Layout view	Home, Views		
Line	Form Design Tools Design, Controls		
Linked Table Manager	Database Tools, Database Tools		
Logo	Form Design Tools Design, Controls		
Make table query	Query Tools Design, Query Type		
Margins	Print Preview, Page Layout		
Merge Access data with Word	External Data, Export	, Merge it with Microsoft Office Word	
Multiple Items form	Create, Forms		
New Query dialog box	Create, Other		
Object Dependencies task pane	Database Tools, Show/Hide	Object Dependencies	
Open dialog box		, Open	Ctrl + O
Page numbering	Report Design Tools Design, Controls		
Page Setup dialog box	Print Preview, Page Layout		
Paste Table As	Home, Clipboard		Ctrl + V
Performance Analyzer	Database Tools, Analyze	Analyze Performance	
PivotChart	Home, Views	, PivotChart View	
PivotTable form	Create, Forms	More Forms ▾, PivotTable	
PivotTable view	Home, Views	, PivotTable View	
Primary key	Table Tools Design, Tools		
Print orientation	Print Preview, Page Layout	,	
Print Preview		, Print, Print Preview	
Print relationships report	Relationship Tools Design, Tools	Relationship Report	
Property Sheet	Report (or Form) Design Tools Design, Tools		F4
Query design window	Create, Other		
Relationships window	Database Tools, Show/Hide		
Remove filter	Home, Sort & Filter	, Clear filter from xxx OR Advanced ▾, Clear All Filters	
Report	Create, Reports		
Report Design	Create, Reports		
Report view	Home, Views		
Report Wizard	Create, Reports	Report Wizard	
Run macro	Macro Tools Design, Tools		
Run query	Query Tools Design, Results		
Save as 2000 Database		, Save As, Access 2000 Database	
Save as 2002 - 2003 database		, Save As, Access 2002 - 2003 Database	
Save As dialog box		, Save As	
Save database		, Save	Ctrl + S
Show or print table		, Print OR	
Show Table in a query	Query Tools Design, Query Setup		
Show Table dialog box	Relationship Tools Design, Relationships		
Simple Query Wizard	Create, Other	, Simple Query Wizard	
Sort, ascending or descending	Home, Sort & Filter	OR	
Spelling checker	Home, Records	Spelling	F7
Split database	Database Tools, Move Data		
Split Form	Create, Forms		
Subform	Form Design Tools Design, Controls		
Subreport	Report Design Tools Design, Controls		
Switch to Datasheet view from Design view	Table Tools Design, Views		
Switch to Design view from Datasheet view	Home, Views		
Switchboard Manager	Database Tools, Database Tools	Switchboard Manager	
Table Analyzer Wizard	Database Tools, Analyze	Analyze Table	
Table templates	Create, Tables		
Title in a form	Form Design Tools Design, Controls	Title	
Title in a report	Report Design Tools Design, Controls		
Ungroup selected controls	Form Design Tools Arrange, Control Layout		
Update query	Query Tools Design, Query Type		
Use control wizards	Form (or Report) Design Tools Design, Controls		